Books In This Series

Web Guru Guide to JavaScript™

WILLIAM STANEK

PAUL WATTERS

PEARSON

Prentice
Hall

Upper Saddle River, New Jersey 07458

Library of Congress Cataloging-in-Publication Data

Watters, Paul A.
  Web Guru guide to JavaScript / Paul Watters, William Stanek.
    p. cm.
  ISBN 0-13-148722-1
    1. JavaScript (Computer program language) 2. Internet programming. I. Stanek, William R. II. Title.

QA76.73.J39W36 2005
005.2'762--dc22   2005042968

Vice President and Publisher: Natalie E. Anderson
Executive Acquisitions Editor, Print: Stephanie Wall
Executive Acquisitions Editor, Certification: Steven Elliot
Executive Acquisitions Editor, Media: Jodi McPherson
Editorial Project Manager: Laura Burgess
Editorial Assistants: Brian Hoehl, B. Marchigano, Alana Meyers
Senior Media Project Manager: Cathi Profitko
Senior Media Project Manager: Steve Gagliostro
Marketing Manager: Sarah Davis
Marketing Assistant: Lisa Taylor
Production Project Manager: Vanessa Nuttry
Manufacturing Buyer: Natacha St. Hill Moore
Design Manager: Maria Lange
Art Director: Blair Brown
Interior Design: Blair Brown
Cover Design: Blair Brown
Cover Illustration/Photo: Gettyimages/Photodisc Blue
Composition/Full-Service Project Management: Laserwords Private Limited/BookMasters, Inc.
Cover Printer: Phoenix Color
Printer/Binder: Phoenix Color

Credits and acknowledgments borrowed from other sources and reproduced, with permission, in this textbook appear on appropriate page within text.

Microsoft® and Windows® are registered trademarks of the Microsoft Corporation in the U.S.A. and other countries. Screen shots and icons reprinted with permission from the Microsoft Corporation. This book is not sponsored or endorsed by or affiliated with the Microsoft Corporation.

Pearson Education LTD.   Pearson Education Australia PTY, Limited
Pearson Education Singapore, Pte. Ltd   Pearson Education North Asia Ltd
Pearson Education, Canada, Ltd   Pearson Educación de Mexico, S.A. de C.V.
Pearson Education–Japan   Pearson Education Malaysia, Pte. Ltd

10 9 8 7 6 5 4 3 2 1
ISBN 0-13-148722-1

Contents in Brief

Table of Contents

Web Guru Series Walk-Through

The Web Guru Series is designed to help you understand the "programming" behind basic Web applications and create a Web page or program that you can add to your portfolio. This walk-through highlights the key elements you'll find in this book created to help you along the way.

Chapter Introduction. Introductory material at the beginning of each chapter explains why these topics are important and how the chapter fits into the overall organization of the book.

Chapter Exercises. These objectives give you short-term, attainable goals. They mirror the titles of the step-by-step exercises.

Chapter Exercises

This unit's exercises will teach you how to:

- Identify JavaScript as the scripting language being used in a Web page
- Add JavaScripts to Web pages
- Use comments inside JavaScripts
- Solve compatibility issues between browsers and JavaScript versions

Visual Summary. This illustrates the project you will complete by the end of the chapter.

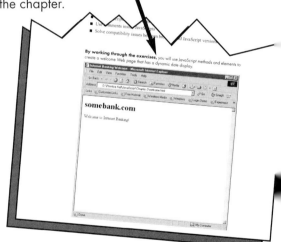

By working through the exercises, you will use JavaScript methods and elements to create a welcome Web page that has a dynamic date display.

---

22   CHAPTER 2 | Adding client-side scripts to web pages

Exercise 2.1 – Identifying JavaScript

JavaScript has several different versions, and different implementations of the s version can have significant differences in functionality. Indeed, other scripting guages may be used instead of JavaScript within a browser. Therefore, it is importa a first step to be able to correctly identify JavaScript as the language of choice for a cific HTML page.

In this exercise, you will learn how to specify JavaScript as the scripting lang to be used within a page and how to read in scripts from an external file into a HT page. This is good programming practice, because different individuals may fil roles of HTML developer and JavaScript programmer. The former is usually respe ble for the HTML markup, whereas the latter is responsible for the scripting.

According to the W3C, the *language attribute* of the <script> tag is depre ed in HTML 4. In addition, it is no longer supported by Internet Explorer 6 or b cent versions of other browsers, such as Mozilla 1.6. In the future, all script tags sh leave off the language attribute, such as <script language="JavaScript1 type="text/javascript">, or include both the MIME type and the lang instead, such as <script language="JavaScript1.5" type="te javascript"> for JavaScript 1.5.

STEP 1 – SELECTING JAVASCRIPT

In your text editor, create a code block by inserting an opening <script> tag a closing </script> tag. All scripts, whether they are JavaScript, VBScript, or other scripting language, must be identified by an attribute in the <script> block. Thus, to identify the code block as JavaScript, you would need to pass the ap priate attribute type="text/javascript", as shown in Exhibit 2.1.

EXHIBIT 2.1

```
<script type="text/javascript">
</script>
```

Step-by-Step Exercises. Hands-on tutorials let you "learn by doing" and include numbered, step-by-step instructions.

Tips. These brief notes offer key insights, helpful advice, and additional information that extend what you read in the chapter text.

For Your Career. These features show you how to take concepts from the book and apply them on your own and in the workplace.

Most str... contain a ... of alphanum... ...ers in the ranges a through z, A through Z, or 1 through 9. However, because in many cases strings represent every... ... characters may also need to be displayed. Generally, characters such as !, @, #, $, %, ...—... ... ... be included. However, other characters that have a special purpose in JavaScript—such as ... ... denoted as being part of a string literal.

A good example of this is the display of file pathnames, such as "C:\My Documents\JavaScript Book\". A variable declaration such as var path="C:\My Documents\JavaScript Book\": would only display C:My Documents-JavaScript Book if printed using the document.write() method. This is because the backslash character is used to denote special characters such as tabs (\t), backspaces (\b), form feeds (\f), new lines (\n), and carriage returns (\r). Thus, to ensure that the path string example is displayed as intended, the variable should be declared as var path="C:\\My Documents\\JavaScript Book\\";.

Exercise 3.3 – Using Variables

Variables are common to all programming languages, and the way that they are declared is quite similar across the various languages. Inside scripts, however, JavaScript variables are used much like Java variables. For example, string variable values can be inserted into string literals by using the addition (+) operator—literally adding strings together inside a method call, such as document.write(). But you can pass a variable to any method or function defined inside your script, and you can even pass multiple variables to many functions.

In this exercise, you will learn how to display variable values inside the strings that are used to dynamically construct the contents of a Web page.

STEP 1 – DEFINING THE VARIABLES

In your text editor, create a new HTML document, news.html, and insert a new <script> section. The variables to be inserted into the script will represent the lines to be displayed in a Web page, as shown in Exhibit 3.8.

EXHIBIT 3.8

TIP 3

Character Escaping

Doubling up backslashes is known as *character escaping*, and it has nothing to do with prisons! A character escape allows the denoted character literal to be quoted inside a string. It is most often used with quote marks inside strings. Specifically, when generating HTML code output using document.write(), you will often encounter double quotes, such as <A HREF="http://www.cassowary.net/">Cassowary Computing</A>. In this case, you would escape both of the double quotes in the variable assignment so that the string would be var site-Name="<A HREF=\"http://www.cassowary.net/\">Cassowary Computing</A>".

Test Your Skills. Extensive end-of-chapter exercises emphasize hands-on skill development. You'll find 5 types of evaluation here.

> Practice Drills

> Multiple-Choice Questions

> Fill-in-the-Blank Questions

> Definitions Questions

> Basic and Intermediate Projects

...problem... ...getting Ja...cripts act... ...different ... ...structs of JavaScript, such as functions, ...variables, and ... touched on here, will be discussed further in ...apter 3.

Test Your Skills

Practice Drill 2.1: String Quoting

In this exercise, you will observe what happens when you use document.write() to display a string that has a backslash (\) embedded inside it, which is known as *escaping*. These strings usually refer to files on a file system, such as C:\WINDOWS, but not HTTP URLs, which use forward slashes (/) to define paths.

If you don't "quote" a backslash inside a JavaScript string, it will simply not appear. You need to place a second backslash immediately in front of the backslash to be displayed. For example, to display the file system path C:\WINDOWS, the document.write() string would be "C:\\WINDOWS". The following example shows how this works in practice:

1. In your text editor, create a HTML page with the appropriate <head> and <body> elements:

```
<html>
    <head>
        <title>String Quoting Example</title>
    </head>
    <body>
    </body>
</html>
```

2. Insert the JavaScript code block between the <body> tags:

```
<script type="text/javascript">
</script>
```

3. Insert a document.write() method call between the <script> tags:

```
document.write("");
```

4. Insert the unquoted string as follows:

```
document.write("Configuration saved to C:\WINDOWS");
```

For Your Career

In this chapter, you will learn basic skills that will enable you to create dynamic Web pages with many layers. JavaScript is an important part of Dynamic HTML; it provides the foundation for all of the computational work required to work with browser objects.

All of the skills you will learn in this chapter will be useful to you when you create your own Web sites. Whether producing structured layouts, designing of scripts, or displaying an understanding of the subtleties of different JavaScript versions and implementations, building robust JavaScripts will impress every user who visits your pages.

Career Builder

Now that you have learned how to insert simple JavaScripts into Web pages with calls to document.write(), you should now create a sample welcome page for a real Internet banking site. Using a search engine, locate the home pages of five different Internet banking sites and examine their layout. What are the main entry points into the various applications that they provide? Use the View Source function of your Web browser to investigate the HTML and JavaScript code used on the page. Has the site used any of the features you have learned about in this chapter?

Using a Web design package or just Notepad and your Web browser, create a front page for an Internet banking site that uses document.write() to display text within the <body> section of the page. A link should be created to the login page, which will be examined in the next chapter.

Career Builder. This is a running project designed to present a real-world business case. It combines the lessons of the entire chapter, and builds on concepts taught in earlier chapters. By the end of the book, you will have a working project that you can present to potential employers.

Preface

JavaScript is the most widely used power tool on the World Wide Web. Just about every commercial Web site uses JavaScript in some way and so do many hobbyist Web sites. You can use JavaScript to implement image rollovers, customize pages for users or browsers, and any of hundreds of others tasks—if you know what JavaScript has to offer and when to use it. If you are a current Web designer or Web programmer, a clear understanding of JavaScript is essential to your long-term success. The same applies if you want to be a Web designer or Web programmer.

Like any power tool, there's a right way and a wrong way to use JavaScript. The good news is that after reading this book you'll know whether and when JavaScript is the right tool for the job and just as important you'll know the real-world solutions necessary to achieve your desired results. A key focus in this book is the capabilities and limitations of JavaScript. The more you know about JavaScript's capabilities and limitations, the more likely you will be to use JavaScript when it is the right tool for the job.

Features

To help you learn the ways of JavaScript, this book offers several features:

For Your Career To discuss real-world issues or provide general discussion of how the text pertains to actual Web sites

Tips To offer insights, helpful advice, or additional information

Practice Drills To offer practical exercises that reinforce the text

Multiple-Choice Questions To test what you have learned by focusing on finding the best real-world solutions to common design and production challenges

Definitions Questions To test your understanding of key definitions in the text

Basic Projects and *Intermediate Projects* To provide you with additional opportunities to work with topics covered in the text

Career Builder To help expand your career portfolio or demonstrate advanced functionality you are likely to use whenever you work with JavaScript

Overview

By following the chapters and exercises in this book, you'll not only learn JavaScript fundamentals, but also the advanced techniques of current designers and programmers. Chapter 1 serves to introduce JavaScript and the scripting options available. From there, the other parts of the book delve into the many features of JavaScript.

Chapter 2 discusses the techniques you can use to add scripts to Web pages. Chapter 3 examines the basic programmatic capabilities of JavaScript including variables, expressions, operators, and data types. In Chapter 4, you will learn to control the way scripts are executed using conditional expressions and looping controls. Chapter 5 discusses functions and how they are used. Chapter 6 explores objects and arrays. Chapter 7 details the essentials for working with strings and manipulating textual input. Chapter 8 details how to use regular expressions and pattern matching. Chapter 9 shows you how to use, precache, and swap images with JavaScript.

Chapter 10 introduces event handlers. Chapter 11 covers working with windows and dialog boxes. Chapter 12 focuses on examining the elements within Web pages. Chapter 13 details scripting embedded objects, such as applets. Chapter 14 examines how you can work with the browser history list and locations. Chapter 15 zeroes in on accessing browser and operating system version information. Chapter 16 shows you how to create client-side cookies and use them to store information. Chapter 17 discusses techniques you can use to script and validate HTML forms. Appendixes A and B provide essential quick references for working with JavaScript. Finally, the Glossary lists common JavaScript terms introduced in the chapters, and their definitions.

Throughout this book you'll see a variety of elements to help keep the text clear. You'll find code terms in `monospace type`, key terms in ***bold italics***, and hypertext links in <u>underline</u>.

Teaching and Student Resources

Instructor's Resource Center on CD-ROM

The Instructor's Resource Center on CD-ROM (IRC on CD) is distributed to instructors only and is an interactive library of assets and links. It includes the tools you expect from a Prentice Hall text:

- Instructor's Manual—provides instructional tips, an introduction to each chapter, teaching objectives, teaching suggestions, and answers to end-of-chapter questions and problems.

- PowerPoint slide presentations for each chapter—provide a convenient means of reviewing the content of the book in the classroom setting.

- Data and Solution Files.

- Complete Test Bank.

- TestGen Software—a test generator that lets you view and easily edit test bank questions, transfer them to tests, and print in a variety of formats suitable to your teaching situation. The program also offers many options for organizing and displaying test banks and tests. A built-in random number and text generator makes it ideal for creating multiple versions of tests that involve calculations and provides more possible test items than there are test bank questions. Powerful search and sort functions let you easily locate questions and arrange them in the order you prefer.

Companion Web Site (www.prenhall.com/webdevelopment)

The Companion Web site is a Pearson learning tool that provides students and instructors with online support. Here you will find the Interactive Study Guide, a Web-based interactive quiz designed to provide students with a convenient online mechanism for self-testing their comprehension of the book material.

About the Authors

William R. Stanek has 20 years of hands-on experience with advanced programming and development. He is a leading technology expert, an award-winning author, and an exceptional instructor who teaches courses in Windows, SQL Server, Exchange Server, and IIS administration. Over the years, his practical advice has helped millions of programmers, developers, and network engineers all over the world. His 50+ books have more than 3 million copies in print. Current or forthcoming books include *Windows Server 2003 Inside Out*, *Microsoft Windows XP Professional Administrator's Pocket Consultant,* Second Edition; *Microsoft Windows Server 2003 Administrator's Pocket Consultant*; and *IIS 6.0 Administrator's Pocket Consultant*. To contact William, visit his Web site (www.williamstanek.com) and send him an e-mail.

Dr. Paul Watters is a Senior Lecturer in the Postgraduate Professional Development Program and Department of Computing at Macquarie University, Sydney, Australia, where he convenes the Web Technologies program. He has developed numerous commercial Web applications and services for clients including the Universities Admissions Centre (UAC), and has served on the CeNTIE information brokering panel exploring future Internet and Web applications at the CSIRO. Dr. Watters currently teaches ITEC833 Web Server Technologies and Web Services. He is the author of *Web Services in Finance*, published by Apress.

Acknowledgments

As ever, I want to thank everyone who has been a part of this book. In my long career as a writer and instructor, this is my first "official" book with Prentice Hall. I say official, because I've written many books for Macmillan, and now they are part of Pearson Education. It really is a small world after all.

After 50 books or so, you wouldn't think Web Guru's *Guide to JavaScript* would be a challenge, but it was—really, really, really—and a lot of fun too. The Web Guru series is entirely new and Prentice Hall also wanted to take the series in many new and exciting directions. So the book you hold in your hands is the result of much hard work and many long hours of working to get it right so the book would be unique. I truly hope we've achieved that.

Working with a new team was also challenging and fun. Joyce Nielsen was the Development Editor. Laura Burgess, the Project Manager. Steven Elliot, the Acquisitions Editor. Together they work very well as a team and I look forward to working with them again in the future.

Thank you also to my agents at Studio B, David Rogelberg and Neil Salkind.

If I've forgotten anyone, it was an oversight, honest. ;-)

—William R. Stanek

I would like to thank my editor, Steven Elliot, for his insight and advice during the development of this book. I would like to acknowledge the outstanding work done by Laura Burgess and Joyce Nielsen for their smooth and efficient management and development. The technical editors and reviewers ensured that the gaps in my knowledge were quickly filled. I would like to thank my family for their patience during my many absent hours during the writing of this book. Finally, I am grateful to Neil Salkind and the team at Studio B and I wish to acknowledge their excellent work.

—Dr. Paul Watters

Quality Assurance

We would like to thank the primary members of our Quality Assurance team for their critical effort and unstinting efforts to make sure we got it right.

Technical Editors

John M. Bunch currently teaches Web development at The International Academy of Design and Technology in Tampa, Florida. He also teaches at The University of South Florida, where he is a PhD candidate in Instructional Technology. Previously, he spent several years as a private consultant and technical trainer.

Brian Eubanks is the founder of Eu Technologies, Inc., a consulting and training firm based in Northern Virginia. Eu Technologies currently provides Java and XML consulting and training services to clients in the Mid-Atlantic region. Clients have included the New York Stock Exchange, government agencies, and public and private firms. Brian holds a master of science degree in computer science from George Mason University. He is the author of *Wicked Cool Java*, a book of interesting and useful things to do in Java, to be released in 2005. Brian also serves as the Flash editor for *MX Developer's Journal*.

Reviewers   We would like to take this opportunity to thank our outstanding reviewer team. Their attention to detail and suggestions for improvements have resulted in a better book.

Carolyn Borne is an instructor in the Information Systems and Decision Sciences Department at Louisiana State University, teaching the Internet Development Course. She holds a BS in Computer Science from Nicholls State University, and a masters in Information Systems and Decision Sciences from Louisiana State University.

George H. Fravel is currently an adjunct professor at LaSalle and Penn State Universities, teaching classes in Web Design and Development, Graphics, and Java Programming. In addition to classroom work, George is Executive Manager of Graham and Fravel Associates, an independent consulting firm devoted to Web development, training, and custom programming. With more than 20 years of systems and operations consulting experience, George brings real-world application to his writings and teaching.

Candace Garrod is a professor of Computer Science/Computer Technology at Red Rocks Community College in Colorado. She has more than 35 years of computer experience in business and industry. She worked at United Airlines for 17 years, was Director of Training at IBSN, and is President of Kaleidoscope Computing. She has also published three computer textbooks, on Authorware, Dreamweaver, and Program Logic and Design.

Heidi Kolen is currently an instructor with Okaloosa Walton College's division of Business and Computer Technology. She has taught a wide range of Computer Science courses including Web Design and Programming. Ms. Kolen also used JavaScript extensively as a Web programmer for iBinder, a Web-based content management tool used by teachers, parents, and mentors of Florida Public Schools, and as a consultant.

Web Guru Guide to JavaScript™

Chapter 1

Introducing JavaScript

This book is about *JavaScript*, the interpreted, object-based, client-side programming and scripting language jointly developed by Netscape Communications and Sun Microsystems. It started out as LiveScript, worked alongside Microsoft's JScript, and was recently standardized as ECMAScript (www.ecma-international.org/publications/standards/Ecma-357.htm). If you have ever used a Web browser to read a *Web page* or to access embedded multimedia content, the Web page probably contained JavaScript code that enabled dynamic behavior within the page. If you do not have a Web browser, Netscape Navigator can be downloaded from home.netscape.com/computing/download; Microsoft Internet Explorer can be downloaded from www.microsoft.com/ie. Put simply, the purpose of JavaScript is to add dynamic behavior to client-side Web browsers, especially when they contain forms for processing client-entered data or when some type of special presentation or layout is required.

The development of dynamic Web pages has been strongly influenced by the rise of "new" architectures for developing Web-based information systems, such as Sun's Java 2 Enterprise Edition (J2EE) architecture, which allows Web pages to be generated from data drawn from relational databases, components, message queues, and legacy systems. We will not discuss these more advanced systems in this book, but once you have mastered JavaScript and dynamic Web pages, there are many more advanced avenues to explore, starting with the simple Common Gateway Interface (CGI) for invoking server-side *scripts* or applications. CGI is an easy way to build dynamic applications that are not tied to a higher-level development environment. If you are already familiar with J2EE, you could move on to develop Java Server Pages (JSPs), or if you are a Microsoft .NET fan, Active Server Pages (ASPs) are the logical choice.

For Your Career

In this chapter, you will examine the high-level issues surrounding Web page design and implementation and why you would use JavaScript when creating dynamic Web pages. JavaScript is not suitable for solving all Web page problems, and it is important to be able to justify why you should use JavaScript on a project rather than alternative technologies based on server-side processing, such as VBScript, Java, CGI, and so on.

Chapter Exercises

This unit's exercises will teach you how to:

- Create Web pages
- Create dynamic Web pages
- Describe the available JavaScript scripting options
- Insert multiple scripts into a single page
- Use scripts and functions
- Determine how and why JavaScript can and should be used
- Determine when not to use JavaScript

By working through the exercises in this chapter, you will learn how and when to use JavaScript.

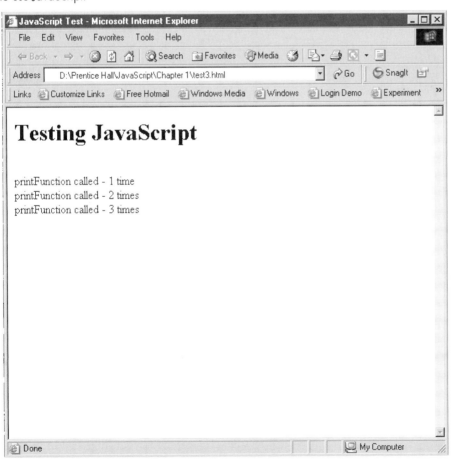

Exercise 1.1 – Creating Web Pages

When the World Wide Web (WWW) was young, Web pages were static. Web sites had to be updated manually to change the information displayed to users who accessed them. However, it quickly became clear that many Web pages were based on information that changed constantly. An individual news story is published and never changed; however, the list of breaking headline news stories changes frequently. A Webmaster or Web programmer should not have to manually change the headline news story page each time a new story is added to a site.

Thus, several approaches for creating dynamic Web pages were developed, some of which were more successful than others. At this point, it is worth pointing out that Java and JavaScript are two completely separate and independent languages even though they share some similarities in name, syntax, and function. For example, Java is an object-oriented, platform-independent, compiled language that can be used for Web development or general-purpose programming. It runs on many different platforms, just like JavaScript, and when compiled to an intermediate byte-code format, it can be executed on any platform that has a Java Virtual Machine (JVM) installed.

In contrast, JavaScript is a scripting language that has a predefined object model that is based on the structure of Web pages; Java is a much more general-purpose programming language. This is why some people refer to Java as being "object oriented" and JavaScript as being "object based." Many Web developers start with HTML, master JavaScript, and then go on to become Java developers, utilizing Web-related Java technologies such as JSPs, servlets, and applets.

Before we review JavaScript in detail, let's explore some basic concepts about Web pages and how they are retrieved. Web users run client applications such as Netscape Navigator or Microsoft Internet Explorer. These applications use the ***Hypertext Transfer Protocol (HTTP)*** to connect with Web servers. HTTP enables clients to request a page—referenced by a ***Uniform Resource Locator (URL)***—and have it returned for interpretation on the client. For example, to access the home page for Prentice Hall, the URL is www.prenhall.com. The client-server communication process is shown in Figure 1.1. Once a page is retrieved from a server, it is interpreted and displayed within the browser window, which is known as the *document* object. The browser has several other objects, including alert windows, buttons, and a status bars. We will discuss how to use each of these in the chapters that follow.

The ***Hypertext Markup Language (HTML)***, a variant of the Standard Generalized Markup Language (SGML), is used to create Web pages. The markup provided for Web page text consists of structural elements, such as `<head>` and `<body>`, as well as display directives, such as `<b>` or `<i>` for bold and italics, respectively. HTML does not provide programming capability for clients, and although HTML is based on a W3C standard (www.w3c.org/), different browsers (and different versions of the same browser) may interpret the markup differently. This problem is historical; SGML was a strict markup language that predated XML, the eXtensible Markup Language. These languages do not specify display logic. Appearing timewise between SGML and XML, HTML unwisely combined both display logic and document layout logic. Browser differences are discussed in detail at www.thewebseye.com/browsers.htm.

In this exercise, you will learn how to specify JavaScript as the scripting language to be used within a page and how to pull scripts from an external file into a HTML page. Creating modular source code is good programming practice, because different individuals usually fill the roles of "HTML developer" and "JavaScript programmer."

FIGURE 1.1

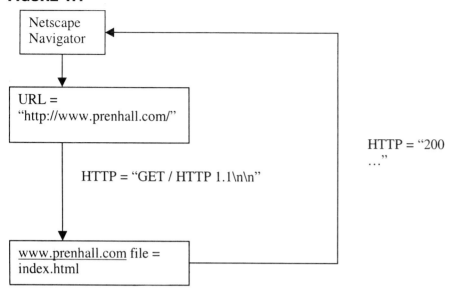

The former is usually responsible for the HTML markup, whereas the latter is responsible for the scripting. Indeed, to encourage proper demarcation, the JavaScript developer may only allow read-only access to his or her JavaScript code to the HTML developer to prevent inadvertent modification of the JavaScript code.

STEP 1 – CREATING A WEB PAGE

In order to introduce some basic concepts, let's start by creating a HTML document. In your text editor, create a new blank page and save it as "stockquote.html." You will create a sample HTML page for a stock price quote by entering the HTML code shown in Exhibit 1.1.

EXHIBIT 1.1

```
<html>
 <head>
  <title>Stock Quote</title>
 </head>
 <body>
  <h1>Stock Quote</h1>
  <p>Sun Microsystems: $4.00</p>
 </body>
</html>
```

In addition to the tags shown here, some tags can accept attributes that modify their behavior in some way. For example, on HTML forms that contain an OK button, the name of the button and its displayed value must be specified by using an attribute, as shown below for the address1 field:

```
<input type="button" name="btnOK" value="OK"></p>
```

When to Use Dynamic HTML

A facility that provides dynamic behavior for Web pages is necessary because the pages themselves contain very little information about the document's structure or the display of items within the document. In this example, because the stock price of Sun Microsystems (and most other stocks) changes many times a day, it would be very inefficient to require someone to manually update the page for each price change. Indeed, if a read lock on the open HTML file was not respected by the Web server, then users would not be able to retrieve the stock price for a large percentage of the trading day. What is really required is the ability to update the contents of Web pages and the ability to control the display of data retrieved from a Web server.

STEP 2 – DISPLAYING A WEB PAGE

Open the HTML file you created in Step 1 in Internet Explorer by using the File, Open command. After parsing the HTML file, the browser will display it, as shown in Figure 1.2. Note the placement and style of the various header and body elements. These can be greatly enhanced through the use of Cascading Style Sheets (CSS), which have increased the display and style options available to Web page designers, but which are beyond the scope of this book.

FIGURE 1.2

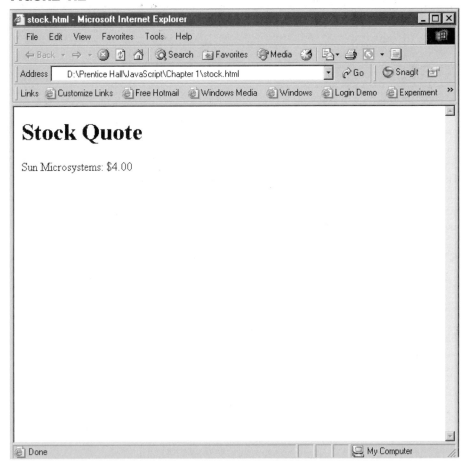

Exercise 1.2 – Creating a Dynamic Web Page

Dynamic behavior can be added to Web pages in one of two ways: programming on the client side or programming on the server side. Server-side programming can generate dynamic Web pages through the use of *Common Gateway Interface (CGI)*, *Java Server Pages (JSPs),* and Java Servlets. In practice, many Web-based applications use both server-side and client-side programming to create dynamic Web pages.

Server-side programming is best suited for situations where all clients perform the same types of tasks, with little knowledge of how the end result is presented. For example, the method used to gather stock prices should be common to many different applications—you wouldn't want each client to have to write their own! However, the stock price information can be used in many different ways, and the server shouldn't dictate to the client how this should be used. This is particularly important when the servers and clients run different operating systems and environments—the type of information display required for a UNIX server may be very different from that required by a Microsoft Windows client! Also, different companies may customize information differently according to their own needs.

All other things being equal, it is best to use client CPU power as much as possible in a distributed system, which is exactly what Web servers do as they service thousands of clients every day. To ensure that the service provided by a Web server is scalable, client systems should use as much of their own processing power as possible to reduce the burden on the server. Thus, although it is possible to do many things on the server side, such as validating data entered on a Web form, in practice, this can be performed by a JavaScript on the client side. In addition, network traffic can be minimized by using JavaScript to perform form validation, because there is no need to connect to the server until all of the fields have been validated on the client side.

Java applets work in a similar way, offloading processing tasks to the client to the greatest extent possible. Both applets and JavaScript enable dynamic behavior to be scripted on the client side. However, applets run as separate, sandboxed applications within a Web page; they are not an integral part of a Web page. Also, applets can normally only connect to the server they were downloaded from. Thus, although the applet security model reduces the chance that untrusted code is malicious, it's really a fat-client technology that requires a high level of technical expertise to work with. In contrast, JavaScript provides a simple, object-based model for development that enables developers to build on their knowledge of HTML page elements to create programmable Web pages.

Exercise 1.3 – Scripting Options

One of the benefits of a scripting language such as JavaScript is that you don't need to "compile" before using it. For example, with a Java applet, you need to design, develop, compile, and deploy the class files before using the applet. With JavaScript, you just edit a script in a text editor and load it into a Web browser. All browsers have a JavaScript interpreter that will execute commands on the fly, meaning that you can debug and test more quickly than with traditional development. In addition, because Web pages have a well-defined object structure, much of the design work is simplified. Writing a Java applet requires an in-depth knowledge of the two major windowing libraries (AWT and Swing) before any development can be undertaken. With JavaScript, you can reuse your knowledge of HTML to develop client-side applications more quickly.

One of the main drawbacks of the quick run and test cycle is that errors will not be picked up before they are executed, unlike a compiled language, where syntax errors are detected before a binary executable is created. Another potential problem is that different browsers have different interpreters, and there are several versions of JavaScript in existence. A JavaScript created and tested in one browser and for one version of the standard may not work in another browser honoring the same specification or any other.

Learn HTML before JavaScript

This book assumes that you have a working knowledge of HTML, that you can use a text editor to create JavaScripts, and that you know how to load HTML pages with embedded JavaScripts into a Web browser. If you do not know how to complete any of these tasks, you will need to read a more basic book on HTML or visit one of the many HTML developer's sites on the Internet (such as www.page resource.com/html). Some HTML editors have integrated support for JavaScript development and debugging. If you already use such an editor, check whether it supports JavaScript.

It certainly pays to test often and broadly when developing JavaScripts that must be supported across different platforms.

Although the reasons for the problems associated with browser incompatibilities are largely historical, it is important to keep in mind that JavaScript was a late addition to the Web and programming in general: It was only in late 1995 that the second version of Netscape Navigator was available with JavaScript 1.0. At present, most browsers, including Microsoft Internet Explorer 5.0 and above and Netscape Navigator 4.5 and above, support JavaScript 1.3. Text-based browsers, such as Lynx and earlier versions of the two main browsers, may support only JavaScript 1.2 and/or 1.1 or no version at all. JavaScript versions 1.4 through 1.7 are currently being developed by Netscape, but their acceptance by Microsoft and other browser vendors is not clear.

STEP 1 – CREATING A STATIC WEB PAGE

In your text editor, create a new static HTML document using the code shown in Exhibit 1.2. You should be able to load this code into your browser as described in Exercise 1.1.

EXHIBIT 1.2

```
<html>
 <head>
  <title>JavaScript Test</title>
 </head>
 <body>
  <h1>Testing JavaScript</h1>
 </body>
</html>
```

STEP 2 – MAKING THE WEB PAGE DYNAMIC

In your text editor, modify the static HTML document created in Step 1 by inserting the code shown in Exhibit 1.3 after the </h1> tag. Save the file as "test.html" and load it into your browser, as shown in Figure 1.3.

EXHIBIT 1.3

```
<script type="text/javascript">
document.write("JavaScript is running OK!");
</script>
```

When the browser loads the HTML file, it parses the normal HTML tags until it reaches <script>, at which point it passes interpretation of the script code to the interpreter specified by the language attribute. Thus, it is technically possible to use languages other than JavaScript in this context. Scripts can be included within the <head> and <body> elements or both. It is also possible to keep the JavaScript source in a separate file from the HTML code. This is useful when one person is responsible for the HTML markup and another is responsible for the scripting. Indeed, to encourage proper demarcation, the JavaScript developer may only allow read-only access to the

FIGURE 1.3

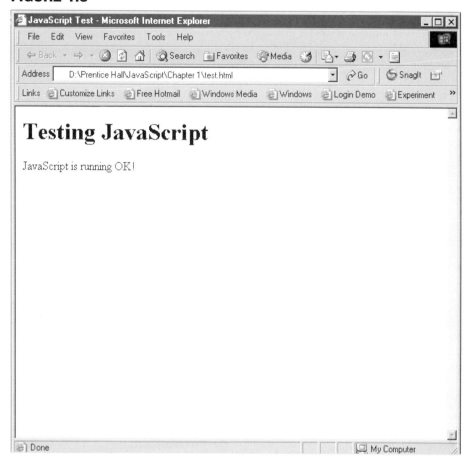

HTML developer for her JavaScript code, to prevent inadvertent modification of the JavaScript code. To include an external script in the previous example, we would change the `<script>` line to the following:

```
<script language="JavaScript" src="testScript.js">
```

Note that the `language="JavaScript"` convention is for JavaScript 1.2 and earlier, whereas JavaScript 1.3 and beyond uses the MIME-style `script type="text/javascript"`, as shown in Exhibit 1.3. In the script shown here, we have only included a single line of code. However, a JavaScript can have many different lines of code that comprise a single script. The scripts can also do many more useful things other than just printing out text; data can be stored in different types of *variables*, representing numbers, strings, and characters, and a large number of operators can be used to transform this data. For example, a DVD shopping basket application may have a variable that contains the number of items contained in the basket. This variable would have to be of an integer type, because it would be impossible to order half a DVD. The list of DVD titles placed in the basket would have to be stored in a string type of array, because titles contain sets of letters that make up the name. An array is required wherever more than one item that belongs to a set—like a list of DVD titles—needs to be stored.

JavaScript also has the ability to repeat the same action a number of times, using various kinds of loops, and can make decisions based on this kind of iteration. For example, the maximum number of DVDs that could be placed in a shopping basket might be 10. Before an order is processed, the number of DVD titles contained in the array would have to be counted using a loop, and if this number exceeded 10, then the order would have to be modified. Although this procedure could just be included as part of the JavaScript body, it could also be spun out into a special counting *function*, allowing it to be reused more than once within the same script or called from multiple scripts to support modular programming. With modular programming, an effort is made to create code that is self-contained and reusable. In object terms, functions are more often referred to as *methods*.

As mentioned previously, JavaScript is an object-based language. One of the main benefits of JavaScript is that the object model is already well defined—Web browsers have document, window, and button objects that have their own methods that can be invoked within the script. You have already seen how the document object has a write method that can be invoked to print text to the screen. The document object has many other methods that we will discuss later in the text.

Another aspect of object orientation that is used heavily in JavaScript is event handling. This means that when something happens to an object, it can be handled in a customizable way. Writing JavaScripts in a Web browser follows an event-driven programming model. For example, the Click event has an event handler called onClick that is called whenever the user clicks on a button, form, or some other object. Although some event handlers specify default behavior, developers generally will want to add their own handling.

Exercise 1.4 – Using Multiple Scripts

A HTML page can contain more than one script, which may or may not be written in JavaScript. This example demonstrates two things: how to include two different scripts in a page and how to invoke methods on two different objects—document and window objects. The `document.write` example just prints out text; the `window.alert` example creates an alert window with an OK button and some text. Other window methods allow text to be entered by the user and processed by the script. At each stage of the incremental development of scripts, it is useful to refresh the loaded page in your Web browser to check your work.

STEP 1 – INSERTING A SECOND SCRIPT

Load the test.html page that you created in Exercise 1.3 into your text editor. Replace its contents with the code shown in Exhibit 1.4. Save the file and then load it into your browser. It should appear as the sample output shown in Figure 1.4.

EXHIBIT 1.4

```
<html>
 <head>
  <title>JavaScript Test</title>
 </head>
 <body>
  <h1>Testing JavaScript</h1>
```

```
 <p>Script 1</p>
 <script type="text/javascript">
  document.write("JavaScript is running OK!");
 </script>
 <p>Script 2</p>
 <script type="text/javascript">
  window.alert("Click OK to continue");
 </script>
 </body>
</html>
```

FIGURE 1.4

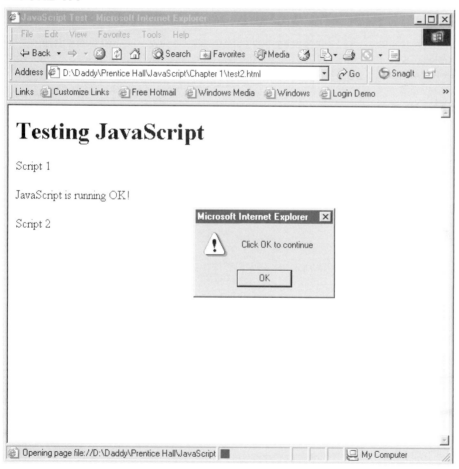

Exercise 1.5 – Scripts and Functions

Another important aspect of JavaScript programming is the use of functions. *Functions* are encapsulated (self-contained) segments of JavaScript that are (a) used repetitively,

(b) separated out from the main script, and (c) can be invoked by using the function's name and passing any required parameters. Sometimes a function returns a discrete value, such as a mathematical function that returns the square root of a passed-in value. In this book, you will learn to use functions extensively to support modular, well-designed scripts that can be reused. However, in the following example, we have removed the `document.write()` method call from the <body> section and defined it as a function called `printFunction(x)` within the <head> element. Because the function is defined in the <head> element, it can then be called anywhere in the <body>—perhaps more than once! Indeed, this example shows that you can pass a single parameter to the function—representing the number of times it has been called from the <body>, represented by the variable x—and the function can use this when it calls `document.write()` after it is passed in as variable y. Each time the function is called, x is incremented by one and passed to the `printFunction`.

STEP 1 – INSERTING A SECOND SCRIPT

Load the test.html page that you created in Exercise 1.3 into your text editor. Replace its contents with the code shown in Exhibit 1.5. Save the file and then load it into your browser. It should appear as the sample output shown in Figure 1.5.

EXHIBIT 1.5

```
<html>
 <head>
  <title>JavaScript Test</title>
  <script type="text/javascript">
   function printFunction(y)
   {
    if (y==1)
    {
     document.write("<br>printFunction called - "+x+"
       time");
    }
    else
    {
     document.write("<br>printFunction called - "+x+"
       times\n");
    }
   }
  </script>
 </head>
 <body>
  <h1>Testing JavaScript</h1>
  <script type="text/javascript">
   var x=1;
   printFunction(x);
   x++;
   printFunction(x);
```

```
   x++;
   printFunction(x);
  </script>
 </body>
</html>
```

FIGURE 1.5

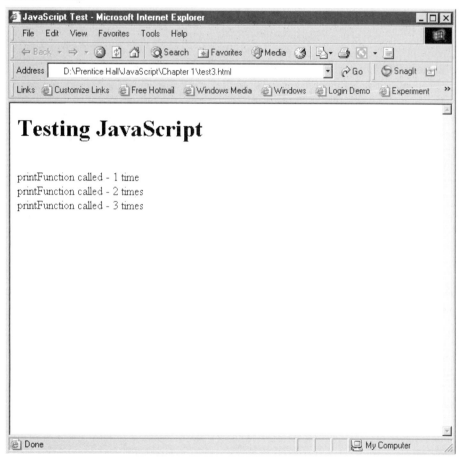

Notice that when the script is run correctly, it prints "1 time," "2 times," "3 times," and so on because we have enabled some decision logic based on the value of the parameter y to correctly enumerate the number of times `printFunction` has been called. Worrying about plural and singular forms may seem trivial, but my current cellular phone has numerous such errors in its user interface, such as "1 entrys is found" in the address book!

In this section, we only examined some basic features of JavaScript and script development. In later chapters, we will examine how all of these characteristics can be used to develop sophisticated client-side applications.

Exercise 1.6 – When to Use JavaScript

JavaScript is most useful for controlling and customizing the display of information that requires the decision logic, data structures, functions, and operators not provided by HTML. It provides a basic level of programmability for all client-side processing. Thus, there is no point in writing expensive server-side scripts to run on the server if all the script does is process and validate user data submitted via a form when the burden of that work can be carried locally. Many of us have tried to access Web pages and online services that have failed because of too many client accesses. By making use of client-side programming through JavaScript and designing applications appropriately, such problems can be avoided. Of course, a JavaScript syntax error could prevent a user from submitting form data that is correct, so it's important to design and test JavaScript code with the same rigor as compiled applications.

Validation of user-entered form data is the most common use of JavaScript by Web applications. In this scenario, a number of checks are performed on the fields supplied on a HTML form, according to specifications typically supplied by a business analyst. For example, name and address fields on a registration form will be subject to a number of checks before submission to the server. Some of these checks can be performed using HTML, such as setting the size attribute of a text field to the maximum allowable by the specification. Others require JavaScript, especially when there is some repetitive checking. For example, a password might need to be checked to ensure that it is secure, does not contain two repeating elements, has at least two numbers as well as characters, and does not contain the corresponding user name in some permuted form. All of these operations can be performed on the client side and can be programmed using JavaScript; these CPU-intensive tasks do not have to performed on the server.

A second important application of JavaScript is in the area of **Dynamic HTML (DHTML)**. DHTML can be used with CSS to spice up Web pages with dynamic elements and various types of special effects with layering. Although this sort of programming is not generally related to the user interface requirements of a Web page, it can be very useful when customizing Web pages for certain types of browsers. We do not cover this type of DHTML in this book, but the Prentice Hall title *DHTML and JavaScript* by Gilorien certainly does.

A more programmatic view of JavaScript is taken when it is used as the client "backplane" for a presentation layer in Web-based enterprise applications. In this case, a JavaScript might be contained within a HTML page that is dynamically generated from a Java Server Page that is itself connected to a database (along the lines of the stock price example we discussed earlier in this chapter). One of the reasons that JavaScript is useful in this context is that it can access state information stored in client-side cookies. *Cookies* are small chunks of data subject that are unique to each user. Cookies are very useful for tracking user state when clients are navigating through long, complicated applications. If a user logs out of an application, then his or her state can be saved on the server side and his or her user name written to a cookie. This cookie can then be used to identify the user on his or her next visit. Using cookies has some security issues, which are discussed later in the chapter.

Another important reason to use JavaScript on the client side has to do with the nature of the HTTP protocol. Remember that HTTP is a request/response protocol. If a form is validated on the server side, every mistake would require four network operations: the original request, the response indicating an error, the modified request, and the final response. By using JavaScript, you can process data without going back to the Web server, thereby reducing network traffic in a significant way. Particularly for users with slow modem connections but fast computers, this can be really useful.

The final benefit of using JavaScript is that scripts can access the local features of a Web browser, which server-side processes cannot. For example, JavaScript can be used to create windows with certain dimensions or to obtain the value of the status bar. This can be very useful when customizing pages for displaying different types of information based on local conditions.

Exercise 1.7 – When Not to Use JavaScript

Although JavaScript is very useful, there are several reasons why you may not use it for every Web site. For example, simple Web applications request data from a server and then display the results on the screen. What if you needed to write data back to the server directly, without requiring the user to press a submit button? In this scenario, you're going to need a "fatter" or "thicker" client that can use different protocols and that has more general-purpose programmability than JavaScripts do. For example, Java applets support Remote Method Invocation (RMI) to execute method calls on remote server objects. JavaScript cannot do this directly, although it can act as the backplane for a servlet that could directly access these objects. In general, if you need applications with this advanced level of functionality, it is probably time to migrate from a simple Web server to a J2EE application server or to Microsoft .NET.

Another problem with JavaScript is its poor security model. When you create a script and include it in a Web page, it is downloaded to the client browsers and executed. However, any user can browse the contents of a downloaded page and its scripts by selecting "View Source" from the menu bar. Developers have devised various tricks and obfuscation methods, such as hiding the menu bar, to avoid this problem, but a really determined hacker could just use HTTP commands directly on the Web server port to download the scripts without executing them. Thus, you need to accept that everyone can see your scripts and download them and reuse them without your permission. Thus, if you need a stronger security model on the client side, applets are probably your best choice, because they can normally only write data to the server from which they were downloaded. However, even applets cannot completely hide the source code, because Java bytecode can be introspected and decompiled fairly easily, even if an obfuscator is used to randomly assign variable and method names to make it hard to follow.

The final situation when JavaScript is not suitable is when you need a more specialized programming architecture on the client, such as a component model. Although Web pages do have a well-defined object model, if you want to create your own, you are going to need something like Java Beans. Again, there is nothing stopping you from creating JSPs that access beans and have JavaScript, but remember that JavaScript can't do everything!

Summary

This chapter introduced how JavaScript can be used to make Web pages programmable. This programmability makes it easy to validate forms and perform CPU-intensive tasks on the client, reducing server and network load. JavaScript also can be used with CSS to make Web pages more dynamic.

Note that although JavaScript provides solutions for some problems with regards to the Web, some problems still remain, such as the fact that URLs are location based rather than content based. When the physical location of Web content changes, the client receives a 404 Not Found message—even if the page requested has just been moved somewhere else on the same server!

You can review some sample JavaScripts by visiting just a few of the many sites on the Internet where people share them. Although it may seem easier to just download scripts rather than use your own, you still need to test the scripts to ensure that they behave as expected. In my experience, it is easier to just learn the basics of JavaScript and the object model rather than debug someone else's scripts! Some of the better JavaScript repositories include www.pageresource.com/jscript and http://www.javascriptcity.com.

Test Your Skills

Practice Drill 1.1: Displaying Web Page Text

In this exercise, you will observe what happens when you use document.write() to display a string. Strings can contain static or dynamically generated text. Normally, you would just embed static text within a HTML <body> section, but dynamic text must be created inside the script. The following example shows how this works in practice:

1. In your text editor, create a HTML page with the appropriate <head> and <body> elements:

```
<html>
        <head>
                <title>Text Display Example</title>
        </head>
        <body>
        </body>
</html>
```

2. Insert the following JavaScript code block between the <body> tags:

```
<script type="text/javascript">
</script>
```

3. Insert a document.write() method call between the <script> tags:

```
document.write("");
```

4. Insert the text to be displayed:

```
document.write("Testing the document.write method!");
```

5. Load the page into your Web browser.

6. The following results will be displayed:

```
Testing the document.write method!
```

MULTIPLE-CHOICE QUESTIONS

1. For which of the following is JavaScript *not* the appropriate technology?
   A. Adding dynamic behavior to client-side Web browsers
   B. Processing client-entered form data
   C. Customized Web page presentations
   D. Gaining access to databases

2. What is the similarity between Java and JavaScript?
   A. One is a script version of a real compiled language.
   B. They are both compiled languages with the same object model.
   C. They always run the same in every browser.
   D. One is a general-purpose compiled language; the other has an object model based on Web page structure.

3. What does the "document" in `document.write()` refer to?
   A. Any type of word processing document
   B. The document object representing a HTML page
   C. A JavaScript document loaded in from a stand-alone file
   D. A variable type defined within the JavaScript language

4. What is the opening tag for a JavaScript script embedded in a Web page?
   A. `<script type="text/javascript">`
   B. `<JAVAscript language="JavaScript">`
   C. `<script language="Script" type="Java">`
   D. `<JAVA language="JavaScript">`

5. Where can a JavaScript function definition appear?
   A. Only in the `<head>`
   B. Only in the `<body>`
   C. In the `<head>` or the `<body>`
   D. After a `<JAVA>` tag

FILL-IN-THE-BLANK QUESTIONS

1. HTTP allows clients to request a page that is described by a _____ Resource Locator.

2. Web pages are crafted with the _____ Markup Language (HTML).

3. Many Web-based applications use both _____-side and client-side programming to create dynamic Web pages.

4. JavaScript provides a simple, _____ model for development.

5. Scripts can be included within the _____ and <body> elements or both.

DEFINITIONS QUESTIONS

1. What is a JavaScript?

2. What is Dynamic HTML?

3. What is a function?

4. What is an object?

5. What is encapsulation?

BASIC PROJECTS

The following short projects provide you with the opportunity to create a new Web
page, create a simple JavaScript, and insert it into the page.

Project 1.1 – Creating a Welcome Web Page

This project will require you to create a welcome page for an Internet banking application. Create a HTML page that has correct <head> and <body> elements. Create a
JavaScript that displays two HTML statements to the user using the document.
write method:

```
"<p>Welcome to Internet Banking</p>"
"<p>Click NEXT to Continue...</p>"
```

Insert the JavaScript into the <body> section of the Web page. Load the Web page into
Internet Explorer and Netscape Navigator. Does it display correctly?

Project 1.2 – Using a Function

This project will require you to extend Project 1.1 by creating a function that calls the
document.write method instead of calling document.write directly. You can
display the same text as in Project 1. Load the page into Internet Explorer and Netscape
Navigator. Does it display correctly?

▶▶Career Builder

In the Career Builder sections at the end of each chapter, you will work toward completing a full-fledged JavaScript project. The Career Builder is challenging, but rewarding, much like a career in Web design.

The actual work for your project begins in Chapter 2. Your task in this Career Builder is an easy but extremely important one: Play around with JavaScript. Test it out. Look up some methods from later chapters and see what they do. Try to get a feel for how scripts are laid out and written.

As you explore, keep in mind that nothing you do in JavaScript can harm the software or your computer, so feel free to experiment. If you get stuck, simply close your text editor and start again. Your objective is to relax, have fun, and become friends with the software. The better acquainted you are, the easier being productive becomes.

Chapter 2

Adding Client-Side Scripts to Web Pages

Browsers and HTML Web pages have a well-defined set of *objects* associated with them. JavaScript operates directly on these objects, such as document objects, instantiating them if necessary and invoking their methods as part of a script. This chapter introduces you to the *document object* and its *write method*, which simply prints text to a Web page. Once you include other programming elements, such as variables, printing dynamic text becomes more interesting, as we will see in the chapters that follow.

In this chapter, you will learn how commonly used objects within browsers and Web pages, such as the document object, can be employed to create effective scripts that work across different browser versions.

The chapter exercises will introduce an Internet banking example that will be used throughout the rest of this book. In the chapter exercises, you will create a welcome Web page using JavaScript methods and elements.

For Your Career

In this chapter, you will learn basic skills that will enable you to create dynamic Web pages with many layers. JavaScript is an important part of Dynamic HTML; it provides the foundation for all of the computational work required to work with browser objects.

All of the skills you will learn in this chapter will be useful to you when you create your own Web sites. Whether producing structured layouts, designing of scripts, or displaying an understanding of the subtleties of different JavaScript versions and implementations, building robust JavaScripts will impress every user who visits your pages.

Chapter Exercises

This unit's exercises will teach you how to:

- Identify JavaScript as the scripting language being used in a Web page
- Add JavaScripts to Web pages
- Use comments inside JavaScripts
- Solve compatibility issues between browsers and JavaScript versions

By working through the exercises, you will use JavaScript methods and elements to create a welcome Web page that has a dynamic date display.

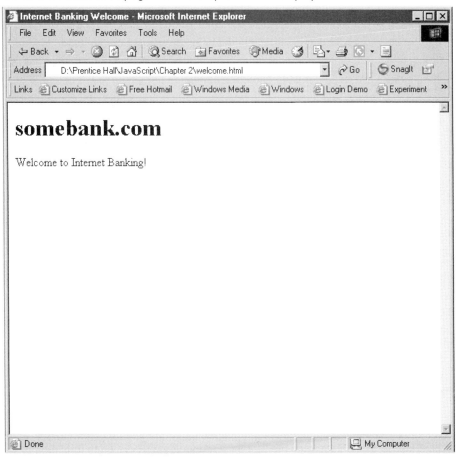

Exercise 2.1 – Identifying JavaScript

JavaScript has several different versions, and different implementations of the same version can have significant differences in functionality. Indeed, other scripting languages may be used instead of JavaScript within a browser. Therefore, it is important as a first step to be able to correctly identify JavaScript as the language of choice for a specific HTML page.

In this exercise, you will learn how to specify JavaScript as the scripting language to be used within a page and how to read in scripts from an external file into a HTML page. This is good programming practice, because different individuals may fill the roles of HTML developer and JavaScript programmer. The former is usually responsible for the HTML markup, whereas the latter is responsible for the scripting.

According to the W3C, the ***language attribute*** of the `<script>` tag is deprecated in HTML 4. In addition, it is no longer supported by Internet Explorer 6 or by recent versions of other browsers, such as Mozilla 1.6. In the future, all script tags should leave off the language attribute, such as `<script language="JavaScript1.5" type="text/javascript">`, or include both the MIME type and the language instead, such as `<script language="JavaScript1.5" type="text/javascript">` for JavaScript 1.5.

In the set of exercises that follow, you will learn how to create basic JavaScripts and insert them into Web pages. This is a fairly easy task, but ensuring that certain browsers execute your scripts correctly is more problematic. That is why it is important for you to always identify the scripting language being used inside your `<script>` blocks and to appreciate some of the differences between HTML pages and JavaScripts. For example, HTML tags are case insensitive, whereas JavaScript elements are mostly case sensitive. Because there are semantic differences between the interpretations of JavaScript in different browsers, sloppy coding that is accepted by one browser may not be accepted by another. Don't be fooled!

Script design and layout is a very important issue for the maintenance of your code. One of the greatest problems with JavaScript is the extent to which novice coders "borrow" other developer's code and insert it into their own. Many Web pages contain the modern day equivalent of "spaghetti code"—unreadable, undebuggable code that is impossible to maintain. Worse still, students copy and paste this code, thereby repeating other's mistakes. By learning good design and commenting skills, you will develop good practices and avoid harmful ones.

STEP 1 – SELECTING JAVASCRIPT

In your text editor, create a code block by inserting an opening `<script>` tag and a closing `</script>` tag. All scripts, whether they are JavaScript, VBScript, or any other scripting language, must be identified by an attribute in the `<script>` code block. Thus, to identify the code block as JavaScript, you would need to pass the appropriate attribute `type="text/javascript"`, as shown in Exhibit 2.1.

EXHIBIT 2.1

```
<script type="text/javascript">
</script>
```

Exhibit 2.1 declares a JavaScript code block and nothing else. If you wanted to do something useful, like dynamically generate a line of text and pipe it to the HTML page, you would use the code shown in Exhibit 2.2.

EXHIBIT 2.2

```
<script type="text/javascript">
        document.write("Using JavaScript 1.5!");
</script>
```

You will learn about the document object and the write method in more detail in the exercises that follow.

Ordinary HTML tags are not case sensitive, so `<H1>` is parsed in the same way as `<h1>`. Although you could write `<script language="JavaScript">`, `<script language="JAVAscript">`, or `<script type="text/javascript">`, and they would be parsed as equivalent, this is not the case for the JavaScript code included between the `<script>` tags. However, because we are using the *XHTML* standard for HTML in this book, all tags are lowercase, making it possible for a *DOM* parser to parse the files correctly.

STEP 2 – READING SCRIPTS FROM FILES

In your text editor, you can create separate files for the JavaScript and the HTML source. This enables different people to develop HTML pages and JavaScript code, and it is a good source-control strategy. Once created, the scripts would be located and loaded from the server where the calling JavaScript resides. For example, to create the welcome Web page for an Internet banking Web site, you would create a HTML page called welcome.html, as shown in Exhibit 2.3.

EXHIBIT 2.3

```
<html>
      <head>
            <title>Internet Banking Welcome</title>
      </head>
      <body>
            <script type="text/javascript"
                src="welcome.js">
      </script>
      </body>
</html>
```

Here, the `<script>` element has an attribute called "src" (usually read as "source"). When the browser loads the page, and after the `<script>` tag is parsed, the browser uses its built-in JavaScript interpreter to load in the script and execute it before loading the remainder of the Web page.

Of course, to actually execute the script stored in welcome.js, you need to create the welcome.js file and insert valid JavaScript. For example, to print a welcome banner for the Internet banking Web page, you would insert the statement shown in Exhibit 2.4 into welcome.js. The output is shown in Figure 2.1.

EXHIBIT 2.4

```
document.write("Welcome to Internet Banking!");
```

FIGURE 2.1

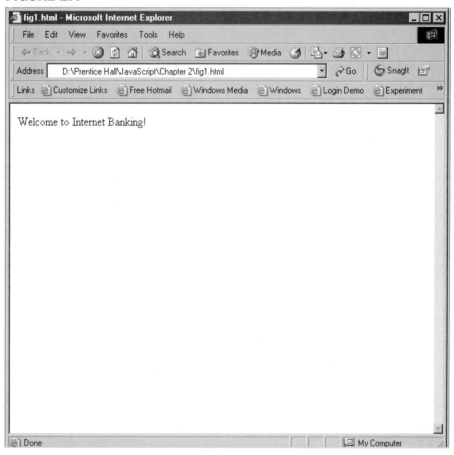

When you create HTML page layouts, you need to identify the sections where you will be inserting JavaScripts. You may decide to have one script per page, in which case you can store scripts in files with the same filename prefix as the corresponding Web page, as shown in Exhibits 2.3 and 2.4 for welcome.html and welcome.js, respectively. However, things become more complicated if you begin using multiple scripts within a page to carry out discrete tasks. In this case, you may want to include that task in the file name. For example, a welcome.html page may have a validation script for a password stored in the file welcome validation.js.

The statement shown in Exhibit 2.4 is pretty self-explanatory when you see the page output; the text enclosed in quotes is simply inserted into the HTML document as it is displayed on the screen. The text in quotes is a collection of characters that is technically known as a *string*. However, under the surface, a number of important things are happening: A *reference* to an object (the HTML document) is being made and one of its methods (`write`) is being invoked. The characters are enclosed in double quotes to create a single string argument, and method arguments are always enclosed within parentheses. Each *method* can take as many *parameters* as required by the script to perform its function. You will learn more about JavaScript objects and their methods in later chapters.

Exercise 2.2 – Adding Scripts to Web Pages

JavaScripts consist of a set of *statements* that are executed sequentially by the interpreter. The code you used to display the string `"Welcome to Internet Banking!"` in Exhibit 2.4 is a statement because it is self-contained and terminated by a semicolon. More formally, a *statement* is a syntactically valid code element that is *encapsulated*. Throughout the book, you will see many examples of JavaScript statements and the various forms that they can take.

Multiple JavaScripts in a single Web page are also executed sequentially; the first script is executed first, the second script is executed next, and so on. It is important for you to design your HTML documents in a way that allows each script to be executed correctly.

STEP 1 – CREATING A HTML DOCUMENT

In your text editor, load the existing HTML document, welcome.html, shown in Exhibit 2.3. Add the single JavaScript statement as shown in Exhibit 2.4 to arrive at the complete code shown in Exhibit 2.5. Notice the indentation between code blocks in the HTML and the JavaScript source. Indentation makes debugging easy because you can match the starting and terminating elements within a code block and identify any missing elements easily. For example, you might start the `<script>` code block, write a series of statements, and then forget to terminate the `<script>` code block with the element `</script>`. This will generate a syntax error in many browsers.

EXHIBIT 2.5

```
<html>
     <head>
          <title>Internet Banking Welcome</title>
     </head>
     <body>
          <script type="text/javascript">
                 document.write("Welcome to Internet
                 Banking!");
          </script>
     </body>
</html>
```

STEP 2 – INSERTING THE SCRIPT

In your text editor, insert a second statement in the first code block, which will be executed after the first statement. Then insert a second JavaScript block to be executed sequentially after the first JavaScript block. This now increases the number of statements to four and the number of code blocks to two, as shown in Exhibit 2.6.

EXHIBIT 2.6

```html
<html>
     <head>
          <title>Internet Banking Welcome</title>
     </head>
     <body>
          <script type="text/javascript">
                  document.write("<p>Welcome to
                      Internet Banking! </p>");
                  document.write("<p>Welcome again to
                      Internet Banking! </p>");
          </script>
          <p>Insert some plain HTML here.</p>
          <script type="text/javascript">
                  document.write("<p>Thanks for using
                      Internet Banking!</p>");
                   document.write("<p>Thanks once
                      again for using Internet
          Banking!</p>");
          </script>
     </body>
</html>
```

STEP 3 – TESTING THE SCRIPT IN A BROWSER

In your browser, select File, Open and use the file browser to select and open the welcome.html file. The output is shown in Figure 2.2. Normally, if a file resides on a Web server, you would simply type the appropriate URL into the browser's Address field to request the HTML page.

Many procedural languages, such as C, and object-oriented languages, such as Java, terminate their statements with a semicolon. JavaScript is no exception! The normal convention is to place each JavaScript on a line of its own, generally with tabbed indenting from the margin. However, there is some looseness in the implementation of JavaScript interpreters. Some interpreters will correctly process valid statements even if they are not terminated by a semicolon. By not including a semicolon, however, you introduce some uncertainty of execution into the code, making it difficult to track down and debug errors across browsers.

JavaScript interpreters read and process statements atomically and in isolation from each other. This means that after the interpreter encounters a semicolon and terminates a

FIGURE 2.2

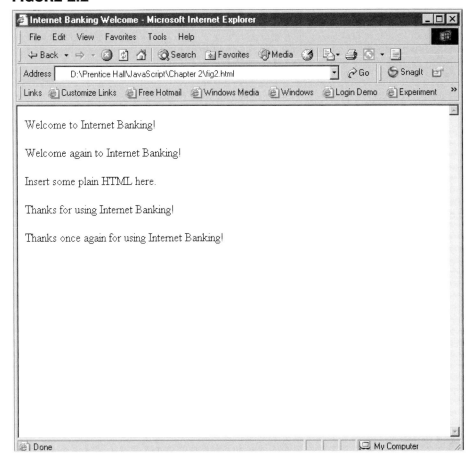

statement, the interpreter skips all empty space (or *whitespace*), including literal space characters and end-of-line characters, until it reads the next nonspace character. It then treats this character as the start of another statement. This means that you can include as much whitespace as you like in your code, depending on your coding style.

Exercise 2.3 – Using Comments

Comments are an excellent way to document your code. When you create your scripts, you may use variables and create functions that make sense to you, but nobody else. Thus, when someone else comes along to maintain your scripts, they won't even know where to start working! It has been estimated that 80 percent of programming time is spent in revisions, and this can increase if scripts are not properly documented. Commenting code is generally necessary even if the same person writes and maintains the code—especially if that person is a beginning programmer.

You should always explain the less-than-obvious aspects of your scripts using *in-line comments*. For example, in your Internet banking application, you may decide to write a function that checks whether a user name has the correct number of letters. You may decide to name this function so that it is self-describing—for example, `checkUsernameNumberOfLettersIsCorrect()`—but that takes a long time to type out every time you want to call the function. You may decide to abbreviate this function name to something like `checkUNOLIC()`, which only makes sense if you can refer it semantically back to the self-describing term `checkUsernameNumber-OfLettersIsCorrect()`. Comments allow you to do this.

STEP 1 – INSERTING SINGLE LINE COMMENTS

In your text editor, load the existing HTML document welcome.html shown in Exhibit 2.6. To insert a single line comment, you enclose it between the comment start element `<!--` and the closing element `//-->`. The reason that these rather strange combinations of characters are used is to prevent the interpreter from mistaking the element as normal text. After all, many documents (such as C++ program listings) on the Web might contain the literal strings `//`, which are standard C++ comments, but few would contain `<!--`.

Many interpreters permit the `//` comment style to be used and also honor the classical C syntax of `/* Insert Comment Here */`.

To insert the comment "Internet Banking Welcome Page" into the script, insert the string enclosed by the comment elements, as shown in Exhibit 2.7.

EXHIBIT 2.7

```html
<html>
    <head>
        <title>Internet Banking Welcome</title>
    </head>
    <body>
        <script type="text/javascript">
            <!-- Internet Banking Welcome
                Page //-->
            document.write("Welcome to Internet
                Banking!");
        </script>
    </body>
</html>
```

STEP 2 – USING MULTIPLE LINE COMMENTS

In your text editor, add a second line to your comment, with the end comment element on the next line, as shown in Exhibit 2.8, and refresh your page. You will probably see the error message shown in Figure 2.3. The error occurs because each additional line of commentary requires a comment continue element to be placed at the beginning of each line. This element is the same as the standard C++ comment element `//`. The correct form of the multiline comment is shown in Exhibit 2.9.

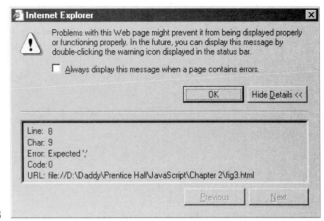

FIGURE 2.3

EXHIBIT 2.8

```
<html>
    <head>
        <title>Internet Banking Welcome</title>
    </head>
    <body>
        <script language="JavaScript">
                <!--Internet Banking
                Welcome Page//-->
                document.write("<p>Welcome to
                    Internet Banking!</p>");
        </script>
    </body>
</html>
```

EXHIBIT 2.9

```
<html>
    <head>
        <title>Internet Banking Welcome</title>
    </head>
    <body>
        <script language="JavaScript">
                <!--Internet Banking
                //Welcome Page//-->
                document.write("<p>Welcome to
        Internet Banking!</p>");
        </script>
    </body>
</html>
```

Hiding Scripts from Older Browsers

Older browsers that do not support JavaScript have a tendency to display scripts in-line because they are not recognized as code. To prevent this from happening, scripts can be enclosed in a set of special comment symbols, as shown in Exhibit 2.10. Ensure that you place the comments after the `<script>` element is declared; otherwise, your script will not work even in newer, compatible browsers!

EXHIBIT 2.10

```html
<html>
    <head>
        <title>Internet Banking Welcome</title>
    </head>
    <body>
        <script type="text/javascript">
            <!--
            document.write("Welcome to
                Internet Banking!");
            //-->
        </script>
    </body>
</html>
```

Exercise 2.4 – Solving Compatibility Issues

The biggest hurdles to developing effective JavaScripts are cross-platform compatibility issues. Browser differences are an enduring problem for JavaScript developers. As previously mentioned, there may be slight differences in the way each browser's JavaScript interpreter interprets the same code. Indeed, if you use a lot of CSSs in your work, you may even decide to have a welcome page that detects whether the user is browsing from one browser or another and maintain one codebase for each. This may sound drastic, but if you are dealing with important applications, such as Internet banking, you need to be able to support different browsers. Even if one browser only holds 10 percent of the market, out of a population of (say) 100 million users, that is still 10 million that need to be supported.

You can specify the JavaScript version used in your scripts as an attribute to ensure that an interpreter knows what version to expect. Alternatively, you also can force execution of a specific version as well.

Another approach is to use a functional testing tool, such as SilkTest, that can process all of your scripts and identify potential compatibility problems before they arise in production.

STEP 1 – USING A SPECIFIC JAVASCRIPT VERSION

In your text editor, load the existing HTML document welcome.html shown in Exhibit 2.5. To set the JavaScript version to 1.5, you simply insert the string `"JavaScript 1.5"` as the version number. This action alters the interpreter to the expected version of the interpreter so that the interpreter can determine whether it is able to process the script. To specify JavaScript 1.2 and 1.1, you would use `"JavaScript 1.2"` and `"JavaScript 1.1"`, respectively. Note that some newer browser versions may not correctly interpret the version when specified using this method.

STEP 2 – ENFORCING VERSION RESTRICTIONS

In your text editor, load the existing HTML document welcome.html shown in Exhibit 2.5. Insert the code shown in Exhibit 2.11 into the code after the first `<script>` block.

This code allows you to change the behavior and actions of the script on the basis of the detected browser type, at a very fine scale. It is also possible to use the logical OR operator (‖) to execute a code block for a number of a different browsers. For example, the expression if (is_ie5up‖ is_nav4) would execute a code block for both Internet Explorer 4 and above and Netscape Navigator 4 and above browsers. Maintaining different code segments for different browsers in this way can be time consuming, but in some cases it is necessary!

EXHIBIT 2.11

```
<script>
<!--
if (is_ie5up)
 {
  // Internet Explorer 4 and above statements
     go here...
 }
 else if (is_nav4)
 {
  // Netscape Navigator 4 and above statements
     go here...
 }
 else if (is_gecko)
 {
  // Netscape Navigator 6 and Mozilla statements
     go here...
 }
 else if (is_nav3)
 {
  // Netscape Navigator 3 statements go here...
 }
 else if (is_opera)
 {
  // Opera browser statements go here...
 }
 else
 {
  // All other versions - probably earlier or just
     incompatible
 }
// -->
</script>
```

If you are not sure what client browser your users are running, you can download and use the Browser Sniffer code from www.mozilla.org/docs/web-developer/sniffer/browser_type.html, but be aware that this is now deprecated for newer browser versions. This code allows for many more options and combinations of options than those just shown. A list of interesting browser-specific bugs is also available at www.posit-ioniseverything.net/.

Expressions are logical phrases that are evaluated using ***Boolean operators*** such as OR and AND. They are used in conjunction with variables that are data structures that can take on different values. Expressions and ***variables*** form the cornerstone of all programming languages, because general cases of very specific problems can be treated by writing single expressions, with the values of variables changing as necessary. You will learn about operators, expressions, and variables in Chapter 3.

The page as it currently appears is shown in Figure 2.4. Although these examples are very simple, they illustrate how important it is to develop JavaScripts incrementally and to test often, especially across platforms, because you need to identify language version and/or browser incompatibilities early on in development.

FIGURE 2.4

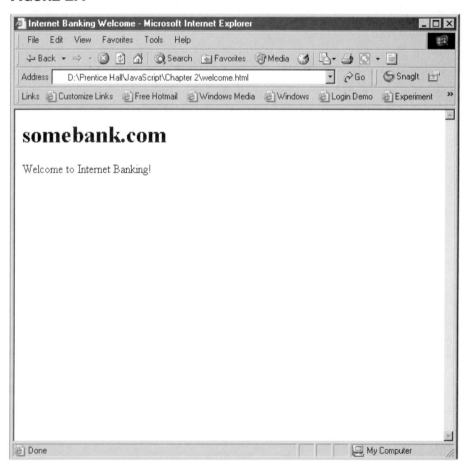

Summary

In this chapter, you learned how to identify JavaScript as the scripting language used in a Web page and how to add JavaScripts to Web pages. In addition, you examined why comments should be used inside JavaScripts and discovered how to solve compatibility issues between browsers and JavaScript versions. You also learned how to create scripts compatible with specific JavaScript versions and previewed how to use the document object and write method to generate dynamic text within Web pages.

The examples in this chapter have been kept very simple so that you could resolve the problem of getting JavaScripts actually running in different browsers. The core constructs of JavaScript, such as functions, expressions, variables, and operators, that were touched on here, will be discussed further in Chapter 3.

Test Your Skills

Practice Drill 2.1: String Quoting

In this exercise, you will observe what happens when you use `document.write()` to display a string that has a backslash (\) embedded inside it, which is known as *escaping*. These strings usually refer to files on a file system, such as C:\WINDOWS, but not HTTP URLs, which use forward slashes (/) to define paths.

If you don't "quote" a backslash inside a JavaScript string, it will simply not appear. You need to place a second backslash immediately in front of the backslash to be displayed. For example, to display the file system path C:\WINDOWS, the `document.write()` string would be `"C:\\WINDOWS"`. The following example shows how this works in practice:

1. In your text editor, create a HTML page with the appropriate `<head>` and `<body>` elements:

```
<html>
    <head>
        <title>String Quoting Example</title>
    </head>
    <body>
    </body>
</html>
```

2. Insert the JavaScript code block between the `<body>` tags:

```
<script type="text/javascript">
</script>
```

3. Insert a `document.write()` method call between the `<script>` tags:

```
document.write("");
```

4. Insert the unquoted string as follows:

```
document.write("Configuration saved to C:\WINDOWS");
```

5. Insert the quoted string as follows:

```
document.write("Configuration saved to
    C:\\WINDOWS");
```

6. Load the page into your Web browser. The following results will be displayed:

```
Configuration saved to C:WINDOWS
Configuration saved to C:\WINDOWS
```

Practice Drill 2.2: Backspace Characters

In this exercise, you will observe what happens when you use `document.write()` to display a string that has a backspace `"\b"` character embedded inside it. This results in the character just prior to the backspace character being deleted when the page is displayed. This technique is often used to hide strings within pages—a search of the page will not reveal the existence of the string that is actually displayed on the screen. In Internet Explorer 6 and in the newest version of Mozilla 1.5, the embedded backspace is displayed as a block and does not erase anything, so this example will only work in previous versions of these browsers.

If you do not use a backspace character inside a JavaScript string, the literal string will appear. You need to place the backspace character immediately after the character to be deleted. To delete the character 'S' from the string showing the path C:\WINDOWS, the `document.write()` string would be `"C:\\WINDOWS\b"`. The following example shows how this works in practice:

1. In your text editor, create a HTML page with the appropriate `<head>` and `<body>` elements:

```
<html>
      <head>
            <title>Backspace Character Example</title>
      </head>
      <body>
      </body>
</html>
```

2. Insert the JavaScript code block between the `<body>` tags:

```
<script type="text/javascript">
</script>
```

3. Insert a `document.write()` method call between the `<script>` tags:

```
document.write("");
```

4. Insert the normal string as follows:

```
document.write("Configuration saved to C:\\WINDOWS");
```

5. Insert the backspace character as follows:

```
document.write("Configuration saved to
    C:\\WINDOWS\b");
```

6. Load the page into your Web browser. The following results will be displayed:

```
Configuration saved to C:\WINDOWS
Configuration saved to C:\WINDOW
```

Practice Drill 2.3: String Quoting Revisited

In Practice Drill 2.1, you escaped a backslash to display pathnames and similar strings in the `document.write()` method. This technique can be used to display other character literals that fall within strings. A good example is the display of quote characters such as `"`, which are used to display strings within strings that have these quotes embedded inside them. These strings usually refer to quotes from text or speech, such as `MyBank: "The People's Bank"`.

If you don't "quote" these quotes inside a JavaScript string, they will cause an error. You need to place a backslash immediately in front of the quote character to be displayed. To display the message for an Internet banking site such as `MyBank: "The People's Bank"`, the `document.write()` string would be `"MyBank: \"The People's Bank\""`. The following example shows how this works in practice:

1. In your text editor, create a HTML page with the appropriate `<head>` and `<body>` elements:

```
<html>
      <head>
            <title>String Quoting Revisited
                  Example</title>
      </head>
      <body>
      </body>
</html>
```

2. Insert the JavaScript code block between the `<body>` tags:

```
<script type="text/javascript">
</script>
```

3. Insert a `document.write()` method call between the `<script>` tags:

```
document.write("");
```

4. Insert the unquoted string as follows:

```
document.write("MyBank: "The People's Bank"");
```

5. Load the page into your Web browser. An error will be displayed because the parser finds two opening quote marks: `""`.

6. Trying the process again, insert the quoted string as follows:

```
document.write("MyBank: \"The People's Bank\"");
```

7. Load the page into your Web browser. The following results will be displayed:

```
MyBank: "The People's Bank"
```

MULTIPLE-CHOICE QUESTIONS

1. How does a JavaScript interpreter identify that a script is being used inside a Web page?

   A. `<JavaScript>` tag

   B. `<script>` tag

   C. `<JAVAscript>` tag

   D. `<HTMLScript>` tag

2. Which of the following is *not* a valid language attribute for a Web page script?

   A. JavaScript

   B. JavaScript 1.2

   C. JavaScript 1.3

   D. JavaScript 2.0

3. Which of the following is true of JavaScripts and XHTML tags?

   A. Only JavaScripts are case sensitive.

   B. Both are case insensitive.

   C. Both are case sensitive.

   D. Only XHTML tags are case sensitive.

4. For the statement `document.write("Welcome to Internet Banking!")`, what is the object and what is the method?

   A. Document is the object; write is the method.

   B. Write is the object; document is the method.

   C. Document is the object; there are no methods.

   D. There are no methods or objects in this statement.

5. How many JavaScripts can be contained in a single page?

   A. One per page

   B. Two, one in the `<head>` and one in the `<body>`

   C. One in the `<head>` and two in the `<body>`

   D. An unlimited number

6. Why should you indent code blocks in JavaScript?

   A. Syntax requires indentation.

   B. Some parsers need it; others don't.

   C. It makes it easy to match the starting and terminating elements.

   D. It is mandated in the ECMA standard.

7. What is the purpose of commenting scripts?

   A. To highlight the purpose of less than obvious aspects of your scripts

B. To explain function names such as

        `checkUsernameNumberOfLettersIsCorrect`

C. To increase developer workloads

D. To ensure that scripts are not recognized as code

8. Which of the following is *not* a valid opening comment element?

A. `<!--`

B. `//`

C. `/*`

D. `@@`

9. What sort of expression can be used to enforce browser compatibility?

A. when

B. after

C. type

D. if

10. What is an expression?

A. A CSS style

B. An implementation of a specific code block

C. A logically evaluated phrase

D. A statement that determines what browser clients need to use

FILL-IN-THE-BLANK QUESTIONS

1. Script design and _____ are very important to the maintenance of your code.

2. Ensuring that certain _____ execute your scripts correctly is problematic.

3. Allowing different people to develop _____ pages and _____ code is a good source-control strategy.

4. The browser uses its built-in JavaScript _____ to load in the script and execute it.

5. A statement is a syntactically valid code element that is _____.

6. JavaScript interpreters read and process _____ atomically and in isolation from each other.

7. _____ JavaScripts in a single Web page are executed sequentially.

8. Text in quotes is a collection of characters technically known as a(n) _____.

9. The interpreter skips all _____, including literal space and end-of-line characters.

10. You can specify the JavaScript version used in your scripts as a(n) _____.

DEFINITIONS QUESTIONS

1. What is a JavaScript?

2. What's the difference between a HTML developer and a JavaScript programmer?

3. What is a string?

4. What is a comment?

5. What is an expression?

BASIC PROJECTS

The following short projects provide you with the opportunity to create a new Web page, develop a simple JavaScript, and insert it into the page. You will then have to modify your JavaScript to display the client version.

Project 2.1 – Inserting a JavaScript into a Web Page

This project will require you to create a better welcome page for the Internet banking application. Create a HTML page that has the correct `<head>` and `<body>` elements. Create a JavaScript that displays two HTML statements to the user using the `document.write` method:

```
"<p>Welcome to Internet Banking</p>"
"<p>Click NEXT to Continue...</p>"
```

Insert the JavaScript into the `<body>` section of the Web page and load it into Internet Explorer and Netscape Navigator. Does it display correctly in both browsers?

Project 2.2 – Checking Out the JavaScript Version

Using the HTML page and JavaScript described in Project 2.1, you should indicate to the user whether his or her browser type has been correctly detected. Using the `if` expression, extend the JavaScript to display the following message if Internet Explorer is detected:

```
"<p>You are using Internet Explorer</p>"
```

Or, if Internet Explorer is not being used or if Netscape Navigator is being used, display the following message:

```
"<p>You are not using Internet Explorer</p>"
```

INTERMEDIATE PROJECTS

The following intermediate projects provide you with the opportunity to further investigate string and character handling and variables.

Project 2.1 – Strings and Variables

A variable is a data item whose value can change. In most languages, variables have a particular type that specifies what kind of values the variable can store, such as numbers, characters, strings, and so on. More complicated values—such as dates—are stored as objects because they can vary in many different ways. For example, although a string can only be stored in one way, such as "a string," a date can be stored in a number of different ways, depending on how it is formatted and ordered. In some countries, such as the United States, dates are ordered by month, day, and then year, but in Europe, it is more common to use day, month, and year ordering. Formatted dates can be expressed using numeric equivalents ("01" for January, for example) or abbreviations ("Feb" for February).

As you'll learn in the next chapter, JavaScript supports many different variable types, even if they are not explicitly declared like other languages. Many different types of operations can be performed on variables, and these will be covered in the chapters that follow. For example, a string variable can be checked to see if it contains certain characters or two integer variables can be added together to produce a result. Operating on variables is the foundation of data processing, and given the main reasons that you might need to use JavaScript in the validation of form data, it is critical that you start thinking about variables when designing your pages.

1. In your text editor, create a HTML page with the appropriate <head> and <body> elements:

```
<html>
      <head>
            <title>String Variable Example</title>
      </head>
      <body>
      </body>
</html>
```

2. Insert the JavaScript code block between the <body> tags:

```
<script type="text/javascript">
</script>
```

3. Define two variables with the Internet banking welcome messages from Project 1 in the Basic Projects:

```
var welcomeString1="<p>Welcome to Internet
      Banking</p>";
var welcomeString2="<p>Click NEXT to
      Continue...</p>";
```

4. Insert two `document.write()` method calls between the `<script>` tags, without any quotes:

```
document.write();
document.write();
```

5. Insert the string names into the method call as follows:

```
document.write(welcomeString1);
document.write(welcomeString2);
```

6. Load the page into your Web browser. The following result will be displayed:

```
Welcome to Internet Banking
Click NEXT to Continue...
```

Does your project look something like this?

Project 2.2 – Quoted Strings and Variables

As described in Practice Drill 2.3 of *Test Your Skills*, you can quote quotation marks within strings to display them on screen. This also works with strings that have been declared as variables. For example, instead of assigning the value "Click NEXT to Continue. . . " to welcomeString2, we might want to display the value "Click "NEXT" to Continue . . ." This project combines string quoting and the use of variables.

1. In your text editor, create a HTML page with the appropriate `<head>` and `<body>` elements:

```
<html>
      <head>
            <title>String Variable Example</title>
      </head>
      <body>
      </body>
</html>
```

2. Insert the JavaScript code block between the `<body>` tags:

```
<script type="text/javascript">
</script>
```

3. Define two variable with the Internet banking welcome messages from Project 1 in the Basic Projects, with the second welcome string containing literal quotes:

```
var welcomeString1="<p>Welcome to Internet
                    Banking</p>";
var welcomeString2="<p>Click \"NEXT\" to
                    Continue...</p>";
```

4. Insert two `document.write()` method calls between the `<script>` tags, without any quotes:

```
document.write();
document.write();
```

5. Insert the string names into the method call as follows:

```
document.write(welcomeString1);
document.write(welcomeString2);
```

6. Load the page into your Web browser. The following results will be displayed:

```
Welcome to Internet Banking
Click "NEXT" to Continue...
```

Does your project look something like this?

Career Builder

Now that you have learned how to insert simple JavaScripts into Web pages with calls to `document.write()`, you should now create a sample welcome page for a real Internet banking site. Using a search engine, locate the home pages of five different Internet banking sites and examine their layout. What are the main entry points into the various applications that they provide? Use the View Source function of your Web browser to investigate the HTML and JavaScript code used on the page. Has the site used any of the features you have learned about in this chapter?

Using a Web design package or just Notepad and your Web browser, create a front page for an Internet banking site that uses `document.write()` to display text within the `<body>` section of the page. A link should be created to the login page, which will be examined in the next chapter.

Chapter | 3

Using Variables, Data Types, Expressions, and Operators

JavaScript shares many basic characteristics with other programming languages. Variables of a specific character, numeric, or string type can be evaluated using different logical operators as part of an expression. JavaScript does not have formal *type declarations*, but values take on one of nine types. This chapter introduces you to JavaScript variables, their basic types, expressions that use variables, and the various *logical operators* used in expressions. These language elements provide the foundation for all programming in JavaScript and allow the contents of pages to be made dynamic.

In this chapter, you will learn how variables can be used to represent unknown values in scripts. These variables can be assigned values at design time, run time, or during a script's lifetime. To allow operations between variables of the same category, a typing system is used, but it is much looser than those used in most other programming languages. This flexibility makes it easy to write scripts, but it can cause problems at run time, when values are assigned to variables that may be out of scope or out of range.

The chapter exercises will continue with the Internet banking example used throughout the book. You will create a "customer details" Web page in which individual HTML form field values are assigned to variables, whose bounds are then checked. This is one of the most common uses of the programmatic aspects of JavaScript.

For Your Career

In this chapter, you will learn basic skills that will allow you to declare and work with variables and constants of different types. As a programming language, JavaScript provides the foundation for common logical operations (including comparisons) that underlie the implementation of different types of business operations. All of the skills in this chapter will be used in every Web site you develop—whether it is writing validation scripts for e-commerce sites or calculating window locations given a certain screen size that can change at run time.

Chapter Exercises

This unit's exercises will teach you how to:

■ Use the fundamental JavaScript language components

■ Create JavaScript statements

■ Name, declare, type, and scope variables

■ Declare and work with data types, basic expressions, and operators

3

By working through the exercises, you will create a "customer details" Web page in which individual HTML form field values are assigned to variables, whose bounds are then checked.

$$x = 10; y = 5$$
$$x \mathrel{+}= y = 15$$
$$x = 15; y = 5$$
$$x \mathrel{-}= y = 10$$
$$x = 10; y = 5$$
$$x \mathrel{*}= y = 50$$
$$x = 50; y = 5$$
$$x \mathrel{/}= y = 10$$
$$x = 10; y = 5$$
$$x \mathrel{\%}= y = 0$$
$$x = 0; y = 5$$

Exercise 3.1 – Identifying JavaScript Language Components

In these exercises, you will learn how to use variables within JavaScripts and how to select the appropriate variable type. This is a very important task when designing scripts, because many variables will be added, subtracted, multiplied, or have some more sophisticated operator applied to them. Ensuring that variable types are honored at run time is sometimes problematic, but explicit typing can avoid these problems. That is why it is important for you to always identify the range and scope of expected variable values before sitting down to write your script—and certainly before you begin creating expressions using variables or using them within logical operations. Some variables are assigned a value at design time that does not change. These special variables are called *constants*. They are used when you are sure that the initial value of a variable will never change.

The real "guts" of any JavaScript program is in the expressions that are created to operate on variables. For example, a credit card validation system takes a 16-digit string from a HTML text box and computes a checksum. The value from the text box must be assigned to a variable before it can be operated on; otherwise, a validation function would have to be written for every possible credit card number! This does not mean that the value of a form element cannot be read without first assigning it to another variable.

JavaScript has a number of different language components, including variables, constants, expressions, operators, and statements, that can be found inside a script. It is very important to be able to distinguish between the different language components, because variables can have any name (apart from a reserved word) and some represent specific members of a system class or instantiated object (such as the `document` object).

In this exercise, you will learn how to recognize JavaScript errors that result from the use of reserved words and unacceptable characters for variable names. This is good programming practice, because run-time errors are quite difficult to debug. For example, the use of the reserved word "if" as a variable name would raise the exception "Expected identifier," which does not exactly indicate what has gone wrong! It is useful to review the exceptions before getting too involved in using variables.

STEP 1 – DECLARING A VARIABLE

In your text editor, create a code block by inserting an opening `<script>` and a closing `</script>` tag. To declare a variable, you need to choose a name that represents the variable. For example, to declare a variable to represent the current temperature, you might name it "temperature."

A variable must be declared inside a statement, which is a single, encapsulated unit of work. A statement may contain variable declarations, operations on variables, logical expressions, or a combination of these things. Statements should be delimited by a semicolon.

Variable declarations are preceded by the reserved word "var," which is short for "variable." Exhibit 3.1 shows the declaration of the variable "temperature" using a valid statement.

EXHIBIT 3.1

```
<script type="text/javascript">
        var temperature;
</script>
```

Exhibit 3.1 declares a single JavaScript code block and the variable temperature. If you wanted to do something useful, like declare variables to store today's temperature and yesterday's temperature, you could use the same code block, as shown in Exhibit 3.2.

EXHIBIT 3.2

```
<script type="text/javascript">
        var temperatureToday, temperatureYesterday;
</script>
```

Variables can also be declared with specific ***initial values***. Even though new values can be assigned during the life cycle of a script, it is sensible to use an initial default value. For example, if you knew what the temperature was yesterday at 11:59 P.M., it would make sense to assume that that would be the same temperature at 12:00 A.M. today. Thus, today's initial temperature could be set to yesterday's temperature initially, as shown in Exhibit 3.3.

EXHIBIT 3.3

```
<script type="text/javascript">
        var temperatureYesterday=100;
        var temperatureToday= temperatureYesterday;
</script>
```

In this example, the value of 100 is assigned to temperatureYesterday, and the value of temperatureToday is then set to the value of temperatureYesterday, which we know is 100.

Traditionally, when programmers worked with systems that had very limited amounts of RAM and narrow bus widths, programs were very compact, and the naming conventions adopted at the time were very economical. Variables were often named with single letters of the alphabet, starting with "a" and ending with "z." When the alphabet was exhausted, numerals would be added to the end of the character; thus, "z" would be followed by "a1," "a2," "a3," and so on. In those days, a data dictionary was rigorously maintained to show the mapping between these arbitrary variable names and their real-life equivalents. Because the computer ultimately assigns arbitrary ***identifiers*** to these variables during processing, the approach seemed logical enough.

Although this sounds great in theory, programmers are not known for their documentation skills. So, although a ***data dictionary*** should always be updated when a new variable is introduced into the system, in practice, programmers often declared arbitrary variables and did not document their referents. This meant that other programmers who came along later to extend the code did not know what each variable actually represented!

These days, computers have large amounts of RAM and bus widths, so we can use more descriptive names like "temperature" to represent the temperature. Unfortunately, I still see many JavaScripts on the WWW that still use "a," "b," and "c" as variable names—and it is not necessary.

STEP 2 – DECLARING A VARIABLE USING A RESERVED WORD

In your text editor, create a code block by inserting an opening `<script>` and a closing `</script>` tag. Normally, to declare a variable you need to choose a name that represents the variable, but what if the variable has the same name as a reserved word? In this situation, you need to choose an alternative name. A ***reserved word*** is part of the core JavaScript language, so if you call a variable by the same name as a reserved word, the interpreter will not know whether you are referring to the variable or to the reserved word. For example, if you wanted to create a variable called "var," it might seem obvious to declare "var var;" which is syntactically legal, but later in the program any other appearance of "var" would be ambiguous. Exhibit 3.4 shows an example of this problem.

EXHIBIT 3.4

```
<script type="text/javascript">
      var var;
</script>
```

When this script is executed, the ***interpreter*** processes the variable declaration and flags an error—probably something like "Expected identifier." This means that "var" is not recognized as a variable identifier, and another variable name must be chosen.

Exercise 3.2 – Declaring and Initializing Variables

A JavaScript consists of a set of statements that are executed sequentially by the interpreter. Many of these statements include operations on variables. These operations include declaration and initialization, which were covered in the previous exercise. In this exercise, you will learn how to assign values to variables and what sorts of values can be assigned. This lays the groundwork for the next exercise, which looks at how to specifically assign types to variables during declaration.

STEP 1 – DECLARING VARIABLES

In your text editor, create a new `<script>` block, as shown in Exhibit 3.5. Create a new set of variables that represent the typical values found in a customer record, including family name, first name, address lines, city, state, country, and so on. A Boolean variable is also set to show that an address belongs to a customer. A Boolean variable can only have two values: true or false. They are very useful as "flag" variables that indicate a discrete state.

Avoiding Reserved Words

You might be wondering how to avoid using reserved words. This can be difficult, because the JavaScript language specification does change occasionally. However, Table 3.1 shows the most commonly used reserved words, and these should definitely be avoided.

Never Use Reserved Words with Different Cases

Although using reserved words can confuse an interpreter, capitalizing reserved words confuses other programmers. Because JavaScript is case sensitive, the reserved word "var" is distinct from the variable name "VAR," "VaR," "vAr," and so on. But using these words in this way will certainly confuse novice programmers who maintain your scripts and should thus be avoided.

TABLE 3.1 Commonly used reserved words.

boolean	break	byte	abstract
case	catch	char	class
const	continue	debugger	default
delete	do	double	else
enum	export	extends	false
final	finally	float	for
function	goto	if	implements
import	in	instanceof	int
interface	long	native	new
null	package	private	protected
public	return	short	static
super	switch	synchronized	this
throw	throws	transient	true
try	typeof	var	void
volatile	while	with	

3

EXHIBIT 3.5

```
<script type="text/javascript">
        var firstName;
        var familyName;
        var address1;
        var address2;
        var city;
        var state;
        var zip;
        var country;
        var ourCustomer;
</script>
```

STEP 2 – INITIALIZING VARIABLES

In your text editor, you will now initialize each of the variables and assign the variable type. The types that can be indirectly assigned to variables in JavaScript include Booleans, nulls, numbers, and strings. In this example, shown in Exhibit 3.6, you will initialize seven string variables, one Boolean variable, and one numeric variable.

EXHIBIT 3.6

```
<script type="text/javascript">
        var firstName="";
        var familyName= null;
        var address1=null;
        var address2= null;
        var city= null;
        var state=";
        var zip=0;
        var country="USA";
        var ourCustomer=true;
</script>
```

Note that string variables can be initialized using either single quotes (' ') or double quotes (" "), but pairs of quotes must always be matched. Therefore, you cannot initialize a string starting with a single quote (') and finishing with a double quote (") or vice versa. In both cases, the JavaScript interpreter will throw an unterminated string exception. Another option is to initialize string variables with no value—literally called "null." Whereas a string set to " " or ' ' is technically a set of no characters that has been initialized, null indicates that the string has no value at all. Boolean variables can take the values true or false. They do not need to be enclosed within quotes, because an unquoted true or false string will be interpreted as initializing a Boolean variable.

STEP 3 – CHANGING VARIABLE VALUES

Variable values can be changed at any time using the ***assignment operator*** (=). This operator assigns the value on the right-hand side of the equals sign to the variable on the left-hand side of the equals sign. You will learn more about expressions and how they work in Exercise 3.4. Exhibit 3.7 shows the assignment of a specific value to each of the variables in address.html. Normally, these may be retrieved from HTML <form> values, as entered by a user.

EXHIBIT 3.7

```
<script type="text/javascript">
        firstName="Elizabeth";
        familyName="Jones";
        address1="Rose Cottage";
        address2="25 City Road";
        city="Richmond";
        state='VA';
        zip=23227;
        country="USA";
</script>
```

Note that numeric variables do not require quotes around their values when assigned to variables. Only strings require a delimiter to enclose the text, especially when the string contains spaces (a numeric variable has no spaces). This hint also helps the interpreter work out which variables are numbers and which are strings.

Most strings contain a series of alphanumeric characters in the ranges a through z, A through Z, or 1 through 9. However, because in many cases strings represent everyday language, special characters may also need to be displayed. Generally, characters such as !, @, #, $, %, ^, &, *, ( ), and so on can be included. However, other characters that have a special purpose in JavaScript—such as /\"''"—need to be denoted as being part of a string literal.

A good example of this is the display of file pathnames, such as `"C:\My Documents\JavaScript Book\"`. A variable declaration such as `var path="C:\My Documents\JavaScript Book\";` would only display `C:My Documents-JavaScript Book` if printed using the `document.write()` method. This is because the backslash character is used to denote special characters such as tabs (\t), backspaces (\b), form feeds (\f), new lines (\n), and carriage returns (\r). Thus, to ensure that the path string example is displayed as intended, the variable should be declared as `var path="C:\\My Documents\\JavaScript Book\\";`.

Exercise 3.3 – Using Variables

Variables are common to all programming languages, and the way that they are declared is quite similar across the various languages. Inside scripts, however, JavaScript variables are used much like Java variables. For example, string variable values can be inserted into string literals by using the addition (+) operator—literally adding strings together inside a method call, such as `document.write()`. But you can pass a variable to any method or function defined inside your script, and you can even pass multiple variables to many functions.

In this exercise, you will learn how to display variable values inside the strings that are used to dynamically construct the contents of a Web page.

STEP 1 – DEFINING THE VARIABLES

In your text editor, create a new HTML document, news.html, and insert a new `<script>` section. The variables to be inserted into the script will represent the lines to be displayed in a Web page, as shown in Exhibit 3.8.

EXHIBIT 3.8

```
<html>
    <head>
        <title>Bank News</title>
    </head>
    <body>
        <script type="text/javascript">
                var headline1="Bank fees increase by
                        10 percent";
```

TIP 3

Character Escaping

Doubling up backslashes is known as **character escaping**, and it has nothing to do with prisons! A character escape allows the denoted character literal to be quoted inside a string. It is most often used with quote marks inside strings. Specifically, when generating HTML code output using `document.write()`, you will often encounter double quotes, such `<A HREF="http://www.cassowary.net/">Cassowary Computing</A>`. In this case, you would escape both of the double quotes in the variable assignment so that the string would be `var siteName="<A HREF=\"http://www.cassowary.net/\">Cassowary Computing</A>";`.

```
                        var headline2="Mortgage rates at
                                       25 year lows";
                        var headline3="NASDAQ closes above
                                       2000";
               </script>
       </body>
</html>
```

Each of these variables (`headline1`, `headline2`, and `headline3`) could be used once or multiple times within a script once they have been declared. They could also be used to refer to other HTML files using hypertext, as shown in the following step.

STEP 2 – DISPLAYING VARIABLE VALUES

In your text editor, you will enter a series of `document.write()` statements to display the value of each variable defined within the script for the news headlines. Each headline will then be linked to a HTML page that is ***content addressable*** (i.e., the file name is the same as the headline text). This makes it easy to automate Web page production and searching and also shows how useful it is to use variables to represent strings that are going to be used multiple times within a single page. You also need to escape the double quotes, enclosing each of the HTML links to ensure that the HREFs are correctly formed. The code is shown in Exhibit 3.9, and the Web page output is shown in Figure 3.1.

EXHIBIT 3.9

```
<script type="text/javascript">
        // Define the headline variables 1, 2 and 3…
        var headline1="Bank fees increase by 10
                       percent";
        var headline2="Mortgage rates at 25 year lows";
        var headline3="NASDAQ closes above 2000";
        // Display a set of headings for today's,
           yesterday's and last week's news…
        document.write("<h1>Breaking news:
                "+headline1+"</h1>");
        document.write("<h2>Yesterday's news:
                "+headline2+"</h2>");
        document.write("<h3>Last week's news:
                "+headline2+"</h3>");
        document.write("<p>News Stories");
        // Display the links to news stories
        document.write("<br><a href=\""+headline1+
                ".html\">"+headline1+"</a>");
        document.write("<br><a href=\""+headline2+
                ".html\">"+headline2+"</a>");
```

```
          document.write("<br><a href=\""+headline3+
             ".html\">"+headline3+"</a>");
</script>
```

FIGURE 3.1

Breaking news: Bank fees increase by 10 percent

Yesterday's news: Mortgage rates at 25 year lows

Last week's news: Mortgage rates at 25 year lows

News Stories
Bank fees increase by 10 percent
Mortgage rates at 25 year lows
NASDAQ closes above 2000

Boolean variables are formally equivalent to any other variable that has two and only two possible values, because they represent whether a particular state is true or false. For logical expressions that have been evaluated in your program, such as `"price > 10"`, it is very useful to be able to store the result of that evaluation. For example, for some grocery items, `price < 10`, in which case your script may perform one action; if `price > 10`, a separate action may be taken. A Web site that displays book prices, for instance, will often be used to only display bargain books (`price < 10`), and ignore everything else. Rather than using a number variable with the values 0 (false) and 1 (true), it is better to use Booleans, because they can only have two values (numeric variables can have many more).

Exercise 3.4 – Using Statements, Operators, and Expressions

A statement is a valid instruction to the Java interpreter that is terminated a by a semicolon. You have already learned how to use some common statement types, such as variable initialization and declaration. However, the true power of JavaScript and other programming languages lies in your ability to create logical expressions using variables and operators and then evaluate them. JavaScript expressions and operators are like mathematical expressions and operators, such as 1 + 2 = 3. In this example, + is the operator, and = represents the act of evaluation. Here, 1 and 2 are constants, but they could just as easily be variables, and 3 is the result of evaluating the expression. You could also frame the expression in a more abstract way, such as a + b = c, just like a mathematical formula. In JavaScript expressions, though, the assignment is framed in the opposite order—the variable is always on the left-hand side and the value to be assigned is on the right-hand side.

When to Use Null Variables

In some programming languages, initializing strings with null rather than " " or ' ' can have dramatic consequences. In JavaScript, the differences are not as important, except that when you process HTML form values, you can determine whether something (anything) has been entered into a field or whether nothing has been entered (null).

STEP 1 – USING MATHEMATICAL OPERATORS WITHOUT ASSIGNMENT

In your text editor, create a new HTML file called maths.html. Several different types of mathematical operators can be used to perform operations on number variables. These are shown in Table 3.2.

TABLE 3.2 Mathematical operators.

Operation	Function	Symbol
Add	Adds numbers together	+
Subtract	Subtracts numbers from each other	–
Multiply	Multiplies numbers with each other	*
Division	Divides numbers by each other	/
Negation	Changes a positive number to a negative one or a negative number to a positive one	–
Increment	Adds one to a number	++
Decrement	Subtracts one from a number	--
Modulus	Returns only the remainder from a division	%

You have already seen how strings can be added (concatenated) together using the addition operator. The semantics for multiplying strings, however, are not defined, so these operators are usually confined to numbers.

In this example, you will use each of these operators on two numbers and verify that the result meets your expectation. First, you need to declare two variables (x and y) and initialize their values. Next, you need to construct a set of expressions based on each operator and use the `document.write()` method to display each of the results. The code is shown in Exhibit 3.10, and the Web page output is shown in Figure 3.2.

$$x + y = 15$$
$$x - y = 5$$
$$x * y = 50$$
$$x / y = 2$$
$$x \% y = 0$$
$$-x = -10$$
$$x-- = 9$$

FIGURE 3.2 $x++ = 10$

EXHIBIT 3.10

```
<script type="text/javascript">
        var x=10;
        var y=5;
        document.write("<br>x + y = "+(x+y));
        document.write("<br>x - y = "+(x-y));
        document.write("<br>x * y = "+(x*y));
        document.write("<br>x / y = "+(x/y));
        document.write("<br>x % y = "+(x%y));
        document.write("<br>-x = "+(-x));
        document.write("<br>x-- = "+(--x));
        document.write("<br>x++ = "+(++x));
</script>
```

Note that evaluating an expression does not modify the values of the variables used in the expression unless the result is assigned to another variable using the assignment operator (=)—except when the increment and decrement operators are used. In each of the examples shown in Exhibit 3.10 for addition, subtraction, multiplication, division, negation, and the modulus, the values of x and y are not affected by the use of an operator. However, incrementing or decrementing a variable can actually change its value: When the operator precedes the variable, the value is changed, and the statement is executed. When the operator comes after the variable, the expression is evaluated using the variable's current value, and only afterwards is the operator applied. Thus, `document.write(++x)` will give a different result than `document.write(x++)` even though the same operator is being used.

STEP 2 – USING MATHEMATICAL OPERATORS WITH ASSIGNMENT

In your text editor, open the HTML file maths.html. In the previous step, you used a number of different operators, such as addition, subtraction, multiplication, division, negation, and the modulus, which operated without assigning the result to a variable. The basic assignment operator (=) takes the result of an expression and assigns it to a variable. In addition, compound assignment operators can combine an assignment with an operation, such as +=, which adds one variable to a second variable and stores the result in the first variable. This is equivalent to writing the expression out longhand using both the + and = operators. In other words, x += 4 is equivalent to x = x + 4. The compound operators are shown in Table 3.3.

You can now modify maths.html with these new operators and observe the different results. In each example, you can see that the value of y is unchanged, because assignment is only ever performed on x. The result of each subsequent operation is dependent on the previous one, because the value of x keeps changing as a result of the previous operation. The code is shown in Exhibit 3.11, and the Web page output is shown in Figure 3.3.

TABLE 3.3 Assignment operators.

Assignment Operation	Function	Symbol
Add/Assign	Adds numbers together and assigns the value to the left-hand variable	+=
Subtract/Assign	Subtracts numbers from each other and assigns the value to the left-hand variable	−=
Multiply/Assign	Multiplies numbers with each other and assigns the value to the left-hand variable	*=
Division/Assign	Divides numbers by each other and assigns the value to the left-hand variable	/=
Modulus/Assign	Returns only the remainder from a division and assigns the value to the left-hand variable	%=

EXHIBIT 3.11

```
<script type="text/javascript">
        var x=10;
        var y=5;
        document.write("<br>x = "+x+"; y = "+y);
        document.write("<br>x += y = "+(x+=y));
        document.write("<br>x = "+x+"; y = "+y);
        document.write("<br>x -= y = "+(x-=y));
        document.write("<br>x = "+x+"; y = "+y);
        document.write("<br>x *= y = "+(x*=y));
        document.write("<br>x = "+x+"; y = "+y);
        document.write("<br>x /= y = "+(x/=y));
        document.write("<br>x = "+x+"; y = "+y);
        document.write("<br>x %= y = "+(x%=y));
        document.write("<br>x = "+x+"; y = "+y);
</script>
```

T I P

Increments and Decrements

If you forget the format of ++ the increment and decrement operators, don't worry, you can always write out the longhand form. For example, ++x is the same as x=x+1.

Dividing a number by zero is mathematically not defined. You cannot divide a pie into zero pieces, otherwise it would not exist! Therefore, before you perform the operation, you need to check every variable on the right-hand side of a division operator to make sure that it is greater than zero or less than zero. Otherwise, users will get an unhandled error, and your script will fail. If the users have entered a zero value into a HTML field, you can always catch it using an event handler and display a pop-up warning window.

$$x = 10;\ y = 5$$
$$x \mathrel{+}= y = 15$$
$$x = 15;\ y = 5$$
$$x \mathrel{-}= y = 10$$
$$x = 10;\ y = 5$$
$$x \mathrel{*}= y = 50$$
$$x = 50;\ y = 5$$
$$x \mathrel{/}= y = 10$$
$$x = 10;\ y = 5$$
$$x \mathrel{\%}= y = 0$$

FIGURE 3.3 $x = 0;\ y = 5$

Summary

In this chapter, you have learned how to work with variables, create statements, and build expressions based on mathematical operators. Although these examples are very simple, some of the following exercises and basic and intermediate projects will illustrate how to use these operators in practice. The following chapters on conditional expressions and branching are all based on the core concepts discussed here, so it is important for you to be comfortable working with variables and expressions before moving on.

In this chapter, you learned how to use different types of JavaScript variables to build logical expressions that can be evaluated within your scripts. All JavaScripts use variables in some way or another, whether to display a dynamically constructed string or to perform a mathematical operation. For example, the modulus operator is used by many encryption algorithms, and some of these may be implemented in a JavaScript as part of an authentication system. To build these more complicated scripts, you will need to explore the chapters on functions and conditional statements.

Test Your Skills

Practice Drill 3.1: Displaying Error Messages

In this exercise, you will observe what happens when you trap a division by zero error before an expression is evaluated. This prevents a user from encountering an unhandled exception.

You will learn about a new object and method in this exercise: `window.alert()`. This method raises a pop-up window with a specific message and is very useful for providing error feedback on forms. The following example shows how this works in practice.

1. In your text editor, create a HTML page with the appropriate `<head>` and `<body>` elements.

```
<html>
      <head>
            <title>Error Message Example</title>
      </head>
      <body>
      </body>
</html>
```

2. Insert the JavaScript code block between the `<body>` tags.

```
<script type="text/javascript">
</script>
```

3. Define two variables, x and y, between the `<script>` tags.

```
var x=1;
var y=0;
```

4. Insert a division expression.

```
document.write("x / y ="+(x/y));
```

5. Insert the warning message before the division occurs.

```
window.alert("Error: Division by Zero detected");
```

6. Load the page into your Web browser. The resulting window will be displayed, as shown in Figure 3.4, following the output shown.

```
x / y = Infinity
```

FIGURE 3.4

x / y =Infinity

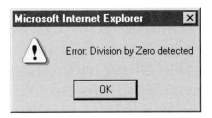

Practice Drill 3.2: Using Logical Operators

In this exercise, you will improve the division by zero example by introducing a check to determine whether an expression is true or false (i.e., Boolean) by using a logical operator. Boolean operators are related to the mathematical operators and include greater than (>), less than (<), and equal to (==). The biggest mistake when using operators is to confuse assignment (=) with equivalence (==). Note that they are completely different; = gives a variable a value but == checks if a variable has a certain value. Thus, x=9 is a statement but x==9 is an expression that returns true or false.

The following example shows how this works in practice using the equivalence operator.

1. In your text editor, create a HTML page with the appropriate <head> and <body> elements.

```
<html>
      <head>
            <title>Error Message Example</title>
      </head>
      <body>
      </body>
</html>
```

2. Insert the JavaScript code block between the `<body>` tags.

```
<script type="text/javascript">
</script>
```

3. Define two variables, x and y, between the `<script>` tags.

```
var x=1;
var y=0;
var result;
```

4. Insert a division expression with a check for division by zero.

```
result=(x/y==Infinity);
```

5. Insert the warning message that shows if division by zero occurs.

```
window.alert("Error: Division by Zero
     detected"+result);
```

6. Load the page into your Web browser. The resulting window will be displayed as shown in Figure 3.5.

FIGURE 3.5

x / y =Infinity

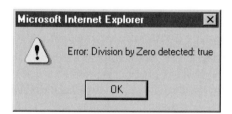

Practice Drill 3.3: Using a Conditional Statement

In this exercise, you will improve the division by zero example by introducing a check to determine whether an expression is true or false (i.e., Boolean) by using a logical operator. Here you will use the logical `if` conditional statement to either print the result of the division or print an error message, but not both! We will cover the syntax of conditional statements in the next chapter, but this example demonstrates the power of Boolean logic.

1. In your text editor, create a HTML page with the appropriate `<head>` and `<body>` elements.

```
<html>
      <head>
            <title>Error Message Example</title>
```

```
          </head>
          <body>
          </body>
     </html>
```

2. Insert the JavaScript code block between the `<body>` tags.

```
<script type="text/javascript">
</script>
```

3. Define two variables, x and y, between the `<script>` tags.

```
var x=1;
var y=0;
var result;
```

4. Insert a division expression with a check for division by zero.

```
result=(x/y==Infinity);
```

5. Insert a conditional branching statement, indicating if the result is true, and display the warning message, showing that the division by zero has occurred.

```
if (result)
{
        var result=x/y;
}
else
{
window.alert("Error: Division by Zero detected");
}
```

6. Load the page into your Web browser. The resulting window will be displayed as shown in Figure 3.6 if y=0.

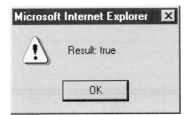

FIGURE 3.6

MULTIPLE-CHOICE QUESTIONS

1. What is a reserved word?

   A. A keyword in the JavaScript language

   B. A variable name that has already been declared

   C. A constant name that has already been declared

   D. A class name that has already been declared

2. A statement should be terminated by which character?

   A. :

   B. ;

   C. *

   D. +

3. Can variables be declared with specific values?

   A. No

   B. Yes

   C. Only for Boolean types

   D. Only for numeric types

4. Which of the following is *not* a reserved word?

   A. static

   B. return

   C. true

   D. dynamic

5. Are JavaScript variable names case sensitive?

   A. Yes

   B. No

   C. Yes, but only upper-case and lower-case names are equivalent

   D. Yes, but only mixed-case names are equivalent

6. What operator is used to change a variable's value?

   A. Addition

   B. Subtraction

   C. Modulus

   D. Assignment

7. What output would be displayed from `"<A HREF=\"http://www.cassowary.net/\">Cassowary Computing</A>"` in `document.write()`?

   A. `<A HREF="http://www.cassowary.net/">Cassowary Computing</A>`

   B. `<A HREF=""http://www.cassowary.net/"">Cassowary Computing</A>`

   C. `<A HREF=\"http://www.cassowary.net/\">Cassowary Computing</A>`

   D. `<A HREF=\\http://www.cassowary.net/\\>Cassowary Computing</A>`

8. Will `document.write(++x)` give a different result than `document.write(x++)`?

   A. Yes

   B. No

   C. Only if x > y

   D. Only if x is positive

9. If x = 10 and y = 5, then what is x%y?

   A. 10

   B. 5

   C. 2

   D. 0

10. Which operator changes a positive number to a negative one or a negative number to a positive one?

    A. Addition

    B. Subtraction

    C. Negation

    D. Modulus

FILL-IN-THE-BLANK QUESTIONS

1. Ensuring that variable types are honored at run time is sometimes problematic, but explicit _____ can avoid these problems.

2. The use of the _____ word "if" as a variable name would raise the exception "Expected identifier."

3. A variable must be declared inside a(n) _____, which is a single, encapsulated unit of work.

4. Variables can be declared with specific _____ values.

5. A variable is declared using the _____ keyword.

6. Boolean variables can take the values _____ or _____.

7. String variable values can be inserted into string literals with the _____ operator.

8. The _____ operator returns only the remainder from a division.

9. The _____ operator adds numbers together and assigns the value to the left-hand variable.

10. `document.write(++x)` will give a different result than
    `document.write(_____)`.

DEFINITIONS QUESTIONS

1. What is a JavaScript variable?

2. What is a Boolean variable?

3. What is an increment?

4. What is a decrement?

5. What is the division by zero problem?

BASIC PROJECTS

The following short projects provide you with the opportunity to use your knowledge of JavaScript variables, expressions, and operators to complete some tasks related to an Internet banking Web site.

Project 3.1 – Checking a Credit Limit

This project will require you to check whether a purchase amount exceeds a credit limit. Create a HTML page that has correct `<head>` and `<body>` elements and the appropriate `<script>` code block. Define one variable that represents the credit limit and another that represents the purchase amount. Use a logical greater-than operator to determine if the purchase price exceeds the credit limit. If it does, raise an exception using the `window.alert()` method, otherwise, print a message saying that the purchase has been approved.

Project 3.2 – Adding Up Items for Credit

Using the HTML page and JavaScript described in Project 1, you should be able to add a list of variables that represent five different purchases—such as a shirt, pants, and underwear items—and see whether that sum exceeds the credit limit. Define a variable that represents the credit limit and five variables that represent the purchase amount for each item. Use a compound addition and assignment operator to add the amounts for all items and use the logical greater-than operator to determine if the total purchase price exceeds the credit limit. If it does, then raise an exception using the `window.alert()` method, otherwise, print a message saying that the purchase has been approved.

INTERMEDIATE PROJECTS

In the following intermediate projects you will work with comparison and logical operators.

Project 3.1 – Working with Comparison Operators

In this chapter, you learned primarily about arithmetic operators, but there are three other sets of operators you need to be able to work with: comparison, logical, and bitwise operators. In this project, you will work with comparison operators; in Project 2, you will use logical operators. Bitwise operators are restricted to performing logical operations on binary rather than base-10 numbers and are not generally used. They will not be discussed further in this chapter.

The comparison operators are summarized in Table 3.4.

TABLE 3.4 Comparison operators.

Comparison Operation	Function	Symbol
Equal To	Is true if and only if the value of the left-hand variable is equal to the value of the right-hand variable	==
Not Equal To	Is true if and only if the value of the left-hand variable is not equal to the value of the right-hand variable	!=
Less Than	Is true if and only if the value of the left-hand variable is less than the value of the right-hand variable	<
Greater Than	Is true if and only if the value of the left-hand variable is greater than the value of the right-hand variable	>
Less Than or Equal To	Is true if and only if the value of the left-hand variable is less than or equal to the value of the right-hand variable	<=
Greater Than or Equal To	Is true if and only if the value of the left-hand variable is greater than or equal to the value of the right-hand variable	>=

In this project, you will create a simple HTML form and accompanying JavaScript that validates a Customer Reference Number (CRN) for Internet banking, given the business rule that all CRNs must be less than 999,999. You will see some advanced concepts being used here—such as referring to the values of text fields on a HTML form (document.Login.CRN.value) and functions (checkCRN())—but see if you can follow the simple logic and see the result!

1. In your text editor, create a HTML page with the appropriate <head> and <body> elements.

```
<html>
    <head>
        <title>Comparison Operators</title>
    </head>
    <body>
    </body>
</html>
```

2. Insert a HTML form with the name "Login." It should have a single text field called "CRN" and a submit button that invokes the function checkCRN() when clicked.

```
<form nameform name="Login">
        CRN: <input type="Text" name="CRN">
        <input type="Submit" value="Submit"
                onClick="checkCRN()">
</form>
```

3. Insert the JavaScript code block between the <body> tags.

```
<script type="text/javascript">
</script>
```

4. Between the <script> tags, enter the definition for the function checkCRN(). It should take the value from the CRN field and compare it with the maximum permitted number (999,999) using the greater-than operator. If the comparison is true, then the user should be prompted to reenter a valid CRN, otherwise, the user should be allowed to continue.

```
function checkCRN()
{
  if (document.Login.CRN.value>999999)
  {
        window.alert("Your CRN must be less than
             999,999. Please enter it again.");
  }
  else
  {
        window.alert("Your CRN appears to be valid.
             You may continue.");
  }
}
```

5. Load the page into your Web browser. Type "1000" into the CRN field. Does the result look like Figure 3.7?

FIGURE 3.7

6. Type "1000000" into the CRN field. Does the result look like Figure 3.8?

FIGURE 3.8

CRN:

Project 3.2 – Using Logical Operators

In the previous project, you learned about comparison operators, but you will often need to work with logical operators as well. In this project, you will use logical operators. These are the standard AND, OR, and NOT used in other programming languages. They are used to compare the truth of two statements. The logical operators are summarized in Table 3.5.

TABLE 3.5 Logical operators.

Logical Operation	Function	Symbol
AND	Is true if and only if both conditions are true	&&
OR	Is true if and only if at least one condition is true	||
NOT	Is true if and only if the right-hand condition is true	!

In this project, you will extend the simple HTML form and accompanying JavaScript that validates a Customer Reference Number (CRN) to include PIN validation, given the business rule that all CRNs must be less than 999,999 and PINs less than 9,999. Again, you will see some advanced concepts being used here—such as referring to the values of text fields on a HTML form (document.Login.CRN.value) and functions (checkCRN())—but see if you can follow the simple logic and see the result!

1. In your text editor, create a HTML page with the appropriate <head> and <body> elements.

```
<html>
        <head>
                <title>Internet Banking Login</title>
        </head>
        <body>
        </body>
</html>
```

2. Insert a HTML form with the name "Login." It should have a single text field called "CRN" and a submit button that invokes the function checkCRNandPIN() when clicked.

```
<form name="Login">
      CRN: <input type="Text" name="CRN">
      PIN: <input type="Text" name="PIN">
      <input type="Submit" value="Submit"
            onClick="checkCRNandPIN()">
</form>
```

3. Insert the JavaScript code block between the <body> tags.

```
<script type="text/javascript">
</script>
```

4. Between the <script> tags, enter the definition for the function check-CRNandPIN(). It should take the value from the CRN field and compare it with the maximum permitted number (999,999) using the greater-than operator. It should also take the value from the PIN field and compare it with the maximum permitted number (9,999) using the greater-than operator. If any of the comparisons are true, then the user should be prompted to reenter a valid CRN and/or PIN, otherwise, the user should be allowed to continue.

```
function checkCRNandPIN()
{
   if ((document.Login.CRN.value>999999)||(document.
      Login.PIN.value>9999))
   {
         window.alert("Your CRN must be less than
               999,999 and PIN less than 9,999.
   Please enter them again.");
   }
   else
   {
         window.alert("Your CRN and PIN appear to
               be valid. You may continue.");
   }
}
```

5. Load the page into your Web browser. Type "1000" into the CRN field and "2000" into the PIN field. Does the result look like Figure 3.9?

6. Type "1000000" into the CRN field and "2000" into the PIN field. Does the result look like Figure 3.10?

FIGURE 3.9

FIGURE 3.10

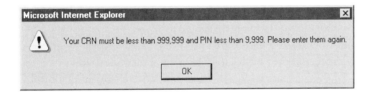

Career Builder

Now that you have learned how to work with variables, operators, and expressions, you are well prepared to move on to more sophisticated topics such as branching and logical evaluation on the language side, and working with forms on the practical side. Almost all JavaScript code written in practice is based around forms, so it is a good idea to become comfortable with them early on. Although the Internet banking examples here are complicated, try and follow the logic—it is not that hard, and it will be very instructive if you continue to apply the concepts in the following chapters to form work.

Can you extend the Intermediate Project 3.2 to display the news headline page from Exhibit 3.8 if someone enters a valid PIN and CRN?

Chapter 4

Controlling the Flow within Scripts

A typical JavaScript application needs to make decisions about what to do when variables have certain values or when values have changed. Often, the decisions are made on the basis of comparisons between variable values using the character, numeric, and logical operators discussed in Chapter 3. For example, client-side processing of forms permits checks and balances to be performed prior to server-side processing. Controlling *script flow* ensures that users follow a certain path through a Web page and only proceed if they have satisfied any number of different requirements.

In this chapter, you will learn how to control script flow by making use of the *conditional statements* `if`, `if . . . else`, and `try . . . catch . . . finally`. You will also learn how to use looping statements, such as `for`, `for . . . in`, `while`, `do . . . while`, `break`, and `continue`, to ensure that statements are repeated a number of times depending on the evaluation of different types of expressions.

The chapter exercises will continue the Internet banking example used throughout the book. You will use JavaScript methods and elements to evaluate customer details and ensure that form data entered on a home loan application is consistent.

For Your Career

In this chapter, you will learn how to use variables to make decisions according to business logic or some other aspect of program flow. The order of execution of blocks of statements, as determined by the execution of conditional or looping statements, makes it very easy to automate tasks.

The skills you will learn in this chapter will be used to develop a home loan application Web page. For example, you could determine if a user may proceed from one field to the next by checking that prerequisites from a previous section have been fulfilled.

Chapter Exercises

This unit's exercises will teach you how to:

- Use conditional statements, including `if` and `if . . . else`
- Implement looping statements, including `for`, `for . . . in`, `while`, `do . . . while`, `break`, and `continue`
- Know when to use `label`, `switch`, and `with` statements

By working through the exercises, you will create a home loan application page and evaluate user data before submitting it to a Web application.

Unsorted
First Pacific
Second Western
Royal Canadian
Swiss Private
Sorted Alphabetically
First Pacific
Royal Canadian
Second Western
Swiss Private
Reverse Sorted
Swiss Private
Second Western
Royal Canadian
First Pacific

4

Exercise 4.1 – Using `if . . . else` Statements

In all of the examples that you have worked through thus far, when a JavaScript is executed, all of the statements are executed once and only once. This is not very useful for general-purpose programming. For example, if you wanted to automatically execute the same task 100 times, such as when printing a batch of address labels, you would need to run the program 100 times. ***Looping statements***, described below, allow you to specify that a code block be executed a certain number of times or according to the result of some logical, numeric, or character expression.

By using the `if . . . else` statement, you are asking for a particular expression to be evaluated as being either true or false. So, if the statement between `if` and `else` is true, then the code block after `if` in the statement will be executed, otherwise, the code block after `else` will be executed. The expression to be evaluated can be any valid expression of the kinds examined in Chapter 3. Typically, a logical or numeric comparison will be made between two variables or a variable and one constant. The result of comparing two constants should be predictable! Note that the parenthetical expression does not have to evaluate strictly to the Boolean true or false, because zero, null, and nonzero/non-null values have meaning in this context as well.

In this exercise, you will learn how to specify the most basic conditional statement that allows decisions to be made within a script. Imagine the scenario where a home loan applicant fills in his or her income and personal details on a Web page before it is processed by the bank's loan approval system running on the server side. Before posting the information to the server, and creating human work in terms of reviewing loan documents and proof of earnings, it makes sense to process some of these basic features on the client side, because some loan applicants will be rejected out of hand. In the following exercise, you will assign the applicant status of "declined" to an applicant with income less than $50,000, and "eligible" otherwise.

STEP 1 – SIMPLE `IF . . . ELSE`

In your text editor, create a code block by inserting opening `<script>` and closing `</script>` tags, as shown in Exhibit 4.1. Define a function called `checkIf Eligible()` that checks whether the value entered in the form field `annual Income` in the form `homeLoanApplication` has a value less than $50,000. If `homeLoanApplication.annualIncome.value` is less than $50,000, then execute a `window.alert()` to tell the user that his or her application has been rejected, otherwise, execute a `window.alert()` to tell the user that he or she is eligible to apply for a loan.

Next, design the simple Web form—homeLoanApplication—with a single field—annualIncome—and ensure that the form executes the `checkIfEligible()` function when submitted.

EXHIBIT 4.1

```
<html>
 <head>
  <title>Home Loan Application</title>
```

```
</head>
<body>
<script type="text/javascript">
function checkIfEligible()
{
 if (document.homeLoanApplication.annualIncome.
   value<50000)
  {
   window.alert("You are not eligible to apply for
     a home loan.");
  }
  else
  {
    window.alert("You are eligible to apply for a
      home loan.");
  }
}
</script>
<form name="homeLoanApplication">
Annual Income: $<input type="Text"
                        name="annualIncome">
<input type="Submit" value="Submit" onClick=
          "checkIfEligible()">
</form>
</body>
</html>
```

The result of entering $1,000 as your annual income into the annualIncome field is shown in Figure 4.1.

FIGURE 4.1

In the exercises that follow, you will learn how to expand upon this basic type of decision logic to increase the number and scope of statements executed after a statement evaluation.

Else? What Else?

Sometimes, you do not need to execute a second block if the evaluation of the expression within the if() statement is true. For example, you may submit the loan application if and only if income is greater than or equal to $50,000 and simply not provide further processing for the else condition. In this situation, you do not need to supply an else part to the statement, and there is no second code block.

The most common issue that arises when using the if . . . else statement is that the assignment (=) and equivalence (==) operators often are confused. The assignment operator sets a variable to have some value, such as loanBalance=100. However, if you want to test whether the value of loanBalance is 100 in an if . . . else context, then you need to use the equivalence operator in the following way: if (loanBalance==100) . . . else. If you used if (loanBalance=100), then the inner expression loanBalance=100 assigns the value 100 to the variable loanBalance, after which the expression is always evaluated true.

STEP 2 – MULTIPLE COMPARISONS

In your text editor, create a code block by inserting an opening <script> and a closing </script> tag, as shown in Exhibit 4.2. Once again, define a function called checkIfEligible() that checks whether the value entered in the form field annualIncome in the form homeLoanApplication has a value less than $50,000 and also whether the applicant has liabilities greater than $100,000.

If homeLoanApplication.annualIncome.value is less than $50,000 or if the applicant has liabilities greater than $100,000, then execute a window.alert() to tell the user that his or her application has been rejected, otherwise, execute a window.alert() to tell the user that he or she is eligible to apply for a loan.

Once again, design a simple Web form—homeLoanApplication—with two fields—annualIncome and liabilities—and ensure that the form executes the checkIfEligible() function when submitted, as shown in Figure 4.2.

EXHIBIT 4.2

```
<html>
 <head>
  <title>Home Loan Application</title>
 </head>
 <body>
 <script type="text/javascript">
 function checkIfEligible()
 {
   if (document.homeLoanApplication.annualIncome.
     value<50000||document.homeLoanApplication.
     liabilities.value>100000)
   {
    window.alert("You are not eligible to apply for
      a home loan.");
   }
   else
   {
    window.alert("You are eligible to apply for a
      home loan.");
   }
 }
```

```
</script>
<form name="homeLoanApplication">
Annual Income: $<input type="Text"
name="annualIncome">
 Current Liabilities: $<input type="Text"
    name="liabilities">
 <input type="Submit" value="Submit" onClick=
    "checkIfEligible()">
 </form>
 </body>
</html>
```

FIGURE 4.2

When you create complex logical expressions that are evaluated within an `if . . . else` statement, things can become very complicated very quickly, and it is critical to ensure that your statement meets the order of operations specified in Chapter 3. One way to ensure that your logical expressions are testing what you intend is to read them aloud (or inside your head) as you construct them. So, while typing `annualIncome.value<50000 || liabilities.value>100000`, you might read aloud "if annual income is less than $50,000 or liabilities are greater than $100,000, then . . . " If what you are thinking does not seem to match what you are writing, you may need to group comparisons within parentheses to ensure that the correct order of operations is used.

STEP 3 – NESTED COMPARISONS

In your text editor, create a code block by inserting opening `<script>` and closing `</script>` tags, as shown in Exhibit 4.3. Once again, define a function called `checkIfEligible()` that performs multiple logical comparisons that cannot be specified within a single expression. In this step, if the value entered in the form field `annualIncome` in the form `homeLoanApplication` has a value less than $50,000 and if the applicant has liabilities greater than $100,000, then the application is rejected, otherwise, a second comparison is made on the basis of the ratio of `annualIncome` in the form `homeLoanApplication`, which is called `liquidity`. If `liquidity` is greater than 1.0, and the applicant's age is greater than 25, then the loan should be approved, otherwise, it is rejected.

T I P

Complex Code Blocks

So far in this chapter, you have only seen code blocks with one statement; however, code blocks that are grouped by braces are not limited in the number of statements that can be executed. Do not evaluate the same expression twice to execute two conditional statements, just group them together in a single code block and a single conditional statement.

4

If the loan is rejected, then open a `window.alert()` to tell the user that his or her application has been rejected, otherwise, execute a `window.alert()` to tell the user that he or she is eligible to apply for a loan.

Once again, you need to design a simple Web form—homeLoanApplication—but now with three fields—annualIncome, liabilities, and age—and ensure that the form executes the `checkIfEligible()` function when submitted, as shown in Figure 4.3.

EXHIBIT 4.3

```html
<html>
 <head>
  <title>Home Loan Application</title>
 </head>
 <body>
 <script type="text/javascript">
  function checkIfEligible()
  {
   if (document.homeLoanApplication.annualIncome.
       value<50000||document.homeLoanApplication.
       liabilities.value>100000)
   {
    window.alert("You are not eligible to apply for
       a home loan because your income is too low or
       your liabilities are too high.");
   }
   else
    {
liquidity=document.homeLoanApplication.annualIncome.
  value/document.homeLoanApplication.liabilities.value;
      if (liquidity>1&&document.homeLoanApplication.
        age.value>25)
      {
       window.alert("You are eligible to apply for a home
         loan.");
      }
      else
      {
       window.alert("You are not eligible to apply for a
         home loan because your liquidity ("+liquidity+")
         is too low to justify the risk based on your
         age.");
      }
     }
   }
 </script>
 <form name="homeLoanApplication">
```

```
   Annual Income: $<input type="Text"
     name="annualIncome">
   Current Liabilities: $<input type="Text"
     name="liabilities">
   Age: <input type="Text" name="age">
   <input type="Submit" value="Submit"
         onClick="checkIfEligible()">
   </form>
   </body>
</html>
```

FIGURE 4.3

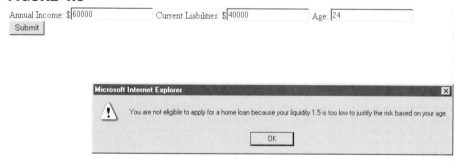

The function `checkIfEligible()` is now quite complicated: It prints customized messages for each type of loan rejection, explaining why the application is being rejected. If the application is rejected because of low liquidity, the applicant's liquidity ratio is shown in the `window.alert()` string. Also, you can see how both the logical OR (||) and logical AND (&&) operators can be used to test the truth of multiple logical conditions simultaneously.

Exercise 4.2 – Using Looping

Looping statements allow repetitive actions to be executed automatically—without the user having to press a button or run a script many times to achieve the desired result. For example, you may want to format 100 address labels or you might want to process 100 loan applications. Whenever you need to repeat operations, you need a loop.

Loops can simply involve repeatedly executing the same set of statements, but they are most powerful when they are combined with conditional statements. For example, if you had a program that printed address labels for both domestic and international customers, you would not print a country field if the customer had a valid zip code. This type of repetitive but selective activity can be well handled by combining looping and conditional statements.

In this exercise, you will learn how to use the `while` statement to continue executing a block of statements until a certain condition (logical or otherwise) has been met.

STEP 1 – USING `WHILE`

In your text editor, create a code block by inserting opening `<script>` and closing `</script>` tags, as shown in Exhibit 4.4. Define a `printPayments()` function that uses two parameters from a Web form—the outstanding loan principal and the number of years to pay—and then computes and displays the outstanding balance of the loan at the beginning of each year, assuming zero interest for simplicity. Four variables are defined: the principal, the number of years to pay, the size of the annual payment, and the year number (y). The logical expression `years>0` is evaluated on each pass of the `while` loop. If the number of years is greater than zero, then a table row is inserted, displaying the year number in the first cell and the outstanding principal at the beginning of that year in the second cell. On each pass, the number of years is decremented using the decrement (--) operator, whereas the year number is incremented using the increment operator (++).

Note the major structural difference between Exercises 4.1 and 4.2. In this exercise, you are using the `document.write()` method to dynamically print the contents of the HTML page because of the loop, whereas in Exercise 4.1 the HTML page contents were static. The approach in this exercise is the most flexible, but it means that you need to escape any quotes embedded in the HTML that is being generated dynamically, including the table border and width sizes.

You also need to design a simple Web form—homeLoanCalculator—with two fields—`principal` and `yearsToPay`—and ensure that the form executes the `printPayments()` function when submitted, as shown in Figure 4.4.

EXHIBIT 4.4

```html
<html>
 <head>
  <title>Home Loan Calculator</title>
 </head>
 <body>
 <script type="text/javascript">
  function printPayments()
  {
   var principal=document.homeLoanCalculator.
              principal.value;
   var years=document.homeLoanCalculator.years.value;
   var annualPayment=principal/years;
   var y=1;
   document.write("<table border=\"1\"
width=\"100%\">");
   document.write("<tr>");
   document.write("<td>Year</td>");
   document.write("<td>Value</td>");
   document.write("</tr>");
   while (years>0)
   {
    document.write("<tr>");
```

```
      document.write("<td>"+y+"</td>");
      document.write("<td>$"+principal+"</td>");
      document.write("</tr>");
      principal-=annualPayment;
      y++;
      years-;
      }
   document.write("</table>");
   }
</script>
<form name="homeLoanCalculator">
 Outstanding Principal: $<input type="Text"
     name="principal">
 Years to Pay: $<input type="Text" name="years">
 <input type="Submit" value="Submit"
     onClick="printPayments()">
</form>
</body>
</html>
```

FIGURE 4.4

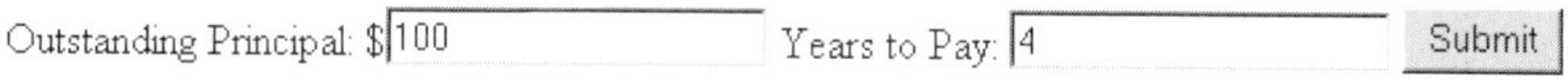

Outstanding Principal: $ 100   Years to Pay: 4   Submit

STEP 2 – USING FOR

In your text editor, create a code block by inserting opening `<script>` and closing `</script>` tags, as shown in Exhibit 4.5. Once again, define a `printPayments()` function that uses two parameters from a Web form—the outstanding loan principal and number of years to pay—and then computes and displays the outstanding balance of the loan at the beginning of each year, assuming zero interest for simplicity. Four variables are again defined—the principal, the number of years to pay, the size of the annual payment, and the year number (y).

The difference between the loan calculators in Steps 1 and 2 is that the former uses a `while` loop, which has an implicit iterator (`years-`), whereas the latter uses a `for` loop, which has an explicit iterator (`i=0; i<years; i++`). Both techniques produce the same result, but the `for` loop has a definite number of iterations declared up front (i starts at zero and is then incremented by one using the increment operator until i is the same value as years), whereas the `while` loop can loop infinitely until the logical condition specified is met. A common mistake that programmers make with implicit iterators is forgetting to increment the iterator on each pass through the loop, which causes the loop to run forever!

The logical expression `i<years` is evaluated on each pass of the `for` loop, starting at `i=0` on the first pass. If `i` is less than the number of years, then a table row is inserted onto the page, displaying the year number in the first cell and the principal outstanding at the beginning of that year in the second cell. On each pass, the year number

is incremented using the increment operator (++), but you do not need to increment the explicit iterator manually, because the `for` loop takes care of this automatically.

You also need to design a simple Web form—homeLoanCalculator—with two fields—`principal` and `yearsToPay`—and ensure that the form executes the `printPayments()` function when submitted, as shown in Figure 4.5.

EXHIBIT 4.5

```html
<html>
 <head>
  <title>Home Loan Calculator</title>
 </head>
 <body>
 <script type="text/javascript">
  function printPayments()
  {
   var principal=document.homeLoanCalculator.
      principal.value;
   var years=document.homeLoanCalculator.years.value;
   var annualPayment=principal/years;
   var y=1;
   document.write("<table border=\"1\"
      width=\"100%\">");
   document.write("<tr>");
   document.write("<td>Year</td>");
   document.write("<td>Value</td>");
   document.write("</tr>");
   for (i=0; i<years; i++)
   {
   document.write("<tr>");
   document.write("<td>"+y+"</td>");
   document.write("<td>$"+principal+"</td>");
   document.write("</tr>");
   principal-=annualPayment;
   y++;
   }
   document.write("</table>");
  }
 </script>
 <form name="homeLoanCalculator">
  Outstanding Principal: $<input type="Text"
     name="principal">
  Years to Pay: <input type="Text" name="years">
  <input type="Submit" value="Submit"
              onClick="printPayments()">
 </form>
 </body>
</html>
```

FIGURE 4.5

Year	Value
1	$1000
2	$875
3	$750
4	$625
5	$500
6	$375
7	$250
8	$125

What happens if you are in the middle of a loop, but you need to interrupt the normal processing of the loop for some reason? You can use the `continue` statement to execute the next iteration of the loop and ignore the rest of the statements in the current loop by using the `if` statement to check against a logical condition. For example, if you were formatting customer addresses on the screen in groups of 10, and you wanted to close a table and start a new one after the 10th iteration, you could do this inside the loop and then execute `continue` to start the loop at the next iteration.

`Break` is similar to `continue` except that the loop will stop iterating completely if it encounters `break` and proceed with the execution of the first statement following the loop statement.

Exercise 4.3 – Controlling Object Flow

In Exercises 4.1 and 4.2, you examined how to manage flow control through loops, conditional statements, and explicit and implicit iterators for simple variables. Recalling that JavaScript is an object-based scripting language, you may be wondering how objects are involved with flow control. The answer is that objects have their own special flow-control statements, which are generally simpler versions of the statements used with simple variables. They are easier to use, because the objects have encapsulated properties that are shared across all objects of the same class.

For example, arrays are objects that allow you to store related items in a single object. Although you can store one bank's name in a string variable called `bank1`, for example, you would need to enumerate 10 string variables to store 10 bank names (`bank1, bank2, bank3, . . . , bank10`). With an array, you can treat all of the bank names as a single object and leave the enumeration to a designated subscript. Therefore, `bank[1]` , `bank[2]` , and `bank [3]` would refer to the first three bank names, and `bank` itself would have all of the normal object characteristics of an array, including methods to sort the contents in alphabetical or reverse order. In Chapter 5, you will learn more about arrays, but to demonstrate the power of object flow control, they have been included in this exercise.

In this exercise, you will learn how to use the `for . . . in` statement to iterate through an array of bank names that supply loan finance and invoke some standard array methods to sort them in various orders for display.

STEP 1 – USING `for . . . in`

In your text editor, create a code block by inserting opening `<script>` and closing `</script>` tags, as shown in Exhibit 4.6. You are again using the `document.`

Counting from Zero

You may be wondering why we generally count from zero rather than one in an `if` statement. The answer is simple: You use the less-than operator (<) to test against the *iterator* associated with the number of years. If you counted from one, you would iterate one less loop than actually required. In this example, if you had counted from one, then you would only print out the payments due from the next year, rather than the current year.

write() method to dynamically print the contents of the HTML page because of the loop, but no Web form is required.

Next, declare an array called banks by using the new Array() statement and initialize the first four bank names by assigning their values to successive locations in the array: banks[0], banks[1], banks[2], and banks[3]. You then need to create a table for displaying the bank names, after which you execute the statement for (i in banks), where i is an explicit object iterator that is used to access each value in order from the banks array. Four bank names are then printed as rows in the table.

The same sequence is then repeated, but only after the banks array has been sorted alphabetically by invoking the sort() method and reverse sorted by invoking the reverse() method, as shown in Figure 4.6.

EXHIBIT 4.6

```
<html>
 <head>
  <title>Home Loan Providers</title>
 </head>
 <body>
 <script type="text/javascript">
  banks = new Array ();
  banks[0]="First Pacific";
  banks[1]="Second Western";
  banks[2]="Royal Canadian";
  banks[3]="Swiss Private";
  document.write("<table border=\"1\"
width=\"100%\">");
  document.write("<tr>");
  document.write("<td><b>Unsorted</b></td>");
  document.write("</tr>");
  for (i in banks)
  {
   document.write("<tr>");
   document.write("<td>"+banks[i]+"</td>");
   document.write("</tr>");
  }
  document.write("<tr>");
  document.write("<td><b>Sorted
     Alphabetically</b></td>");
  document.write("</tr>");
  for (i in banks.sort())
  {
   document.write("<tr>");
   document.write("<td>"+banks[i]+"</td>");
   document.write("</tr>");
  }
  document.write("<tr>");
```

```
   document.write("<td><b>Reverse Sorted</b></td>");
   document.write("</tr>");
   for (i in banks.reverse())
   {
    document.write("<tr>");
    document.write("<td>"+banks[i]+"</td>");
    document.write("</tr>");
   }
   document.write("</table>");
  </script>
  </body>
</html>
```

4

FIGURE 4.6

Unsorted
First Pacific
Second Western
Royal Canadian
Swiss Private
Sorted Alphabetically
First Pacific
Royal Canadian
Second Western
Swiss Private
Reverse Sorted
Swiss Private
Second Western
Royal Canadian
First Pacific

Summary

In this chapter, you have learned how to control flow within JavaScripts using iterators and simple variables types and previewed how to use arrays in the context of control flow for objects. Flow control allows you to build more sophisticated scripts, because you can manage the way in which certain code blocks are executed based on various conditional statements. As you will learn in the chapters that follow, making use of JavaScript objects, such as arrays, gives you access to common features, such as object iterators, that simplify code development.

You also learned to use conditional and looping statements to ensure that certain blocks of statements are executed only under certain conditions or for a specific number of iterations. The number of iterations can be predetermined or evaluated on each pass through the loop. Looping and iteration are the cornerstones of implementing logical decision making within scripts and are critical for developing flexible applications that work equally well with simple scripts and complex objects, such as arrays.

Test Your Skills

Practice Drill 4.1: Using `do...while`

In this exercise, you will examine the effect of using a `do . . . while` statement rather than a `while` statement to perform conditional looping.

As you learned in Exercise 4.2, the major difference between `do . . . while` and `while` is that `do . . . while` executes a code block before checking if a logical condition is true, for example, whereas the `while` loop does the checking first. You should use a `while` statement when you are not sure whether a code block should be executed; you should use a `do . . . while` statement when the code block will always be executed irrespective of the evaluation of the `while` statement.

The following example revisits Exercise 4.2 and shows how `do . . . while` works in practice.

1. In your text editor, create a HTML page with the appropriate `<head>` and `<body>` elements.

```
<html>
 <head>
  <title>do...while example</title>
 </head>
 <body>
  </body>
  </html>
```

2. Insert the JavaScript code block between the `<body>` and `</body>` tags.

```
<script type="text/javascript">
</script>
```

3. Declare the `printPayments()` function.

```
function printPayments()
{
}
```

4. Declare the function's local variables.

```
var principal=document.homeLoanCalculator.
              principal.value;
var years=document.homeLoanCalculator.years.value;
var annualPayment=principal/years;
var y=1;
```

5. Print the table headers.

```
document.write("<table border=\"1\"
     width=\"100%\">");
document.write("<tr>");
document.write("<td>Year</td>");
document.write("<td>Value</td>");
document.write("</tr>");
```

6. Insert the `do . . . while` loop.

```
 do
 {
  document.write("<tr>");
  document.write("<td>"+y+"</td>");
  document.write("<td>$"+principal+"</td>");
  document.write("</tr>");
  principal-=annualPayment;
  y++;
  years--;
 } while (years>0);
 document.write("</table>");
 }
</script>
```

4

7. Insert a form definition for `homeLoanCalculator` after `</script>` but before `</form>`.

```
<form name="homeLoanCalculator">
 Outstanding Principal: $<input type=
     "Text" name="principal">
 Years to Pay: $<input type="Text" name="years">
 <input type="Submit" value="Submit"
     onClick="printPayments()">
</form>
</body>
</html>
```

MULTIPLE-CHOICE QUESTIONS

1. What is the difference between a `while` and a `do . . . while` loop?

   A. A `while` loop can be nested; a `do . . . while` loop cannot be nested.

   B. A `while` loop can have a multiple statements inside a code block; a `do . . . while` loop can only have one statement inside its code block.

   C. A `while` loop executes the code block before statement evaluation; a `do . . . while` loop executes the code block only after statement evaluation.

   D. A `while` loop executes the code block after statement evaluation; a `do . . . while` loop executes the code block before statement evaluation.

2. Does an `if` statement require an `else` statement?

   A. Yes

   B. No

   C. Yes, but only when there are multiple statements inside a code block

   D. No, except when the loop is nested

3. What is the difference between the expressions x=1 and x==1?

   A. They are the same.

   B. x==1 adds one to x.

   C. x=1 is assignment, whereas x==1 is equivalence.

   D. x==1 is assignment, whereas x=1 is equivalence.

4. Which of the following is *not* a valid way of performing multiple comparisons in an `if` statement?

   A. Logical OR

   B. Logical AND

C. Both logical AND and logical OR

D. Neither logical AND or logical OR

5. What is the value of i after the following loop has been completed: `for (i=0; i<10; i++)`?

A. 0

B. 1

C. 9

D. 10

FILL-IN-THE-BLANK QUESTIONS

1. If an `if` statement is true, then its code block will be executed, otherwise, the code block after _____ will be executed.

2. The _____ operator sets a variable to have some value, such as `loanBalance=100`.

3. The _____ operator checks if a variable has a certain value, such as `loanBalance==100`.

4. `document.x.y.` _____ is the amount stored in field y of form x.

5. `document.homeLoanApplication.x.y.value` _____ `50000` checks that the value of y is less than $50,000.

6. `document.homeLoanApplication.x.y.value` _____ `50000` checks that the value of y is greater than or equal to $50,000.

7. `("+liquidity+")` displays the value of the _____ liquidity enclosed in parentheses inside a string.

8. `<input type="Submit" value="Submit" onClick="printPayments()">` invokes a JavaScript _____ called `printPayments()`.

9. The expression x-=y combines assignment with _____.

10. _____ is similar to `continue` except that the loop will stop iterating completely if it encounters the former.

DEFINITIONS QUESTIONS

1. What is the difference between `break` and `continue`?

2. How do `while` and `do . . . while` loops differ?

3. Why do `for` iterators often start from zero?

4. What is an array?

5. What is object flow control?

BASIC PROJECT

The following short project provides you with the opportunity to work with loops and conditional statements.

Project 4.1 – Using the `join` Method

This project will require you to improve the home loan provider's list display script shown in Exhibit 4.5. The `join` method of arrays can be used to join together all of the elements of an array that are separated by a certain delimiter, such as a colon or a comma. In an Internet banking application, `join` would be used to gather together a list of all home loan providers who might consider a certain applicant.

After the `banks.sort()` for statement, add another statement that uses the `join` method on the banks array to create a new string called `approvedLenders`, delimited by commas. Does it display correctly?

INTERMEDIATE PROJECT

The following intermediate project provides you with the opportunity to conduct advanced work with loops and conditional statements.

Project 4.1 – Using the Conditional Operator Statement ( ) ?

The conditional operator statement [( ) ?] is a simple, two-shot version of the `if` statement. It tests a single condition and then assigns one value to a variable if the condition is true, otherwise, it assigns a second value to the variable. For example, to assign the value "eligible" to `applicantStatus` for an applicant with an age greater than 25 but assign the value "ineligible" otherwise, the conditional operator statement could be constructed as follows:

```
var applicantStatus = (age>25) ? "eligible" :
"ineligible";
```

In your text editor, load each of the scripts developed in this chapter that have `if` statements and change them so that they use conditional operators. What advantages does the conditional operator statement bring in terms of readability?

Career **Builder**

In this chapter, you have learned how to implement a home loan approval form that is part of an Internet banking system. You have considered factors such as liquidity, debt, annual earnings, and the applicant's age and implemented methods for preapproving or rejecting the application based on these factors. What other variables could be included to make this form more realistic? You should investigate three bank Web sites and examine what variables they ask applicants to provide before the applicant can proceed to the formal approval process and extend the application in this chapter accordingly.

4

Chapter | 5

Working with Functions

Functions support modular programming in JavaScript. They provide the capacity to *encapsulate* related parts of an application's logic into an entity that can be reused multiple times by the same script or other scripts. For example, a set of functions to calculate various interest payments could be used on an Internet banking site to provide income estimates for new investors, but it also could be reused by the bank to calculate interest for existing investors.

In object terms, a **method** is a function that forms part of an object. The object often models the behavior and data of a real-world object. JavaScript objects are based on the structures in a Web browser—dialog boxes, text fields, and so on—and numerous JavaScript methods are available to operate on these objects. However, note that programmers also can create objects that are not based on structures in the Web browser. These will be discussed in the next chapter.

For Your Career

In this chapter, you will learn how to create new functions for your scripts to encapsulate application logic. This will enable you to implement sophisticated client-side browser applications that reuse functions.

Chapter Exercises

This unit's exercises will teach you how to:

- Use functions and function calls
- Differentiate between global and local scope of function variables

By working through the exercises, you will become more familiar with the functional approach to JavaScript design.

Welcome to WizBank!

Username:

Password:

Login

5

Exercise 5.1 – Introduction to Functions

Functions are the basis of modular programming. They promote good application design by moving discrete chunks of script logic into reusable modules. These modules can then be called one or more times by a single script to realize the higher-level goals of the program. A well-designed, modular application composed of many scripts provides a set of reusable building blocks for other applications and reduces the amount of time needed to develop new applications, because sets of functions will already have been tested.

A function should logically perform only one job, and a function may need to call many other functions to complete its work. Some functions return a result after they are finished in the same way that a mathematical expression always returns an answer. However, JavaScript functions are more general than mathematical expressions; they are not required to return a result on completion.

Functions are encapsulated, or self-contained, and can be identified by their name, which must be unique. For example, a function to compute compound interest rates might be called `computeCompoundInterestRate()`. As when naming variables, function names should be as descriptive as possible.

STEP 1 – CREATING A FUNCTION

To introduce some basic function concepts, let's start by creating a script that forecasts the simple interest on a promissory note issued by a corporation. In your text editor, create a new blank page and save it as promissory.html. In your text editor, create a code block by inserting opening `<script>` and closing `</script>` tags, as shown in Exhibit 5.1.

Define two functions—`displayInterest()` and `simpleInterest()`—that compute the simple interest on a promissory note after a certain number of years given a certain principal and interest rate, as passed from a HTML form. In this case, the form is called `promissoryNote`. The form allows the user to enter three parameters: `principal`, `annualInterestRate`, and `years`.

When the user clicks the Calculate Interest button, the `displayInterest()` function is called. This in turn calls the `simpleInterest()` function, which calculates the simple interest using the formula `principal` × `annualInterestRate` (in decimal terms) × `years` and returns the result to the calling function `displayInterest()`. This function then displays the simple rate using `window.alert()` after changing the text to account for the potentially singular and plural number of years supported by the script. A sample output is shown in Figure 5.1.

EXHIBIT 5.1

```
<html>
 <head>
  <title>Promissory Note Application</title>
 </head>
 <body>
 <script type="text/javascript">
 function displayInterest()
```

```
{
 var interest= simpleInterest();
 if (document.promissoryNote.time.value==1)
 {
  window.alert("Interest after one year is
     $"+interest+".");
 }
 else
 {
  window.alert("Interest after
"+document.promissoryNote.
     time.value+" years is $"+interest+".");
 }
}
function simpleInterest()
{
 return document.promissoryNote.principal.value *
     document.promissoryNote.annualInterestRate.
        value/100 *
     document.promissoryNote.time.value;
}
</script>
<form name="promissoryNote">
 Principal: $<input type="text" name="principal"/><p>
 Annual Interest Rate: < input type="text"
       name="annualInterestRate"/> %<p>
 Time: < input type="text" name="time"/> years<p>
 <input type="submit" value="Calculate Interest"
       onClick="displayInterest()"/>
 </form>
 </body>
</html>
```

FIGURE 5.1 Note the essential features of a function: (1) It must be declared using the function keyword. (2) It must be delimited by curly braces. The two functions in this example do not pass any parameters, so the round brackets after the function name are empty.

STEP 2 – MULTIPLE INVOCATIONS

In the previous example, you called parameters directly from the form using the object model of the JavaScript document to access the values of the variables entered by the user on the form `promissoryNote` (`document.promissoryNote.principal.value`, etc.). However, functions are most useful when they can accept parameters that can be modified within the local scope of the function, as shown in the call to the `window.alert()` method, in which the string to be displayed inside the alert window is passed as a parameter.

In this step, you will modify the script to allow the `simpleInterest()` function to be called multiple times from the `displayInterest()` function. This demonstrates how useful functions can be in terms of saving time and in allowing multiple operations to be performed by a single encapsulated code block. If you were not able to use a function to compute simple interest for an arbitrary number of years, then you would have to insert the function code in-line for a fixed number of years, which would limit the functionality of your script.

You will use a `for` statement to create a loop that iterates once for each year and adds the interest calculated for that year to the cumulative interest calculated for all years. The cumulative interest is then displayed by a call to the `window.alert()` method, as shown in Exhibit 5.2 and Figure 5.2.

EXHIBIT 5.2

```
<html>
 <head>
  <title>Promissory Note Application</title>
 </head>
 <body>
<script type="text/javascript">
 function displayInterest()
 {
  var msg="Cumulative interest. ";
  var cumInterest=0;
  for (i=0; i<document.promissoryNote.time.value; i++)
  {
   var interest= simpleInterest();
   cumInterest=cumInterest+interest;
   msg=msg+" Yr "+(i+1)+": $"+cumInterest;
  }
  window.alert(msg);
 }

 function simpleInterest()
 {
  return document.promissoryNote.principal.value *
       document.promissoryNote.annualInterestRate.
          value/100;
 }
```

```
  </script>
 <form name="promissoryNote">
  Principal: $<input type="text" name="principal"/><p>
  Annual Interest Rate: <input type="text"
     name="annualInterestRate"/> %<p>
  Number of Years: <input type="text"
     name="time"/> years<p>
  <input type="submit" value="Calculate Interest"
     onClick="displayInterest()"/>
  </form>
 </body>
</html>
```

FIGURE 5.2

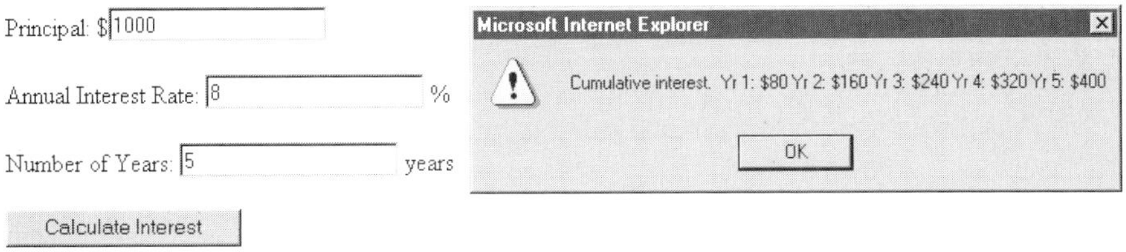

STEP 3 – PASSING PARAMETERS

Functions can take parameters and make a computation without changing the original values of the variables passed as parameters. This is because JavaScript passes variables by value and not by reference to the variables being passed. Thus, the local copies of the variable values can have different names than their antecedents. Modifying the values of these local copies does not affect their values in the calling function.

In the following step, you will create a new function called `computeCum Interest(a, b)` that takes two parameters: the value of `cumInterest` is passed as a and the value of interest is passed as b, as shown in Exhibit 5.3 and Figure 5.3.

EXHIBIT 5.3

```
<html>
 <head>
  <title>Promissory Note Application</title>
 </head>
 <body>
<script type="text/javascript">
 function displayInterest()
 {
  var msg="Cumulative interest. ";
  var cumInterest=0;
```

```
for (i=0; i<document.promissoryNote.time.value; i++)
{
 var interest= simpleInterest();
 cumInterest=computeCumInterest(cumInterest,
    interest);
 msg=msg+" Yr "+(i+1)+": $"+cumInterest;
}
window.alert(msg);
}
 function computeCumInterest(a,b)
 {
 var _interest=a+b;
 a=a*1000;
 return _interest;
}

function simpleInterest()
{
 return document.promissoryNote.principal.value *
    document.promissoryNote.annualInterestRate.
       value/100;
}
</script>
<form name="promissoryNote">
 Principal: $<input type="text" name="principal"/><p>
 Annual Interest Rate: <input type="text"
    name="annualInterestRate"/> %<p>
 Number of Years: <input type="text" name="time"/>
    years<p>
 <input type="submit" value="Calculate Interest"
    onClick="displayInterest()"/>
 </form>
</body>
</html>
```

FIGURE 5.3

Principal: $ 5000

Annual Interest Rate: 10   %

Number of Years: 5   years

Calculate Interest

Microsoft Internet Explorer

⚠ Cumulative interest. Yr 1: $500 Yr 2: $1000 Yr 3: $1500 Yr 4: $2000 Yr 5: $2500

OK

Exercise 5.2 – Variable Scope in Functions

One problem that you will face when you begin splitting an application's functionality into functions is *variable scope.* When all of the variables are declared in a single script, they have *global scope,* meaning that they can be referenced anywhere within the script. Global variables also can be referenced inside functions, which is problematic if you wish to create local variables of the same name inside a function.

Why would you need to do this? Imagine that you have a variable representing a bank balance, and you simply want to check what would happen to the balance after a year's worth of interest. Increasing the global variable bankBalance by the computed interest would be incorrect, because you are only computing an estimate and not actually increasing the bankBalance by the projected amount. In this case, you can declare a new, local copy of bankBalance inside the function, using the var keyword, and then assign the value of the global variable bankBalance to this local copy, even if it has the same name.

In this exercise, you will investigate issues associated with variable scope to ensure that global and local variables do not conflict.

STEP 1 – IGNORING GLOBAL VARIABLES

In your text editor, copy the source code shown in Exhibit 5.3. After the <script> block, define a global variable called cumInterest. Assign a value of 1,000,000 to cumInterest. Ensure that the local cumInterest variable in the function displayInterest() is initialized to zero. When you run the script shown in Exhibit 5.4 and use the same test cases as Exhibit 5.3, do you get the same results as shown in Figure 5.4? Or, is the global variable cumInterest going to make the customer a virtual millionaire?

The answer is that the global variable's value does not affect the value of a local variable that happens to have the same name. As far as the JavaScript interpreter is concerned, they are different variables, even though they look the same to us.

EXHIBIT 5.4

```
<html>
 <head>
  <title>Promissory Note Application</title>
 </head>
 <body>
<script type="text/javascript">
 var cumInterest=0;
 function displayInterest()
 {
  var interest= simpleInterest();
  if (document.promissoryNote.time.value==1)
  {
   window.alert("Interest after one year is
      $"+interest+".");
  }
```

```
  else
  {
   window.alert("Interest after
"+document.promissoryNote.
     time.value+" years is $"+interest+".");
  }
 }
 function simpleInterest()
 {
  return document.promissoryNote.principal.value *
      document.promissoryNote.annualInterestRate.
        value/100 *
      document.promissoryNote.time.value;
 }
 </script>
 <form name="promissoryNote">
  Principal: $<input type="text" name="principal"/><p>
  Annual Interest Rate: < input type="text"
     name="annualInterestRate"/> %<p>
  Time: < input type="text" name="time"/> years<p>
  <input type="submit" value="Calculate Interest"
     onClick="displayInterest()"/>
  </form>
 </body>
</html>
```

FIGURE 5.4

Principal: $ 1000

Annual Interest Rate: 5 %

Time: 10 years

Calculate Interest

STEP 2 – LOCAL PROTECTION

In your text editor, copy the source code shown in Exhibit 5.3. Note that there is a local variable called _interest in the function computeCumInterest(a,b) that stores the value of the cumulative interest calculated within the script. If you now define a new local variable inside the function displayInterest(), which calls computeCumInterest(a,b) several times, do you think that the value of _interest inside computeCumInterest(a,b) will be affected? When you run the script, as shown in Exhibit 5.5, and you use the same test cases as Exhibit 5.3, do you get the same results as shown in Figure 5.5? Or, is the local variable _interest once again going to make the customer a virtual millionaire?

Because a local variable's scope only extends to the function where it is defined, the variable defined inside computeCumInterest(a,b) is not able to influence the value of the variable with the same name declared inside displayInterest(), and vice versa.

EXHIBIT 5.5

```
<html>
 <head>
  <title>Promissory Note Application</title>
  </head>
  <body>
<script type="text/javascript">
 function displayInterest()
  {
    var _interest=1000000;
   var msg="Cumulative interest. ";
   var cumInterest=0;
   for (i=0; i<document.promissoryNote.time.value; i++)
   {
    var interest= simpleInterest();
    cumInterest=cumInterest+interest;
    msg=msg+" Yr "+(i+1)+": $"+cumInterest;
   }
   window.alert(msg);
  }

  function simpleInterest()
  {
   return document.promissoryNote.principal.value *
       document.promissoryNote.annualInterestRate.
            value/100;
  }
  </script>
  <form name="promissoryNote">
   Principal: $<input type="text" name="principal"/><p>
```

```
   Annual Interest Rate: <input type="text"
        name="annualInterestRate"/> %<p>
  Number of Years: <input type="text" name="time"/>
        years<p>
  <input type="dubmit" value="Calculate Interest"
        onClick="displayInterest()"/>
  </form>
 </body>
</html>
```

FIGURE 5.5

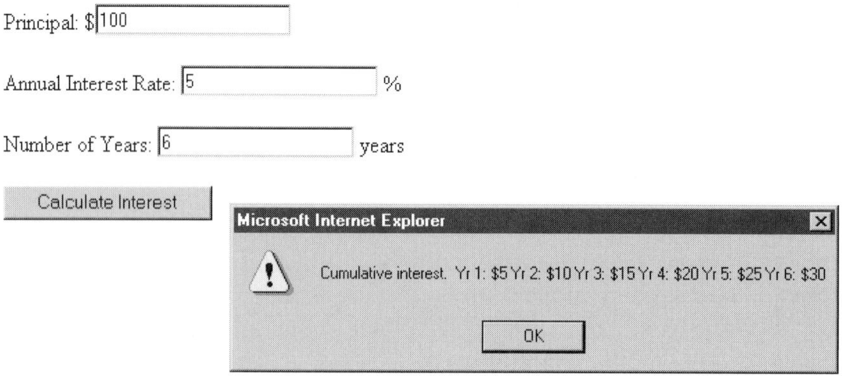

Principal: $ [100]

Annual Interest Rate: [5] %

Number of Years: [6] years

[Calculate Interest]

Microsoft Internet Explorer ⚠ Cumulative interest. Yr 1: $5 Yr 2: $10 Yr 3: $15 Yr 4: $20 Yr 5: $25 Yr 6: $30 [OK]

STEP 3 – LOCAL AND GLOBAL SCOPE

In your text editor, copy the source code shown in Exhibit 5.3. At the local level, function scope ensures that if a local variable has not been defined with the same name as a global variable, then the global variable can be referenced within a function. The value of that global variable is modified globally when it is modified locally. It is poor application design to rely on global variables, because they break the rules of encapsulation: You never know which other functions may have modified the value of a global variable before you modify it within a function.

Good script design ensures that functions call other functions as required. If operations need to be repeated several times, or in different contexts, then it makes sense to refactor existing functions to ensure optimal reuse.

In your text editor, move the declaration and initialization of the `msg` variable from the function `displayInterest()` to have global scope (i.e., outside of any particular function's declaration but within the scope of `<script>` code block). When you run the script, as shown in Exhibit 5.6, and you use the same test cases as Exhibit 5.3, do you get the same results as shown in Figure 5.6? Or, is the wrong message provided to the customer?

EXHIBIT 5.6

```
<html>
 <head>
  <title>Promissory Note Application</title>
 </head>
 <body>
<script type="text/javascript">
 var msg="Cumulative interest. ";
 function displayInterest()
 {
  var cumInterest=0;
  for (i=0; i<document.promissoryNote.time.value; i++)
  {
   var interest= simpleInterest();
   cumInterest=computeCumInterest(cumInterest,
interest);
   msg=msg+" Yr "+(i+1)+": $"+cumInterest;
  }
  window.alert(msg);
 }

 function computeCumInterest(a,b)
 {
  var _interest=a+b;
  a=a*1000;
  return _interest;
 }

 function simpleInterest()
 {
  return document.promissoryNote.principal.value *
      document.promissoryNote.annualInterestRate.
        value/100;
 }
 </script>
 <form name="promissoryNote">
  Principal: $<input type="text" name="principal"/><p>
  Annual Interest Rate: <input type="text"
     name="annualInterestRate"/> %<p>
  Number of Years: <input type="text" name="time"/>
     years<p>
  <input type="submit" value="Calculate Interest"
     onClick="displayInterest()"/>
  </form>
 </body>
</html>
```

FIGURE 5.6

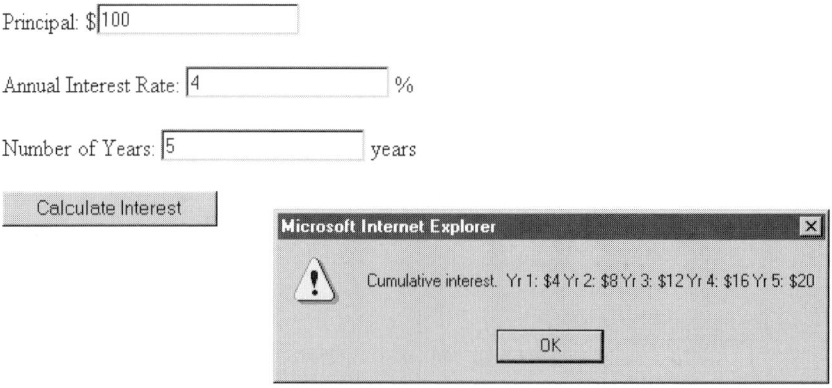

Principal: $ [100]

Annual Interest Rate: [4] %

Number of Years: [5] years

[Calculate Interest]

```
Microsoft Internet Explorer                                    [X]

    /!\    Cumulative interest.  Yr 1: $4 Yr 2: $8 Yr 3: $12 Yr 4: $16 Yr 5: $20

                        [    OK    ]
```

Exercise 5.3 – Encapsulation

One of the key features of JavaScript functions is that they can be used to encapsulate functionality that can be reused or kept separate from the main program. In Exercise 5.2, you saw how variable scope can be used to implement encapsulation.

In this exercise, you will learn how to use a function to "wrap" existing statements so that their parameters can be used for more general purposes. The example will use a window object to setup a login page for an Internet banking Web site. The login page will be spawned from a parent Web page, with the size and location set on creation. Other functions could then be enabled, such as printing the page or requesting user input. A well-designed script will separate all of these activities into separate functions.

STEP 1 – CREATING A NEW WINDOW

In your browser, create a new Web page that displays a <h1> heading for an Internet banking site called WizBank. Then, create a form called "Start" with a single Submit button that displays the value "Start Internet Banking" and set the onClick method to the JavaScript function openWindow().

Create a new JavaScript code block. In the code block, define the openWindow() function, which contains a single statement, to open a new 640 × 480 pixel window that opens the HTML page login.html, with the name "login," as shown in Exhibit 5.7.

To observe the result shown in Figure 5.7, you will need to create a login page, which is described in Step 2.

EXHIBIT 5.7

```
<html>
 <head>
  <title>Internet Banking</title>
 </head>
 <body>
 <h1>Welcome to WizBank!</h1>
```

```
<script type="text/javascript">
 function openWindow()
 {

window.open("login.html","login",width=640,height=480);
 }
</script>
<form name="start">
 <input type="submit" value="Start Internet Banking"
     onClick="openWindow()"/>
</body>
</html>
```

FIGURE 5.7

Welcome to WizBank!

Start Internet Banking

Internet Banking Login - Microsoft Internet Explorer

Welcome to WizBank!

Username:

Password:

Login

STEP 2 – CREATING THE LOGIN PAGE

In the previous example, you created a page that spawned a new page when a user clicks a button. But what you really want to do is to allow the user to login using the new page login.html.

In your browser, create a new Web page called login.html that displays a <h1> heading for the Internet banking login. Then, create a form called myLogin that has an input text field, a password text field, and a single Submit button that displays the value "Login" and set the onClick method to be the JavaScript function login().

Create a new JavaScript code block. In the code block, define the login() function, which displays a window.confirm() with the message "Are you sure these details are correct?" as shown in Exhibit 5.8 and Figure 5.8.

EXHIBIT 5.8

```html
<html>
 <head>
  <title>Internet Banking Login</title>
 </head>
 <body>
 <h1>Welcome to WizBank!</h1>
 <script type="text/javascript">
  function login()
  {
   window.confirm("Are you sure these details are
       correct?");
  }
 </script>
 <form name="myLogin">
  Username: <input type="text" name="username"/><p>
  Password: <input type="password" name="password"/><p>
  <input type="submit" value="Login"
onClick="login()"/>
 </body>
</html>
```

FIGURE 5.8

Welcome to WizBank!

Username: [   ]

Password: [   ]

[Login]

When the user types in his or her user name and password credentials, the user will be prompted to see if the details are correct before they are passed on to the authentication system.

After the required operations for the login page have been specified, a new function can be created to implement the functionality. If the function is going to be invoked multiple times with slightly different requirements, then the appropriate parameters, such as the screen size, can be passed as arguments.

Summary

In this chapter, you have learned about JavaScript functions. These entities allow you to encapsulate application logic for reuse where that logic can be expressed in functional terms. JavaScript functions provide a simple method for validating HTML form data, but could potentially be used for more sophisticated applications. As you will see in the next chapter, it is possible to use functions to define new objects within a script.

Test Your Skills

Practice Drill 5.1: Functions and Decisions

In this exercise, you will learn how to call a function where the function selected depends on the logical evaluation of an expression using `if . . . else`. The following example shows how this works in practice.

1. In your text editor, create a HTML page with the appropriate `<head>` and `<body>` elements.

   ```
   <html>
           <head>
                   <title>Debt Application</title>
           </head>
           <body>
           </body>
   </html>
   ```

2. Insert the following JavaScript code block between the `<body>` tags:

   ```
   <script type="text/javascript">
   </script>
   ```

3. Insert the definitions for the functions.

   ```
   function displaydebt()
   {
    var debt=simpleInterest();
    if (debt>10000)
     {
     highDebt();
     }
     else
   ```

5

```
  {
   lowDebt();
  }
}

function highDebt()
{
 document.write("You have a very high debt.
    Consider paying off your loan principal more
    quickly.");
}

function lowDebt()
{
 document.write("You have a reasonable debt level.
    Continue paying off your loan principal at
    current rates.");
}

function simpleInterest()
{
 return document.debt.principal.value *
     document.debt.interest.value/100;
}
```

4. Insert the definitions for the form.

```
<form name="debt">
 Principal: $<input type="text" name="principal"/><p>
 Interest Rate: %<input type="text"
    name="interest"/><p>
 <input type="submit" value="Calculate Debt"
    onClick="displaydebt()"/>
 </form>
```

5. Load the page into your Web browser. The following results will be displayed if the total debt is over $10,000:

```
You have a very high debt. Consider paying off your
loan principal more quickly.
```

Practice Drill 5.2: Functions Calling Functions

In this exercise, you will learn how to call a function from inside a function. The following example shows how this works in practice.

1. In your text editor, create a HTML page with the appropriate <head> and <body> elements.

```
<html>
      <head>
            <title>Debt Application</title>
      </head>
      <body>
      </body>
</html>
```

2. Insert the following JavaScript code block between the <body> tags:

```
<script type="text/javascript">
</script>
```

3. Insert the definitions for the functions.

```
function displaydebt()
{
 var debt=simpleInterest();
 if (debt>10000)
 {
   highDebt();
 }
 else
 {
   lowDebt();
 }
}

function highDebt()
{
 document.write("You have a very high debt. Consider
    paying off your loan principal more quickly.");
    warning();
}

function warning()
{
 document.write(" See a financial planner for more
    details.");
}
function lowDebt()
{
```

5

```
      document.write("You have a reasonable debt level.
         Continue paying off your loan principal at
         current rates.");
   }

   function simpleInterest()
   {
    return document.debt.principal.value *
    document.debt.interest.value/100;
   }
```

4. Insert the definitions for the form.

```
<form name="debt">
 Principal: $<input type="text" name="principal"/><p>
 Interest Rate: %<input type="text"
    name="interest"/><p>
 <input type="submit" value="Calculate Debt"
    onClick="displaydebt()"/>
</form>
```

5. Load the page into your Web browser. The following results will be displayed if the total debt is over $10,000:

```
You have a very high debt. Consider paying off your
loan principal more quickly. See a financial planner
for more details.
```

MULTIPLE-CHOICE QUESTIONS

1. Can you pass multiple parameters to a function?

    A. Yes

    B. No

    C. Yes, but only with functions of type int

    D. Yes, but only with functions of type char

2. What types can be returned from a function?

    A. char

    B. int

    C. void

    D. Any valid type

3. How many values can be returned from a function?

    A. 0

    B. 1

    C. 2

    D. Unlimited

4. Can global variables be accessed from within a function?

    A. Yes

    B. No

    C. Yes, but only when they have been declared using the var keyword

    D. No, except when they have been declared as global using the global keyword

5. Can local variables be accessed from outside a function?

    A. Yes

    B. No

    C. Yes, but only when they have been declared using the var keyword

    D. No, except when they have been declared as global using the global keyword

FILL-IN-THE-BLANK QUESTIONS

1. A function may need to call many other _____ to complete its work.

2. Encapsulation ensures that a function's activities are _____.

3. Both _____ and _____ variables can be accessed inside functions.

4. Functions can take parameters that allow them to compute something without affecting the original values of the variables passed as _____.

5. A function must be declared using the _____ keyword, and it must be delimited by curly braces.

DEFINITIONS

1. What is encapsulation?

2. What is a function?

3. What is the result of a function?

4. What are function parameters?

5. What is variable scope?

BASIC PROJECTS

The following basic projects provide you with the opportunity to work with functions.

Project 5.1 – Writing a Bolding Function

Create a simple printing function that takes a string argument and then bolds the text inside the string for display. This will make it easier to bold text on a page, because you will no longer have to insert starting and ending tags for bold display.

Project 5.2 – Passing More Function Parameters

In this project, you will use the `window.open()` method to open a new HTML window that is 800 × 600 pixels. You will enable the directory, menu, and status bars, but disallow resizing of the window. This can be achieved by setting the appropriate parameters within a method call that itself resides inside a function. If these parameters needed to be modified—in the situation where the function was called multiple times from different entry points—then they could be passed as parameters to the function.

INTERMEDIATE PROJECTS

The following intermediate projects provide you with additional opportunities to work with functions.

Project 5.1 – Recursion

A recursive function is one that calls itself many times before finally completing. Several mathematical functions act this way, such as those that compute the Fibonacci sequence. In this project, you will create a recursive function that calls itself to compute the factorial of an integer (in this case, `fact(10)`). You must define a termination condition for the function, otherwise it will continue in a perpetual loop. To avoid perpetual looping, you will decrement the variable that keeps track of the index once each loop, using a single argument that is passed to the function. This argument is itself generated as a result of the function.

Project 5.2 – Extending Recursion

To prove that the recursion function from the previous project is actually calling itself the same number of times as its argument, display the iteration number for each iteration.

Career Builder

In this chapter, you have continued to develop small elements of an Internet banking application. In this project, you will create a login function that validates a user's entered data for the Internet banking application. The user will then be asked to check his or her entered credentials before proceeding. Use the `window.confirm` method to accept the user's response.

5

Chapter | 6

Getting Started with Objects and Arrays

JavaScript is an object-based language that allows you to program predefined data and methods for your Web browser. You can create your own objects, but JavaScript objects are intended to be embedded within HTML and interpreted by browsers, so you will obviously want to make use of these existing JavaScript objects.

Objects have variables (known as *properties*), and their values can be initialized and/or modified by a script once the object has been instantiated. Early versions of JavaScript instantiated objects and initialized their properties by calling a *constructor method* from within a `<script>` block. The more modern method is to use an explicit *object initializer*. In this chapter, you will learn how to use both techniques. Object methods can be defined to operate on the values of properties.

An *array* is an *ordered set* of variables or objects. You can use arrays to store copies of similar data items inside a single *data structure* so that they can be sorted and referenced as a set. For example, a set of bank customer numbers would be stored in an array, rather than in individual variables, because they are related items of data. Arrays are useful when you need to display a list of a customers' bank accounts numerically by account balance or alphabetically by account name. Functions also can be applied to the data contained in arrays, which are sets of related data of the same type that can be indexed and iterated through sequentially.

For Your Career

In this chapter, you will learn how to create new functions for data structures such as arrays and work with the existing methods defined for browser objects. This will enable you to implement sophisticated client-side browser applications that make use of data structures for operating on data sets.

Chapter Exercises

This unit's exercises will teach you how to:

- Work with JavaScript objects
- Create user-defined objects
- Use arrays

By working through the exercises, you will be able to work more effectively with standard JavaScript objects, as well as those that you create yourself.

Existing customers: Eric Kwok, Jane Yu

6

Exercise 6.1 – Using JavaScript Objects

JavaScript has many different types of standard objects. These include objects such as arrays, whereby methods are provided that operate on the data that you supply, or objects such as the `window` objects, which supply much of their own data as well as associated methods. In previous chapters, you have used some simple examples of the `window` object, so it is appropriate to begin our explanation of objects with the `window` object before moving on to self-defined objects.

Each time a window is produced on the screen, a JavaScript `window` object is instantiated. The `window` object has many properties and methods that allow you to work with frames, alerts, or the main browser window. Many complex Web applications, such as Internet banking Web sites, make use of multiple windows, frames, and alerts. In this exercise, you will explore how to create a more interactive, menu-driven system for the Internet banking application.

The properties of `window` objects are accessed by using a reference to the `window` object and then using the dot (.) operator to access the required property. For example, `window.name` returns the name of the current window. Just like `window` object properties, `window` object methods can be invoked with the dot operator. For example, `window.close()` will close a window, and `window.open()` will open a new window. Note that some methods, such as `window.open()`, have a number of attributes that can be modified at creation. For example, you can set the height and width of a new `window` and place scrollbars or menubars on the window or remove them. Dialog boxes allow users to enter information, acknowledge alerts, and accept or deny requests that are made to them, providing an ideal set of input and output routines. However, such routines are limited because `window.prompt()` can only accept one input parameter at a time. In the following example, you will use dialog boxes, rather than a HTML form, to obtain user input.

STEP 1 – GETTING USER DATA FROM PROMPTS

In the previous chapter, you used a HTML form to obtain username and password parameters. However, JavaScript's `window` object allows users to enter such details into a special prompt window called by `window.prompt()`. In the following example, you will extend the login.html page from Chapter 5 to permit a user's details to be reentered for authentication if they click Cancel in the `window.confirm()` screen.

In your browser, modify the Web page login.html and the `login()` function. After displaying a `window.confirm()` with the message, "Are you sure these details are correct?" assign the result of `window.confirm()` to the variable `correct`. If `correct` is false, then use `window.prompt()` to ask the user to reenter his or her username and password, as shown in Exhibit 6.1 and Figure 6.1. If the username, password, or both are null, then alert the user appropriately.

EXHIBIT 6.1

```
<html>
 <head>
   <title>Internet Banking Login</title>
 </head>
```

```
<body>
<h1>Welcome to WizBank!</h1>
<script type="text/javascript">
 function login()
 {
  var correct=window.confirm("Are you sure these details
     are correct?");
  if (correct==false)
  {
  var newUsername=window.prompt("Please re-enter your
     username","");
  var newPassword=window.prompt("Please re-enter your
     password","");
  if (newUsername==null)
  {
  window.alert("Error: You must re-enter your
username");
  }
  else if (newPassword==null)
  {
  window.alert("Error: You must re-enter your
password");
  }
  else if (newUsername==null&&newPassword==null)
  {
  window.alert("Error: You must re-enter your username
     and password");
  }
  }
 }
 </script>
 <form name="myLogin">
  Username: <input type="text" name="username"/><p>
  Password: <input type="password" name="password"/><p>
  <input type="submit" value="Login"
onClick="login()"/>
 </body>
</html>
```

STEP 2 – REMINDING THE USER TO ENTER DATA

In the previous step, you extended login.html to permit a user's details to be reentered for authentication if the user clicks Cancel in the window.confirm() screen,
and you checked that the user's username and password were non-null. However, what
if the user continued to ignore these requests to reenter his or her details?

FIGURE 6.1

Welcome to WizBank!

Username: james

Password: ****

Login

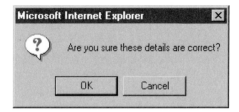

One possibility, and a potentially annoying one to the user, is to recall the `login()` function periodically to tell the user that he or she needs to authenticate. This can be achieved by using the `window.setInterval` method, which allows you to invoke a function at a regular interval (measured in milliseconds).

Use the `setInterval` method to recall the `login()` function at an interval of 1,000 milliseconds, as shown in Exhibit 6.2 and Figure 6.2.

EXHIBIT 6.2

```html
<html>
 <head>
  <title>Internet Banking Login</title>
 </head>
 <body>
 <h1>Welcome to WizBank!</h1>
 <script type="text/javascript">
  window.setInterval("login()", 1000);
  function login()
  {
   var correct=window.confirm("Are you sure these
details
       are correct?");
   if (correct==false)
   {
    var newUsername=window.prompt("Please re-enter your
        username","");
    var newPassword=window.prompt("Please re-enter your
        password","");
    if (newUsername==null)
    {
```

```
      window.alert("Error: You must re-enter your
          username");
      }
      else if (newPassword==null)
      {
        window.alert("Error: You must re-enter your
            password");
      }
      else if (newUsername==null&&newPassword==null)
      {
        window.alert("Error: You must re-enter your
username
          and password");
      }
     }
    }
  </script>
  <form name="myLogin">
   Username: <input type="text" name="username"/><p>
   Password: <input type="password" name="password"/><p>
   <input type="submit" value="Login" onClick="login()"/>
  </form>
  </body>
</html>
```

FIGURE 6.2

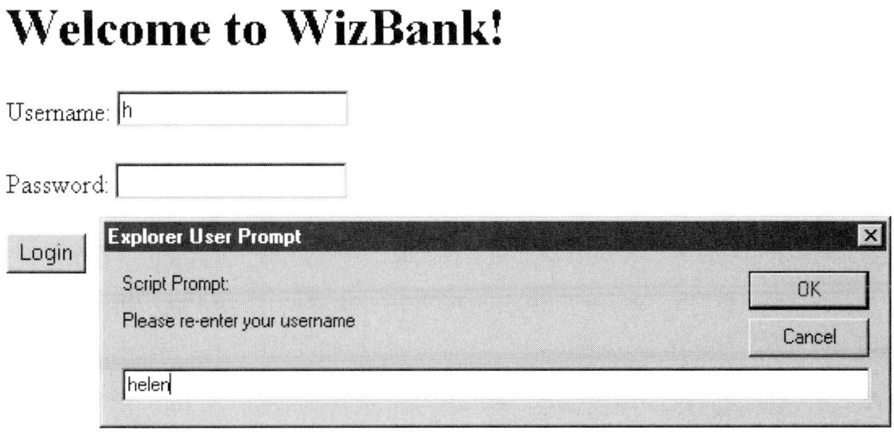

Welcome to WizBank!

Username: h

Password:

Login

Explorer User Prompt

Script Prompt:

Please re-enter your username

OK

Cancel

helen

Exercise 6.2 – Creating User-Defined Objects

In this exercise, you will create an object that represents a customer's personal data. The properties of the object will define the customer's contact details. The associated object methods will be used to determine whether a new customer's data, captured from a HTML form, is valid.

STEP 1 – CREATING AN OBJECT

As shown in Exhibit 6.3, you will create an object called `customer`. This object has three properties (`firstName`, `lastName`, and `zip`) that are initialized from values passed to a script called `checkDetails()` from a HTML form called `customerAccount`. The purpose of the form is to determine whether the customer is eligible to apply for an Internet banking account. In Step 2, you will define methods to verify whether the customer is eligible; this first step will lay the foundation for creating and instantiating the `customer` object.

After a customer enters his or her data into the `customerAccount` HTML form, the `checkDetails()` method is called. Inside this method, the `customer` object is defined as having three properties and is initialized based on the values typed in by the customer. The user's details are then retrieved from the object instantiation and displayed in a message window, as shown in Figure 6.3.

Creating Objects with a Constructor

In Exhibit 6.3, you instantiated an object by using a direct object initializer. However, in older versions of JavaScript, objects are implicitly instantiated by calling a constructor. The `customer` object could just as easily have been created by using the following syntax:

```
function customer
  (firstName,
  lastName, zip)
{
 thisfirstName
  =document.
  customerAccount.
  firstName.value;
 this.lastName=
  document.
  customerAcc
ount.
  lastName.value;

this.zip=document.
  customerAccount.
  zip.value;
}
```

EXHIBIT 6.3

```html
<html>
 <head>
  <title>Customer Account Application</title>
 </head>
<body>
<script type="text/javascript">
function checkDetails()
{
 customer={firstName:document.customerAccount.
           firstName.value,
  lastName:document.customerAccount.lastName.value,
  zip:document.customerAccount.zip.value};
  window.alert("Dear "+customer.firstName+"
     "+customer.lastName+", you are eligible to enroll
     for Internet Banking.");
}
</script>
<form name="customerAccount">
 First Name: <input type="text" name="firstName"/><p>
 Last Name: <input type="text" name="lastName"/><p>
 Zip: <input type="text" name="zip"/><p>
 <input type="submit" value="Verify Details"
           onClick="checkDetails()"/>
</form>
</body>
</html>
```

FIGURE 6.3

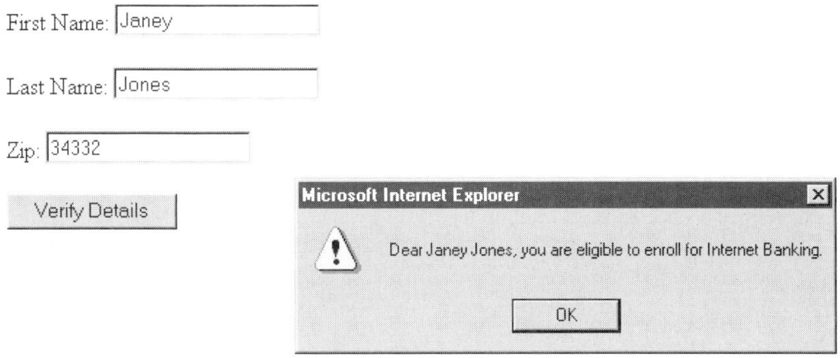

First Name: Janey

Last Name: Jones

Zip: 34332

Verify Details

Microsoft Internet Explorer

⚠ Dear Janey Jones, you are eligible to enroll for Internet Banking.

OK

STEP 2 – CREATING AN OBJECT METHOD

You now will define a method called `verifyZip` for the `customer` object, as shown in Exhibit 6.4,. This method checks whether the user can apply for an Internet banking account based on the user's zip code. In this example, all zip codes less than 23228 are valid, but all other zip codes are invalid. The `customer.zip` property is passed to the method for verification as a parameter.

If the user's zip code is not in the correct range, he or she will receive an alert, as shown in Figure 6.4.

EXHIBIT 6.4

```
<html>
 <head>
  <title>Customer Account Application</title>
 </head>
 <body>
 <script type="text/javascript">
 function checkDetails()
 {
  customer={firstName:document.customerAccount.
   firstName.value,lastName:document.customerAccount.
   lastName.value,zip:document.customerAccount.
   zip.value};
  if(verifyZip(customer.zip))
  {
   window.alert("Dear "+customer.firstName+"
     "+customer.lastName+", you are eligible to enroll
     for Internet Banking.");
  }
  else
```

```
  {
  window.alert("Dear "+customer.firstName+" "+customer.
      lastName+", you are not eligible to enroll for
      Internet Banking.");
  }
}

function verifyZip(zip)
{
 if (zip<23228)
 {
  return true;
 }
 else
 {
  return false;
 }
}
</script>
<form name="customerAccount">
 First Name: <input type="text" name="firstName"/><p>
 Last Name: <input type="text" name="lastName"/><p>
 Zip: <input type="text" name="zip"/><p>
 <input type="submit" value="Verify Details"
     onClick="checkDetails()"/>
 </form>
</body>
</html>
```

FIGURE 6.4

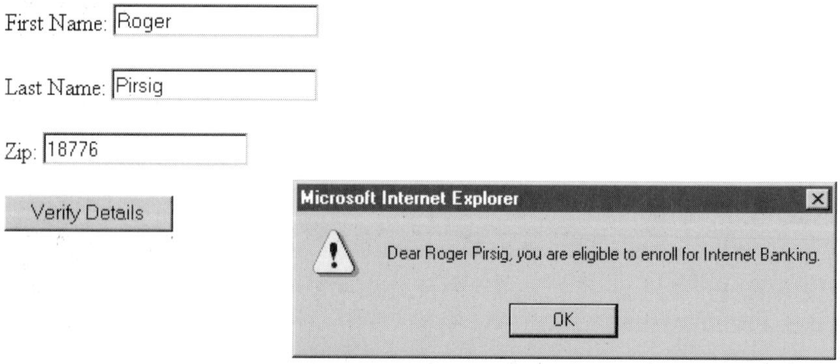

First Name: Roger

Last Name: Pirsig

Zip: 18776

Verify Details

Microsoft Internet Explorer

⚠ Dear Roger Pirsig, you are eligible to enroll for Internet Banking.

OK

Exercise 6.3 – Working with Arrays

An array is an ordered set of variables or objects. In Chapter 4, you learned how to create an array to store related items in a single object. For example, although you can store one customer's name in a string variable called `customer1`, you would need to enumerate 10 string variables to store 10 customer names (`customer1`, `customer2`, `customer3`, . . . , `customer10`). With an array, you can treat all of the customer names as a single object and leave the enumeration to a designated subscript. Thus, `customer[0]`, `customer[1]`, and `customer[2]` would refer to the first three customer names, and `customer` itself would have all of the normal object characteristics of an array, including methods to sort the contents in alphabetical or reverse order.

Arrays contain a number of different standard methods:

- `concat()`—Merges two or more arrays into a single array.

- `join()`—Takes all of the elements from one array and inserts them into a string.

- `pop()`—Pops the last element from an array and returns it to the array.

- `push()`: Pushes a new element onto the end of array and returns the new length of the array.

- `reverse()`: Reverses the order of the array's elements.

- `shift()`: Pops the first element from an array and returns it to the array.

- `unshift()`: Pushes a new element onto the beginning of array and returns the new length of the array.

- `slice()`: Takes a range of array members and inserts them into a new array.

- `splice()`: Substitutes or deletes elements from an array.

- `sort()`: Arranges array elements in alphabetical order.

STEP 1 – SORTING AND JOINING ARRAYS

In your text editor, create a code block by inserting opening and closing `<script>` tags, as shown in Exhibit 6.5. You will again use the `document.write()` method to dynamically print the contents of the HTML page , but no Web form is required.

Next, declare an array called `customer` by using the `Array()` statement and initialize the first four customer names by assigning their values to successive locations in the array: `customer[0]`, `customer[1]`, `customer[2]`, and `customer[3]`. You will then display all four customer names after sorting them alphabetically and then use the `join()` method to concatenate all customer entries with a comma and a space as a delimiter. This demonstrates the power of objects because it shows how multiple methods can be combined together to perform multiple operations, as shown in Figure 6.5.

EXHIBIT 6.5

```
<html>
  <head>
    <title>Customers</title>
  </head>
  <body>
```

```
<script type="text/javascript">
 customer = new Array ();
 customer[0]="Wu Cheng En";
 customer[1]="Eric Kwok";
 customer[2]="Jane Yu";
 customer[3]="Yukio Ashihara";
 document.write("Existing customers:
   "+customer.sort().join(", "));
</script>
</body>
</html>
```

FIGURE 6.5

Existing customers: Eric Kwok, Jane Yu, Wu Cheng En, Yukio Ashihara

STEP 2 – SLICING ARRAYS

As shown in Exhibit 6.6, you will now slice the first two entries from the alphabetically sorted customer array before using the join() method to concatenate all of the customer entries with a comma and a space as a delimiter. This further demonstrates the power of objects, because in this case three methods have been combined together, as shown in Figure 6.6.

EXHIBIT 6.6

```
<html>
 <head>
  <title>Customers</title>
 </head>
 <body>
 <script type="text/javascript">
  customer = new Array ();
  customer[0]="Wu Cheng En";
  customer[1]="Eric Kwok";
  customer[2]="Jane Yu";
  customer[3]="Yukio Ashihara";
  document.write("Existing customers:
    "+customer.sort().slice(0,2).join(", "));
 </script>
 </body>
</html>
```

FIGURE 6.6

Existing customers: Eric Kwok, Jane Yu

Summary

In this chapter, you learned about JavaScript objects, their methods and properties, and the array data structure. You can use these entities to model real-world data and activities within JavaScript and process ordered data sets. For applications that involve large amounts of data, objects can be used to represent the data, and their methods can be used to operate on that data.

Test Your Skills

Practice Drill 6.1: Shifting Array Elements

In this exercise, you will observe what happens when you use the `shift()` method to insert a new element at the beginning of an array. The following example shows how this works in practice.

1. In your text editor, create a HTML page with the appropriate `<head>` and `<body>` elements.

```
<html>
        <head>
                <title>unshift() Example</title>
        </head>
        <body>
        </body>
</html>
```

2. Insert the following JavaScript code block between the `<body>` tags:

```
<script type="text/javascript">
</script>
```

3. Insert the definitions for the customer elements.

```
customer = new Array ();
customer[0]="Wu Cheng En";
customer[1]="Eric Kwok";
customer[2]="Jane Yu";
customer[3]="Yukio Ashihara";
```

4. Insert the new element at the beginning and display the results.

```
customer.unshift("Yoko Fujiyama");
document.write("All customers: "+customer.join(", "));
```

5. Load the page into your Web browser. The following results will be displayed:

```
Customers: Yoko Fujiyama, Wu Cheng En, Eric Kwok,
Jane Yu, Yukio Ashihara
```

6

Practice Drill 6.2: **Reversing Array Elements**

In this exercise, you will observe what happens when you use the `reverse()` method to insert a new element at the beginning of an array. The following example shows how this works in practice.

1. In your text editor, create a HTML page with the appropriate `<head>` and `<body>` elements.

```
<html>
        <head>
                <title>reverse() Example</title>
        </head>
        <body>
        </body>
</html>
```

2. Insert the following JavaScript code block between the `<body>` tags.

```
<script type="text/javascript">
</script>
```

3. Insert the definitions for the customer elements.

```
customer = new Array ();

customer[0]="Wu Cheng En";

customer[1]="Eric Kwok";

customer[2]="Jane Yu";
customer[3]="Yukio Ashihara";
```

4. Reverse the new elements and display the results.

```
customer.reverse();
document.write("All customers: "+customer.join(", "));
```

5. Load the page into your Web browser. The following results will be displayed:

```
Customers: Eric Kwok, Jane Yu, Wu Cheng En, Yoko
        Fujiyama, Yukio Ashihara
```

MULTIPLE-CHOICE QUESTIONS

1. Is it legal to use two different methods to perform multiple operations on an array?

A. Yes

B. No

C. Yes, but only when the # operator is used

D. No, except when the $ subscript is used

2. If cheese is an array, what does `cheese.sort().slice(1,2). join(", ")` do?

    A. Sorts the entries in cheese alphabetically and then takes the first two entries and joins them with a comma delimiter

    B. Sorts the entries in cheese alphabetically and then takes the second entry and joins it with a comma delimiter

    C. Sorts the entries in cheese alphabetically and adds the first two entries and joins them with a comma delimiter

    D. Sorts the entries in cheese in reverse and takes the first two entries and joins them with a comma delimiter

3. What does the `pop()` method do?

    A. It pops the first element from an array and then returns it to the array.

    B. It pops the last element from an array and then returns it to the array.

    C. It pops the average element from an array and then returns it to the array.

    D. It pops the maximum element from an array and then returns it to the array.

4. What does the `push()` method do?

    A. It adds a new element to the end of an array.

    B. It adds the last element from an array.

    C. It adds the average element from an array

    D. It adds the maximum element from an array.

5. What does the `shift()` method do?

    A. It removes the first element of an array.

    B. It removes the last element of an array.

    C. It removes the middle element of an array.

    D. It adds a new element to an array.

6

FILL-IN-THE-BLANK QUESTIONS

1. `slice()` _____ elements from an array.

2. `push()` pushes a new element onto the _____ of an array and then returns the new length of the array.

3. `unshift()` pushes a new element onto the _____ of an array and then returns the new length of the array.

4. The prototype _____ makes it possible to extend existing objects.

5. The _____ property contains the number of array elements.

DEFINITIONS QUESTIONS

1. What is an array?

2. What is a constructor?

3. What is a property?

4. What does the `sort()` method do?

5. What does the `slice()` method do?

BASIC PROJECTS

The following basic projects provide you with the opportunity to work with objects and arrays.

Project 6.1 – Adding Entries to the End of an Array

This project will require you to add an element to the beginning of the customer array displayed in Exhibit 6.6. Insert a new element at the end of the array for the customer "Yoko Fujiyama" and then sort the array alphabetically. Join the array elements together using a forward slash (/) delimiter. Load the page into Internet Explorer and Netscape Navigator. Does it display correctly?

Project 6.2 – Combining and Sorting Two Arrays

This project will require you to concatenate two customer arrays together—one representing Japanese customers (`jpCustomer`) and one representing Australian customers (`auCustomer`)—and then sort the array alphabetically. Join the array elements together using a colon delimiter. Load the page into Internet Explorer and Netscape Navigator. Does it display correctly?

INTERMEDIATE PROJECTS

The following intermediate projects provide you with the additional opportunities to work with objects and arrays.

Project 6.1 – Splicing an Array

This project will require you to splice the customer array displayed in Exhibit 6.6. Remove the entry for the customer "Eric Kwok" and then sort the array alphabetically. Use the length property to verify that there are now only three elements in the array. Load the page into Internet Explorer and Netscape Navigator. Does it display correctly?

Project 6.2 – Associative Arrays

Associative arrays do not use numbers as indexes for each element; instead, a string is "associated" with each element. Associative arrays have the benefit of being more descriptive than simple integer indexes. Assigning elements to an associative array is similar to a normal array, except that a string, rather than an index, is specified. Assuming that there is one sales representative per state, signing up user for the Internet banking site. Create an associative array for four reps, using their state code as the reference. Sort the array alphabetically by name and then load the page into Internet Explorer and Netscape Navigator. Does it display correctly?

Career Builder

In this chapter, you have continued to develop small elements of an Internet banking application. Customer data, for example, are likely to be represented by objects. Large amounts of customer data are likely to be arranged in array structures so that names, addresses, and so on can be sorted and presented for display in a number of different ways.

Extend Intermediate Project 6.2 so that a sales manager can enter the state where he or she wants to find the name of the local sales representative and have that name displayed. If there is no representative available for the state entered by the manager, then return an error message.

6

Chapter 7

Manipulating Strings

Strings are some of the most important objects in JavaScript. **String** data literally form the body of dynamically generated HTML. String methods provide the ability to process string data and change its format as well as modify a string's display properties.

Although a string contains a set of characters, String objects have accessible properties, such as length, that are extremely useful for checking whether user-entered data is valid. For example, in a back-end database, a field size for a surname may only permit a maximum of 40 characters to be stored. Thus, if you use JavaScript to validate form data, you can use the String object's length property to generate a user error without tying up valuable database server time by submitting incorrect data. You can use JavaScript String objects to address individual characters in the string's data as individual characters so that you can sort, replace, and otherwise manipulate their values.

For Your Career

In this chapter, you will learn how to use JavaScript String objects and their extensive set of methods and properties for manipulating sets of character data. String management is one of the most important skills for building complex form processing. This chapter will continue developing aspects of the Internet banking site with an emphasis on string processing.

Chapter Exercises

This unit's exercises will teach you how to:

- Work with String objects
- Format string data
- Convert between string data and numbers

By working through the exercises, you will learn about String objects and their methods and properties.

customer1 and customer2 are identical in length.

customer3 and customer4 are identical in length.

customer1.toString() and customer2.toString() are identical in length.

7

Exercise 7.1 – Creating and Using the `String` Object

The JavaScript `String` object encapsulates the data, methods, and properties that are associated with strings. String data comprises an ordered set of characters. Among many other things, `String` methods can be used to test the properties of a string (such as matching), convert the case of the string, concatenate strings together, or break them apart using substring methods.

Table 7.1 contains a list of just a few of the available string data manipulation operations. As you can see, these are method invocations that change the underlying form of the string's data, including extracting the character value of a character at a specific position within the string or replacing some characters within the string with another set of characters.

In this exercise, you will learn how to create a `String` object and access its basic data manipulation operations for HTML form validation.

TABLE 7.1 String data manipulation operations.

Method Name	Description
`charAt(c)`	Returns the character at location "c" within the string.
`charCodeAt(c)`	Returns the character's value at location "c" within the string in Unicode.
`concat()`	Returns two strings concatenated or merged together.
`fromCharCode()`	Returns the character's value from Unicode.
`indexOf()`	Returns the index of a character when it first occurs in the string.
`lastIndexOf()`	Returns the index of a character when it last occurs in the string.
`link()`	Returns the string as a hyperlink.
`match()`	Returns a string if it is found in another string.
`replace()`	Replaces a substring with another substring.
`search()`	Searches for a substring within a string.
`slice()`	Removes a substring from a string
`split()`	Turns a string into a set of substrings
`substr()`	Returns a substring at a specific starting location and with a certain number of characters.
`substring()`	Returns a substring at a specific starting and ending location.
`toLowerCase()`	Returns the string in lowercase.
`toUpperCase()`	Returns the string in uppercase.

STEP 1 – CREATING A STRING

A string can be created implicitly or explicitly. An implicit definition creates a new variable and assigns a string value to it. This creates what is known as a ***string literal***. An explicit definition uses the new keyword to indicate that a new String object is being created. Although string literals can be used to access all of the normal properties and methods of a full String object, string literals and String objects differ in one very important way: If you compare the values of two string literals using the equivalence operator (==), then they will be treated as equivalent. However, if you compare two String objects using the equivalence operator, then the match will be false, because objects contain both data and methods, and you cannot compare them in such a simple way.

In fact, a string literal is associated with a String object, but the object is implicitly created when the string literal is declared. As a programmer, you do not obtain a reference to this implicit object, but you can access its methods and properties by using the string literal reference.

Exhibit 7.1 demonstrates the difference between the two approaches. Two window alerts will be produced after two surname string literal objects are compared (yielding a positive result). Two surname String objects that have been initialized with the same value will return a false result. Note that if we use the toString() methods to access the string literal of the String object in each case, the comparison will return true, as shown in Figure 7.1.

EXHIBIT 7.1

7

```
<html>
 <head>
  <title>Customers</title>
 </head>
 <body>
 <script type="text/javascript">
  customer1 = new String("Eric Kwok");
  customer2 = new String("Eric Kwok");
  var customer3 = "Jane Yu";
  var customer4 = "Jane Yu";
  if (customer1==customer2)
  {
   document.write("<p>customer1 and customer2 are
     identical.</p>");
  }
  else
  {
   document.write("<p>customer1 and customer2 are
     different.</p>");
  }
  if (customer3==customer4)
  {
   document.write("<p>customer3 and customer4 are
     identical.</p>");
```

```
  }
  else
  {
   document.write("<p>customer3 and customer4 are
     different.</p>");
  }
  if (customer1.toString()==customer2.toString())
  {
   document.write("<p>customer1.toString() and
     customer2.toString() are identical.</p>");
  }
  else
  {
   document.write("<p>customer1.toString() and
     customer2.toString() are different.</p>");
  }
 </script>
 </body>
</html>
```

FIGURE 7.1

customer1 and customer2 are different.

customer3 and customer4 are identical.

customer1.toString() and customer2.toString() are identical.

Note that the string literal associated with a `String` object could correctly be equated with a string literal as long as the string literals are equivalent in terms of the set of characters they contain, in which case a comparison will return true.

STEP 2 – WORKING WITH PROPERTIES

In the previous example, you explicitly created the `customer1` and `customer2` strings as objects. Declaring a `String` object in this way has a number of advantages over the string-literal approach. For example, you can access the **constructor** *property* for a `String` object called `customer1` by using the reference `customer1.constructor`. Its value will be displayed as `function String() { [native code] }`. If any public code was involved in the construction of the object by the *constructor function*, then it would be displayed.

Another property that is associated only with `String` objects and not string literals is the **prototype** *property*. This allows new methods and properties to be inserted into JavaScript objects. For example, to add a property called `dateCreated` to the `String` object, then the statement `String.prototype.dateCreated="01/01/2004";` could be used. Any later instantiation of a string within the local scope would then have the property `dateCreated`, which is accessed using the dot operator. For the `String` object `customer1`, the property `dateCreated` would be accessed using `customer1.dateCreated`.

The third key property of `String` objects is shared by string literals—the `length` property. This returns the number of characters that comprise the string data.

In this step, you will modify the script to use the `length` property of all objects to perform the comparisons, as shown in Exhibit 7.2. The results are shown in Figure 7.2.

EXHIBIT 7.2

```html
<html>
 <head>
  <title>Customers</title>
 </head>
 <body>
 <script type="text/javascript">
  customer1 = new String("Eric Kwok");
  customer2 = new String("Eric Kwok");
  var customer3 = "Jane Yu";
  var customer4 = "Jane Yu";
  if (customer1.length==customer2.length)
  {
   document.write("<p>customer1 and customer2 are
     identical in length.</p>");
  }
  else
  {
   document.write("<p>customer1 and customer2 are
     different in length.</p>");
  }
  if (customer3.length==customer4.length)
  {
   document.write("<p>customer3 and customer4 are
     identical in length.</p>");
  }
  else
  {
   document.write("<p>customer3 and customer4 are
     different in length.</p>");
  }
  if (customer1.toString().length==customer2.
     toString().length)
  {
   document.write("<p>customer1.toString() and
     customer2.toString() are identical in
     length.</p>");
  }
```

```
  else
  {
   document.write("<p>customer1.toString() and
     customer2.toString() are different in
     length.</p>");
  }
 </script>
 </body>
</html>
```

FIGURE 7.2
customer1 and customer2 are identical in length.

customer3 and customer4 are identical in length.

customer1.toString() and customer2.toString() are identical in length.

STEP 3 – USING DATA MANIPULATION METHODS

Many of the String object's functions are designed to manipulate data, such as changing case, extracting a substring from a larger string, or breaking a large string into a number of substrings. Many of these operations rely on the underlying representation of data in the string's literal representation. Imagine that the string's data is just an array of characters. Each character in the string is associated with a specific location, starting at index 0. Thus, a String object that has 18 characters of data will have 18 character locations addressed from index 0 through to index 17. You can use these locations to perform the substring methods referred just discussed.

In the following step, you will use a range of text-matching methods to determine if a customer's name as entered on a form is on a list of delinquent cardholders for an Internet banking application. Cardholders' names are represented as string literals, whereas the delinquent cardholders' names are contained in an array of string literals of mixed case. Because the cardholders' names are downloaded from a legacy system that only has 7-bit bytes, all characters are uppercase. Therefore, the first step is to convert the uppercase variables to lowercase. You can then iterate through all entries in the delinquent cardholder array for each customer name after you convert each delinquent cardholder's name to lowercase (the same characters with different case will not result in a match). This code is shown in Exhibit 7.3, and the results are shown in Figure 7.3.

EXHIBIT 7.3

```
<html>
 <head>
  <title>Customers</title>
 </head>
```

```
<body>
<script type="text/javascript">
 // New customer entries
 var customer1 = "ERIC KWOK";
 var customer2 = "JANE YU";
 // Delinquent customer entries
 var delinquents=new Array(4);
 delinquents[0]="John Smith";
 delinquents[1]="Eric Kwok";
 delinquents[2]="Jane Doe";
 delinquents[3]="John Lee";
 // Converting case
 customer1=customer1.toLowerCase();
 customer2=customer2.toLowerCase();
 document.write("<p>Checking customer details for
     "+customer1+" and "+customer2+".</p>");
 // Checking delinquents
 for (i=0; i<4; i++)
 {
  if (customer1==delinquents[i].toLowerCase())
  {
   document.write(customer1+" is on the delinquent
     cardholder's list.");
  }
 }
 for (i=0; i<4; i++)
 {
  if (customer2==delinquents[i].toLowerCase())
  {
   document.write(customer2+" is on the delinquent
     cardholder's list.");
  }
 }
</script>
</body>
</html>
```

FIGURE 7.3

Checking customer details for eric kwok and jane yu.

eric kwok is on the delinquent cardholder's list.

This script could be improved by creating a second array for the customers' names and then having two nested arrays to do the string matching, with one pass through the outer loop for each customer and one check per delinquent per customer on the inner loop.

Improving Efficiency

If you have m customers and n delinquents, then you need to perform m x n checks unless you break the loop when the customer's name has been found on the list. This will reduce the number of matching operations if and only if at least one customer's name is matched to a delinquent cardholder's name.

Exercise 7.2 – Formatting Strings

Methods from the `String` object can be used to format string text. In most cases, the methods simply insert some HTML markup around the text of the string. You might ask why, if this is just HTML, would you need to use JavaScript to format the text in the first place? The answer is that if you embed the formatting inside plain HTML, then HTML does not allow you to reuse the same string text later on when it may need to be reformatted in some way. For example, you may define literal strings for different standard heading styles that may be presented in different colors on different parts of the page. Alternatively, you may change the color of a customer's name depending on the customer's bank account status. If the balance after being tallied is positive, it should be displayed in black; if the balance is negative, it should be displayed in red. Because these items may depend on dynamic data, it is not possible to statically code the string-formatting information in HTML.

A number of different methods can be used to format JavaScript strings, as shown in Table 7.2.

TABLE 7.2 Methods for formatting strings.

Method Name	Description
`big()`	Increases the size of the string text using `<big>`
`blink()`	Makes the string text blink using `<blink>`
`bold()`	Turns the string text into bold using `<bold>`
`fontcolor()`	Changes the font of the string text using `<font color>`
`fontsize()`	Changes the size of a font using `<font size>`
`italics()`	Italicizes the string text using `<i>`
`small()`	Decreases the size of the string text using `<small>`
`strike()`	Strikes through the string text using `<strike>`
`sub()`	Subscripts the text using `<sub>`
`sup()`	Superscripts the text using `<sup>`

In this exercise, you will add a customer's credit card purchases that have been entered into a HTML form and display the sum in black if it is a positive balance or red if it is a negative balance.

STEP 1 – ASSEMBLING THE DATA

In this example, you will create a HTML form called `purchases` in which the customer enters his or her weekly purchases. This data is then passed to a JavaScript function called `calculate()`, which lists entries in black for a positive balance or red for a negative balance.

The code for this step is shown in Exhibit 7.4. The results are shown in Figure 7.4.

EXHIBIT 7.4

```html
<html>
 <head>
  <title>Credit Card Balance</title>
 </head>
 <body>
 <script type="text/javascript">
 function calculate()
 {
  var items=new Array(5);
  items[0]=document.purchases.item1.value;
  items[1]=document.purchases.item2.value;
  items[2]=document.purchases.item3.value;
  items[3]=document.purchases.item4.value;
  items[4]=document.purchases.item5.value;
  document.write("<h1>Purchase Summary</h1>");
  document.write("<ul>");
  for (i=0; i<5; i++)
  {
   if (items[i]<0)
   {
    document.write("<li>"+items[i].fontcolor("red"));
   }
   else
   {
    document.write("<li>"+items[i].fontcolor("blue"));
   }
  }
  document.write("</ul>");
 }
 </script>
 <form name="purchases">
  Item 1: <input type="Text" name="item1"><p>
  Item 2: <input type="Text" name="item2"><p>
  Item 3: <input type="Text" name="item3"><p>
  Item 4: <input type="Text" name="item4"><p>
  Item 5: <input type="Text" name="item5"><p>
  <input type="Submit" value="Tabulate Items"
    onClick="calculate()">
  </form>
 </body>
</html>
```

Purchase Summary

- 10
- -25
- -15
- 24
- 12

FIGURE 7.4

STEP 2 – ADDING THE DATA

In this example, you will perform an addition operation on the purchase data to arrive at a positive or negative balance. At first glance, it may appear to be very simple: You have an array of items, and you simply use the addition operator to add them together. If you do this, you will end up adding the literal string values together, so $1 + 2 + 3 + 4 + 5$ is 12345 and not 15.

   Converting text to numbers and back requires the use of a parsing method to explicitly convert the text representation of a number to its numeric representation. Conversely, a numeric representation should be converted to a string before it is used as such. JavaScript provides several methods to do this:

- `parseInt(s)`—Parses the strings and returns an integer

- `parseFloat(s)`—Parses the strings and returns a floating point number

- `toString()`—Converts a numeric variable to a literal string

- `isNaN(n)`—Checks whether a value is numeric or not

In Exhibit 7.5, when the value of each item is added to the balance, the string representing the value is parsed to a floating point number. A check is then made as to whether the balance is less than zero. If the number is negative, then the balance is converted to a string so that the string method `fontcolor` can change the font color to red. Conversely, if the balance is greater than or equal to zero, the balance is converted into a string and the color is changed to blue, as shown in Figure 7.5.

EXHIBIT 7.5

```
<html>
 <head>
  <title>Credit Card Balance</title>
 </head>
 <body>
 <script type="text/javascript">
 function calculate()
 {
  var items=new Array(5);
  items[0]=document.purchases.item1.value;
  items[1]=document.purchases.item2.value;
  items[2]=document.purchases.item3.value;
```

```
 items[3]=document.purchases.item4.value;
 items[4]=document.purchases.item5.value;
 //document.write("<h1>Credit Card Balance</h1>");
 var balance=0.0;
 for (i=0; i<5; i++)
 {
  balance=balance+parseFloat(items[i]);
 }
 if (balance<0.0)
 {
  document.write("Dear customer, your balance is
    $"+balance.toString().fontcolor("red"));
 }
 else
 {
  document.write("Dear customer, your balance is
    $"+balance.toString().fontcolor("blue"));
 }
}
</script>
<form name="purchases">
 Item 1: <input type="Text" name="item1"><p>
 Item 2: <input type="Text" name="item2"><p>
 Item 3: <input type="Text" name="item3"><p>
 Item 4: <input type="Text" name="item4"><p>
 Item 5: <input type="Text" name="item5"><p>
 <input type="Submit" value="Calculate"
   onClick="calculate()">
</form>
</body>
</html>
```

FIGURE 7.5
Dear customer, your balance is $19

Exercise 7.3 – String Matching

A String object has methods to extract substrings with specific starting and ending locations or with a specific starting location for a certain length. This is very useful if you
are processing fixed field-size data that may be extracted from a flat file or from a database. For example, a record may consist of surname, firstName, creditCard,
and expiryDate fields with 20, 10, 16, and 4 characters, respectively, but the record
may be formatted as a single string with 20 + 10 + 16 + 4 = 50 characters. If the fields
were delimited by spaces, then there would be three extra characters.

An example string value is shown in Exhibit 7.6. If the string were called `record` and you extracted the substrings using the `substring()` method, then you could assign each of these substrings to a new string literal.

EXHIBIT 7.6

```
Watters          Paul    5654332322124454 0905
```

In this exercise, you will create a script that extracts the substring representing the credit card number from a set of credit card records and displays the name of the customer if the card is on a delinquent cardholder list.

STEP 1 – EXTRACTING THE SUBSTRINGS

In your text editor, create a new HTML page with the title "Credit Card Records." Create a new JavaScript block and declare a new `Array` with five elements called `customer`. Assign five sample customer records to an array element using the structure shown in Exhibit 7.6. Iterate through the array elements using a `for` loop, writing out the credit card number from each record. This is achieved by extracting the substring starting at index 31 for a total of 16 characters using the `substring()` method, as shown in Exhibit 7.7. The results are shown in Figure 7.6.

EXHIBIT 7.7

```
<html>
 <head>
  <title>Credit Card Records</title>
 </head>
 <body>
 <script type="text/javascript">
  var customer=new Array(5);
  customer[0]="Watters     Paul    5654332322124454 0905";
  customer[1]="Smith       Zoe     7463889595066414 1005";
  customer[2]="Jackson     Bill    5425458458437575 0407";
  customer[3]="Johnson     Kelly   8548578383838456 0205";
  customer[4]="Withers     June    3298514094598547 0206";

  document.write("<h1>Credit Card Records</h1>");
  for (i=0; i<5; i++)
  {
  document.write("<p>Card #"+(i+1)+":
    "+customer[i].substr(31,16)+"</p>");
  }
 </script>
 </body>
</html>
```

FIGURE 7.6

Credit Card Records

Card #1: 565433232212445

Card #2: 746388959506641

Card #3: 542545845843757

Card #4: 854857838383845

Card #5: 329851409459854

STEP 2 – COMPARISONS

In your text editor, modify the HTML page you created in Step 1. Declare a new `Array` with five elements called `delinquents`. Assign five sample delinquent credit card numbers to an array element using the structure shown in Exhibit 7.7. Add another `for` loop. Iterate through both loops, comparing each customer's extracted credit card record with each delinquent credit card number by parsing each string as an integer. If the comparison is true, then extract the customer's name (first name and surname) using the `substring()` method and then break the loop to ensure efficiency (this assumes that you only want to know if each customer has at least one delinquent card). Exhibit 7.8 shows the code. The results are shown in Figure 7.7.

EXHIBIT 7.8

```
<html>
 <head>
  <title>Credit Card Delinquents</title>
 </head>
 <body>
 <script type="text/javascript">
  var customer=new Array(5);
  customer[0]="Watters    Paul    5654332322124454 0905";
  customer[1]="Smith      Zoe     7463889595066414 1005";
  customer[2]="Jackson    Bill    5425458458437575 0407";
  customer[3]="Johnson    Kelly   8548578383838456 0205";
  customer[4]="Withers    June    3298514094598547 0206";
  var delinquents=new Array(5);
  delinquents[0]="5654332322124454";
  delinquents[1]="7463889595066444";
  delinquents[2]="3298514094598547";
  delinquents[3]="5654332322124457";
  delinquents[4]="5425444045843757";
  document.write("<h1>Credit Card Delinquents</h1>");
```

```
   for (i=0; i<5; i++)
   {
    var s1=customer[i].substr(31,17).toString();
    for (j=0; j<5; j++)
    {
     var s2=delinquents[j].toString();
     if (parseInt(s1)==parseInt(s2))
     {
     document.write("<p>Customer "+customer[i].
        substr(21,11)+" "+customer[i].substr(0,21)+"
        has a delinquent card.</p>");
     break;
     }
    }
   }
  </script>
  </body>
</html>
```

FIGURE 7.7

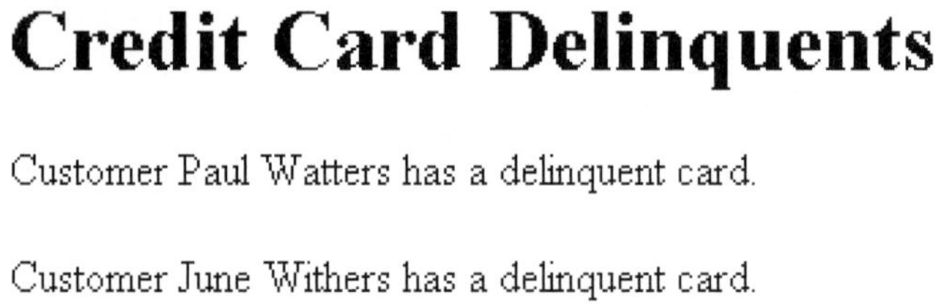

Credit Card Delinquents

Customer Paul Watters has a delinquent card.

Customer June Withers has a delinquent card.

Note that although the credit card field has 16 characters, we mark the end character as 16+1, hence the use of 17 characters in the call to substr. In addition, the parseInt and parseFloat methods should technically have a second argument (the radix), but because many Web applications are only concerned with base-10 arithmetic, the default of 10 is implied in this example.

Summary

In this chapter, you learned about JavaScript `String` objects and their methods and properties. These entities allow you to manipulate ordered sets of character data by extracting substrings and allowing HTML formatting to be applied programmatically to string data. String literals act as an implicit form of the `String` object. However, the `String` object provides you with extra functionality, such as being able to access constructors and define prototypes.

Test Your Skills

Practice Drill 7.1: Converting String Data from Lowercase to Uppercase

In this exercise, you will observe what happens when you use the `toUpperCase()` method to convert string data from lowercase to uppercase. The following example shows how this works in practice.

1. In your text editor, create a HTML page with the appropriate `<head>` and `<body>` elements.

```
<html>
        <head>
                <title>toUpperCase Example</title>
        </head>
        <body>
        </body>
</html>
```

2. Insert the JavaScript code block between the `<body>` tags.

```
<script type="text/javascript">
</script>
```

3. Insert the definitions for the customer elements.

```
customer = new Array ();
customer[0]="Wu Cheng En";
customer[1]="Eric Kwok";
customer[2]="Jane Yu";
customer[3]="Yukio Ashihara";
```

4. Iterate through the array, converting each name to uppercase.

```
for (i=0; i<4; i++)
{
 customer[i]=customer[i].toUpperCase();
 document.write("<p>"+customer[i]+"</p>");
}
```

7

5. Load the page into your Web browser. The following results will be displayed:

```
YOKO FUJIYAMA
WU CHENG EN
ERIC KWOK
JANE YU
YUKIO ASHIHARA
```

Practice Drill 7.2: Searching Text for a Specific String

You learned about one of the more frequently used methods of the `String` object in the previous exercise. Programmers and Web developers will often convert user and file input to a common case to ensure that matches are not missed due to typographical errors or differences in capitalization when comparing text entries. This is very common when using form input. Another method often used in conjunction with form input is `indexOf()`. This method can be used in form validation and to determine if specific input is present, which you will do here. In this example, comments/inquiries entered by a user are scanned for keywords. Depending on the keyword found, an alert box is displayed telling the user the appropriate bank employee to contact.

1. In your text editor, create a HTML page with the elements as shown. In the `<title>` element, add the text "Text Search using indexOf()."

```
<html>
<head>
<title>Text Search using indexOf()</title>
</head>
<body>
 <center>

 </center>
</body>
</html>
```

2. Within the body of the page (between the `<center>` tags), add the input form that will be used to access user inquiries. For the purposes of this exercise, the Reset button has the default function of resetting all default values and a user-defined button is used to initiate script processing. Add the following HTML between the `<body>` tags:

```
<body>
 <center>
 <form name="inputForm" action="" method="post">
  <h2>User Inquiry Form</h2>
  <p>
  Please enter your comment, or inquiry, below.<br />
  You will be advised as to whom to contact based
     <br /> on the specific area of concern.
  </p>
  <textarea cols="25" rows="10"
     name="commentArea"> </textarea>
```

```
  <p>
   <input type="button" value="Submit"
     onClick="idContact()" />
   <input type="reset" value="Reset Form" />
  </form>
  </center>
 </body>
```

3. Enter the JavaScript code block between the `<head>` tags (below the `<title>` tags).

```
<script type="text/javascript">
</script>
```

4. Use two parallel arrays, one of keywords and one of contact persons, to match customer issues with bank contacts. Enter the following JavaScript code within the `<script>` block to define these arrays:

```
var keywords = new Array (4);
keywords[0]="concerned";
keywords[1]="incorrect";
keywords[2]="wrong";
keywords[3]="incompetent";

var contacts = new Array (4);
contacts[0]="Ms. Jones at 555-1212";
contacts[1]="Mr. Smith at 555-1213";
contacts[2]="Mrs. Rasham at 555-1234";
contacts[3]="Ms. Hammon at 555-2222";
```

5. Enter a function named `idContact()` following the array declarations and initializations. This function will access text area input.

```
function idContact()        {
      textIn = document.inputForm.commentArea.value;
      }
```

6. Use a loop and the `indexOf()` method to identify to whom inquiries should be directed. If it is present in the test string, `indexOf()` returns the starting position/index (starting at zero) of the search string. A default contact (Mr. Jamison) is identified for all inquiries where a keyword is not present. Enter the additional code so that the `idContact()` function appears.

```
function idContact()       {
 textIn = document.inputForm.commentArea.value;
 contactPerson = "";
 for(i=0; i<keywords.length; i++)       {
  if(textIn.indexOf(keywords[i])>=0) {
    contactPerson=contacts[i];
    break;
   }
 }
```

7

```
if(contactPerson=="")    {    // set default contact
 contactPerson="Mr. Jamison at 555-5555";
 }
 alert("For additional information please
    contact \n" + contactPerson);
}
```

MULTIPLE-CHOICE QUESTIONS

1. What is the difference between a string literal and a `String` object?
   A. They do not differ.
   B. A `String` object is created by assigning string data to a variable; a string literal is created using the `new` keyword.
   C. A string literal is created by assigning string data to a variable; a `String` object is created using the `new` keyword.
   D. A `String` object uses 8-bit bytes; a string literal uses 7-bit ASCII encoding.

2. What is the role of the `constructor` property?
   A. To define private data members for an existing object
   B. To define private data members for a new object
   C. To return the value of the constructor function
   D. To access abstract methods in a class

3. What is the role of the `prototype` property?
   A. To add properties to an object
   B. To provide an abstract version of a class
   C. Provides links to a superclass
   D. Allows HTML formatting to be performed dynamically

4. What is the name of the method that changes string data to title case?
   A. `titleCase()`
   B. `changeCase(title)`
   C. `toUpperCase(first, last)`
   D. No such method exists

5. What does the `strike()` method do?
   A. Strikes out an element from an array
   B. Strikes out a number of letters specified by the parameter L
   C. Strikes out a range of letters specified by the R
   D. Inserts `<strike>` and `</strike>` tags into string data

FILL-IN-THE-BLANK QUESTIONS

1. The `replace()` method replaces a(n) _____ with a substring.

2. The `toString()` _____ takes nonstring data and converts it to string data.

3. The _____ method creates an array of substrings from a string.

4. The `concat()` method takes a number of _____ and adds them together.

5. A _____ string is formatted by using the `sup()` method.

DEFINITIONS QUESTIONS

1. What is string data?

2. What is the opposite of the `toLowerCase()` method?

3. What are the two types of methods available to the `String` object?

4. What is the `small()` method?

5. What is `blink()` method?

BASIC PROJECTS

The following basic projects provide you with the opportunity to work with `String` objects and their methods.

Project 7.1 – Using the `toString()` Method

This project will require you to modify the script given in Exhibit 7.1. Modify the script so that the two strings will be matched by using the `toString()` method for the `String` object references, even if the data is given in different cases. Load the page into Internet Explorer or Netscape Navigator. Does it display correctly?

Project 7.2 – Using the `charAt()` and `toUpperCase()` Methods

Sometimes you do not want or need to examine the entire string entered by a user. For example, if you ask for gender, place of residence (house or apartment), or city where there are restricted but known possibilities, you may simply check for the first character. In this project, you create a page that uses the `charAt()` method to determine user input.

For the exercise, create a simple HTML page with two text boxes, one for gender and one for residence, and two buttons (Submit and Reset). (Hint: It would be easy to modify the form used in Practice Drill 7.2, "Searching Text for a Specific String" for this purpose.) Using static text on the page, tell the user to enter his/her gender and residence in the two boxes. Use `charAt()` to check the first character of input in each box to determine the input. For example, if the user enters "male" or "m" in the gender box, the same result is achieved. When the user clicks the Submit button, call a function to display the answer in an alert box. For example, when the user enters "male," the alert box will show the text "You are male." To account for users entering upper- and lowercase letters, you should combine this with the `toUpperCase()` method.

INTERMEDIATE PROJECTS

The following intermediate projects provide you with the opportunity to work with `String` objects and their methods in an advanced way.

Project 7.1 – Using a Word Counter

Anyone who has submitted a Web site to a search engine has probably found that there is a limit to the number of words that may be entered for the site's description, keywords, and the like. In this exercise, you use the `split()` method to divide (split) the contents of a text area. The `split()` divides a string into substrings and stores these substrings in an array that you declare. The length of the array is the number of substrings created.

Modify the input page created in Practice Drill 7.2, "Searching Text for a Specific String," and save the document under a new name. Delete the original function and create a new function that accepts user input from the text area, determines the number of words entered, and displays an alert box stating the number of words. Delimit the words with spaces. Note that spaces entered at the beginning or end of the text result in a higher word count.

Project 7.2 – Creating an E-Mail Checker

Checking the format of e-mail addresses is a classic use of `String` object methods and pattern matching (regular expressions), which will be discussed in the next chapter. In this exercise, you will write the code to make a simple check of an e-mail address to ensure the presence of the @ and period (.) characters.

Create a Web page similar to the one in Basic Project 7.2, but with only one text box. The user will type an e-mail address into this box. When the user clicks the Submit button, call a function that checks the e-mail address for the @ and a period. Use the `<input type="button" ...>` tag to define the button. Do not use the default Submit button. As you will learn later, the default Submit button has built-in functionality that will impact the process shown here.

Remember, the @ character cannot be at the very first position of the string, it must be in front of (have a lower index than) the period, and there must be at least one character between the two characters. The period (.) cannot be in front of the @, and it cannot be the last character in the string. Therefore, you must check the positions of the two characters in the string and in relation to one another.

Hint: You will have to go through multiple checks, each of which must be passed to ensure you have a valid e-mail address. To avoid long, confusing expressions, it is a good idea to create one or more Boolean variables that indicate whether or not (true or false) the address passes each test of the validation process. If the address passes each individual test, it is valid. Failing any test makes the address invalid.

►► Career Builder

In this Career Builder exercise, you are going to develop a simple URL validator. You will work with the `subString()` and `lastIndexOf()` methods of the `String` object and learn techniques for using flags and concatenating strings for output in message boxes and prompts. This validator is simplified only in the sense that we are limiting the number of allowed protocols and site types.

To set the background, you are to create a Web page that will validate a URL entered in a text box by a user. You are to allow only commercial (.com), educational (.edu), and governmental (.gov) sites. The only protocol that will be accepted is HTTP. Your checks will verify only these two items.

To start, you will need a Web page with a text box and input and reset buttons.

```
<html>
<head>
 <script language="javascript"
     type="text/javascript" >
 <!-

 //-->
 </script>
 <title>URL Validation</title>
</head>
<body>
 <center>
 <form name="inputForm" action="" method="post">
  <h2>URL Validator</h2>
  <p>
   Please enter a URL in the box below and click
     the "submit" button.
  </p>
  <p>
   <input type="text" name="txtURL" value="" />
   <input type="button" value="Submit"
     onClick="checkURL()" />
   <input type="reset" value="Reset Form" />
 </form>
 </center>
</body>
</html>
```

(continued)

Because several errors may be present, we want to display them all in one alert box, rather than having multiple boxes appear one after the other. Therefore, we have created a generic error message that will appear whenever an error occurs. This message simply states that there is an error present. Specific errors will be listed in the error message. We also declare a variable that will be used as a flag, which tells us if an error is present. The code is as follows:

```
// The generic start of any error message shown.
errorMsg ="The form has the following errors:";
inputErrorFlag=false;
```

To begin processing, create a function called `checkURL` that is called when the user clicks the Submit button. The first step in this function is to ensure that content has been entered into the text box. In this case, if there is no input, the error message is set and, other than displaying the error message, processing stops. Note how the `+=` operator is used to concatenate the message with the generic intro line. Also see how the `\n` escape sequence is used to place the error on a new line.

```
function checkURL()     {
 URL = document.inputForm.txtURL.value;
 // Is there a URL entered? If not display error
    message and stop other checks
 if(URL=="")       {
  errorMsg +="\nURL missing";
  inputErrorFlag=true;
}
```

If there is content in the text box, processing continues and other checks are made. This code is placed within an `else` block immediately following the `if` block shown above.

The first check will be to determine if the proper protocol is used. We have created a variable to hold the substring and then test the substring. In this situation, the protocol is found in the first seven positions of the URL (starting at index 0 and ending at index 6). The `subString()` method specifies the first character to include and the next character to exclude.

```
else     {
 // check for a proper protocol
 protocol = URL.substring(0,7);
 if(protocol != "http://")    {
    errorMsg += "\nincorrect protocol";
    inputErrorFlag=true;
 }
```

Notice that the `inputErrorFlag` is set to `true` if the protocol is incorrect. This flag is checked later to determine if an error message is required.

(continued)

We do not stop processing if the protocol is wrong, because we want to advise the user of all of the errors, giving the user the opportunity to make all of the corrections at one time.

Our next check is to determine if the user has entered a URL with the proper site type. To accomplish this, the position of the last period is determined and a substring starting at the period and going to the end of the URL string is obtained. This substring is then checked to see if it is equal to one of those permitted. As we saw earlier, if there is not a valid site type, additional content is added to the error message and the `inputErrorFlag` is set to true.

```
// check that URL has allowable site type ... ends in
   .com or .edu or .gov
endStart = URL.lastIndexOf(".");
ending = URL.substring(endStart,URL.length);
if(ending !=".com" && ending !=".gov" && ending
   !=".edu")       {
  errorMsg+="\nincorrect site type";
  inputErrorFlag = true;
}
} // this ends the 'else' code block
```

It is now time to check to see if an error message should be displayed. If `inputErrorFlag` is true, an error message will be displayed that lists all of the errors that were identified. If the flag is false, a message stating that the URL is valid is displayed.

If errors are found, the `errorMsg` and `inputErrorFlag` variables are reset. If these were not reset, the `inputErrorFlag` would remain true and an error message would appear if a valid URL were entered on subsequent tries. The `errorMsg` must be reset because, if left alone, new errors would simply be concatenated to the existing message.

```
// do we display an error message?
if(inputErrorFlag)       {
  alert(errorMsg);
  errorMsg ="The form has the following errors:";
  inputErrorFlag=false;
}
else     {
  alert("Very good. You have a valid URL");
 }
} // END OF FUNCTION
```

Chapter 8

Exploring Expressions in Arithmetic and Pattern Matching

So far, you have learned how to use simple arithmetic and logical expressions in conjunction with conditional statements to implement program logic in JavaScript. However, checking whether simple values are greater than zero or whether a comparison operator yields true or false is really only the first step in exploring the power of JavaScript expressions.

Going one step further, you can begin to apply arithmetic expressions to JavaScript objects such as Date and Math. For the Internet banking we have been developing, this would allow you to use the Date object to check credit card expiration dates or use the regular expression object known as RegExp to search for a set of dates matching certain criteria.

You can use regular expressions to specify certain patterns in string data, allowing you to search for items that match specific criteria. In a file system, for example, you can specify regular expressions using *wildcards* such as * to match certain parts of a file name or file extension. You can use the **RegExp** object to create similar pattern specifications and apply them to string data.

For Your Career

In this chapter, you will learn how to use JavaScript pattern-matching techniques to search in String objects. You will also discover how to form and evaluate expressions using sophisticated objects such as Date and Math. This chapter will continue developing aspects of the Internet banking site, with an emphasis on pattern matching.

Chapter Exercises

This unit's exercises will teach you how to:

- Specify and evaluate arithmetic expressions using the Date and Math objects
- Create regular expressions using the RegExp syntax
- Perform pattern matching

By working through the exercises, you will learn about JavaScript Math, Date, and RegExp objects and their methods and properties.

Internet Banking Customer Registration

Account: 6666732423

Surname: Watters3

First Name: Paul

Email Address: paul@cassowary.net

Phone: 8876654434

Register Account

Microsoft Internet Explorer

⚠ Your name contains invalid characters. Please enter a new name.

OK

8

Exercise 8.1 – Using the `Math` Object

The JavaScript `Math` object has many properties and methods that allow you to compute advanced mathematical functions. This is especially important for Web sites, such as Internet banking ones, that need to compute interest rates and investment returns for bank clients.

The most commonly used `Math` object properties are shown in Table 8.1. They are accessed by creating a reference to the `Math` object and then using the dot operator to access the required property. For example, `Math.E` provides the numeric approximation to Euler's constant, *e*, which can then be used in more complex expressions.

TABLE 8.1 Commonly used `Math` object properties.

Property	Description
E	Numeric approximation of Euler's constant, *e*, which is approximately 2.71828.
LN10	Numeric approximation of the natural logarithm of 10, which is approximately 2.302585.
LN2	Numeric approximation of the natural logarithm of 2, which is approximately 0.693147.
LOG10E	Numeric approximation of the logarithm of *e* base-10, which is approximately 0.43429.
LOG2E	Numeric approximation of the logarithm of *e* base-2, which is approximately 1.442695.
PI	Numeric approximation of π, the ratio of a circle's circumference to its diameter, which is approximately 3.14159.
SQRT2	Numeric approximation of the square root of 2, which is approximately 1.4142.
SQRT1_2	Numeric approximation of the square root of one-half, which is approximately 0.7071.

Just like `Math` object properties, `Math` object methods can be invoked with the dot operator. For example, `Math.random()` will return a value generated by a **pseudorandom number generator**, which can be very useful in applications that rely on probability. For example, if your Internet banking pages support advertising, you might randomly select an integer between 1 and 20, each representing a different image, whose file name is dynamically inserted into the Web page by using the `document.write()` method. Table 8.2 shows the most commonly used `Math` methods.

In this exercise, you will learn how to use the `Math` object to randomly select an advertising slogan for placement at the top of an Internet banking Web page every time it is loaded.

TABLE 8.2 Commonly used Math methods.

Method	Description
abs *(n)*	Returns the absolute value of n.
acos *(n)*	Returns the arc-cosine of n.
asin *(n)*	Returns the arc-sine of n.
atan *(n)*	Returns the arc-tangent of n.
ceil *(n)*	Returns n if n is an integer or the next integer above n if n is real.
cos *(n)*	Returns the cosine of n.
exp *(n)*	Returns the value of e to the power of n.
floor *(n)*	Returns n if n is an integer or the next integer below n if n is real.
log *(n)*	Returns the value of the natural logarithm of n.
max *(m, n)*	Returns m if m > n otherwise returns *n*.
min *(m, n)*	Returns m if m < n otherwise returns *n*.
pow *(m, n)*	Raises m to the power of n.
random *()*	Returns a pseudorandomly generated floating point number between zero and one.
round *(n)*	Rounds up n to the nearest integer.
sin *(n)*	Returns the sine of n.
sqrt *(n)*	Returns the square root of n.
tan *(n)*	Returns the tangent of n.

STEP 1 – CREATING THE SLOGANS

In your browser, create a new Web page that displays a <h1> heading for an Internet banking site called "WizBank." Then, define an array of string literals using the new Array keyword called slogan. Assign each string literal within slogan to a string of advertising text.

In this step, you will simply print out each slogan, in turn, using a for loop. In addition, you will apply the String method bold() to each slogan to display it in bold type, as shown in Exhibit 8.1. The results are shown in Figure 8.1.

EXHIBIT 8.1

```
<html>
 <head>
  <title>Internet Banking Slogan</title>
 </head>
 <body>
 <h1>Welcome to WizBank!</h1>
 <script type="text/javascript">
```

```
    var slogan=new Array(10);
    slogan[0]="WizBank - excellence in customer service";
    slogan[1]="WizBank - the choice of tomorrow's
      generation";
    slogan[2]="WizBank - future financial services today";
    slogan[3]="WizBank - bringing you the best in
      technology";
    slogan[4]="WizBank - customer service with a smile";
    slogan[5]="WizBank - 6% home loans (first 25
      customers only)";
    slogan[6]="WizBank - discount credit card rates
      until tomorrow";
    slogan[7]="WizBank - serving you financially";
    slogan[8]="WizBank - #1 in finance for homes";
    slogan[9]="WizBank - mortgages are our business";
    for (i=0; i<10; i++)
    {
      document.write("<p>"+slogan[i].bold()+"</p>");
    }
  </script>
  </body>
</html>
```

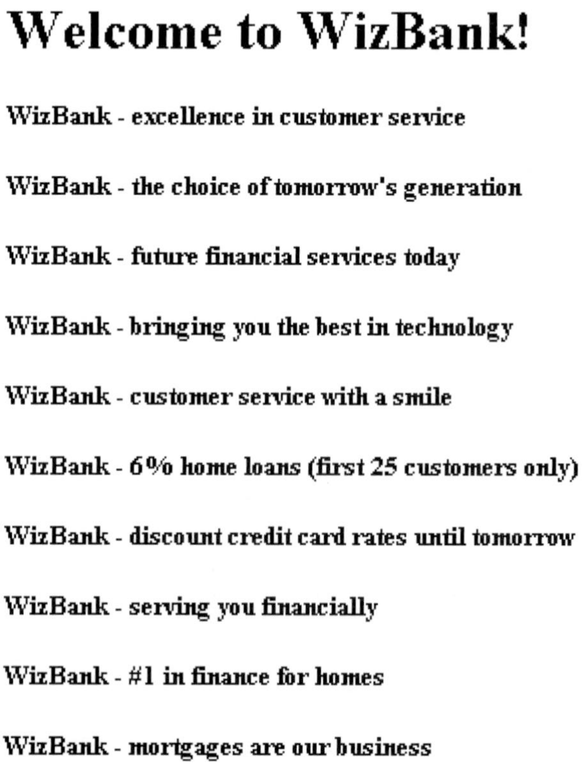

Welcome to WizBank!

WizBank - excellence in customer service

WizBank - the choice of tomorrow's generation

WizBank - future financial services today

WizBank - bringing you the best in technology

WizBank - customer service with a smile

WizBank - 6% home loans (first 25 customers only)

WizBank - discount credit card rates until tomorrow

WizBank - serving you financially

WizBank - #1 in finance for homes

FIGURE 8.1   WizBank - mortgages are our business

STEP 2 – RANDOM SELECTION

In the previous example, you displayed all of the slogans stored in the slogan array on the page. But what you really want to do is select one slogan randomly every time the page is loaded so that a customer has an equal chance of seeing each slogan in his or her first 20 visits.

To achieve this goal, you must randomly select the subscript of the array slogan every time the script is executed. To do this, you call the Math.random() method, which returns a floating point value between 0 and 1, which you then multiply by 10 to scale the result to lie between 0 and 9, which corresponds to the range of subscripts in slogan.

In this step, you will modify the code from the previous step to randomly select the subscripts, as shown in Exhibit 8.2. The results are shown in Figure 8.2.

EXHIBIT 8.2

```
<html>
 <head>
  <title>Internet Banking Slogan</title>
 </head>
 <body>
 <h1>Welcome to WizBank!</h1>
 <script type="text/javascript">
  var slogan=new Array(10);
  slogan[0]="WizBank - excellence in customer service";
  slogan[1]="WizBank - the choice of tomorrow's
    generation";
  slogan[2]="WizBank - future financial services today";
  slogan[3]="WizBank - bringing you the best in
    technology";
  slogan[4]="WizBank - customer service with a smile";
  slogan[5]="WizBank - 6% home loans (first 25
    customers only)";
  slogan[6]="WizBank - discount credit card rates
    until tomorrow";
  slogan[7]="WizBank - serving you financially";
  slogan[8]="WizBank - #1 in finance for homes";
  slogan[9]="WizBank - mortgages are our business";
  var subscript=Math.floor(Math.random()*10);
  document.write("<p>"+slogan[subscript].bold()+"</p>");
 </script>
 </body>
</html>
```

Random Number Generators

Although the random numbers generated using the Math.random() method are random enough for advertising slogans, you would not want to use them for developing gaming or gambling applications. Because you cannot explicitly set the seed (or starting value) of the random number generator in JavaScript, you have no way of ensuring that repeatable sequences do not occur, because the number selection is only **pseudorandom**. More full-fledged programming languages, such as Java, allow you to select the algorithm used and the seed value. Only a hardware device can generate **true random** numbers, for example, by measuring radiation. See http://www.random.org/ for more details.

Welcome to WizBank!

FIGURE 8.2   WizBank - bringing you the best in technology

Note that you could easily be randomly selecting image URLs to display rather than lines of text, which may be more visually effective. The `slogan` array would simply contain URLs to images rather than text.

Exercise 8.2 – Using the `Date` Object

In some programming languages, dates are stored as strings in which the day, month, and year occupy fixed positions. This makes dates easy to display, but notoriously difficult to work with. Typically, date operations might include working out how many days there are between a start and an end date or converting between different time zones. Although you could use the JavaScript substring and pattern-matching methods to write your own date-processing classes, these are actually provided to you in JavaScript's `Date` class. The **Date** class has methods for getting and setting time and date values. In addition, it has auxiliary methods for converting dates into Greenwich Mean Time (GMT) format and for returning the number of milliseconds since January 1, 1970, which is often used with UNIX systems.

Instantiating a `Date` object allows you to access two properties: `constructor` and `prototype`. You can access the `constructor` property for a `Date` object called `date1` by using the reference `date1.constructor`. Its value will be displayed as `function Date() { [native code] }`. If any public code was involved in the construction of the `Date` object by the `constructor` function, then it would be displayed. The `prototype` property allows new properties to be inserted into JavaScript objects. For example, the statement `Date.prototype.appName= "Internet Banking";` could be used to add a property called `appName` to the `Date` object. Any later instantiation of a `Date` within the local scope would then have the property `appName`, which could be accessed by using the dot operator. For the `Date` object `date1`, the property `appName` would be accessed by using `date1. appName`. The most commonly used `Date` methods are described in Table 8.3.

In this exercise, you will create an application that displays the current date and time of an account transfer in the browser's alert window for an Internet banking application.

STEP 1 – DISPLAYING THE DATE AND TIME

In this example, you will create a script that displays the current date and time in the browser's status window. First, you need to retrieve the current date by instantiating a new `Date` object and then create new variables for the day of the week, day, month, and year for the date and the hours, minutes, and seconds for the time. You then need to define two arrays of string literals to store the day names and month names, respectively, because `Date` only returns numbers. Note that these numbers always start with zero; Sunday represents the zero day and January represents the zero month. Finally, the values for the time and date can be assembled and displayed using the `document.write()` method.

The code for this step is shown in Exhibit 8.3, and the results are shown in Figure 8.3.

TABLE 8.3 Commonly used Date methods.

Method Name	Description
getDate()	Gets the current date
getDay()	Gets the current day
getHours()	Gets the current hour
getMinutes()	Gets the current number of minutes
getMonth()	Gets the current month
getSeconds()	Gets the current number of seconds
getTime()	Gets the current time
getTimezoneOffset()	Gets the difference (in minutes) between the current time zone and GMT
getYear()	Gets the current year (two digits)
getFullYear()	Gets the current year (four digits)
parse()	Gets the milliseconds elapsed since January 1, 1970
setDate()	Sets the current date
setDay()	Sets the current day
setHours()	Sets the current hour
setMinutes()	Sets the current number of minutes
setMonth()	Sets the current month
setSeconds()	Sets the current number of seconds
setTime()	Sets the current time
setYear()	Sets the current year (two digits)
setFullYear()	Sets the current year (four digits)
toGMTString()	Gets a date in GMT format
toLocaleString()	Formats a date based on the internationalized locale

8

EXHIBIT 8.3

```
<html>
 <head>
  <title>Date Display</title>
 </head>
 <body>
 <script type="text/javascript">
  // Current date variables
```

```
    var currentDate=new Date();
    var dayOfTheWeek=currentDate.getDay();
    var month=currentDate.getMonth();
    var day=currentDate.getDate();
    var year=currentDate.getYear();
    var hours=currentDate.getHours();
    var minutes=currentDate.getMinutes();
    var seconds=currentDate.getSeconds();
    // Day text
    var dayNames=new Array(7);
    dayNames[0]="Sun";
    dayNames[1]="Mon";
    dayNames[2]="Tue";
    dayNames[3]="Wed";
    dayNames[4]="Thu";
    dayNames[5]="Fri";
    dayNames[6]="Sat";
    // Month text
    var monthNames=new Array(12);
    monthNames[0]="Jan";
    monthNames[1]="Feb";
    monthNames[2]="Mar";
    monthNames[3]="Apr";
    monthNames[4]="May";
    monthNames[5]="Jun";
    monthNames[6]="Jul";
    monthNames[7]="Aug";
    monthNames[8]="Sep";
    monthNames[9]="Oct";
    monthNames[10]="Nov";
    monthNames[11]="Dec";
    // Display date and time
    document.write("<p>Current date: "+dayNames
      [dayOfTheWeek]+" "+day+" "+monthNames[month]
        +" "+year);
    document.write("<p>Current time: "+hours
      +":"+minutes+":"+seconds);
  </script>
  </body>
</html>
```

Current date: Wed 29 Sep 2004

FIGURE 8.3 Current time: 21:12:9

STEP 2 – IMPLEMENTING THE TRANSFER

In this example, shown in Exhibit 8.4, you will create a HTML form called `transfer` that has three fields: an account number to transfer money from, an account number to transfer money to, and the amount of money to be transferred.

Once these details have been submitted, the JavaScript `calculate()` function is called. This function calculates the current date and time and then raises an alert window to display a message confirming that the transfer has taken place, as shown in Figure 8.4.

EXHIBIT 8.4

```
<html>
 <head>
  <title>Money Transfer</title>
 </head>
 <body>
 <script type="text/javascript">
 function calculate()
 {
  // Current date variables
  var currentDate=new Date();
  var dayOfTheWeek=currentDate.getDay();
  var month=currentDate.getMonth();
  var day=currentDate.getDate();
  var year=currentDate.getYear();
  var hours=currentDate.getHours();
  var minutes=currentDate.getMinutes();
  var seconds=currentDate.getSeconds();
  // Day text
  var dayNames=new Array(7);
  dayNames[0]="Sun";
  dayNames[1]="Mon";
  dayNames[2]="Tue";
  dayNames[3]="Wed";
  dayNames[4]="Thu";
  dayNames[5]="Fri";
  dayNames[6]="Sat";
  // Month text
  var monthNames=new Array(12);
  monthNames[0]="Jan";
  monthNames[1]="Feb";
  monthNames[2]="Mar";
  monthNames[3]="Apr";
  monthNames[4]="May";
  monthNames[5]="Jun";
  monthNames[6]="Jul";
  monthNames[7]="Aug";
```

8

```
    monthNames[8]="Sep";
    monthNames[9]="Oct";
    monthNames[10]="Nov";
    monthNames[11]="Dec";
    // Display date and time
    window.alert("$"+document.transfer.amount.value+"
      transferred from "+
      document.transfer.account1.value+" to "+
        document.transfer.account2.value+
      " on "+dayNames[dayOfTheWeek]+" "+day+" "+
      monthNames[month]+" "+year+
      " at "+hours+":"+minutes+":"+seconds);
    }
    </script>
    <h1>Transfer Funds</h1>
    <form name="transfer">
     Account 1: <input type="Text" name="account1"><p>
     Account 2: <input type="Text" name="account2"><p>
     Amount: <input type="Text" name="amount"><p>
     <input type="Submit" value="Transfer Funds"
       onClick="calculate()">
     </form>
    </body>
</html>
```

FIGURE 8.4

Transfer Funds

Exercise 8.3 – Using Regular Expressions

In Chapter 7, you learned how to work with the `String` object to extract substrings with specific starting and ending locations or with a specific starting location for a certain length. This is very useful if you are processing fixed field-size data that might be extracted from a flat file or database, for example. However, it does not allow you to search for specific substrings within a string or to create a specification to identify substrings that match a certain pattern.

JavaScript regular expressions allow you to specify patterns—both simple and complex—to determine whether a string matches specific criteria. For example, in an Internet banking application, you may want to validate input being entered into a form, such as a customer's e-mail address, to ensure that it is valid. To validate the e-mail address, you would need to ensure that it contains an @ symbol and has a recognized top-level domain, such as .edu, .org, .com, and so on

Regular expressions can be specified by a string literal that follows a certain format and implemented using the `RegExp` object. The `RegExp` literal takes a similar form as the UNIX Visual Editor (vi) syntax: Forward slashes are used to delimit the pattern to search for and the actions that are to be performed when a match is made.

In this exercise, you will use regular expressions to verify aspects of a customer's data entered into a form to register an existing bank account for Internet banking.

STEP 1 – SPECIFYING A PATTERN

In your text editor, create a new HTML page with the title "Internet Banking Customer Registration." Insert a HTML form called `register`, with fields for the customer's surname, first name, e-mail address, and phone number. When submitted, the form should call a JavaScript function called `verifyDetails`; this function should have three patterns to be matched with the customer's e-mail address. These correspond to the three excluded e-mail domains (yahoo.com, hotmail.com, and google.com) that customers may not use when registering their account. The three patterns are then evaluated inside an `if` statement and logically OR'ed. If any of them return a match, then the customer is prompted to reenter his or her e-mail address. Exhibit 8.5 shows the code. The results are shown in Figure 8.5.

EXHIBIT 8.5

```
<html>
 <head>
  <title>Internet Banking Customer Registration</title>
 </head>
 <body>
 <script type="text/javascript">
 function verifyDetails()
 {
  var excludedDomain1=/yahoo.com/;
  var excludedDomain2=/hotmail.com/;
  var excludedDomain3=/google.com/;
  if (excludedDomain1.test(document.register.
    email.value)||
```

```
          excludedDomain2.test(document.register.
            email.value)||
          excludedDomain3.test(document.register.
            email.value))
  {
     window.alert("Your e-mail address is from an
       excluded domain. Please enter a new e-mail
       address.");
  }
  else
  {
     window.alert("Your account has been registered.");
  }
}
</script>
<h1>Internet Banking Customer Registration</h1>
<form name="register">
 Account: <input type="Text" name="account"><p>
 Surname: <input type="Text" name="surname"><p>
 First Name: <input type="Text" name="firstName"><p>
 Email Address: <input type="Text" name="email"><p>
 Phone: <input type="Text" name="phone"><p>
 <input type="Submit" value="Register Account"
    onClick="verifyDetails()">
 </form>
 </body>
</html>
```

FIGURE 8.5
Internet Banking Customer Registration

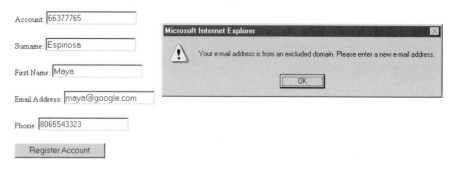

STEP 2 – CASE SENSITIVITY

In your text editor, modify the HTML page you created in Step 1 to perform the match regardless of the case, because the matching process is usually case sensitive. This can be achieved by modifying each of the RegExp literals and adding a flag to indicate case insensitivity. Exhibit 8.6 shows the code. The results are shown in Figure 8.6.

EXHIBIT 8.6

```html
<html>
 <head>
  <title>Internet Banking Customer Registration</title>
 </head>
 <body>
 <script type="text/javascript">
 function verifyDetails()
 {
  var excludedDomain1=/yahoo.com/i;
  var excludedDomain2=/hotmail.com/i;
  var excludedDomain3=/google.com/i;
  if (excludedDomain1.test(document.register.
    email.value)||
     excludedDomain2.test(document.register.
       email.value)||
     excludedDomain3.test(document.register.
       email.value))
   {
     window.alert("Your e-mail address is from
       an excluded domain. Please enter a new e-mail
       address.");
   }
   else
   {
     window.alert("Your account has been registered.");
   }
 }
 </script>
 <h1>Internet Banking Customer Registration</h1>
 <form name="register">
  Account: <input type="Text" name="account"><p>
  Surname: <input type="Text" name="surname"><p>
  First Name: <input type="Text" name="firstName"><p>
  Email Address: <input type="Text" name="email"><p>
  Phone: <input type="Text" name="phone"><p>
  <input type="Submit" value="Register Account"
    onClick="verifyDetails()">
 </form>
 </body>
</html>
```

Other flags can also be used: g indicates that the matching should be global—every match in the string is performed (the default is to stop matching after one positive result). You can also combine flags together, thus ig indicates that the matching should be case insensitive and global.

FIGURE 8.6
Internet Banking Customer Registration

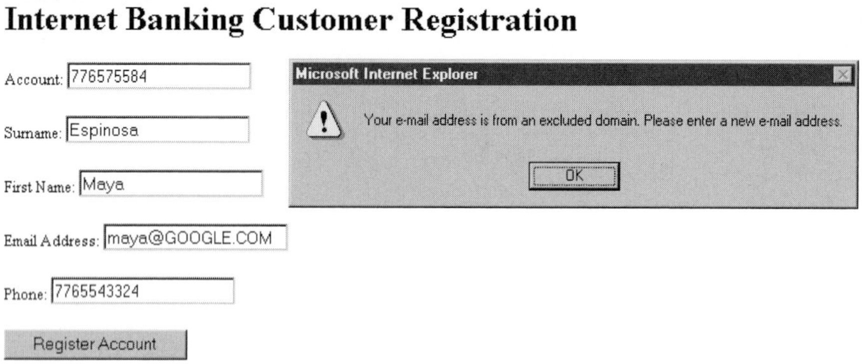

STEP 3 – COMPLEX PATTERNS

In your text editor, modify the HTML page you created in Step 1 to verify whether each of the text fields (surname and firstName) only contain alphabetical characters. This can be achieved by specifying the appropriate character ranges in the RegExp literals and adding a flag to indicate case insensitivity. Exhibit 8.7 shows the code. The results are shown in Figure 8.7.

EXHIBIT 8.7

```html
<html>
 <head>
  <title>Internet Banking Customer Registration</title>
 </head>
 <body>
 <script type="text/javascript">
 function verifyDetails()
 {
  var validCharacters=/[A-Z]/i;
  if (!validCharacters.test(document.
   register.surname.value)||
     !validCharacters.test(document.
       register.firstName.value))
   {
     window.alert("Your name contains invalid
       characters.Please enter a new name.");
   }
   else
   {
     window.alert("Your account has been registered.");
   }
 }
 </script>
```

```
<h1>Internet Banking Customer Registration</h1>
<form name="register">
 Account: <input type="Text" name="account"><p>
 Surname: <input type="Text" name="surname"><p>
 First Name: <input type="Text" name="firstName"><p>
 Email Address: <input type="Text" name="email"><p>
 Phone: <input type="Text" name="phone"><p>
 <input type="Submit" value="Register Account"
    onClick="verifyDetails()">
 </form>
 </body>
</html>
```

FIGURE 8.7

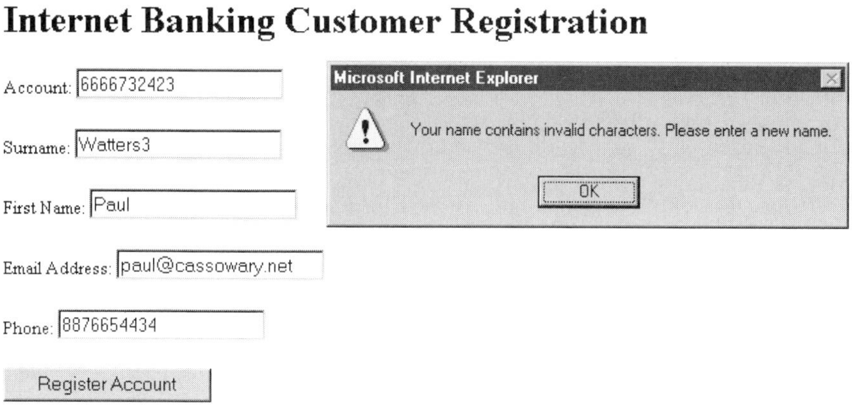

Internet Banking Customer Registration

Account: 6666732423

Surname: Watters3

First Name: Paul

Email Address: paul@cassowary.net

Phone: 8876654434

Register Account

Microsoft Internet Explorer

⚠ Your name contains invalid characters. Please enter a new name.

OK

8

Summary

In this chapter, you have learned about JavaScript `Math`, `Date`, and `RegExp` objects and their methods and properties. These entities allow you to formulate and evaluate expressions in very powerful ways. Simple scripts rely on arithmetic and logical operators; more complex data, such as dates, require a set of ready-made methods. When combined with pattern-matching techniques, these methods (and other `Math` object methods) make it easy to validate form data against business logic.

Test Your Skills

Practice Drill 8.1: Checking for Illegal Characters

In this exercise, you will observe what happens when you use regular expressions to check for inappropriate whitespace characters (form feeds, new lines, carriage returns, tabs, or vertical tabs) in HTML form data. The following example shows how this works in practice.

1. In your text editor, create a HTML page with the appropriate `<head>` and `<body>` elements.

```
<html>
      <head>
            <title>Internet Banking Customer
                    Registration</title>
      </head>
      <body>
      </body>
</html>
```

2. Insert the JavaScript code block between the `<body>` tags.

```
<script type="text/javascript">
</script>
```

3. Insert the definition for the `verifyDetails()` function.

```
function verifyDetails()
{
 var invalidCharacters=/\f\n\cr\t\v/;
 if (invalidCharacters.test(document.register.
   surname.value)||
     invalidCharacters.test(document.register.
       firstName.value))
 {
    window.alert("Your name contains invalid
      characters. Please enter a new name.");
 }
```

```
else
{
    window.alert("Your account has been registered.");
}
}
```

4. Create the HTML form.

```
<h1>Internet Banking Customer Registration</h1>
 <form name="register">
   Account: <input type="Text" name="account"><p>
   Surname: <input type="Text" name="surname"><p>
   First Name: <input type="Text" name="firstName"><p>
   Email Address: <input type="Text" name="email"><p>
   Phone: <input type="Text" name="phone"><p>
   <input type="Submit" value="Register Account"
      onClick="verifyDetails()">
   </form>
```

5. Load the page into your Web browser. If you enter form feeds, new lines, carriage returns, tabs, or vertical tabs into the `surname` or `firstName` fields, you will receive the following error message:

```
Your name contains invalid characters. Please enter a
new name.
```

Practice Drill 8.2: Calculating a New Date

It is often necessary to determine dates based on a certain number of days or months into the future. For example, say that you take a short-term, 45-day loan from the bank. When is this loan due? On a Web site, it is common practice to specify expiration dates for cookies (a topic for future discussion) based on the number of days or months you want the cookie to be valid. In this exercise, you will calculate future dates based on a specified number of days or months from information entered into a form by the user.

1. In your text editor, create a HTML page with the appropriate `<head>` and `<body>` elements.

```
<html>
    <head>
     <title>Date Calculator</title>
    </head>
    <body>
    </body>
    </html>
```

2. Create a HTML form that will allow user input of either the number of days or months by placing the following between the `<body>` tags:

```
<center>
    <h2>Calculating Future Dates</h2>
      <form name="dateForm">
```

```
Please enter the number of days
   <b>or</b>months in
<br /> the future for which you want to
   calculate the date.
<p>
   Days: <input type="text" name="txtDays" />
   <input type="button" value="Calculate
      Date" onClick="calcDays()" />
</p>
<p>
   Months: <input type="text" name=
      "txtMonths" />
   <input type="button" value="Calculate
      Date" onClick="calcMonths()" />
</p>
   </form>
</center>
```

3. Insert the JavaScript code block between the `<body>` tags.

```
<script type="text/javascript">
</script>
```

4. Now it is time to create the calculation functions. First create a function that will calculate the new date based on the number of days. Note that you simply add the number of days to the current `Date` object's date and reset the date. Insert the `calcDays()` function between the `<script>` tags.

```
function calcDays(){
        var days = parseInt(document.dateForm.
          txtDays.value);
        var today = new Date();
        var date = today.getDate();
        date += days;
        today.setDate(date);
        alert("The future date is: " + today);
}
```

5. As you may guess, calculating a future date based on the number of months given follows the same pattern as that for days. The difference is that you change the `Date` object's month value. Insert the `calcMonths()` function into the JavaScript block following the `calcDays()` function.

```
function calcMonths()    {
        var months = parseInt(document.dateForm.
          txtMonths.value);
        var today = new Date();
        var month = today.getMonth();
        month += months;
```

```
            today.setMonth(month);
            alert("The future date is: " + today);
    }
```

6. Load the page into your Web browser. Unless it is a leap year, when you calculate a new date with 365 days the result is today's date next year. Likewise, if you calculate a date 12 months in the future you get today's date, but a year in the future. On leap years, you will have one day difference. What happens if you use negative numbers?

MULTIPLE-CHOICE QUESTIONS

1. What is the `Math` object property that gives the value of the square root of one-half?

    A. SQRT

    B. SQRT(1/2)

    C. SQRT1_2

    D. SQRT(0.5)

2. What is the role of the `Date` object `constructor` property?

    A. To define private data members for an existing object

    B. To define private data members for a new object

    C. To return the value of the `constructor` function

    D. To access abstract methods in a class

3. What is the role of the `Date` object's `prototype` property?

    A. To add properties to an object

    B. To provide an abstract version of a class

    C. To provide links to a superclass

    D. To allow HTML formatting to be performed dynamically

4. What is the name of the `Math` object method that returns a random number between zero and one?

    A. rnd()

    B. random(0,1)

    C. rnd(0,1)

    D. random()

5. What does the `RegExp` literal `/date/i` match?

    A. Any global instance of "date" (case insensitive)

    B. Any global instance of "date" (case sensitive)

    C. First instance of "date" (case sensitive)

    D. First instance of "date" (case insensitive)

8

FILL-IN-THE-BLANK QUESTIONS

1. The `/total/ig` _____ string matches all instances of "total" in a string (case insensitive).

2. The _____ method sets the year in a `Date` object with four numbers (e.g., 2004).

3. The _____ property returns the value of π.

4. The _____ method returns an integer equal to or less than a number passed as a parameter.

5. The _____ method returns the smallest of two numbers passed as parameters.

DEFINITIONS QUESTIONS

1. What is the difference between the `LN10` and the `LN2` `Math` object properties?

2. What does the `pow()` `Math` object method do?

3. What `Math` object method returns the sine of a single parameter?

4. What `Math` object property returns the value of Euler's constant?

5. What `Math` object method returns the square root of a parameter?

BASIC PROJECTS

The following basic projects provide you with the opportunity to work with `RegExp` objects and their methods.

Project 8.1 – Using the `replace()` Method

This project will require you to modify the script given in Exhibit 8.7. Modify the script so that if the e-mail address contains the string "aol.com," it will be replaced by "google.com." This can be achieved by using the `String replace()` method (described in Chapter 7) and passing the replaced string parameter as a `RegExp` string literal.

Project 8.2 – Using the Date to Determine Page Displays

In Exercise 8.1, you used the `Math` object's `random()` method to generate random slogans. To make their sites more personal and/or seasonal, many designers will place special greetings and images on their Web pages based on the date or season. If you wish, you can even change content based on the time of day, for example, saying "good morning" or "good afternoon."

This project requires you to generate greetings based on the day of the week. Use the script provided in Exhibit 8.2 as a template and modify it to check for the day of the week. Then, depending on the day, display a different greeting or slogan.

To test this script properly, you will have to change the system date. Just remember to change it back to the proper date when you are finished.

INTERMEDIATE PROJECTS

The following intermediate projects provide you with the opportunity to work with `Date` objects and their methods in an advanced way.

Project 8.1 – Creating a Digital Clock

Many Web pages display the date and time. In this exercise, you will create a simple Web page that displays a digital clock. Use the `Date` object methods that you have learned to capture the hours, minutes, and seconds and display them in the format "hh:mm:ss." This is easily achieved by updating (assigning the value of) a form's text box.

To initiate a function that will create this display, place an `onload` event in the `<body>` tag (e.g., `<body onload="`*functionName*`()">`). Also, the last line in your function should be `setTimeout("`*functionName*`()",1000);`, where *functionName* is the name of your function. The `setTimeout()` calls your function every 1,000 milliseconds (each second). In the next chapter, you will see how `setTimeout()` can be used within a different function than the one being called.

Hint: To achieve the desired two-digit display, you must check each value and add the leading zero when there are less than 10 minutes, seconds, or hours.

Your output should look similar to this—`10:05:55`—with the value for seconds changing every second.

Project 8.2 – Determining the Days Remaining Until Special Events

In both Practice Drill 8.2 and Basic Project 8.2, you used methods of the `Date` object to determine and calculate new dates. In this exercise, you will expand the use of the `Date` object methods by determining the days remaining until some future date. It is essentially the reverse of what was done in the previous exercises.

Create a Web page that displays the number of days remaining until three special days. For this exercise, create a `Date` object of January 1, 2000: `var today = new Date("January 1, 2000")`. Then create three special event `Date` objects (these dates are suggested so that you can verify output with the solution code):

- Your uncle's birthday: January 2, 2000
- Fourth of July: July 4, 2000
- New Year's day: January 1, 2001

Calculate and display the number of days until each special event. Output should be similar to this: `There are 184 days until July 4th.`

Hint: JavaScript does not have a simple subtraction function for dates. Remember that when a `Date` object is created, it contains the number of milliseconds since January 1, 1970. Therefore, if you want to compare two dates, you cannot simply subtract one from the other; the result would be in milliseconds. Rather, you must subtract the dates and then calculate the specific value you want by dividing the resulting milliseconds. To get seconds, you must divide the result by 1,000. To get minutes, you must divide the seconds by 60 (60 seconds/minute). To get hours, you must divide the minutes, and so on.

Career Builder

Pattern matching using regular expressions allows you to create search patterns to validate input of almost any format. In this exercise, you will create regular-expression patterns to verify the input of zip codes and telephone numbers, adding to what you have already learned. To begin to appreciate the strength and versatility of regular expressions, you will be introduced to new pattern designations and characters.

Create a Web page that holds two input text boxes and Process and Reset buttons. When the user clicks the Process button, call a function that checks the zip code and telephone number input values against acceptable patterns. If the input is not acceptable, display an alert box that states which pattern is wrong. The JavaScript block and function should be placed in the <head> section of your HTML page.

(This is a good point to verify that your HTML and JavaScript are correct. You do not want to confuse errors in the basic layout with the script code you will be writing.)

To alert the user to form errors, simply place an alert message in the function that does the evaluation. Then, when you click the Process button, the alert box will appear. You may even want to display the content of the text boxes in your alert box. Now that you have a form that displays properly and a button that calls the function, you can proceed.

To construct a regular expression pattern, you must first examine the field you want to check. For the zip code, only consider the basic five-digit code. The code must have five numbers, and nothing can appear before or after the five numbers—this is the pattern you want to create.

The character set "\d" in a pattern indicates that you want to match a digit (number). A slash is used to identify the letter "d" as having special meaning, not the literal character "d." Placing a single number inside braces (e.g., {3}) indicates that you want to match exactly the number of the immediately preceding item. Therefore, to state that your input must have exactly five digits, the pattern is \d{5}. Finally, because it is possible for users to accidentally enter spaces and/or letters before or after the five numbers, you must indicate that the pattern begins with and ends with the digit string. The caret (^) indicates that the string must begin with whatever follows, and the dollar sign ($) indicates that the string must end with the immediately preceding item. Therefore, the pattern ^\d{5}$ can be used to check the zip code. Putting this pattern into words, it states that the input string must consist of five digits (no more, no less), and the five digits must begin and end the input string (i.e., there is nothing before or after the five numbers).

As shown in Exercise 8.3, you can construct your regular expression as follows:

```
var reZipCode = /^\d{5}$/
```

where the slashes (/) surround and designate the content as a regular-expression pattern.

(continued)

Continuing with the approach used in Exercise 8.3, you can use the following code to determine if the desired string has been entered:

```
if (reZipCode.test(document.formName.
  textBoxName.value))
```

This will check to see if the regular expression is *found* in the input string. Placing the exclamation point at the beginning of the expression will tell you if a match is *not found*.

```
if (!reZipCode.test(document.formName.
  textBoxName.value))
```

Now look at the telephone number input requirements. For this exercise, use the following format: (999) 999-9999 (where the 9s represent any number). Therefore, for user input to match the desired pattern:

1. It must begin with an opening parenthesis: `^\(` (the backslash in front of the parenthesis indicates that it is used as a simple character to be matched, not to enclose a group of characters).
2. The opening parenthesis is followed by three digits: `\d{3}`.
3. The three digits are followed by a closing parenthesis: `\)`.
4. It must have a space.
5. It must have three digits: `\d{3}`.
6. The three digits are followed by a dash: `-`.
7. The input must end with four digits: `\d{4}$`..

Construct your expression as follows:

```
var rePhone = /^\(\d{3}\) \d{3}-\d{4}$/
```

Now write the expression that will check user input:

```
if (!rePhone.test(document.formName.textBoxName.value))
```

Following the `if` statements, you will want to create messages to indicate that errors have been made and include them in alerts.

As you can see, regular expressions can appear to be very complex, but they are not difficult to create once they have been broken down into their individual components. They are also very powerful and can be used to check for patterns that would require many lines of code to accomplish otherwise. If you want to experiment with regular expressions, several commonly used pattern characters follow:

- `\w`—Matches any alphanumeric character (all letters and numbers)
- `[a-z]`—Matches any lowercase letter
- `[A-Z]`—Matches any uppercase letter
- `[a-zA-Z]`—Matches any letter
- `{n,m}`—Matches the previous item(s) at least *n* times, but not more than *m* times

Chapter 9

Using, Precaching, and Swapping Images

A picture is worth a thousand words, or so the saying goes. To create a spectacular Web site, you need a high-impact design that includes plenty of graphical elements that will capture the attention of your site's visitors. The good news is that JavaScript can add life to your site's graphics and help you better manage the way graphics are used. Not only can you use JavaScript to precache images so graphics are displayed without delay, you can also use JavaScript to dynamically update graphics. This allows you to change graphics on demand, rotate between a set of graphics, and configure timed updates of graphics.

You may be wondering why this is so useful. Have you ever wondered how to make buttons change when you roll over them with the mouse? Typically, the image swapping is handled by JavaScript. When you move the mouse over the graphical button, JavaScript is used to swap the image displayed. Or, say your site has several advertisers or that you are running a series of advertising campaigns, and you want to rotate the banner ads on your site. With JavaScript, you can easily script the display of the banners so that they change automatically at a timed interval, thereby rotating the ads between advertisers or advertising campaigns automatically.

For Your Career

Good design techniques are essential when working with images. To ensure that browsers can process and display pages as quickly as possible, you should specify the `height` and `width` attributes for every graphic in the associated `<img>` tag. This enables a browser to determine how a page should flow without having to load all of the images in the page, which, in turn, allows the browser to display the page more quickly.

Chapter Exercises

This unit's exercises will teach you how to:

- Handle images in scripts
- Precache and swap images
- Rotate images automatically

By working through the exercises, you will learn how to script graphics in Web pages. The techniques you will learn will help you use graphics more effectively, which ultimately should improve the browsing experience for anyone who visits your site and make it easier for you to manage your site's graphics.

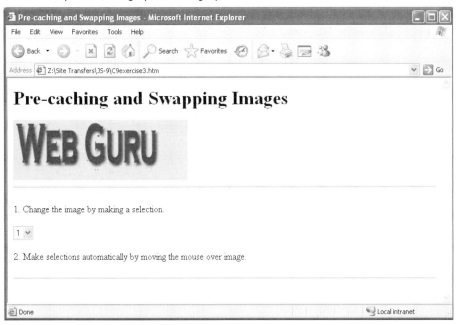

Exercise 9.1 – Getting Started with the `Image` and `<img>` Element Objects

The `Image` and `<img>` element objects are used to support images in browsers. Although these objects share similar features, they differ fundamentally in the way they are used and created.

In your scripts, you use `Image` objects to precache images that you will later use in a Web page. `Image` objects are created when you instantiate them in scripts using the `new` keyword (in much the same that `Array` objects are created using the `new` keyword). In contrast, `<img>` element objects are created by the browser when it loads a page that contains `<img>` elements. Each `<img>` element defined in an HTML page has a corresponding `<img>` element object that can be scripted in JavaScript.

The `Image` objects you create are completely separate from any `<img>` element objects in a page. Typically, a page loads with initial images defined with `<img>` tags. In a script defined in the page, you create instances of the images you want to work with using `Image` objects. This precaches the images by loading them into the browser's image cache in memory. These precached images are not displayed by the browser; they are just loaded into cache. Because the images are already loaded, when the user wants to access them, they can be displayed on demand and without delay. Thus, one reason to create instances of images in a script is simply to precache them so that they can be displayed quickly when a user accesses them.

Table 9.1 shows the most commonly used properties, methods, and event handlers of the `Image` object. Because `Image` objects are not displayed, and therefore not

TABLE 9.1 The `Image` and `<img>` element objects.

Properties	Methods	Events
align	(none)	onabort
alt		onerror
border		onload
complete		
height		
hspace		
lowsrc		
name		
src		
vspace		
width		
border		
x		
y		

affected by elements on the page, the `Image` object does not have as many properties, methods, or event handlers as some of the other objects we have looked at. Still, the properties that the `Image` object does have are very useful. Additionally, because the base set of properties, methods, and event handlers for `<img>` element objects are the same as those for `Image` objects, a separate table is not provided.

As you can see in Table 9.2, most of the `Image` object's properties are used to either set attributes that determine how the image is used when it is later displayed or to read the existing attributes of an image. The exception to this is the `complete` property, which allows you to determine if an image has completely loaded. For example, you could use the `complete` property to make sure that an image is completely loaded before trying to work with it.

The `<img>` object element is easier to work with than the `Image` object. Each `<img>` object element created when a page is loaded can be accessed via the `document.images[]` array, either according to its index in the array or by the value assigned to the `name` attribute. The first image on the page is at index 0 in the `document.images[]` array. This means that if the first image in a page is defined as:

```
<img name="cards" src="cards.gif" width="50" height="75" />
```

it could be accessed using a reference to its index position:

```
document.images[0]
```

or a reference to its name:

```
document.images["cards"]
```

Knowing this, you can easily read a property of this `<img>` element object. For example, you could use the following to check if the associated image has finished loading:

```
if (document.images["cards"].complete) {
  //the image has completely loaded so do this.
}
```

Here, you test to see if the image has completely loaded. If it has, the browser executes the conditional code.

In this exercise, you are going to use the `document.images[]` array to display the properties of an image loading into a page. By following this exercise, you will learn how to access and work with properties of `<img>` object elements. The image file for this and other exercises in this chapter can be found on the Companion Web site for this book (*www.prenhall.com/webguru*). Before you begin, you should copy the necessary images for this chapter to your current working folder (the one in which you will save the document for this exercise).

STEP 1 – CREATING A PAGE

In your text editor, create a new Web page using the markup shown in Exhibit 9.1 and then save it as C9exercise1.htm. As you enter the source for the page, note that the page has two `h1` headings. After the second heading, you insert a clickable image. Clickable images are created by defining an `img` element within an `a` element. Note that most browsers display this type of image with a 2-pixel-wide border unless you specify that no border should be displayed (using `border="0"`).

TABLE 9.2 The `Image` object properties summary.

Property	Value	Type	Description
`align`	String	Read/Write	Sets the alignment of the image; the value assigned to the `align` attribute of an image. Accepted values are string constants: `absbottom`, `absmiddle`, `baseline`, `bottom`, `left`, `middle`, `right`, `texttop`, and `top`. Supported by Netscape Navigator 6 and later, Internet Explorer 4 and later, Mozilla, and Safari.
`alt`	String	Read/Write	Sets the alternate text to display if the image cannot be displayed; the value assigned to the `alt` attribute of an image. Supported by Netscape Navigator 6 and later, Internet Explorer 4 and later, Mozilla, and Safari.
`border`	Integer	Read/Write	Sets the size of the image's border; the value assigned to the `border` attribute of an image. Use `border="0"` to hide the link border of an image placed within an `a` element. Supported by Netscape Navigator 3 and later, Internet Explorer 4 and later, Mozilla, and Safari.
`complete`	Boolean	Read-only	Returns `true` when the `lowsrc` for an image finishes loading; if no `lowsrc` is assigned, returns `true` when the source image finishes loading. Supported by Netscape Navigator 3 and later, Internet Explorer 4 and later, Mozilla, and Safari.
`height`	Integer	Read/Write; Read-only	The value assigned to the `height` attribute of an image. Read/Write in Internet Explorer 4, Netscape Navigator 5, and later. Read-only in Internet Explorer 3 and Netscape Navigator 4. Not supported by earlier versions of these browsers.

TABLE 9.2 (*Continued*)

Property	Value	Type	Description
hspace	Integer	Read/Write; Read-only	The value assigned to the hspace attribute of an image. Read/Write in Internet Explorer 4, Netscape Navigator 5, and later. Read-only in Internet Explorer 3 and Netscape Navigator 4. Not supported in earlier versions of these browsers.
lowsrc	URL String	Read/Write	Sets a low-resolution source for an image; the value assigned to the lowsrc attribute of an image. Supported by Netscape Navigator 3 and later, Internet Explorer 4 and later, Mozilla, and Safari.
name	String	Read/Write	The value assigned to the name attribute of an image. Supported by Netscape Navigator 2 and later, Internet Explorer 3 and later, Mozilla, and Safari.
src	URL String	Read/Write	The value assigned to the src attribute of an image. Supported by Netscape Navigator 3 and later, Internet Explorer 4 and later, Mozilla, and Safari.
vspace	Integer	Read/Write; Read-only	The value assigned to the vspace attribute of an image. Read/Write in Internet Explorer 4, Netscape Navigator 5, and later. Read-only in Internet Explorer 3 and Netscape Navigator 4. Not supported by earlier versions of these browsers.
width	Integer	Read/Write; Read-only	The value assigned to the width attribute of an image. Read/Write in Internet Explorer 4, Netscape Navigator 5, and later. Read-only in Internet Explorer 3 and Netscape Navigator 4. Not supported by earlier versions of these browsers.

9

EXHIBIT 9.1

```
<html>
<head>
<title>Working with an Image's Properties</title>
</head>
<body>
<h1>Set the Image Properties</h1>
<hr />
<hr />
<h1>View the Image</h1>
<p><a href="C9exercise1.htm"><img alt="[Web Guru]"
   src="webguru.jpg" height="100" width="300" /></a>
   JavaScript is a very powerful scripting language.
   You can use it to help you create more dynamic
   Web sites.
The more you know about JavaScript, the better you'll
   be as a Web site designer and programmer.</p>
</body>
</html>
```

STEP 2 – MODIFYING THE PAGE

In your text editor, edit the page you created in the previous step by adding the form shown in Exhibit 9.2. Insert the form between the two horizontal rules following the "Set the Image Properties" heading. Note that the form defines two selection menus. When you make a change to the first selection menu, the onchange event is triggered and then handled by a call to the setBorder() function. When you make a change to the second selection menu, the onchange event is triggered and then handled by a call to the setAlign() function. When a selection is made on either menu, the browser calls the appropriate function and uses the this reference to pass the function a reference to the current selection object.

EXHIBIT 9.2

```
<form>
<p>1) Change the image border by making a selection.
<select onchange="setBorder(this)">
<option value="0">Remove Border</option>
<option value="1">Add Thin Border</option>
<option value="2" selected="selected">Add Thick
   Border</option>
</select></p>
<p>2) Change the image alignment by making a selection.
<select onchange="setAlignment(this)">
<option value="absbottom">Align Absbottom</option>
```

```
<option value="absmiddle">Align Absmiddle</option>
<option value="baseline">Align Baseline</option>
<option value="bottom">Align Bottom</option>
<option value="left" selected="selected">Align
  Left</option>
<option value="middle">Align Middle</option>
<option value="right">Align Right</option>
<option value="texttop">Align Texttop</option>
<option value="top">Align Top</option>
</select></p>
</form>
```

STEP 3 – ADDING THE FUNCTIONS

In your text editor, edit the page you created in the previous step. Add a header-defined script that defines the `setBorder()` and `setAlign()` functions using the source provided in Exhibit 9.3. As stated previously, these functions are called with a reference to the current `selection` object. Following good scripting form, you perform a conditional test to ensure that the document has one or more images before trying to work with those images. (Basically, if the document has an images array, it has one or more images.) You use the `options[]` array of this object, as discussed in Chapter 17, to determine the currently selected item and its value. You then set the appropriate property of the related `<img>` element object to this value, which changes the image border or alignment, as appropriate.

EXHIBIT 9.3

```
<script type="text/javascript">
function setBorder(sel) {
if (document.images) {
document.images[0].border=sel.options
  [sel.selectedIndex].value;
}
}
function setAlignment(sel) {
if (document.images) {
document.images[0].align=sel.options
  [sel.selectedIndex].value;
}
}
</script>
```

9

STEP 4 – LOADING AND TESTING THE PAGE

Open the C9exercise1.htm page in Internet Explorer. If you have edited the page correctly, you should see the page as shown in Figure 9.1. To change the appearance of the

FIGURE 9.1 Updating image properties in scripts.

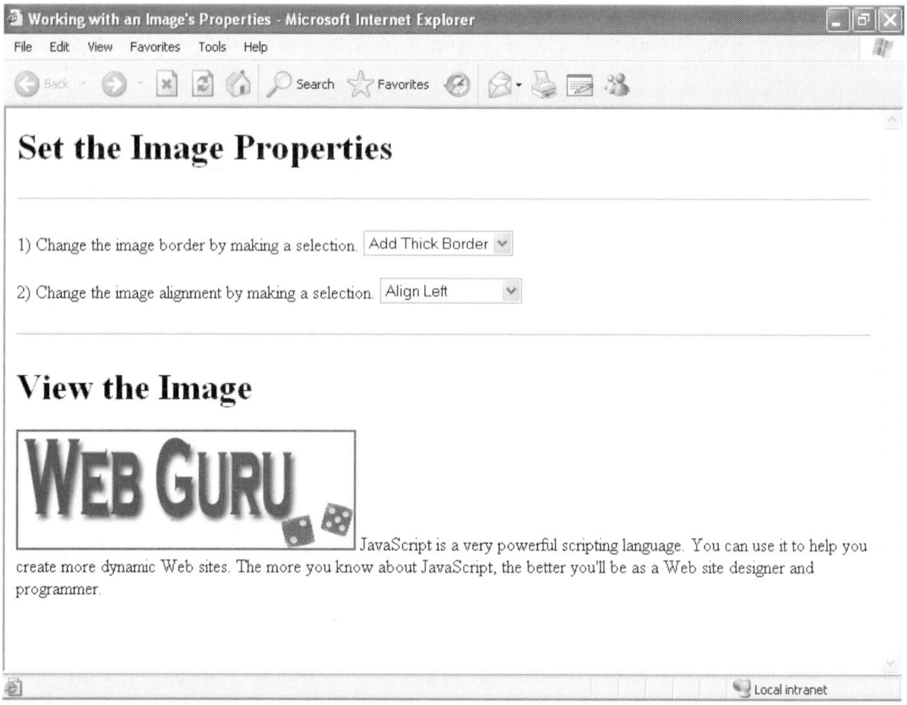

image, make selections on the border and alignment selection menus. You should be able to remove or add the image border and change the image's alignment.

Exercise 9.2 – Precaching and Swapping Images

`Image` objects are not as easy to work with as `<img>` element objects. Before you can work with `Image` objects in scripts, you will need to create instances of the images you want to work with in the browser's memory. Once you have an instance of an image in memory, you can then script the image's properties.

Like `Array` objects, you create `Image` objects using the `new` keyword. The basic syntax for creating an `Image` object is:

```
imageName = new Image([width, height]);
```

The two parameters you can pass to the `Image` object are the pixel width and the pixel height of the image. The width and height are optional. They help the browser allocate memory for the image.

Precaching an image is a two-step process. First, you create an instance of an `Image` object, which allocates memory for the image. Second, you define the source of the image, which tells the browser to load the image into the image cache in memory. Consider the following example:

```
theImage = new Image(150,200);
theImage.src = "tshirt.jpg";
```

Here, you create an instance of an image and set its source, which is a .JPG image file located in the same directory as the current Web page. If the image were in a different directory, you could specify a relative or absolute path to the image. In this example, the .JPG image file is located in the images subfolder of the current directory:

```
theImage.src = "images/tshirt.jpg";
```

In this example, the .JPG image file is located on another Web server:

```
theImage.src = "http://www.robertstanek.com/images/
  tshirt.jpg";
```

If you then wanted to use this image in your Web page, you would need to replace the <img> element object that appears on the page with this image in memory. Here is how you would do this:

```
document.images[0].src = theImage.src;
```

The browser would then replace the first image on the page. In your Web pages, you can use image-swapping technique to change images based on user selections and actions. For example, if a user clicks on a button graphic, you may want to display another version of the graphic to make it appear as if the button is selected.

Again, the steps for precaching and swapping images are as shown in Exhibit 9.4.

EXHIBIT 9.4

```
//1) Create a new instance
//of the Image object
theImage = new Image(150,150);
//2) Assign a source image
theImage.src = "cards.jpg";
//3) Swap the image on the page
//typically in response to a
//user action or selection.
document.images["display"].src = theImage.src;
```

In this exercise, you are going to precache and swap images based on a user selection. By following this exercise, you will learn these essential image-scripting techniques. Once you know how to precache and swap images, you can apply these techniques in a variety of ways to your Web pages. By handling events related to the image, you could swap images based on user actions. By adding a timer, you could swap images based on a schedule.

STEP 1 – CREATING A PAGE

In your text editor, create a new Web page using the markup shown in Exhibit 9.5 and then save it as C9exercise2.htm. As you enter the source for the page, note that the name of the <img> tag is set as "webguru." Note also that the image source is a file called webguru1.jpg. There are also image files called webguru2.jpg, webguru3.jpg, webguru4.jpg, and webguru5.jpg. These images will be used in this example. As mentioned previously, the image files for this exercise can be found on the Companion Web site for

---

TIP

Different Browsers May Handle Image Updates in Different Ways

When you use JavaScript to update images, you should keep in mind how different browsers update graphics. Browsers prior to Internet Explorer 4.0 and Netscape Navigator 6.0 swap images by replacing the original image with a new one in the same space. If the image being swapped is a different pixel size than the original image, the image can be scaled up or down in size to fit the existing space. Starting with Internet Explorer 4.0 and Netscape Navigator 6.0, browsers automatically reflow the page to accommodate the change in the image size. This means that the image can be displayed in the size it was created and the content around the image may change its position when the page is updated. (Keep in mind that you must either update the height and width attributes or omit them in the first place to achieve this effect, however.)

9

this book (*www.prenhall.com/webguru*). If you have not already done so, you should copy these images to your current working folder (the one in which you will save the document for this exercise).

EXHIBIT 9.5

```
<html>
<head>
<title>Precaching and Swapping Images</title>
</head>
<body>
<h1>Precaching and Swapping Images</h1>
<img alt="webguru" src="webguru1.jpg" name="webguru"
  height="100" width="300" border="0"/>
<hr />
<hr />
</body>
</html>
```

STEP 2 – MODIFYING THE PAGE

In your text editor, edit the page you created in the previous step by adding the form shown in Exhibit 9.6. Insert the form between the two horizontal rules following the "Precaching and Swapping Images" heading. Note that the form defines a selection menu. When you make a change to the first menu, the onchange event is triggered and then handled by a call to the loadprecached() function. Thus, when a selection is made, the browser calls the function and uses the this reference to pass the function a reference to the current selection object.

EXHIBIT 9.6

```
<form name="myform">
<p>Change the image by making a selection.</p>
<select name="precached" onchange=
  "loadprecached(this.form)">
<option value="webguru1">1</option>
<option value="webguru2">2</option>
<option value="webguru3">3</option>
<option value="webguru4">4</option>
<option value="webguru5">5</option>
</select>
</form>
```

STEP 3 – ADDING THE PRECACHING FUNCTIONALITY

In your text editor, edit the page you created in the previous step. Add a header-defined script using the source provided in Exhibit 9.7. The first section is used to precache the images. When the page loads, two global variables are created: cacheImages and webguruImages. The `webguruImages` variable is used to create an array of string names as index values (webguru1, webguru2, webguru3, webguru4, webguru5). These strings names will be used to set the first part of the file names for the images you want to precache. Next, you create a second array, called `cacheImages[]`, and size the array so that it can have the same number of elements as there are image files (five in this case). You then use a `for` loop to create the `Image` objects and precache the related image sources. As you can see, the `Image` objects are created with a width of 300 pixels and a height of 100 pixels. The string in the current index of the `webguruImages[]` array is then used to set the file name for the image source as webguru1.jpg, webguru2.jpg, and so on.

EXHIBIT 9.7

```
<script type="text/javascript">
var cacheImages;
if (document.images) {
var webguruImages = new Array("webguru1", "webguru2",
  "webguru3", "webguru4", "webguru5");
cacheImages = new Array(5);
for (var i = 0; i < cacheImages.length ; i++) {
cacheImages[webguruImages[i]] = new Image(300,100);
cacheImages[webguruImages[i]].src = webguruImages[i]
  + ".jpg";
}
}
</script>
```

STEP 4 – ADDING THE LOADPRECACHED FUNCTION

In your text editor, edit the page you created in the previous step. Add the function shown in Exhibit 9.8 to the header-defined script. The function must follow the image precaching statements and come before the end script element, `</script>`. The `loadprecached()` function is called with a reference to the current `form` object. Following good scripting form, you perform a conditional test to ensure that the document has one or more images before trying to work with it. You use the `options[]` array of the `selection` object within the form to determine the currently selected item and its value. You then set the new image source to use for the `<img>` element object, which swaps the image on the page.

EXHIBIT 9.8

```
function loadprecached(form) {
if (document.images) {
var jpgIndex = form.precached.options[form.precached.
  selectedIndex].value;
document.images[0].src = cacheImages[jpgIndex].src;
}
}
</script>
```

STEP 5 – LOADING AND TESTING THE PAGE

Open the C9exercise2.htm page in Internet Explorer. If you have edited the page correctly, you should see the page as shown in Figure 9.2. To swap images on the page, make a selection on the selection menu. You should see the image change each time you make a new selection. Note that the images were automatically precached when the page was loaded. Precaching allows visitors to your Web site to see the images on demand without having to wait for them to download. Without precaching, a visitor to your site might have to wait for images to download, and this delay, even if short, could make visiting your site less enjoyable.

FIGURE 9.2 Precaching and swapping images.

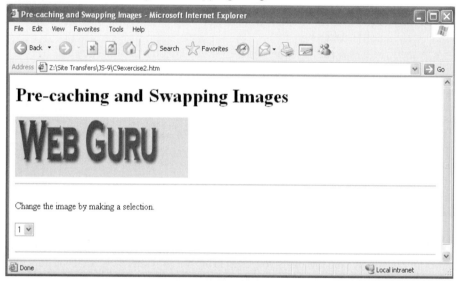

Exercise 9.3 – Rotating Images

In your Web pages, you will often want to update images based on user selections. You have already read about an example of updating images based on user selections in a form. Another way to handle user selections is to use the built-in event handlers that are part of JavaScript. Although you will learn more about these event handlers in Chapter 10, for now, you will focus on one particular event handler: onmouseover. This event handler is triggered when a user moves the mouse over an element or object in a Web page.

Most of the time, handling events is fairly easy. However, handling image-related events is a bit tricky. If you refer back to Table 9.1 you will see that onmouseover is not listed as a *standard* event handler (i.e., those event handlers supported by the widest set of browsers). So the best way to achieve the desired affect is to use another object's event handler, namely the event handler for anchor objects. Consider the following example:

```
<a href="C9exercise2.htm" onmouseover="rotate()">
<img alt="webguru" src="webguru1.jpg" name="webguru"
  height="100" width="300" border="0"/>
</a>
```

Because the image is included in a hypertext link, the `anchor` object's events are triggered when you interact with the image. In this case, when you move the mouse pointer over the image, the `onmouseover` event handler is triggered.

To see how you can use the `onmouseover` event handler with the image-swapping techniques you have learned earlier in this chapter, complete the following exercise.

STEP 1 – CREATING A PAGE

In your text editor, open the page created in Exercise 9.2 and then save it as C9exercise3.htm. Find the following line of markup:

```
<img alt="webguru" src="webguru1.jpg" name="webguru"
  height="100" width="300" border="0"/>
```

Replace this markup with the following code snippet:

```
<a href="C9exercise2.htm" onmouseover="rotate()">
  <img alt="webguru" src="webguru1.jpg" name="webguru"
  height="100" width="300" border="0"/></a>
```

STEP 2 – ADDING THE ROTATE() FUNCTION

In your text editor, edit the page you created in the previous step. Add the function shown in Exhibit 9.9 to the header-defined script. The function must follow the existing script source and come before the end script element, `</script>`. The `rotate()` function is called when you move the mouse pointer over the image. It rotates the image by determining which image is currently selected or in use and then changing to the next image in the sequence. Because there are a fixed number of images, you want to ensure that only the `jpgIndex` values of 0, 1, 2, 3, or 4 are used. You do this by checking the length of the `cacheImages[]` array and resetting the current index pointer (`jpgIndex`) to zero this length is exceeded.

EXHIBIT 9.9

```
function rotate() {
if (document.images) {
var jpgIndex = document.myform.precached.selectedIndex;
if (++jpgIndex > cacheImages.length - 1) {
jpgIndex = 0;
}
document.myform.precached.selectedIndex = jpgIndex;
loadprecached(document.myform);
}
}
```

STEP 3 – LOADING AND TESTING THE PAGE

Open the C9exercise3.htm page in Internet Explorer. If you have edited the page correctly, you should see the page as shown in Figure 9.3. To swap images on the page,

---

T I P

Using onmouseover to Display a Message When a Mouse Is Over an Image

When working with linked images, the `onmouseover` event handler can be used in a number of different ways. One way the `onmouseover` event handler can be used is in helping you use JavaScript to display a message when the mouse pointer is over the image. The technique used is almost the same as the one discussed in this exercise, but instead of calling a function to rotate the image, you call a function to display a message on the browser's status bar. You can also display the message directly. Here is an example code snippet that shows how to do this:

```
<a href="home.htm"
  onMouseOver=
  "window.status
  = 'Visit Our
  Web Guru Home
  Page'" ><img
  alt="webguru"
  src="webguru1.
  jpg" name=
  "webguru"
  height="100"
  width="300"
  border="0"/></a>
```

In Chapter 13, you will find complete details on working with links and linked objects.

FIGURE 9.3 Rotating images based on user actions.

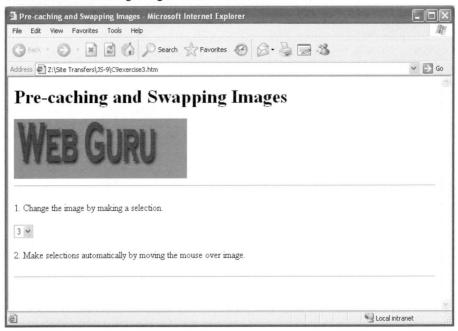

move the mouse pointer over the image or make a selection on the selection menu. You should see the image change each time you move the mouse pointer over the image or make a new selection.

Summary

Images are important parts of Web pages. Using JavaScript, you can precache images and then dynamically update images in your pages. Precaching images loads them into the browser's image cache so that they are ready for use. When you want to use a precached image, you swap its image source for the existing image source on the page. This causes the browser to update the image on the page. In the case of older browsers, the image may be scaled up or down to fit the dimensions of the previous image. In the case of newer browsers, the page is updated so the content around the picture is reflowed.

Test Your Skills

Practice Drill 9.1: Updating Images Based on User Actions

Previously, you learned how to swap an image on the page based on a user action. The example showed how image swapping could be handled in conjunction with other elements in an HTML page. In most of the examples, a form was used to allow users to make a selection, and this form was also updated as the image was rotated, either by the user making a selection or moving the mouse pointer over the image. These examples highlight the interaction of page elements.

Often, you will want to update an image without updating other elements. The following example shows how this can be done.

1. In your text editor, create a HTML page with the elements shown here. Use a `<title>` element with the text "Rotating Images."

```
<html>
<head>
<title>Rotating Images</title>
</head>
<body>
</body>
</html>
```

2. Within the body of the page, add the main text, which includes the image you want to rotate. The `onmouseover` event handler is used to call a function when you move the mouse pointer over the image.

```
<h1>Rotating Images</h1>
<a onmouseover="rotate()"><img alt="webguru"
  src="webguru1.jpg" name="webguru" height="100"
  width="300" border="0"/></a>
<hr />
<p>Move the mouse over the image.</p>
<hr />
```

3. Add a header-defined script to the page. Note that the script creates the necessary array of images. Unlike the `cacheImages[]` array used in the chapter text, the `cacheImages[]` array used in this example is indexed by numbers rather than a set of string values. This allows you to call the array with a numeric index value rather than a string value (the string value corresponded to the values on the selection menu, which you are not using).

```
<script type="text/javascript">
var cacheImages;
var jpgIndex = 0;
if (document.images) {
var webguruImages = new Array("webguru1",
  "webguru2", "webguru3", "webguru4", "webguru5");
cacheImages = new Array(5);
for (var i = 0; i < cacheImages.length ; i++) {
cacheImages[i] = new Image(300,100);
cacheImages[i].src = webguruImages[i] + ".jpg";
}
}
```

4. Add the `rotate()` function to the header-defined script. This function must follow the existing source code and be entered before the end script tag, `</script>`. The way this function works is fairly straightforward. `jpgIndex` is used to track the current index in the array. The value is incremented using `++jpgIndex` and then checked to see if its value is greater than the number of items in the `cacheImages[]` array. If it is, the `jpgIndex` is reset to zero. Otherwise, the incremental value is unchanged. The image in the document is then swapped with the image that has the corresponding index value in the `cacheImages[]` array.

```
function rotate() {
if (document.images) {
if (++jpgIndex > cacheImages.length - 1) {
jpgIndex = 0;
}
document.images[0].src = cacheImages[jpgIndex].src;
}
}
</script>
```

5. Load the page into a Web browser. If you move the mouse pointer over the image, the image should change. When you move through all of the precached images in the array, you should see the first image in the set again.

Practice Drill 9.2: Associating Links with the Updated Images

Oftentimes, images on the page are used as graphical menus that, when selected, take you to other pages. In the case of banner ads, you typically want users to be able to click the banner ad and access a jump page on your site that takes them to your sponsor's Web site or accesses the sponsor's Web site directly. The normal way to link images is to place the image within a hypertext link, such as:

```
<a href="http://www.robertstanek.com/">
<img src="webguru1.gif"></a>
```

When you swap images, however, you need a way to update the link associated with the image. One way to do this is to remove any `href` attribute associated with the link and use the `onclick` event to call a function when the link is clicked. This function could then be used to load the appropriate page into the browser.

To see how this could be handled, complete the following exercise.

1. In your text editor, create a HTML page with the elements as shown here. Use a `<title>` element with the text "Linking Rotated Images."

```
<html>
<head>
<title>Linking Rotated Images</title>
</head>
<body>
</body>
</html>
```

2. Within the body of the page, add the main text that includes the image you want to rotate and link. Note that two event handlers are defined for the image. The first, `onmouseover`, is used to call the `rotate()` function when you move the mouse pointer over the image. The second, `onclick`, is used to call the `goLink()` function when you click the image.

```
<h1>Linking Rotated Images</h1>
<a onmouseover="rotate()" onclick="goLink()"><img
   alt="webguru" src="webguru1.jpg" name="webguru"
   height="100" width="300" border="0"/></a>
<hr />
<p>Move the mouse over the image and then click on
   the image to access the linked page. Try using
   different images to test the results.</p>
<hr />
```

3. Add a header-defined script to the page. Note that this script is the same as the one used in the Practice Drill 9.1 except that it defines a new array and a new function. The `goAddress[]` array contains a series of URL strings and is used to set the pages that should be accessed when the various images are clicked. The `goLink()` function uses the `location` object (discussed in Chapter 11) to load the proper page. It does this by setting the browser location to the value of the current index into the `goAddress[]` array.

```
<script type="text/javascript">
var cacheImages;
var jpgIndex = 0;
if (document.images) {
var webguruImages = new Array("webguru1", "webguru2",
   "webguru3", "webguru4", "webguru5");
```

9

```
cacheImages = new Array(5);
for (var i = 0; i < cacheImages.length ; i++) {
cacheImages[i] = new Image(300,100);
cacheImages[i].src = webguruImages[i] + ".jpg";
}
}

function rotate() {
if (document.images) {
if (++jpgIndex > cacheImages.length - 1) {
jpgIndex = 0;
}

document.images[0].src = cacheImages[jpgIndex].src;
}
}

var goAddress = new Array("page1.htm", "page2.htm",
   "page3.htm", "page4.htm", "page5.htm");

function goLink() {
location = goAddress[jpgIndex];
}
</script>
```

4. Load the page into a Web browser. Move the mouse over the image and then click the image to access the linked page. Try using different images to test the results.

MULTIPLE-CHOICE QUESTIONS

1. Which of the following shows the correct way to create an `<img>` element object?

   A. `var myImage = new img();`

   B. `var myImage = new img(100+200);`

   C. `<img>myimage.jpg</img>`

   D. `<img src="myimage.jpg" />`

2. Which of the following shows the correct way to create an `Image` object?

   A. `var myImage = new Image();`

   B. `var myImage = new img(100+200);`

   C. `<img>myimage.jpg</img>`

   D. `<img src="myimage.jpg" />`

3. Which `Image` object property do you use to determine if an image has completely loaded?

   A. `src`

   B. `complete`

   C. `border`

   D. `alt`

4. Which property of the Image object do you use to read the `<img>` element's name attribute?

    A. `name`

    B. `src`

    C. `alt`

    D. `lowsrc`

5. How would you reference the first image loaded on the page?

    A. `document.images["0"]`

    B. `document.images[0]`

    C. `window.images["0"]`

    D. `window.images[0]`

FILL-IN-THE-BLANK QUESTIONS

1. To help the browser load the page faster, you should always set the _____ and _____ attributes in `<img>` tags.

2. An `<img>` object element is created when a browser reads the _____ tags in the page that it is loading.

3. An Image object is created when it is instantiated in a script using the _____ keyword.

4. If you want a linked image to be displayed without a border, you should set the _____ attribute value to zero.

5. To load an Image object into the browser's image cache, you define its _____ attribute.

6. The _____ property of `<img>` element objects only accepts string constants, which are used to set the alignment of the related image.

7. If an `<img>` element object has a name attribute set as "books," you can use _____ to access the related image in the `document.images[]` array.

8. If an `<img>` element object is the third image on the page, you can use _____ to access the related image in the `document.images[]` array.

9. You define a new Image object with a width of 100 and height of 200 using a declaration of _____.

10. To swap an image on the page, you must set the _____ property of the image in the `document.images[]` array equal to the _____ property of an Image object.

DEFINITIONS QUESTIONS

1. What is the `new` keyword used for with regard to Image objects?

2. Which type of image-related objects are precached and not displayed by the browser?

3. What is the purpose of precaching images rather than accessing them directly when they are needed?

4. What technique can you use to make an image clickable?

5. How do browsers display the images you have cached once you swap the Image object's source for the `<img>` object element's source?

INTERMEDIATE PROJECTS

The following projects provide you with additional opportunities to script images.

Project 9.1 – Rotating Images Automatically with a Timer

In many cases, you will want to change images automatically rather than as a result of a user action or selection. You may, for example, want to rotate between the banners of your site's sponsors at a timed interval. To do this, you can create a simple image-swapping engine that allows you to rotate images on a timed schedule.

Getting the timer to work is somewhat tricky. First, you need to start the timer when the page is loaded. You can do this by adding an `onload` event handler to the document's `body` element, as follows:

```
<body onload="init()">
```

Here, when the document finishes loading, the `onload` event is triggered and the browser calls the `init()` function.

The `init()` function is a basic timer that sets a timeout and calls another function at a specific interval. In this example, the timer calls the `rotate()` function once every second (1,000 milliseconds):

```
function init() {
setTimeout("rotate()",1000);
}
```

The `init()` function starts the first automatic rotation. To keep the automatic rotation going, you need a similar statement in the `rotate()` function.

In this project, you will create a page that uses a timer to automatically rotate a banner image. The timer interval should be of short duration (say, 1,000 to 5,000 milliseconds) to make it easy to test and ensure that the banner rotation is working.

Once you have created the HTML page, load it into Internet Explorer to see if it displays correctly. The page should look similar to Figure 9.4. If you need help getting started, you can use the final source code from Practice Drill 9.2. Be sure to save the file as C9practice1.htm before you start working with it.

Project 9.2 – Rotating an Image Each Time a Page Is Loaded

Rather than displaying a specific banner or rotating a banner at an interval, you might want a random banner to be displayed each time a page is loaded. For example, you might have several similar Welcome! graphics. You want to rotate them randomly to give the page a different appearance each time it is accessed.

The `Math.random()` method allows you to generate random numbers. By basing the random number on the actual number of banners and setting this equal to your image index, a random banner could be generated every time a page is loaded.

FIGURE 9.4 Automatic image rotation.

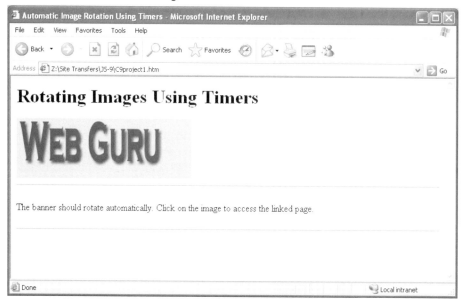

In this project, you will create a page that uses the `Math.random()` method to randomly rotate a banner on a page each time it is loaded. The banner should be linked to a specific set of pages, as in the previous examples. The browser should try to load the correct page when the banner is clicked. For example, if banner 4 is being displayed, the browser should try to display page4.htm when you click the banner.

Once you have created the HTML page, load it into Internet Explorer to see if it displays correctly. The page should look similar to Figure 9.5. If you need help getting

FIGURE 9.5 Rotating an image randomly.

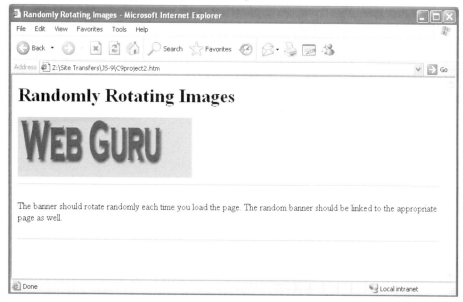

started, you can use the final source code from Practice Drill 9.2. Be sure to save the file as C9practice2.htm before you start working with it.

Career Builder

In this Career Builder exercise, you are going to develop a date-based, image-swapping engine. If you have followed the in-chapter exercises, you know the essentials for swapping images. Now you will look at more advanced techniques that you can use in your career.

- The image-swapping engine should be easy to work with. To ensure this, you should make placeholder variables for the key values and then initialize these variables in the beginning of the script, as shown here:

```
//The value of the banner image's name attribute in
//the page
bannerName = "banner";
//the number of banners to swap
bannerCount = 5;
//the file name string
bannerPrefix = "webguru";
//the image file name suffix, such as .gif or .jpg
bannerSuffix = ".jpg";
```

- Sometimes you will want to rotate banners on a daily basis. Instead of changing links and image references in your pages every day, you can create a banner function that handles this process for you. One way to update banners daily would be to base the current banner on the value returned by the `getDay()` function. This would allow you to have a different banner for each day of the week. Using a straightforward approach, your banner-rotation function would use a simple assignment and display a different banner every day of the week, as shown here:

```
var aDate = new Date ()
var today = aDate.getDay()
document.banner.src = "banner" + today + ".gif"
```

- If your Web site's needs are limited, being able to use up to seven different banners would probably be okay. Still, if you want to go beyond seven banners, what do you do? A typical commercial Web site may rotate 20 different banners. A better approach is to base the current banner on the value returned by `getDate()`, which allows you to use up to 31 different banners. Although you may not use 31 different banners, having additional choices is certainly better than not having enough. However, unless you have 31 banners, you can no longer directly assign

(continued)

the banner source. This means that you have to think of a way to assign the appropriate banner on a given day whether you have 3 banners or 30.

- One way to assign the appropriate banner on any given day is with a `for` loop that cycles for the day count. Within the `for` loop, use two variable indexes to continually cycle through the available banner numbers until the current day of the month is reached. When the current day of the month is reached, the first index points to the appropriate banner, and you can then use the index to assign the image source. The code for the `scheduledRotate()` function follows:

```
function scheduledRotate() {
var aDate = new Date ();
var today = aDate.getDate();
var index = 0;
var currIndex = 0;
for (x = 0; x < today; x++) {
if (currIndex < bannerCount + 1) {
index = currIndex;
currIndex++;
}
if (currIndex >= bannerCount ) {
currIndex = 1;
}
}
document.images[bannerName].src = bannerPrefix +
   index + bannerSuffix;
}
```

- Now that the banner function is complete, you need a way to call it in a Web page. The `onload` event handler provides the perfect mechanism for this:

```
<body onload="scheduledRotate()">
<h1>Rotating Banners According to A Schedule</h1>
<img alt="banner" src="webguru1.jpg" name="banner"
   height="100" width="300" border="0"/>
```

- You can then use the `scheduledRotate()` function in a sample page. Test the page by loading it into your browser. You can customize the banner using the variables set at the beginning of the script.

9

Chapter | 10

Introducing Events and Event Handlers

A s you have seen in previous chapters, JavaScript is a powerful scripting language that can be used to perform behind-the-scenes manipulation of Web pages. In this chapter, you will look at the more interactive features of the language, starting with a look at events and event handlers and continuing with a look at windows and dialog boxes.

An *event* is a procedure that is executed automatically when a certain condition exists. There are events for mouse clicks, mouse movements, button clicks, and so on. An *event handler* is an object property or method that specifies how an object reacts to an event. Events can be triggered by a user action, such as a button click, or a browser action, such as the completion of a document load.

In JavaScript, you create windows and dialog boxes using the window object. The *window object* is at the top of the browser object model for all scriptable browsers. As such, window is the top-level container for all content you view in a Web browser. Whenever you start a Web browser, the window object is defined in memory—even if no document is loaded.

For Your Career

In this chapter, you will examine event handling and simulation. A solid understanding of these concepts is necessary to create interactive Web pages. Because this chapter is an introduction to these concepts, it serves to provide the essential foundation. You will build on that foundation in the chapters ahead.

Chapter Exercises

This unit's exercises will teach you how to:

- Use event handlers with HTML elements
- Simulate events for HTML elements
- Use event-related methods for form controls

By working through the exercises, you will learn not only how to handle user and browser actions, but also how to simulate them.

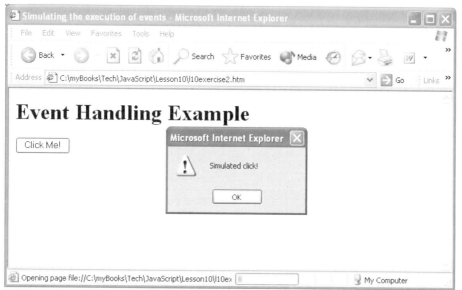

Form Elements Can Be Scripted

Form elements that are manipulated by scripts are often called **HTML controls**. HTML controls include check boxes, radio buttons, push buttons, text windows, text areas, and selection menus.

Exercise 10.1 – Using Event Handlers

Most scriptable browsers, including Internet Explorer, Netscape, and Mozilla, use an object model to represent the HTML elements of a Web page. Every HTML element you use in a Web page has a corresponding object. The object name is the same as the HTML element name without the < > characters. For example, the <p> element's related object is the p object, and the <h1> element's related object is the h1 object.

In this exercise, you will learn how to define an event handler for an HTML object. Like other objects discussed previously, all HTML objects have properties and methods. Generally speaking, a **property** defines a setting of an object and a **method** is a command that a script can give to an object. HTML objects can also have event handlers. **Event handlers** specify how an object reacts to a user or browser action.

Generally, you reference an event handler as an attribute of a related markup tag, such as the <input> tag. Event handlers can call functions or execute statements directly. To make an input button that calls a function when clicked, you would enter the code shown in Exhibit 10.1.

EXHIBIT 10.1

```
<form>
<input type="button" name="clickit" value="Click Me"
   onclick="doThis()" />
</form>
```

A Web page containing this form would have a button labeled Click Me. When you click the button, the onclick event occurs and the doThis() function is called.

STEP 1 – CREATING A BUTTON WITH AN EVENT HANDLER

You can also execute statements directly, as shown in Exhibit 10.2. The value assigned to the onclick event handler is an actual script that has many important elements. A semicolon is used to separate successive lines in the script. The script contains the statement return true. This statement ensures that when you close the alert box by clicking on the OK button, execution continues properly. Generally, whenever you execute statements—other than simple function calls—directly within markup, you want to include a return true statement. Finally, you should note the use of the single quotation marks within the double quotation marks, which prevents a syntax error, because quotes can only be one level deep.

EXHIBIT 10.2

```
<form>
<input type="button" name="clickit" value="Click Me"
   onclick="alert ('Click detected!'); return true" />
</form>
```

STEP 2 – TESTING THE EVENT HANDLER

In Internet Explorer, open the page you created and then click the button to test the event handler. When the button control is clicked, the execution of the `onclick` event causes an alert box to be displayed, as shown in Figure 10.1.

Although `onclick` is one of the most used event handlers, it is not the only event handler you can use. Commonly used event handlers and their meanings are shown in Table 10.1. Keep in mind that not all of these event handlers are appropriate or available for all HTML elements.

FIGURE 10.1 Using event handlers in a Web page.

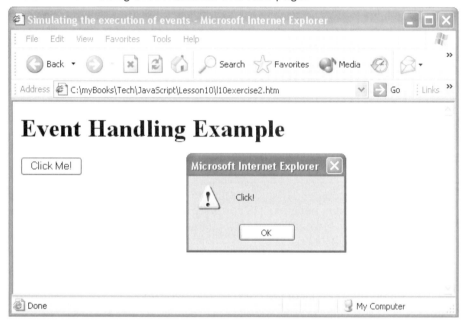

Exercise 10.2 – Simulating Events

Methods are normally used to cause events to occur in the code; they do not require interaction with the user. Thus, a method can be thought of as a controlled event. Unlike user-driven events, controlled events are not executed automatically. Although you can call a method, you must reference it via the object to which it relates. To call a method, you use the following syntax:

objectName.methodName(parameters), where *objectName* is the name of the object you are referencing, *methodName* is the name of the method you want to execute, and *parameters* is an optional comma-separated list of parameters you are passing to the method.

One use of a method would be to simulate button presses during a product tutorial. Instead of the user driving the event, you would simulate the event to trigger an identical response. Following this scenario, you could simulate execution of the button control shown in Exhibit 10.3.

TABLE 10.1 Common event handlers and their uses.

Event Handler Name	Description
onabort	The onabort event is triggered when an element stops loading because a user clicked the Stop button in his or her browser. This event can also be triggered when a user clicks a link in a page that is loading, which interrupts the page-loading process.
onblur	The onblur event is triggered when an element that has focus (meaning it is selected) is about to lose focus because some other element is about to receive focus. The onblur event fires before the onfocus event of the next element.
onchange	The onchange event is triggered when an element is changed, such as when text is entered into an input field.
onclick	The onclick event is triggered when an element, such as a button, is clicked.
onerror	The onerror event is triggered when an unexpected error occurs during the transfer or loading of the related element.
onfocus	The onfocus event is triggered when an element receives focus because it is currently selected or active. Typically an element receives focus after another element loses focus.
onload	The onload event is triggered when an element finishes loading. For a Web page or windows, this event is triggered when all of the page or window components, including images and other embedded media objects, have loaded into the browser. For an image, this event is triggered when the first image source is loaded. Thus, if an img element has a lowsrc property defined, the event fires when this lowsrc is loaded.
onmouseout	The onmouseout event is triggered when the mouse was over an element and then moves away.
onmouseover	The onmouseover event is triggered when the mouse moves over an element.
onreset	The onreset event is triggered when a form is reset.
onselect	The onselect event is triggered when an element is selected. If the element did not have focus before, an onfocus event occurs immediately before the onselect event.
onsubmit	The onsubmit event is triggered when a form is submitted.
onunload	The onunload event is triggered when an element is unloaded.

EXHIBIT 10.3

```
<form name="myform">
<input type="button" name="mybutton" value="Click Me"
   onclick="alert ('Button click detected!');
   return true">
</form>
```

The following code will simulate a button click on the form:

```
<script type="text/javascript">
document.myform.mybutton.onclick();
</script>
```

In reviewing the previous statement, you see that the `onclick` event is simulated by referencing it via the object to which it pertains as a method. When you simulate events, the event name must always be in lowercase text, as shown.

If you continue to examine this simple example, you can learn many things about JavaScript's object hierarchy. Just as you must reference a method via the object to which it pertains, you must also reference the object via its parents in the object hierarchy. In this case, the parent of a button control is the form object named `myform` and the parent of the named form is the `document` object.

It is important to note, however, that `window` is the top-most object in the JavaScript object hierarchy. As long as you are referring to the active window, the `document` object is usually at the top of the object hierarchy in script references. This means that the following reference:

```
document.myform.mybutton.onclick();
```

is generally assumed to be the following:

```
window.document.myform.mybutton.onclick();
```

10

STEP 1 – USING AN EVENT-RELATED METHOD

You can also assign the `onclick` event directly to an action. To do this, you reference the event without the open and close parentheses and assign an action, as in the following example:

```
document.myform.mybutton.onclick = alert ('Simulated
  Click!');
```

To see how simulating events could work in an actual Web page, create a new HTML document using the code shown in Exhibit 10.4. Notice that the `onclick` event is used as a method and referenced via the named elements in its object hierarchy: `document` refers to the current instance of the Web page; `myform` is the current instance of the form object; and `mybutton` is the current instance of the button object.

EXHIBIT 10.4

```
<html>
<head>
<title>Simulating the execution of events </title>
</head>
<body>
<h1>Event Handling Example</h1>
<form name="myform">
<input type="button" name="mybutton" value="Click Me!"
   onclick="alert ('Click!'); return true">
</form>
<script type="text/javascript">
document.myform.mybutton.onclick = alert ('Simulated
   click!');
</script>
</body>
</html>
```

STEP 2 – LOADING THE PAGE AND TESTING IT

In Internet Explorer, open the page you created. Notice that the simulated event occurs immediately after the page is loaded. You do not have to click the button to test the event handler. Figure 10.2 shows what the page looks like.

FIGURE 10.2 Simulating an event and then handling it with a new action.

Exercise 10.3 – Using Event-Related Methods

Technically, the button element you have been working with is a form control. A *form control* is a form-related HTML element, such as `input`, `button`, and `textarea`. In Chapter 17, you will learn more about form-related HTML elements and a method called `click()`.

There is an important difference between simulating the `onclick` event and invoking the `click()` method. When you simulate an event with a method call, actions related to the event occur, such as the display of the *alert* dialog box. When you use an event-related method, such as `click()`, JavaScript simulates the pressing of the button, but it does not necessarily invoke related actions. This means that the following code would simulate the pressing of the button, but might not display an associated alert dialog box as expected:

```
document.myform.mybutton.click();
```

The exact behavior for the `click()` method call depends on the browser version. With browser versions prior to Internet Explorer 4 and Netscape Navigator 4, the `click()` method invoked on a button does not trigger the `onclick` event handler, and if there was a related action, it would not be invoked. With later browser versions, the `click()` method does trigger the `onclick` event handler, and any related actions are invoked as well.

STEP 1 – USING AN EVENT-RELATED METHOD

Modify the HTML document shown in Exhibit 10.4 so that it uses the `click()` method instead of the `onclick` event. To do this, you can replace this line of code:

```
document.myform.mybutton.onclick = alert ('Simulated
  click!');
```

with the following code:

```
document.myform.mybutton.click();
```

STEP 2 – LOADING THE PAGE AND TESTING IT

In Internet Explorer, open the page you just modified. Notice that the `click()` method triggers the `onclick` event immediately after the page is loaded. You do not have to click the button to test the event handler.

Most form controls have event-related methods that you can invoke. Table 10.2 summarizes the most common event-related methods of form controls. Keep in mind that not all of these methods are appropriate or available for all HTML elements.

Keep in mind that you will typically handle events by calling a function in the HEAD element of an HTML document. Remember the doThis() function call in Exhibit 10.1? Exhibit 10.5 extends the original example to show how events would be handled with a function call.

10

TABLE 10.2 Common event-related methods of form controls.

Method Name	Description
blur()	The blur() method removes focus from an element. This deselects whatever may have been selected in the form field and causes the text insertion pointer to leave the field.
click()	The click() method simulates clicking on an element. Because the behavior of the method varies by browser version, you may want to invoke the onclick event handler directly instead.
focus()	The focus() method gives focus to an element. An element that has focus is selected for use. For a text field, this means the insertion pointer is at the beginning of the field.
select()	The select() method selects all text within a text field that has focus. If you invoke an element's focus() method and then the element's select() method, you can give the element focus and then select its contents.

EXHIBIT 10.5

```
<html>
<head>
<title>Continue Tutorial</title>
<script type="text/javascript">
function doThis() {
window.location.href =
"http://www.robertstanek.com/step2.html";
}
</script>
</head>
<body>
<h1>Do you want to continue?</h1>
<form name="myform">
<input type="button" name="clickit" value="Click To
    Continue" onclick="doThis()" />
</form>
</body>
</html>
```

Summary

Every HTML element you use in a Web page has a corresponding object that can be scripted. Most HTML elements have event handlers and event-related methods as well. As shown in this chapter, events that are triggered by a user or browser action can be handled in many ways. You can handle events directly or use function calls. You can also simulate events when you need to trigger an event automatically.

For the purposes of example in this chapter, you have worked primarily with the onclick event handler, the button element, and directly handled events. As shown in Tables 10.1 and 10.2 many other events can be handled or simulated as well. These events can be used with other HTML elements and with form controls, as appropriate. Other chapters in this book will make use of the essential foundation provided here to show you how to create highly interactive and dynamic Web pages. Now that you are familiar with events, you can move on to more advanced interactive topics, such as using windows and dialog boxes, which are covered in the next chapter.

Test Your Skills

Practice Drill 10.1: Using onblur and onfocus Event Handlers

Starting with Internet Explorer 5, the onblur and onfocus events can be triggered for just about any HTML element. In this exercise, you will use the onblur and onfocus events to observe what happens when you change focus from one HTML element to another. The onblur event is triggered when a user tabs from one element to the next in a form or clicks on another form element. It is supposed to occur when an element that has focus is about to lose focus and before the onfocus event of the next element is triggered. However, browser behavior can sometimes yield unexpected or undesirable results.

The following example shows how this works in practice:

10

1. In your text editor, create a HTML page with the appropriate HEAD and BODY elements. Use a TITLE element with the text "Using the onblur and onfocus Event Handlers."

```
<html>
 <head>
  <title>Using the onblur and onfocus Event
     Handlers</title>
 </head>
 <body>
 </body>
</html>
</HTML>
```

2. Insert the JavaScript code block after the `TITLE` element but before the `</head>` tag.

```
<script type="text/javascript">
</script>
```

3. Insert the following Javascript functions into the code block. The first function, `forBlur()`, handles the case when an element loses focus. The second function, `forFocus()`, handles the case when an element gains focus. Notice that in both cases, the ID of the element that triggered the event is obtained using the `event.srcElement.id` property. This ID is then displayed in an alert dialog box.

```
function forBlur() {
 var id = event.srcElement.id;
 alert("Element \"" + id + "\" has lost focus.");
}

function forFocus() {

 var id = event.srcElement.id;

 alert("Element \"" + id + "\" has received focus.");
}
```

4. In the BODY element, insert the text to be displayed. Note that each paragraph of text is given an ID and a `tabindex`. The ID sets an identifier for the paragraph. By adding a `tabindex` to an HTML element, you specify that the user can bring the paragraph into focus by clicking the paragraph or by pressing the [Tab⇆] key. HTML elements receive focus in sequence, according to the tab indexes assigned.

```
<h1>onblur and onfocus Event Handlers</h1>
<p id="Paragraph1" tabindex="1" onblur="forBlur()"
    onfocus="forFocus()">Paragraph 1.</p>
<p id="Paragraph2" tabindex="2" onblur="forBlur()"
    onfocus="forFocus()">Paragraph 2.</p>
<p id="Paragraph3" tabindex="3" onblur="forBlur()"
    onfocus="forFocus()">Paragraph 3.</p>
```

5. Load the page into Internet Explorer 5.0 or later.

6. Experiment with pressing [Tab⇆] and clicking on paragraphs to give or remove focus. Note what happens. Did you notice something odd about the alert dialog boxes? The received focus dialog box is displayed before the lost focus dialog box.

7. Select one of the paragraphs and then close all open dialog boxes. Click a blank area of the page. Note what happens and then click one of the paragraphs.

8. Clicking a blank area of the page causes the selected paragraph to lose focus. Then when you click a paragraph, you select it and give it focus. However, the lost focus event is reported because the action is not tracked for the page itself.

Practice Drill 10.2: Using `onload` and `onabort` Event Handlers

The `onload` event handler can be used with the `<body>` tag, the image, layer, link, and window objects as well as with frames. With images, the behavior of `onload` depends on which attributes of the image object are used. With an image that has a `lowsrc` attribute, the `onload` event is triggered when the `lowsrc` image loads, but not when the `src` image is later loaded. With an animated GIF image, the `onload` event occurs when each frame of the animated GIF is displayed.

The `onabort` event handler is triggered when a user clicks the browser's Stop button before an element completely loads. If you want to activate a script when a user clicks Stop, use the `onabort` event handler. The `onabort` event handler can also be triggered when a user clicks a link in a page that is loading because it interrupts the page-loading process.

To see how these events can be used, complete the following exercise:

1. In your text editor, create a HTML page with the appropriate HEAD and BODY elements. Use a TITLE element with the text: "Using the `onload` and `onabort` Event Handlers."

```html
<html>
 <head>
  <title>Using the onload and onabort Event
     Handlers</title>
 </head>
 <body>
 </body>
</html>
```

2. Insert the JavaScript code block after the TITLE element but before the `</head>` tag.

```html
<script type="text/javascript">
</script>
```

3. Insert the following Javascript functions into the code block. The `stopLoad()` function handles the case when a user clicks the Stop button in the browser before the images load completely. In this case, a confirmation dialog box is displayed giving the user a chance to reload the page.

```javascript
function stopLoad() {
 if(confirm("You've stopped the page from loading.
   Do you want to try to reload the page?"))
 {
  location.reload();
 }
}
```

4. In the BODY element, insert the elements to be displayed. Note that a form is used to display the status of the load as 'true' if the image load is completed. The C10image1.jpg and C10image2.jpg files can be found on the companion Web site

10

for this book (*www.prenhall.com/web development*) and should be copied to your current working folder (the one in which you have saved the document for this exercise).

```
<img alt="image" src="C10image2.jpg"
lowsrc="C10image1.jpg" width="300"
height="255" onload="if (document.forms[0].result)
document.forms[0].result.value='true'"
onabort="stopLoad()" />
<form>
 <p>Load completed? <input type="text"
 name="result" /> <input type="hidden" /></p>
</form>
```

5. Load the page into a Web browser. Note what happens when the image loads. You may not be able to click the Stop button in time, because loading from disk is much faster than loading from the Web.

MULTIPLE-CHOICE QUESTIONS

1. What is the difference between an event and an event handler?
   A. An event is a user or browser action triggered by an event handler.
   B. An event handler specifies how an object reacts to a user or browser action.
   C. An event handler is a procedure that is executed automatically; an event is triggered only by a user.
   D. An event and an event handler are the same thing.

2. Why would you simulate an event?
   A. You simulate an event to ensure that it can be triggered by a user action.
   B. You simulate an event to execute it.
   C. You simulate an event to cause an event to occur in code.
   D. You simulate an event to call it and then execute it.

3. What does `onclick="doThis()"` mean if assigned to an HTML element?
   A. If you click the HTML element, the `doThis()` event is called.
   B. If you change the HTML element, the `doThis()` event is triggered.
   C. If you click the HTML element, the function `doThis()` is called.
   D. If you change the HTML element, the function `doThis()` is called.

4. When does the `onchange` event handler occur?
   A. When you click the browser's Stop button
   B. When you modify an element's contents or enter text in an element

C. When you change the browser's window size

D. When you close the browser window

5. When is the `onload` event triggered?

   A. For a Web page with images, `onload` is triggered when all of the page text has loaded.

   B. For an image, `onload` is triggered whenever a `lowsrc` or `src` is loaded.

   C. For an image, `onload` is triggered when the first image source is loaded.

   D. For an image, `onload` is triggered when the last image source is loaded.

FILL-IN-THE-BLANK QUESTIONS

1. _____ is the top-level object for all scriptable browsers.

2. You reference an event handler as a(n) _____ of a related markup tag.

3. Form elements that are manipulated by scripts are often called _____.

4. The object name is the same as the HTML element name without the _____ characters.

5. The _____ event is triggered when an element that has focus is about to lose focus.

6. The _____ event is triggered when an unexpected error occurs during transfer or loading of the related element.

7. When you call a method, you must reference it via the _____ to which it relates.

8. The _____ method gives focus to an element.

9. The _____ method selects the contents of a field that has focus.

10. Typically, you handle events by calling a function in the _____ element of an HTML document.

DEFINITIONS QUESTIONS

1. What is a property?

2. What is a method?

10

3. What is an event?

4. What is an event handler?

5. What is a window?

INTERMEDIATE PROJECTS

The following short projects provide you with the opportunity to create a new Web page that uses common event handlers as well as event simulation.

Project 10.1 – Adding Event Handlers to a Web Page

This project will require you to use the onmouseover and onmouseout event handlers. When the mouse pointer is over an image, the overImage() function should be called. When the mouse pointer moves away from the image, the offImage() function should be called. For now, the functions do not need to perform any specific tasks. You can use the final document you created in Exercise 10.2 as a starting point if you need help getting started.

Once you've created the HTML page, load it into Internet Explorer or Netscape Navigator to see if it displays correctly.

Project 10.2 – Creating Functions for Handling the onmouseover and onmouseout Events

This project will require you to extend Project 10.1 by creating functions that handle the onmouseover and onmouseout events. The way the events are handled is up to you. However, a unique action should be triggered for both events. For example, when the onmouseover event is triggered, the browser could call the overImage() function shown in the following example.

```
function overImage() {
 alert("The mouse pointer is over the image.");
}
```

When you are finished, load the page into Internet Explorer or Netscape Navigator and test the techniques you have used. Are the events handled as expected?

▶▶Career **Builder**

The purpose of this chapter was to introduce event handling. In your career, you will use these event-handling techniques frequently. The Career Builder exercise for this chapter is to design the main page for a new application.

The main page for the application should be called cb-main.htm. Create this page in your text editor using the following template as a starting point.

```
<html>
<head>
<title>Main Page</title>
</head>
<body>
<h1>Our Application</h1>
</body>
</html>
```

Think about the functions that you could add to this page to handle events triggered when a user loads the page. Consider adding an onabort event handler to handle the case when a user clicks the Stop button before the page has completely loaded. Think about how you could possibly do this.

In the upcoming chapters, event handling will be used more extensively. You'll have opportunities to modify and extend the application you have started in this chapter.

10

Chapter | 11

Working with Windows and Dialog Boxes

You can use scripts to manipulate the browser window and to create additional sub-windows and various types of dialog boxes. In this chapter, you will learn techniques for working with windows and dialog boxes. As you will learn, the `window` object is much more than the base of the object hierarchy. It is the most dynamic object available in JavaScript. Using the `window` object, you can create new windows of many types, including:

- New browser windows
- Alert dialogs
- Prompt dialogs
- Confirmation dialogs

In addition to the properties and methods of the `window` object that help you track and update the many windows you can create, events of the `window` object help you interact with the user when windows are activated or deactivated.

For Your Career

In this chapter, you will examine issues related to browser windows and dialog boxes. Not only will you learn how to create windows, you will also learn techniques for effectively working with windows as you would in real-world applications. It is important to not only be able to create windows, but also to understand the conditions that should be tested before trying to open or close windows. Keep in mind that pop-up blockers can interfere with opening additional windows. On the Web, this means some users may not see pop-up windows. On an internal intranet, however, browsers can be configured with different security to allow pop-ups to be used so your intranet applications work properly.

Chapter Exercises

This unit's exercises will teach you how to:

- Access window properties
- Create and close windows
- Set the features of new windows
- Use confirm dialog boxes
- Use prompt dialog boxes

By working through the exercises, you will learn many things about windows and dialog boxes, such as how to set the window status, size windows, and bring windows to the front or put them to the back.

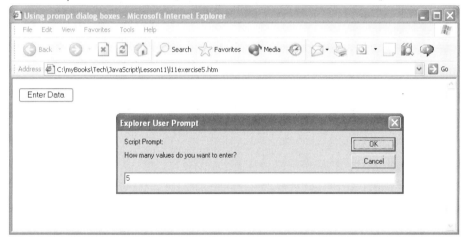

Exercise 11.1 – Accessing Window Properties

Properties of the window object allow you to script various window settings and to check the status of windows. Generally speaking, the most common way to reference a property of a window is to reference the property name in the form:

```
window.propertyName
```

Because window is the top-level object and it always exists, you can also omit the reference to window any time you are referencing objects in the current window. This means another way to reference a property of the current window is

```
propertyName
```

In this exercise, you will learn techniques for accessing window properties by working with the status property. You use status to update the status bar at the bottom of the browser window. Normally, status messages appear when the browser is loading a document, when you move the mouse pointer over a hypertext link, and so on. You can also use status to display your own messages. For example, instead of displaying the URL of a link, you might want to display a custom message that provides more detail about the link.

STEP 1 – CREATING THE HTML PAGE

In your text editor, create a new blank page. You will create a sample HTML page as shown in Exhibit 11.1. Use the TITLE and H1 elements as shown.

EXHIBIT 11.1

```
<html>
<head>
<title>Accessing window properties</title>
</head>
<body>
<h1>Updating the window Status</h1>
</body>
</html>
```

STEP 2 – SETTING THE STATUS MESSAGE

In your text editor, add a hypertext link to the page and define the onmouseover event handler as shown in Exhibit 11.2. Here, you define the event handler directly, which is the most common way to use the window.status property. Closely examine the script statement assigned to the onmouseover event handler. Note that the entire statement is surrounded by double quotes (""). Within the double quotes, you use single quotes to surround the string to display in the status area.

EXHIBIT 11.2

```
<p><a href="http://www.robertstanek.com" onmouseover=
  "window.status='Visit the Robert Stanek Home
  Page'">RobertStanek.com</a></p>
```

STEP 3 – DISPLAYING THE PAGE

In Internet Explorer, open the page you created and then activate the status update by moving the mouse pointer over the link. Figure 11.1 shows the page in a browser.

Note what happens. Did the status display as expected? Not really, and here's why: Internet Explorer and most other browsers require event handlers to return a value. Remember we assigned `return true` in the previous chapter when we handled events directly. If you do not do this, the link is displayed `onmouseover` and the status message is displayed `onmouseout`.

FIGURE 11.1 Creating a status message.

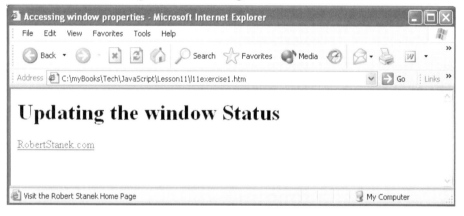

STEP 4 – UPDATING THE PAGE

In your text editor, update the page to add a `return true` statement as shown in Exhibit 11.3.

EXHIBIT 11.3

```
<p><a href="http://www.robertstanek.com" onmouseover=
  "window.status='Visit the Robert Stanek Home Page';
  return true">RobertStanek.com</a></p>
```

STEP 5 – RELOADING THE PAGE

In Internet Explorer, open the page you updated. You can force Internet Explorer to refresh the page by holding [Ctrl] when you click the Refresh button. Move the mouse pointer over the link and note what happens. The status update should work properly now—well, almost. When you move the mouse pointer over the link, the status message is displayed. When you move the mouse pointer away, however, the status message remains.

STEP 6 – CLEARING THE STATUS MESSAGE

In your text editor, update the page to add an `onmouseout` event handler that sets a blank status message as shown in Exhibit 11.4.

EXHIBIT 11.4

```
<p><a href="http://www.robertstanek.com"
onmouseover="window.status='Visit the Robert Stanek
Home Page'; return true" onmouseout="window.status='';
return true">RobertStanek.com</a></p>
```

STEP 7 – TESTING THE FINAL PAGE

In Internet Explorer, open the page you updated. Move the mouse pointer over the link and note that the message is set as expected. Move the mouse pointer away from the link and note that the message is cleared as expected.

Although `status` is a very useful property of the `window` object, you will want to know about the many other `window` properties as well. Table 11.1 provides an overview of the most commonly used properties of the `window` object. Using this table, you can tell the values the properties accept, whether you can set the properties, and whether you can get the current settings of the property; you also get a brief description of how the property is used.

Exercise 11.2 – Creating and Closing Windows

The main browser window is created when the browser is started by a user. When working with scripts, you will often want to create additional windows to display additional information to users. The way you do this is to create a subwindow with the `window.open()` method.

The `window.open()` method has three standard parameters that define window characteristics:

- The URL of the document to load in the new window

- The name for the window, which can be referenced in the target attribute of an HTML tag

- An optional parameter string that details the features of the window in a comma-separated list

To see how windows can be created, consider the following example:

```
var newWindow = window.open("display.htm","display",
  "height=300,width=400");
```

TABLE 11.1 Commonly used properties of the `window` object.

Property	Value	Type	Description
`closed`	Boolean	Read-only	Returns true if the specified `window` object has been closed by a user or by a script. You should test for the `closed` property before trying to work with a window that a user might have closed. Supported by NN3, IE4 and later as well as Mozilla and Safari.
`defaultStatus`	String	Read/Write	Sets or gets the default status message for the browser window. This message is displayed any time the mouse pointer is not atop an object that has precedence over the status bar. Supported by NN2, IE3 and later as well as Mozilla and Safari.
`name`	String	Read/Write	Sets or gets the name of the window so it can be referenced in other windows. The window name helps you determine which window you are working with. Supported by NN2, IE3 and later as well as Mozilla and Safari.
`onerror`	Undefined/ Null	Read/Write	Can be custom error messages or to simply turn off error dialogs. When a browser starts, this property is set to undefined by default. To turn off error dialogs, you set `onerror` to `null`. Supported by NN3, IE4 and later as well as Mozilla and Safari.
`opener`	`window` object	Read/Write	Allows new windows to refer to the window that opened them. This makes it possible to reference

11

TABLE 11.1 *(Continued)*

Property	Value	Type	Description
			objects or properties of the original window. Supported by NN3, IE3 and later as well as Mozilla and Safari.
`self`	`window` `object`	Read-only	Represents the same object as the `window` object. Like a reference to `window`, you can usually omit a reference to `self`. However, if you are working with multiple windows using the `self` property makes it easier to determine which window you are referring to. Although technically a property of `window`, you never use a reference in the form `window.self.` `propertyName`. Instead you make references as `self.propertyName`. Supported by NN2, IE3 and later as well as Mozilla and Safari.
`status`	String	Read/Write	Sets a status message for the browser window. Status messages are normally displayed in the status bar at the bottom of the browser window and are used with temporary events such as document loading progress or when the mouse pointer is over a link. Supported by NN2, IE3 and later as well as Mozilla and Safari.
`window`	`window` `object`	Read-only	Refers to the current `window` object. Generally, the `window` object is assumed in references and need not be included. Supported by NN2, IE3 and later as well as Mozilla and Safari.

This example creates a new window named "display" that loads an HTML document from the same server directory as the current document. The window is sized so it is 400 pixels wide and 300 pixels high (400 × 300).

It is also important to note that you use an assignment statement to create the window. The reason this is required is that the `window.open()` method returns an object reference to the window and that object reference is assigned to the variable. Because the variable holds a valid object reference to the window, you can use the variable to access the properties and methods of the newly created window from a script in the main window. For example, if you wanted to move the window to the back and make it inactive, you could use this reference to the `blur()` method for the subwindow:

```
newWindow.blur();
```

However, if a window does not open successfully, the variable holds a null value, and an error may be generated. Therefore, before you work with a new window, you should test for the null value, as in the following:

```
newWindow = window.open("","");
if (newWindow) {
 newWindow.blur();
}
```

You can close a window as easily as you open it. To close the active window from a script in that window, use the following:

```
self.close();
```

If you wanted to close the window from a script in the main window, you would use this reference to the `close()` method for the subwindow:

```
newWindow.close();
```

When you close a window, the `onUnload` event occurs, and if the associated page handles this event, the defined action is executed. Most browsers will not let you close the main browser window unless the user confirms that he or she wants to close this window. Therefore, if you try to close the main window, users will see a confirm dialog box.

In this exercise, you will learn techniques for creating subwindows. Ideally, any subwindow you create should be initialized using a global variable rather than as a new variable within a function. Using a global variable ensures that the variable holding the window reference is valid for as long as the main document is loaded in the browser. It also allows you to work with the window in multiple functions. You could, for example, have one function that creates the window and another that closes the window.

STEP 1 – CREATING THE SUBWINDOW

In your text editor, create a new blank page. You will create a sample HTML page as shown in Exhibit 11.5. Use the `TITLE` and `H1` elements as shown.

Watch Out for Pop-up Blockers

Windows XP with Service Pack 2 or later includes a built-in pop-up blocker that will block `window.open()` if it is enabled. This pop-up blocker is configured as a privacy feature. In Control Panel, double-click the Internet Option utility and then click the Privacy tab of the Internet Properties dialog box. Use the options on the Pop-up Blocker panel to configure how pop-ups are used. Keep in mind that some firewall and antivirus programs also include pop-up blockers. For example, with Norton Personal Firewall, pop-up blocking is enabled or disabled by turning the Ad Blocking feature on or off.

Use a Full Reference to Subwindows

Keep in mind that you must use a full reference to a subwindow. If you were to use `window.close()`, `self.close()`, or `Close()` in the main browser window, you would close the main browser window instead of the subwindow. Because of this, always reference the subwindow you want to work with by its variable name.

11

EXHIBIT 11.5

```
<html>
<head>
<title>Working with subwindows</title>
</head>
<body>
<h1>Create or close the subwindow</h1>
</body>
</html>
```

STEP 2 – DEFINING THE WINDOW FUNCTIONS

Add a header-defined script to the HTML page as shown in Exhibit 11.6. Note that the newWindow variable is defined as a global variable. This allows the newWindow variable to be accessed in the createWindow() and closeWindow() functions.

EXHIBIT 11.6

```
<script type="text/javascript">
var newWindow;
function createWindow() {
 newWindow = window.open("","mywindow","height=300,
  width=400");
}
function closeWindow() {
 newWindow.close();
}
</script>
```

STEP 3 – UPDATING THE BODY OF THE PAGE

In the body of the page, add a form that can be used to create and close the subwindow after the H1 element. The form should define two buttons as shown in Exhibit 11.7. Note that the first button is used to create the subwindow and the second button is used to close the subwindow.

EXHIBIT 11.7

```
<form>
<input type="button" value="Create a new window"
  onclick="createWindow()">
<input type="button" value="Close the new window"
  onclick="closeWindow()">
</form>
```

STEP 4 – DISPLAYING AND TESTING THE PAGE

In Internet Explorer, open the page you created and then create the subwindow by clicking the appropriate button (see Figure 11.2). Close the window by clicking the other button. Now play around with the window. Note what happens when you click one of the buttons twice. Examine the script to see what is happening behind the scenes. Do you see anything in the coding that could be handled in a better way? Hint: Look at the way the window is closed.

FIGURE 11.2 Creating a subwindow.

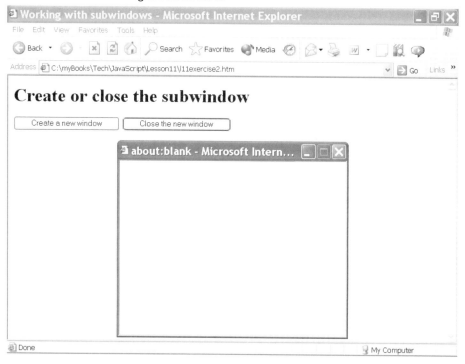

STEP 5 – UPDATING THE PAGE

In your text editor, update the script in the page header to add the `if` condition to the `closeWindow()` function as shown in Exhibit 11.8. With this addition, you test to ensure that the window has been created before you try to close it. When a variable is declared but has no value assigned to it, its initial value is null, which is interpreted by JavaScript to be a false condition. If the variable has a nonzero value assigned to it, it is interpreted by JavaScript to be a true condition. Because of this, the conditional expression in the `closeWindow()` function tests two conditions. The first condition determines whether the window has been created before calling the window's `close()` method. The second condition determines whether the window was previously created and has since been closed. If both conditions evaluate to true, the function closes the open window and then sets the `newWindow` variable to null. This ensures that if you were to try to close the window again, the test conditions would not be met and the function would not try to close a nonexistent window.

EXHIBIT 11.8

```
<script type="text/javascript">
var newWindow;
function createWindow() {
 newWindow = window.open("","mywindow","height=300,
   width=400");
}
function closeWindow() {
 if (newWindow && !newWindow.closed) {
  newWindow.close();
  newWindow = null;
 }
}
</script>
```

STEP 6 – RELOADING THE PAGE

In Internet Explorer, open the page you updated. You can force Internet Explorer to re-fresh the page by holding Ctrl when you click the refresh button. Click the form buttons to open and close the window. Click the open and close buttons several times. Although the page behaves the same as it did before, behind the scenes, the script is better managing the closing of the window. This will prove helpful when you are working with multiple windows and more complex scripts.

As you probably know, the open() and close() methods are not the only methods of the window object. If you are wondering what other methods are available, take a look at Table 11.2. This table provides a brief overview of the most commonly used methods of the window object. You can use this table to quickly learn how to use

TABLE 11.2 Commonly used methods of the window object.

Method	Example	Description
alert()	alert("message")	Displays an alert dialog box with an OK button. Until this dialog box is closed, no other actions are possible. Supported by NN2, IE3 and later as well as Mozilla and Safari.
blur()	self.blur()	Moves the referenced window to the back, making it inactive. Does not work in some versions of Mozilla. Supported by NN2, IE3 and later as well as Safari.

TABLE 11.2 *(Continued)*

Method	Example	Description
clearInterval()	clearInterval (intervalID)	Clears an interval loop; used with the setInterval() method. Supported by NN4, IE4 and later as well as Mozilla and Safari.
clearTimeOut()	clearTimeOut (timerID)	Cancels a timer that is waiting to run; used with the setTimeOut() method. Supported by NN2, IE3 and later as well as Mozilla and Safari.
close()	window.close()	Closes the referenced browser window; a confirmation dialog is displayed if you attempt to close the main browser window. Supported by NN2, IE3 and later as well as Mozilla and Safari.
confirm()	confirm ("message")	Displays a dialog box with OK and Cancel buttons that allows users to confirm or cancel an action. Supported by NN2, IE3 and later as well as Mozilla and Safari.
focus()	window.focus()	Brings the referenced window to the front and makes it active. Supported by NN2, IE3 and later as well as Mozilla and Safari.
open()	window.open ("URL", "Name", "Features")	Creates a new browser window. The first parameter sets the URL of a page you want to open in the new window. The second parameter sets the name of the window. The final property sets the features of the window. Supported by NN2, IE3 and later as well as Mozilla and Safari.

11

TABLE 11.2 (Continued)

Method	Example	Description
print()	window.print()	Allows you to send the current window to the printer, displaying the Print dialog box so the user can set the print settings or cancel the action. Supported by NN4, IE5 and later as well as Mozilla and Safari.
prompt()	prompt("message", "defaultReply")	Creates a dialog box with an input field and two buttons: OK and Cancel. The first parameter is the message to display. The second parameter is the default text for the input field. Supported by NN2, IE3 and later as well as Mozilla and Safari.
scroll()	window.scroll(x, y)	Scrolls the referenced window to the specified x,y coordinates; coordinates are referenced in pixels. Supported by NN3, IE4 and later as well as Mozilla and Safari.
setInterval()	setInterval("function or expression", delay)	Calls a function or evaluates an expression repeatedly at a fixed interval. Supported by NN4, IE4 and later as well as Mozilla and Safari.
setTimeOut()	setTimeOut("function or expression", delay)	Sets a timer that calls a function or evaluates an expression after the specified period of time has elapsed. Supported by NN2, IE3 and later as well as Mozilla and Safari.

a specific method. If you examine the table, you will see that the default syntax for parameter passing is included as well. Parameters enclosed in quotation marks are strings. All other parameters are numbers—unless noted otherwise.

As shown in Table 11.3, the `window` object also has several event handlers. As you saw earlier, you can use events to call functions as well as directly execute statements.

TABLE 11.3 Commonly used events of `window` objects.

Event	Description
`onBlur=`	Executes when a window is deactivated or put to the back.
`onFocus=`	Executes when a window is activated or brought to the front.
`onLoad=`	Executes whenever a document finishes loading into the window.
`onUnload=`	Executes when a document is closed, when a new document is loaded into the current window, and when HTML markup is written to the page with `document.write`.

Exercise 11.3 – Setting the Features of New Windows

Customizing a new window is more difficult than simply creating a window. To customize the window, you must use the parameters of the `open()` method. The first parameter is the URL of the page you want to load into the new window. When you open a new window, supply an URL only if you want to load an existing page into the window. If you plan to insert your own markup within your script, do not fill in the first parameter and instead assign an empty string ("") to this parameter.

The second parameter is the name of the window. Do not confuse the name of the window with the title of the document loaded into the window. Giving the window a unique name enables you to target the window.

If you omit the optional third parameter, JavaScript opens a window that looks exactly like a new browser window. When you use the optional third parameter, you specify the features to include in a comma-separated list. Features not specified in the list are not displayed—which is very important to understand. It means that if you specify any window feature in the third parameter, all windows features not specified are turned off.

Table 11.4 lists the windows features supported by both Internet Explorer and Netscape browsers. By carefully selecting the features and size of a new window, you can create custom windows that only allow users to perform the actions you want them to perform. All the Boolean values listed default to yes if you do not specify the third parameter.

11

Exceptions for the Mac

The menubar and resizable features are not available on Macs. On a Mac, the menu bar is not in the browser window and all windows are resizable.

TABLE 11.4 Feature parameters for JavaScript windows.

Feature Name	Type	Description
copyhistory	Boolean	Creates a Go menu using the current history list.
directories	Boolean	Adds the directory buttons to the window.
height	Integer	Sets the height of the window in pixels.
left	Integer	Sets the horizontal (x) position for the top-left corner of the window. For Netscape Navigator, must be version 6.0 or later.
location	Boolean	Adds the location field for entering and displaying URLs.
menubar	Boolean	Adds the pull-down menus, such as File, Edit, and View.
resizable	Boolean	Allows the user to resize the window.
scrollbars	Boolean	Displays scrollbars when necessary.
status	Boolean	Places the status bar at the bottom of the window.
toolbar	Boolean	Adds toolbar buttons, such as Back, Forward, and Home.
top	Integer	Sets the vertical (y) position for the top-left corner of the window. For Netscape Navigator, must be version 6.0 or later.
width	Boolean	Sets the width of the window in pixels.

Although, you can enter the features as a sequence of Boolean values, it is a lot easier to simply enter the name of the feature you want to turn on, as in the following example:

```
myWindow = window.open("study.htm","StudyWin",
  "location,status,resizable");
```

When using the width and height features, you must set them equal to a specific pixel value. Consider the following example:

```
myWindow = window.open("study.htm","Study",
  "status,width=200,height=250");
```

Here, you set a window width of 200 pixels and a window height of 250 pixels.

In this exercise, you will learn techniques for creating subwindows with additional features. You will also learn techniques for working with multiple windows.

STEP 1 – CREATING THE MAIN PAGE

In your text editor, create a new blank page. You will create a sample HTML page as shown in Exhibit 11.9. Take a close look at the script. The script has all the elements necessary to create a usable window in your own scripts. The new `window` object reference is assigned to a global variable called `newWind`. The `createWindow()` function has the appropriate logic to handle several important conditions. Before it creates a new window, the script checks to see if the window exists or if it has been previously created and then closed. If the window does not exist, it has a `null` value and the `!newWind` condition evaluates to `true`. If the window existed previously but was closed (which is a required check for new browsers), the `newWind.closed` condition evaluates to `true`. If either condition is true, the window is created with the `open()` method. Otherwise, the existing window is brought to the front using the `focus()` method.

EXHIBIT 11.9

```
<html>
<head>
<title>Creating Windows </title>
<script type="text/javascript">
var newWind;

function createWindow() {
 if (!newWind || newWind.closed) {
  newWind = window.open("sample.htm","window2","status,
    resizable,location,height=200,width=450");
 }
 else {
  newWind.focus();
 }
}
</script>
</head>
<body>
<h1>Creating windows</h1>
<form>
<p> <input type="button" value="Make Window Directly"
  onclick="window.open('sample.htm','','status,
  resizable,height=200,width=450')"></p>
<p><input type="button" value="Make Window in Function"
  onclick="createWindow()"></p>
</form>
<hr size=5 noshade>
</body>
</html>
```

11

STEP 2 – CREATING THE SAMPLE.HTM DOCUMENT

In your text editor, create a new blank page. You will create a sample HTML page as shown in Exhibit 11.10. This is the source document for the subwindow.

EXHIBIT 11.10

```
<html>
<head>
<title>Sample Window</title>
</head>
<body>
<h1>The Sample Window</h1>
<p>This is the sample window. You can add or modify
  contents if you want.</p>
</body>
</html>
```

STEP 3 – DISPLAYING AND TESTING THE PAGE

In Internet Explorer, open the page you created in Step 1. You can learn a great deal about windows from working with this simple example in your browser (see Figure 11.3).

FIGURE 11.3 Creating subwindows with additional features.

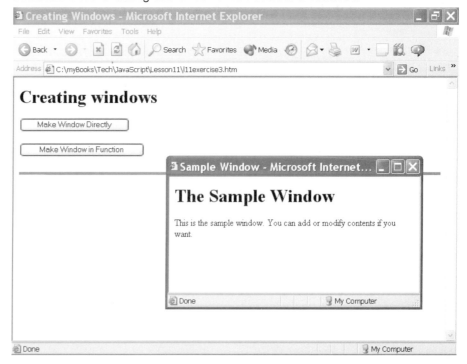

The first button makes a window by directly calling the `window.open()` method in the `onclick` event. This window is not named and loads a document called sample.htm. Each time you click this button JavaScript will create a new window. If you make the main window the active window, the subwindow is usually hidden from view behind the main window. In this case, the only way to see the subwindow again is to access it from the taskbar or close/minimize the main window.

The second button calls a function that creates a window. This window also loads the sample.htm document. If you click on the button a second time, the `createWindow()` function invokes the `focus()` method to bring the window to the front. In this way, if the window is hidden from view, you can bring it to the front simply by clicking on the button.

Note also the features of the windows. Windows created by the first button are resizable and have a status bar. Windows created by the second button are resizable, have a status bar, and also have a location field.

STEP 4 – MODIFYING THE MAIN PAGE

In your text editor, open the HTML page created in Step 1. Change the feature parameters to try out some of the other features. While you are editing the features, give the window created directly with the first input button a name—call it window3. Hint: You give the window a name by setting the second parameter of the `window.open()` method.

STEP 5 – LOADING THE FINAL PAGE

In Internet Explorer, open the modified page. Use both input buttons to create the subwindows and see how the windows' features affect the browser window. Load the subwindows several times. Did you notice any different behavior other than the features you modified? You probably did. Now that the first button creates a named window, clicking the button will only create the window if it does not already exist.

Exercise 11.4 – Using Dialog Boxes

JavaScript provides three types of dialog boxes that you can use to communicate with the user:

- Alert
- Confirm
- Prompt

You will look at alert and confirm dialog boxes first. You create an *alert* dialog box with the `window.alert()` method. An alert dialog box is used to present a message to users and has an OK button users can click on to close the dialog box (see Figure 11.4). While the alert dialog is displayed, no other window can be made active. The `alert()` method of the `window` object accepts a single parameter. This parameter is a string containing the message you want to display, such as the following:

```
alert("Input error, please check the data!");
```

You create a confirm dialog box with the `window.confirm()` method. A *confirm* dialog box is more versatile than an alert dialog box. With a confirm dialog box, you

FIGURE 11.4 An alert dialog box.

can display a message to the user with OK and Cancel buttons (see Figure 11.5). This type of dialog box can be used to ask the user a question.

Because there are two different buttons, your scripts can test to see which button the user clicked and take the appropriate action. Similar to the `alert()` method, the `confirm()` method of the `window` object accepts a single parameter. This parameter is a string containing the message you want to display, such as the following:

```
confirm("Do you want to continue?");
```

When the user clicks the OK button, the `confirm()` method returns `true`. When the user clicks the Cancel button, the `confirm()` method returns `false`. This means you can check the user's response with conditional statements, such as `if...else`.

In the following exercise, you will learn techniques for handling output from dialog boxes. This is an important skill that you will need to learn so that you can create scripts that respond appropriately to user selections. For example, if a user clicks the Cancel button instead of the OK button, your script should be able to handle this. After all, there is no reason to use dialog boxes if you do not want to collect information from a user.

FIGURE 11.5 A confirm dialog box.

STEP 1 – CREATING THE PAGE

In your text editor, create a new blank page. You will create a sample HTML page as shown in Exhibit 11.11. Note that the HTML page contains a form that has an input field whose `onclick` event handler calls a function.

EXHIBIT 11.11

```html
<html>
 <head>
  <title>Using confirm dialog boxes</title>
 </head>
 <body>
  <form>
   <input type="button" name="clearData" value="Reset
      Data" onclick="resetData()" />
  </form>
 </body>
</html>
```

STEP 2 – DEFINING THE FUNCTION

In your text editor, add the script shown in Exhibit 11.12 to the page you previously created. Because the confirm dialog box returns a Boolean value (true for OK or false for Cancel), you can use the method as part of a comparison expression in an if...else statement.

EXHIBIT 11.12

```javascript
<script type="text/javascript">
function resetData() {
 if (confirm("Are you sure you want to reset the
   data?")) {
 //insert statements to reset the data
 alert("Clearing out the data.");
 }
 else {
 alert("Action cancelled.");
 //insert statements to return to previous activity
 }
}
</script>
```

STEP 3 – DISPLAYING AND TESTING THE PAGE

In Internet Explorer, open the page you created in Steps 1 and 2 as shown in Figure 11.6. Click the Reset Data button and test the example by clicking either OK or Cancel. Does the example behave as expected? It should. Clicking OK in the confirm dialog box results in the if condition being executed, which would clear out the data if this were a real application. Clicking Cancel in the confirm dialog box results in the else condition being executed.

11

FIGURE 11.6 Using a confirm dialog box in a page.

STEP 4 – MODIFYING THE PAGE

Another way to handle the output from a confirm dialog box is to use an assignment expression. Here, you assign the result of the `confirm()` method to a variable and then check the variable to determine the action the user performed. In your text editor, modify the script shown in Exhibit 11.12 so that the confirm dialog box is assigned to a variable and then define `if` and `else` statements to handle the true or false result. Exhibit 11.13 provides the necessary code, but first try this modification on your own without looking at the exhibit.

EXHIBIT 11.13

```
<script type="text/javascript">
var response;
function resetData() {
 var response = confirm("Are you sure you want to reset
   the data?");
 if (response) {
 alert("Clearing out the data.");
 //insert statements to reset the data
 }
 else {
 alert("Action cancelled.");
 //insert statements to return to previous activity
 }
}
</script>
```

STEP 5 – LOADING THE FINAL PAGE

In Internet Explorer, open the modified page. Click the Reset Data button and test the example by clicking either OK or Cancel. Clicking OK in the confirm dialog box should still result in the `if` condition being executed; clicking Cancel should still result in the `else` condition being executed.

Exercise 11.5 – Using Prompts

In this exercise, you will learn techniques for using prompts and handling responses to prompts. A ***prompt*** dialog box presents a message and allows users to enter information in response to the message. As you can see from Figure 11.7, this dialog box also has OK and Cancel buttons. To create a prompt, you will use the `prompt()` method, which has two mandatory parameters. The first parameter is the message to display, the second parameter is a default reply. Because the parameters are mandatory, you must use an empty string for the second parameter if you do not want to enter a default reply. See the following example:

```
prompt("Please enter your name.","");
```

You can handle responses from prompt dialog boxes in several different ways. As with confirm dialogs, clicking the OK or Cancel button returns `true` or `false`, respectively. Although checking a true/false condition will work in some respects, you also want to see if the user entered information.

When the user clicks the prompt dialog box's OK button but does not enter text into the input field, the value returned by the `prompt()` method is an empty string (""). When the user clicks Cancel, however, any variable you set equal to the output of the prompt will contain a null value. Because of this, you should always test for both an empty string and a null value when trying to determine if a user entered information in the prompt.

FIGURE 11.7 A prompt dialog box.

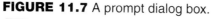
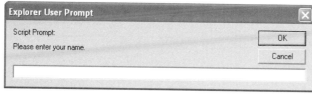

STEP 1 – CREATING THE PAGE

In your text editor, create a new blank page. You will create a sample HTML page as shown in Exhibit 11.14. Note that the HTML page contains a form that has an input field whose `onclick` event handler calls a function.

EXHIBIT 11.14

```
<html>
 <head>
  <title>Using prompt dialog boxes</title>
 </head>
 <body>
  <form>
   <input type="button" name="enterData" value="Enter
     Data" onclick="getData()" />
  </form>
 </body>
</html>
```

STEP 2 – DEFINING THE FUNCTION

In your text editor, add the script shown in Exhibit 11.15 to the page you previously created. To handle the output from a prompt dialog box, you should use an assignment expression as shown. This way you can test the data and store the results as necessary.

EXHIBIT 11.15

```
<script type="text/javascript">
var currVal;
function getData() {
 var currVal = prompt("How many values do you want to
   enter?","");
 if (currVal != null && currVal != "") {
 alert("Preparing to enter " + currVal + " values.");
 //insert statements to handle value entry
 }
}
</script>
```

STEP 3 – DISPLAYING AND TESTING THE PAGE

In Internet Explorer, open the page you created in Steps 1 and 2. Test the page by clicking the Enter Data button. Enter a numeric value in the prompt as shown in Figure 11.8 and click OK. You should see an alert confirming that you are preparing to enter that number of values. Repeat this process and test the error conditions by clicking OK without entering a value or clicking Cancel. Because the function first checks to make sure the return value is not null or an empty string, these error conditions should be handled.

FIGURE 11.8 Handling prompts.

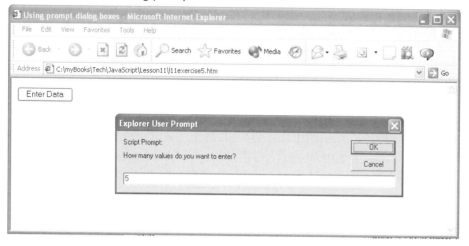

STEP 4 – MODIFYING THE PAGE

Checking for error conditions is a good programming technique. You should also handle error conditions. In this example, you could add an `else` statement to handle the case when the user fails to input a value. You could also use a `while` loop to continually display the prompt until the user enters information. To test this feature, replace the script entered in Step 2 with the script shown as Exhibit 11.16.

EXHIBIT 11.16

```
<script type="text/javascript">
 var currVal;
 function getData() {
  var currVal = prompt("How many values do you want to
   enter?","");
  while (currVal == null || currVal == "") {
   currVal = prompt("How many values do you want to
    enter?","");
  }
  alert("Preparing to enter " + currVal + " values.");
  //insert statements to handle value entry
}
</script>
```

STEP 5 – LOADING THE FINAL PAGE

In Internet Explorer, open the modified page. Click the Enter Data button and test the example by clicking OK without entering a value or by clicking Cancel. Performing either action should cause the `while` loop conditions to evaluate to true, in which case the prompt dialog box is displayed again. To close the prompt dialog box, you must enter a value.

As you have seen, the window object is quite complex. It has many properties, methods, and event handlers. The most important things to remember are the techniques to properly create and close windows. Exhibit 11.17 shows a script with createWindow() and closeWindow() functions that you can use for future reference.

EXHIBIT 11.17

```
<script type="text/javascript">
var newWind;

function createWindow() {
 if (!newWind || newWind.closed) {
  newWind = window.open("sample.htm","window2",
    "height=200,width=450");
 }
 else {
  newWind.focus();
 }
}

function closeWindow() {
 if (newWind && !newWind.closed) {
  newWind.close();
  newWind = null;
 }
</script>
```

Summary

Most scripts you use will work with the browser window in some way. As you have learned in this chapter, `window` is the top-level object, and it always exists. This means you can reference properties of the current window by name without referencing the `window` object. However, for clarity, it is usually a good idea to reference the property you want to work with fully in the form `window.propertyName`.

You can also create custom windows. These custom windows can have a variety of features that you specify when you instantiate the window, including the window height, width, toolbars, and buttons. Another type of window available in a script is a dialog box. JavaScript supports alert, confirm, and prompt dialog boxes, all of which have different uses and purposes. Alert dialog boxes display a message, typically a warning, to users. Confirm dialog boxes display a message with OK and Cancel buttons that allow users to confirm or cancel an action. Prompt dialog boxes display a message and have an input field as well as OK and Cancel buttons. This allows users to answer questions or input information.

Test Your Skills

Practice Drill 10.1: Setting a Default Status

Previously, you learned how to set a status message. The browser window also has a default status message, which is normally set to an empty string (""). After a document is loaded into a window, the default status message is displayed any time the mouse pointer is not over an element that updates the status bar. Moving the mouse pointer over a link or other object that updates the status bar overrides the default status message. Although you can set a default status message at any time, the best time to do so is when a document loads into a window.

The following example shows how you can use a default status along with other status messages:

1. In your text editor, create a HTML page with the appropriate HEAD and BODY elements. Use a TITLE element with the text "Using status messages."

```
<html>
 <head>
  <title>Using status messages</title>
 </head>
 <body>
 </body>
</html>
```

2. Insert the following JavaScript code block after the TITLE element but before the </head> tag. This script sets the default status of the browser window.

```
<script type="text/javascript">
window.defaultStatus = "Welcome to my Web site!
  Thank you for visiting.";
</script>
```

11

3. In the BODY element, insert the text to be displayed. This paragraph tag contains a link that updates the status message onmouseover.

```
<p><a href="http://www.robertstanek.com"
  onmouseover="window.status='Visit the Robert
  Stanek Home Page'; return true" onmouseout=
  "window.status=''; return true">
  RobertStanek.com</a></p>
```

4. Load the page into Internet Explorer 5.0 or later. The default status message should be displayed.

5. Move the mouse pointer over the link to update the status message. When you move the mouse pointer away, the default status message should be displayed again.

6. Remove the onmouseout event handler from the example and reload the page. Move the mouse pointer over the link to update the status message and then move it away. Note the behavior. Because you set a specific default status message, you technically do not need to reset the status message with the onmouseout event.

Practice Drill 10.2: Using the `print()` Method

On the Web, you will often see that pages with multiple columns of information have a print feature that lets you print the main text of the page without printing all of the extraneous information. To do this, Web sites redirect the user to a printer-friendly version of a page and then invoke the window.print() method to send the current window to the printer. Invoking the print() method displays the Print dialog box of the user's operating system so the user can make printing choices.

To see how this method could be used with the techniques your have learned in this chapter, complete the following exercise:

1. In your text editor, create a HTML page with the elements shown here. Use the appropriate HEAD and BODY elements. Use a TITLE element with the text: "Welcome to my Web site!"

```
<html>
<head>
<title>Welcome to my Web site!</title>
</head>
<body>
</body>
</html>
```

2. Insert the following JavaScript code block after the TITLE element but before the </head> tag. The printWindow() function loads a sample document, which for the purposes of this example is considered to be a simplified version of the current page, and then invokes the print() method.

```
<script type="text/javascript">
var newWind;
function printWindow() {
```

```
  if (!newWind || newWind.closed) {
    newWind = window.open("sample.htm","window2",
      "status,height=200,width=450");
    newWind.print()
  }
}
</script>
```

3. In the BODY element, insert the elements to be displayed. Note that a form is used to display a button labeled "Print Page."

```
<h1>Printing example</h1>
<form>
<p><input type="button" value="Print Page" onclick=
  "printWindow()"></p>
</form>
<hr size=5 noshade>
```

4. Load the page into a Web browser. Note what happens when you click the Print Page button. With all browser versions, the Print dialog box should be displayed, allowing you to print the document.

MULTIPLE-CHOICE QUESTIONS

1. How should a script defined in the current window reference a window property?
   A. window.propertyName
   B. propertyName
   C. self.propertyName
   D. All of the above

2. What is the difference between a status message and a default status message?
   A. A status message is displayed when the browser window is loaded; a default status message is displayed when the mouse pointer is over an object that updates the status bar.
   B. Status messages are displayed when the browser window is loaded; default status messages are never used.
   C. A default status message is displayed when the browser window is loaded; a status message is displayed when the mouse pointer is over an object that updates the status bar.
   D. None of the above

3. What are the accepted parameters of the window.open() method?
   A. URL of the document to load
   B. The name of the window
   C. The features of the window in a comma-separated list
   D. All of the above
   E. A and B only

4. Which types of dialog boxes have OK and Cancel buttons?

A. Alert only

B. Confirm only

C. Prompt only

D. Alert and confirm

E. Confirm and prompt

FILL-IN-THE-BLANK QUESTIONS

1. The _____ method is used to bring a window to the front.

2. In a window opened by another window, you reference the window that opened the window using the _____ property.

3. The _____ method accepts a single parameter, which is the message you want to display, but it does not allow the user to confirm his or her response.

4. The _____ method creates a dialog box with OK and Cancel buttons and accepts a single parameter, which is the message you want to display.

5. The _____ method has two parameters: the message you want to display and a default reply.

6. You use the _____ method to create a new window.

7. If you do not want to set the features of a new window, you use a(n) _____ as the third parameter for the `window.open()` method.

8. The _____ method moves the referenced window to the back.

9. You use the _____ property to determine whether a window has been closed by a user or a script.

10. The _____ method is used to close a window.

DEFINITIONS QUESTIONS

1. When working with windows, to what does `opener` refer?

2. When working with windows, to what does `self` refer?

3. When working with windows, to what does a default status refer? When is it displayed?

4. What is a confirm dialog box? How is it used?

5. What is a prompt dialog box? How is it used?

INTERMEDIATE PROJECTS

The following short projects provide you with the opportunity to work with and create custom windows.

Project 11.1 – Creating Status Message Functions

This project requires you to create a function that handles status messages. When the mouse pointer is over a link in a document, the function `displayStatus()` should be called to display a status message for that specific link. The page should have at least two links. The first link should be labeled "Home Page" and the second link should be labeled "Main."

When the mouse pointer moves away from the link, the function `displayStatus()` should be called to set the status message to an empty string. You can use the final document created in Exercise 11.1 as a starting point if you need help getting started.

Once you have created the HTML page, load it into Internet Explorer and Netscape Navigator to see if it displays correctly. The page should look similar to Figure 11.9.

FIGURE 11.9 Working with status messages.

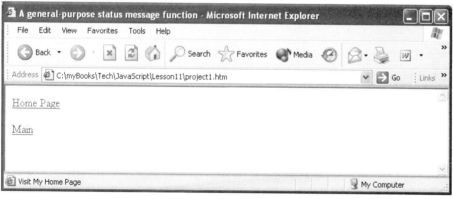

Project 11.2 – Creating and Managing a Subwindow

With this project, you will create a subwindow management page. The page should have buttons that enable you to create and close the window. It should also have buttons that send the window to the back or bring it to the front.

The functions being called should test for all the appropriate conditions before trying to create or work with the window. Thus, although you may be able to use the final document created in Exercise 11.3 as a starting point, you may need to modify the existing functions to ensure they test for the appropriate conditions.

When you are finished, load the page into Internet Explorer and Netscape Navigator and test the window management functions you have defined. The page should look similar to Figure 11.10.

FIGURE 11.10 A window management page.

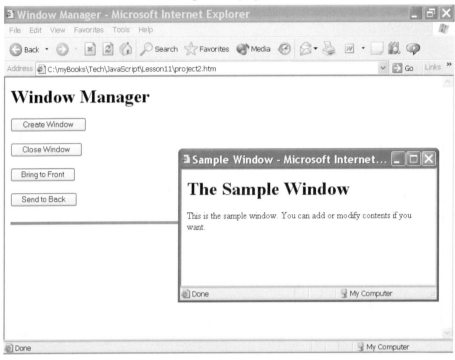

Career Builder

In this chapter, you have learned many useful skills for working with windows and dialog boxes. After following this chapter, you should have a number of functions for managing windows and handling responses to dialog boxes. You should be able to easily modify the functions shown in this chapter so that you can use them in your real-world scripts.

The Career Builder exercise for this chapter is to use the skills you have learned in this chapter to create a scrolling text banner. Shortly after Netscape released JavaScript, Web developers discovered that they could scroll messages in the status bar. At first, these messages were embraced as something new and cool. After a while, developers started hearing from annoyed users who could not read link references or get other information in the status bar while messages were scrolling—and they were right.

(continued)

- The key to using scrolling banners in the status bar is to limit the duration of the message. You can do this by controlling the number of times the message scrolls. One way to do this is to count the number of characters in the banner and then set a counter equal to the number of characters in the banner times the count of the scroll.

- You will need to track the current character count. To handle this, you need variables for the message, the current count, the maximum count, and the number of times to scroll. These variables are set by the following statements.

```
//Set the banner message
var bText = "        Welcome to our site!        We hope
  you enjoy your visit . . .  ";
//set the number of times to scroll
var numScroll = 3;
//initialize count variables
var curCount = 1;
var maxCount = 0;
```

- After you determine the variables you need, you can create the function to scroll the banner. The scrolling is handled by continuously shifting the first character to the end of the banner. The function must stop scrolling the message when the maximum character count is reached. This function is as follows:

```
function scrollText() {
 if (maxCount == 0) {
 //set maximum characters to scroll
 maxCount = numScroll * bText.length;
 }
 window.status = bText;
 //track the number of characters that have
 //been displayed
 curCount++;
 //shift first character to end for continuous
 //scroll
 bText = bText.substring (1, bText.length) +
   bText.substring (0, 1);
 //test for maximum character count
 if (curCount >= maxCount) {
  window.status = "";  //clear status bar
  return;          //break out of function
  } else {
  //if not max count continue to scroll
  scrollText();
 }
}
```

(continued)

- Although the function scrolls the banner, there is no mechanism for controlling the speed of the banner. The result is that messages scroll by faster than you can read them. To control the speed of the banner, you need to build in a delay mechanism.

- This can be handled by a timer that recursively calls the `scrollText()` function only after a specified period of time. The `setTimeout()` method is perfect for this purpose. The method accepts two parameters: a function to call and a delay in milliseconds. The timer definition that follows calls the `scrollText()` function after waiting 150 milliseconds:

```
timerId = setTimeout ("scrollText()", 150);
```

- With a variable initialized at the top of your script, you can make it easier to track timers. Here we will replace the numeric value with a variable called `delay`:

```
timerId = setTimeout ("scrollText()", delay);
```

- When you are finished with a timer, it is always a good idea to zero it out. Setting the timer's value to zero frees system resources and prevents the timer from running amuck on your system. For this reason, in the `scrollText()` function, the timer is zeroed out when the maximum character count is reached. The reworked function is as follows:

```
function scrollText() {
 if (maxCount == 0) {
 //set maximum characters to scroll
 maxCount = numScroll * bText.length;
 }
 window.status = bText;
 //track the number of characters that have
 //been displayed
 curCount++;
 //shift first character to end for continuous
 //scroll
 bText = bText.substring (1, bText.length) +
  bText.substring (0, 1);
 //test for maximum character count
 if (curCount >= maxCount) {
  timerId = 0;      //zero out timer
  window.status = ""; //clear status bar
  return;          //break out of function
  } else {
  //if not max count continue to scroll
  timerId = setTimeout ("scrollText()", delay);
  }
}
```

(continued)

- Now that the banner function is complete, you need a way to call it in a Web page. The `onLoad` event provides the perfect mechanism for this:

```
<body onLoad="scrollText()">
```

- Save the completed Web page that uses the `scrollText()` function. Test the page by loading it into your browser. You can customize the banner using the variables set at the beginning of the script.

11

Chapter | 12

Examining Documents

In this chapter, we begin our look at the document object. The document object is a child of the window object and is the key to creating highly interactive Web pages. In fact, most communication between users and scripts takes place via the document object. The document object is important because it is the container for all of the elements in a Web page. With newer Web browsers—those capable of using dynamic HTML—the document object can be used to update the page on-the-fly, allowing you to update or replace elements with ease. Behind the scenes, Internet Explorer 4.0 or later and Netscape Navigator 6.0 or later automatically redraw the page if the size of content changes when you alter the page using a script.

In older browsers, such as Netscape Navigator 3.0 or Internet Explorer 2.0, you are limited to a small set of objects that you can modify, which includes images, links, embedded objects, and forms. Because of this, if you are creating scripts to have the widest compatibility, you will be limited to changing only a small number of properties after the page loads. Of course a workaround is available. If you need to update pages based on user input or make timed updates to pages, you could design the page so that scripts write the contents and then let the scripts rewrite the entire page with the new settings. Best of all, the updates can be handled completely using client-side scripts; this means the browser does not need to go back to the Web server to request an updated page.

For Your Career

In this chapter, you will examine issues related to the elements in a page. You will learn how to manipulate page elements and how to effectively write and rewrite the contents of the page. Because the document object and its capabilities are so extensive, we have divided its discussion into several chapters. Many of the remaining chapters in this book cover related groups of objects, all of which are contained within the document object. By following the exercises in this chapter, you will learn more about customizing pages and gain some important utility functions for managing content. You should be able to easily modify these functions and add them to your JavaScript toolbox.

Chapter Exercises

This unit's exercises will teach you how to:

- Customize pages using the `document` object
- Use arrays of objects contained in a document
- Write the contents of pages using scripts

By working through the exercises, you will learn many things about the `document` object and how it can be used to access the elements in a page.

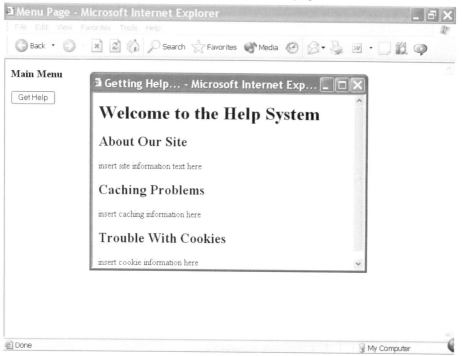

Exercise 12.1 – Customizing Pages Using the document Object

As a developer using JavaScript, you will rely heavily on the document object. Its most commonly used properties, methods, and events are summarized in Table 12.1. Properties of the document object allow you to dynamically update page properties as well as embedded images and objects. Methods of the document object allow you to open, close, and generate documents. Event handlers, which were discussed in an earlier chapter, are triggered when an event occurs on the page.

The document object has numerous properties that you can put to immediate use in your scripts. When you want to customize pages based on user preferences or check current color settings, use the properties in Table 12.2. Although you can read color properties at any time with older browsers, you can only set colors when you generate a

TABLE 12.1 The document object.

Properties	Methods	Event Handlers
activeElement	attachEvent()	onactivate
alinkColor	captureEvents()	onclick
anchors[i]	clear()	ondblclick
applets[i]	clearAttributes()	onkeydown
bgColor	close()	onkeypress
cookie	focus()	onkeyup
domain	getElementById()	onmousedown
embeds[i]	getElementsByName()	onmousemove
fgColor	getElementsTagByName()	onmouseout
forms[i]	getSelection()	onmouseover
frames[i]	handleEvent()	onmouseup
height	hasFocus()	onselectionchange
images[i]	open()	onstop
lastModified	recalc()	
linkColor	releaseEvents()	
links[i]	routeEvent()	
location	setActive()	
referrer	write()	
title	writeln()	
url		
vlinkColor		
width		

TABLE 12.2 The document object properties for preferences and color settings.

Property	Value	Type	Description
alinkColor	"#rrggbb"	Read/Write	Checks or sets the color setting for active links. Supported by NN2, IE3 and later as well as Mozilla and Safari.
bgColor	"#rrggbb"	Read/Write	Checks or sets the background color setting. Supported by NN2, IE3 and later as well as Mozilla and Safari.
fgColor	"#rrggbb"	Read/Write	Checks or sets the color of text on the page. Supported by NN2, IE3 and later as well as Mozilla and Safari.
height	Integer	Read-only	Returns the pixel height of the content in the current window. Supported by NN4 and later as well as Mozilla and Safari. For IE 4 and later, use scrollHeight.
lastModified	Date string	Read-only	Returns the modification timestamp for the document. Supported by NN2, IE3 and later as well as Mozilla and Safari.
linkColor	"#rrggbb"	Read/Write	Checks or sets the color setting for links. Supported by NN2, IE3 and later as well as Mozilla and Safari.
vlinkColor	"#rrggbb"	Read/Write	Checks or sets the color setting for visited links. Supported by NN2, IE3 and later as well as Mozilla and Safari.
width	Integer	Read-only	Returns the pixel width of the content in the current window. Supported by NN4 and later as well as Mozilla and Safari. For IE 4 and later, use scrollWidth.

Watch Out for Deprecated Elements

Although supported by all browsers since Netscape Navigator 2.0 and Internet Explorer 3.0, the following properties listed in Table 12.2 have been deprecated in the JavaScript Document Object Model (DOM): alinkColor, bgColor, fgColor, linkColor, and vlinkColor. The reason for this is that the creators of the JavaScript DOM would prefer that script writers use a style sheet and then script the color changes via the style sheet.

12

page in your script. Afterward, the colors cannot be changed unless you rewrite the page. With newer browsers, pages are automatically redrawn as necessary to allow updating at any time.

Values for the color-related properties can be set as common HTML hexadecimal triplet values, such as "#FF0808," or as any of the Netscape color names. The Netscape color names are recognized by Internet Explorer as well. However, with either browser, users may need to have their monitors set to 16- or 24-bit color settings.

In this exercise, we are going to put the color setting properties to work to see how they can be used to update page colors.

STEP 1 – CREATING THE PAGE

In your text editor, create a new blank page. You will create a sample HTML page, as shown in Exhibit 12.1. Use the TITLE and BODY elements as shown. Note that the <body> tag has the bgcolor property set so the background color of the page is white.

EXHIBIT 12.1

```
<html>
<head>
<title>Custom Color Page</title>
</head>
<body bgcolor="#FFFFFF">
</body>
</html>
```

STEP 2 – DEFINING THE PAGE BODY

Add the elements shown in Exhibit 12.2 to the body of the page. As you examine the exhibit, note that a table is used to lay out the form elements. This is a common design technique to ensure exact placement of form elements. Note also that the form has three selection menus. These selection menus contain color choices for the page background, text, and links with a default option of "Choose." When you choose a different value, the onChange event is triggered and a function is called with two parameters. The first parameter is this.form, which is a placeholder for the form object itself. The second parameter is a reference to the name of the selection menu you are working with, which is either bgColor, textColor, or linkColor.

EXHIBIT 12.2

```
<h1>Welcome to the custom color page!</h1>
<p>You can use the color customization techniques in
    your own pages.</p>
<form>
<table>
<tr><th align=left>Background</th></tr>
<tr><td><select name="backColor" size=1 onChange=
    "setBColor(this.form,'bgColor')">
```

```
<option>Choose</option>
<option>Aqua</option>
<option>Black</option>
<option>Blue</option>
<option>Fuchsia</option>
<option>Gray</option>
<option>Green</option>
<option>Lime</option>
<option>Maroon</option>
<option>Navy</option>
<option>Olive</option>
<option>Purple</option>
<option>Red</option>
<option>Silver</option>
<option>Teal</option>
<option>White</option>
<option>Yellow</option>
</select></td></tr>
<tr><th align=left>Text</th></tr>
<tr>
<td><select name="textColor" size=1
    onChange="setTColor(this.form,'textColor')">
<option>Choose</option>
<option>Aqua</option>
<option>Black</option>
<option>Blue</option>
<option>Fuchsia</option>
<option>Gray</option>
<option>Green</option>
<option>Lime</option>
<option>Maroon</option>
<option>Navy</option>
<option>Olive</option>
<option>Purple</option>
<option>Red</option>
<option>Silver</option>
<option>Teal</option>
<option>White</option>
<option>Yellow</option>
</select></td></tr>
<tr><th align=left>Links</th></tr>
<tr>
<td><select name="linkColor" size=1
onChange="setLColor(this.form,'linkColor')">
<option>Choose</option>
<option>Aqua</option>
<option>Black</option>
```

12

```
<option>Blue</option>
<option>Fuchsia</option>
<option>Gray</option>
<option>Green</option>
<option>Lime</option>
<option>Maroon</option>
<option>Navy</option>
<option>Olive</option>
<option>Purple</option>
<option>Red</option>
<option>Silver</option>
<option>Teal</option>
<option>White</option>
<option>Yellow</option>
</select></td></tr>
</table>
</form>
<p><a href="http://www.robertstanek.com/">Go back
   to home page</a></p>
```

STEP 3 – DEFINING THE CUSTOM COLOR SCRIPT

Add a header-defined script to the HTML page, as shown in Exhibit 12.3. Three separate functions are defined: `setBcolor()` is used to set the background color, `setTcolor()` is used to set the text (foreground) color, and `setVcolor()` is used to set the link color. All three functions expect to be passed a form object and a second value that could be used as an index if needed. The basic functionality of these scripts is to examine the selection menu and determine which option was selected and then to read the text of that option so it can be used to change the color setting as necessary.

EXHIBIT 12.3

```
<script type="text/javascript">
function setBColor(form,index) {
  var userColor = "";
  for (var i = 0; i < form.backColor.length; i++) {
    if (form.backColor.options[i].selected) userColor
        = form.backColor.options[i].text;
  }
  document.bgColor = userColor;
}

function setTColor(form,index) {
  var userColor = "";
  for (var i = 0; i < form.textColor.length; i++) {
    if (form.textColor.options[i].selected) userColor
        = form.textColor.options[i].text;
```

```
  }
  document.fgColor = userColor;
}
function setLColor(form,index) {
  var userColor = "";
  for (var i = 0; i < form.linkColor.length; i++) {
    if (form.linkColor.options[i].selected) userColor
        = form.linkColor.options[i].text;
  }
  document.linkColor = userColor;
  document.vlinkColor = userColor;
  document.alinkColor = userColor;
}
</script>
```

STEP 4 – DISPLAYING AND TESTING THE PAGE

In Internet Explorer, open the page you created, which should look like Figure 12.1. Experiment by changing the colors of the page using the options provided. After changing a color, the page is automatically updated to reflect the change. As long as you are using a newer browser, the changes are automatic. If you are using an older browser, some of the features may work, but others may not.

FIGURE 12.1 Creating a page to dynamically change page colors.

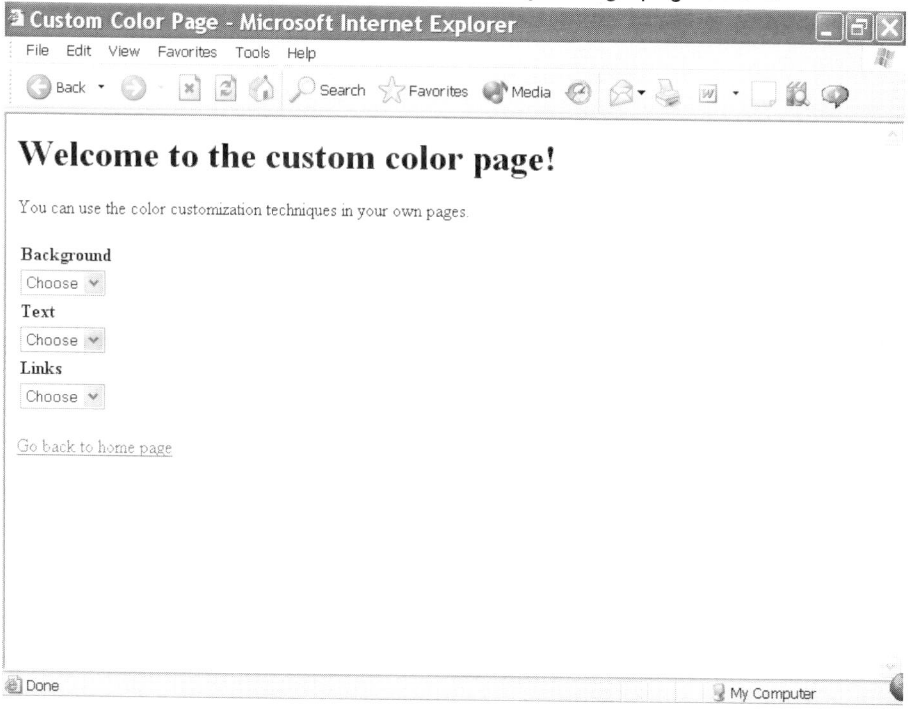

12

Exercise 12.2 – Accessing Objects within a Document

Many objects within documents can be accessed by special arrays. You can use these arrays to access anchors, frames, images, forms, and links as well as other embedded elements and objects in your Web pages according to their index. For a summary of these properties, see Table 12.3.

Use the *frames[]* Array Carefully

The `document.frames[]` property is available only in Internet Explorer 4.0 or later. It is used to reference any `frame` elements of a frame source page or any `iframe` elements defined in a document. If a script is in a frame source page, the `frames[]` array contains the windows objects from the frames you have defined. If a script is in a page with iframe elements, the `frames[]` array contains the `window` objects from the iframes you have defined. Being able to distinguish frame and iframe elements in Internet Explorer is sometimes important, because frame and iframe elements have different methods and properties from `window` objects. If a document isn't a framesource page or doesn't have any iframe elements, the `document.frames[]` array has a length of zero.

TABLE 12.3 Indexed properties of the `document` object.

Property	Value	Type	Description
anchors[i]	Array	Read-only	Allows you to reference named anchors in your page by their index. Supported by NN2, IE3 and later as well as Mozilla and Safari.
applets[i]	Array	Read-only	Allows you to reference applets in your page by their index. Supported by NN2, IE3 and later as well as Mozilla and Safari.
embeds[i]	Array	Read-only	Allows you to reference embedded objects in your page by their index. Supported by NN3, IE4 and later as well as Mozilla and Safari.
forms[i]	Array	Read-only	Allows you to reference forms in your page by their index. Supported by NN2, IE3 and later as well as Mozilla and Safari.
frames[i]	Array	Read-only	Allows you to reference the `window` objects of any frame elements in your page by their index. Only supported by IE4 and later.
images[i]	Array	Read-only	Allows you to reference images in your page by their index. Supported by NN3, IE4 and later as well as Mozilla and Safari.
links[i]	Array	Read-only	Allows you to reference links in your page by their index. Supported by NN2, IE3 and later as well as Mozilla and Safari.

You will learn more about these arrays in later chapters. For now, let's look at basic usage. If you use these properties, keep in mind that index zero always points to the first element or object of a particular type. Following this, you could refer to elements of the first form on the page as follows:

```
document.forms[0].objectName.property
```

If the second form on the page had a text field called `currAddress`, you could access its value with the following:

```
enteredValue = document.forms[1].currAddress.value
```

Because you are working with an array, you can use the properties and methods of the array object to work with the related objects. For example, you can use the following statement to get the number of elements in the first form on the page:

```
document.forms[0].length
```

In this exercise, we are going to extend the example created in the previous exercise to obtain information about the form.

STEP 1 – CREATING THE PAGE

In your text editor, open the completed example created in Exercise 12.1. In the body of the document, replace the end table and end form tabs (`</table></form>`) with the markup shown in Exhibit 12.4. Note that this markup adds two elements to the form. A text area with the name `results` and a button with the name `elements`. When you click the button, it calls a function called `numElements()`.

EXHIBIT 12.4

```
<tr><th align=left>Form Elements</th></tr>
<tr>
<td><textarea name="results" rows="2"
cols="40"></textarea></td></tr>
<tr>
<td><input type="button" name="elements" value="Number
of Elements" onclick="numElements()" />
</td></tr>
</table>
</form>
```

12

STEP 2 – ADDING THE FUNCTION

Add the `numElements()` function to the header-defined script. The source of the function is shown in Exhibit 12.5. Although at first glance the `numElements()` function seems very simple, it does have a bit of complexity. It uses a variable called `result` as a placeholder for the information you want to display. It sets this value so that it reflects the number of elements in the first form in the document (`forms[0]`) and then writes its current contents to the value of the text area named `results`. The value of any input field can be read or written using the `value` property.

EXHIBIT 12.5

```
function numElements() {
  var result ="";
  result += "Number of form elements in the page: " +
      document.forms[0].length + "\n";
  document.forms[0].results.value = result;
}
```

STEP 3 – DISPLAYING AND TESTING THE PAGE

In Internet Explorer, open the modified page. Click the button to update the contents of the text area as shown in Figure 12.2. A key advantage to using the `document.forms[]` array to address a form object or element is that it makes code reuse easier and also allows you to create a library of common functions that could be used in multiple pages.

FIGURE 12.2 Using the `forms[]` array to work with the elements of a form.

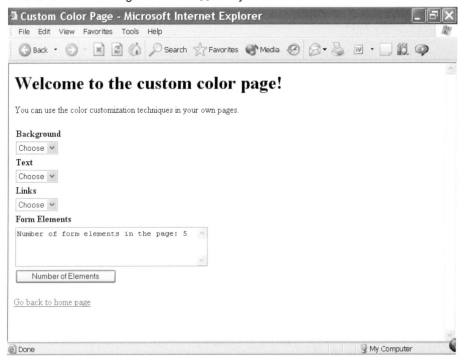

STEP 4 – EXTENDING THE EXAMPLE

In your text editor, open the completed example created in this exercise. In the body of the document, replace the end table and end form tabs (`</table></form>`) with the markup shown in Exhibit 12.6. Note that this markup adds a button with the name Colors. When you click the button, it calls a function called `currColors()`.

EXHIBIT 12.6

```
<td><input type="button" name="Colors" value="Current
    Hex Color Values" onclick="currColors()"
/>
</td></tr>
</table>
</form>
```

STEP 5 – ADDING THE FUNCTION

Add the `currColors()` function to the header-defined script. The source of the function is shown in Exhibit 12.7. Clicking the Colors button displays the current color values in the results text area. As before, the `value` property of the text area is used.

EXHIBIT 12.7

```
function currColors() {

  var result ="";
  result += "bgColor " + document.bgColor + "\n";
  result += "textColor " + document.fgColor + "\n";
  result += "linkColor " + document.linkColor + "\n";
  document.forms[0].results.value = result;
}
```

STEP 6 – DISPLAYING AND TESTING THE PAGE

In Internet Explorer, open the modified page. Click the Colors button to update the contents of the text area as shown in Figure 12.3. Although you set the colors using the color constants, the properties are returned as hexadecimal triplet values. You can experiment further by changing the color values and clicking the Colors button to determine the related hexadecimal values.

12

Exercise 12.3 – Creating Pages On-the-Fly

One of the most common uses for the methods of the `document` object is to create pages on-the-fly. Table 12.4 provides a summary of the methods that will help you do this. Dynamic writes to a page must take place when the page is loading into the user's browser. When you write to the page after the page has completely loaded, the browser will replace the current page with a new page that contains the output of your `write` statements.

FIGURE 12.3 Other contents can be displayed as well, such as the current color values.

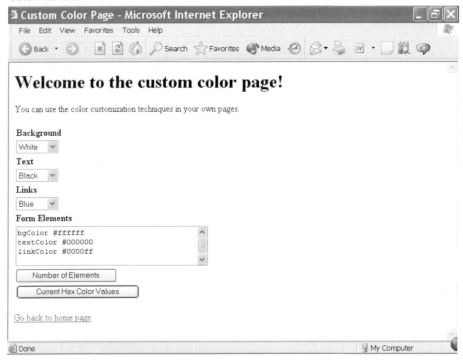

TABLE 12.4 Creating pages with document object methods.

Method	Example	Description
clear()	document.clear()	Clears the current page out of the browser window. Rarely used because if you clear the contents of the page, the scripts you need typically are gone as well. Supported by NN2, IE3 and later as well as Mozilla and Safari.
close()	document.close()	Closes the write stream to a window after it is opened. In many cases, elements on a page will not display properly until you close the write stream, including images. If you don't close the write stream, any subsequent writes are appended to the bottom of the document. Supported by NN2, IE3 and later as well as Mozilla and Safari.
open()	document.open ("text/html")	Opens a write stream for the window using the specified MIME type. If you do not specify a MIME type, the

TABLE 12.4 (*Continued*)

Method	Example	Description
		browser assumes the type is text/html. Supported by NN2, IE3 and later as well as Mozilla and Safari.
write()	document.write ("This string.")	Writes a string to the current page but does not insert a carriage return and line feed. If you use document.write(), you can mark the end of a line—similar to as if you had used the document.writeln() method, using the \n special character. Supported by NN2, IE3 and later as well as Mozilla and Safari.
writeln()	document.writeln ("This line.")	Writes a string to the current page that includes a carriage return and line feed. The carriage return and line feed will make the text more readable in a text editor, although they may not affect the appearance of the page in a browser. Supported by NN2, IE3 and later as well as Mozilla and Safari.

Contrary to what some people think, you cannot use these methods to update the text of existing documents. There is a workaround that allows you to update a document after it is written, but the implementation causes problems on most platforms. Still, if you need to update a document, try this: Assemble the additional markup as a complete object, pass the object to a single document.write() statement, and then issue a document.close() instruction as the next line of the script. This forces the browser to rewrite the contents of the document. If you do not use this technique, the first document.write() or document.writeln() method call will overwrite the contents of the page and there will be no script to execute further. Consider the example in Exhibit 12.8 to see how this would work:

EXHIBIT 12.8

```
var myPage = "<html><head>" + "\n";
myPage += "<title>Test Page</title>" + "\n";
myPage += "</head>" + "\n";
myPage += "<body>" + "\n";
myPage += "<h1>Placeholder</h1>" + "\n";
myPage += "</body>" + "\n";
myPage += "</html>" + "\n";
parent.side.document.open();
parent.side.document.write(myPage);
parent.side.document.close();
```

12

More typically, when you use these document methods, you will write content to a different window, thereby preserving the existing document and the ability to update the window later as necessary. You can do this by opening a new window and then writing the content. If you are using frames, you could use scripts in one of the frames to write to the contents of the other frames, such as after the user makes a selection from a selection menu.

In this exercise, you are going to see how `document.write()` and `document.writeln()` can be used to create documents in new windows. This exercise uses frames.

STEP 1 – CREATING THE MAIN FRAMES PAGE

In your text editor, create a new blank page. You will create the main frames page shown in Exhibit 12.9 and save it as exhibit12-9.htm. This example creates a frame-enhanced page with a small side frame and a large main frame. The source for the frameset will be developed in subsequent steps. These source files should be named exhibit12-10.htm and exhibit12-11.htm.

EXHIBIT 12.9

```
<html>
<head>
<title>Welcome to our site!</title>
</head>

<frameset cols="15%,85%" border=0>
  <frame name="side" src="exhibit12-10.htm">
  <frame name="main" src="exhibit12-11.htm">
</frameset>
</html>
```

STEP 2 – CREATING THE SIDE FRAME

In your text editor, create a new blank page. You will create the side frame as shown in Exhibit 12.10 and save the page as exhibit12-10.htm. This frame defines a script that creates a window when a button is clicked. As you can see from Exhibit 12.10, one way to add text to the help window is with a series of `write` statements. After the method `document.write()` is used to write output to the new window, the `document.close()` method is used to close the write stream to the window.

EXHIBIT 12.10

```
<head>
<title>Menu Page</title>
</head>

<script type="text/javascript">
var helpWindow;
```

```
function createHelpWindow() {
  if (!helpWindow || helpWindow.closed) {
    helpWindow = window.open("","Help","resizable,
      scrollbars,height=300,width=480");
    helpWindow.document.write("<html><head><title>
      Getting Help...</title></head>");
    helpWindow.document.write("<body bgcolor=
      '#FFFFFF'>");
    helpWindow.document.write("<h1>Welcome to the Help
      System</h1>");
    helpWindow.document.write("<h2>About Our
      Site</h2>");
    helpWindow.document.write("<p>insert site
      information text here</p>");
    helpWindow.document.write("<h2>Caching
      Problems</h2>");
    helpWindow.document.write("<p>insert caching
      information here</p>");
    helpWindow.document.write("<h2>Trouble With
      Cookies</h2>");
    helpWindow.document.write("<p>insert cookie
      information here</p>");
    helpWindow.document.close();
  }
}
</script>
<body>
<h3>Main Menu</h3>
<form><input type="button" Value="Get Help"
  onclick="createHelpWindow()" />
</form>
</body>
</html>
```

12

STEP 3 – CREATING THE MAIN FRAME

In your text editor, create a new blank page. You will create the main frame as shown in Exhibit 12.11 and save the page as exhibit12-11.htm. This frame defines the main text of the Web site. Although in this example you are using placeholder text, you could easily update the example to work for an actual Web site. As you study the example, compare the writeSide() function in this exhibit with the createHelpWindow() function in the previous exhibit. Note how the button in the body of the page is used to call the writeSide() function, which when called rewrites the side frame. In this example, parent is a reference to the parent of the current frame document, which is the frame source page, and parent.side is a reference to the frame page we named "side" within our frameset tag. Another way to reference this frame would have been to use the index of zero in the `frames[]` array, as in `parent.frames[0]`.

EXHIBIT 12.11

```
<head>
<title>Main Page</title>
<script type="text/javascript">

function writeSide() {

  var page = "<html><head>" + "\n";
  page += "<title>Menu Page</title>" + "\n";
  page += "</head>" + "\n";
  page += "<body>" + "\n";
  page += "\n";
  page += "<h3>News</h3>" + "\n";
  page += "\n";
  page += "<form><input type='button' Value='Current
     News' onclick='alert()' />" + "\n";
  page += "</form>" + "\n";
  page += "</body>" + "\n";
  page += "</html>" + "\n";

  parent.side.document.open();
  parent.side.document.write(page);
  parent.side.document.close();
}

</script>
</head>
<body bgcolor="#000000" text="#FFFFFF">
<h3>Welcome to our site!</h3>
<p>This is the main page for our site!</p>
<form>
<input type="button" value="Additional News"
   onclick="writeSide()" />
</form>
</body>
</html>
```

STEP 4 – DISPLAYING AND TESTING THE PAGE

In Internet Explorer, open the main frames page from Exhibit 12.9. When you click the button in the side frame, the help window should be displayed, as shown in Figure 12.4. When you are writing to a separate window, you can use multiple `write()` or `writeln()` statements, as shown in Exhibit 12.10, or you can assemble the necessary markup as a complete object, pass this object to a single `document.write()` statement, and then issue a `document.close()`, as shown in Exhibit 12.11. Although

FIGURE 12.4 Writing to a window using the methods of the `document` object.

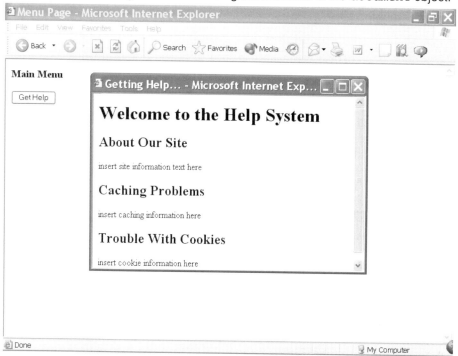

some situations may require you to use one technique or the other, performance should always be considered. You will get better performance when you use fewer `write()` or `writeln()` statements.

It is also important to note that if you want to write embedded objects (such as images or applets) as part of the page you are creating, you should use a complete URL reference instead of a relative URL. If you set the width and height attributes for images and other objects, you will make it so the browser can render the page faster because it can layout the page before the image/object contents are loaded.

You should note the technique used to write content to a window. If you want to write content to the current window, you can use the following technique:

```
document.open()
document.write(contents)
document.close()
```

To write to a named window, you can use:

```
windowName.open()
windowName.write(contents)
windowName.close()
```

In both examples, `contents` is a variable that contains the source of the page you want to write.

12

Summary

In this chapter, you have learned techniques for customizing pages using the `document` object, using arrays of objects contained in documents, and writing the contents of pages using scripts. As you have seen, the `document` object has many useful properties, methods, and event handlers. A key thing to remember is that this chapter only touches the tip of the iceberg with regard to the `document` object.

As you learned in this chapter, the `document` object is the container for all elements in a Web page. You can customize pages using the `document` object, access arrays of objects, and change the page contents using the `document` object. Other chapters in this book will continue the discussion of the `document` object and related objects.

Test Your Skills

Practice Drill 12.1: Customizing a Frame

Previously, you learned how to use `document` object properties to help manage user preferences and color settings. This was the subject of Exercise 12.1. In this exercise, you are going to update this source code to work with frames. To write to a frame, you first reference the main frame source page (the parent) and then either reference the name of the frame or the frame's index in the `frames[]` array, as shown in this example:

```
parent.frames[1].document.open()
parent.frames[1].document.write(contents)
parent.frames[1].document.close()
```

Here, you are referencing the second frame in a frameset.

The following example shows how you can use one window to update the contents of another window.

1. In your text editor, create a main frameset page. Use a frameset with a side frame and a main frame. Save the page as C12frames.htm.
   ```
   <html>
   <head>
   <title>Welcome to our site!</title>
   </head>

   <frameset cols="20%,80%" border=0>
     <frame name="side" src="side.htm">
     <frame name="main" src="main.htm">
   </frameset>
   </html>
   ```

2. In your text editor, open the final page created in Exercise 12.1 and save it as side.htm.

3. In your text editor, modify side.htm so that when you make a color selection, the main frame is updated as appropriate for the selection. Hint: You can reference the main frame by name or by its index in the `frames[]` array.

4. In your text editor, create the main frame page. Use the source as shown and save it as main.htm.

```
<head>
<title>My Web Site</title>
</head>
<body>
<h3>My Web Site</h3>
<p>Welcome to my web site. There is lots to do and
   see here so stick around for awhile!</p>

<h3>Other Sites</h3>
<p>Looking for other sites to visit? Here's a list
   of my favorite sites.</p>
<p><a href="http://www.robertstanek.com/">Robert
   Stanek's Site</a></p>
<p><a href="http://www.ruinmist.com/">The Ruin Mist
   Site</a></p>
</body>
</html>
```

5. Load C12frames.htm into Internet Explorer 5.0 or later. The page should display as shown in Figure 12.5.

FIGURE 12.5 Updating other windows is easy once you know how to reference them.

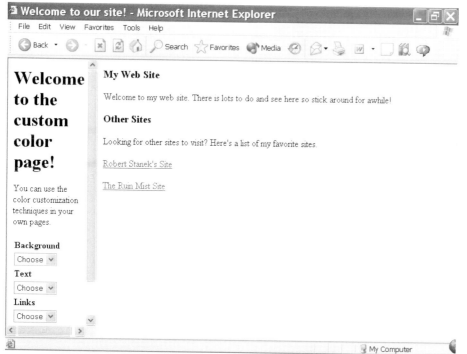

6. Using the selection options on the side frame, try changing the colors of the main page. If you have updated the page correctly, the colors should change to whatever you set.

Practice Drill 12.2: Writing Custom Content to a Page

On the Web, you will often find pages that have different content every time you visit them. You can use the `document.write()` method to create pages that are customized for users as well. In this exercise, you will learn two simple techniques for making the user's browsing experience unique every time the user visits your site. This exercise builds on the main frame created in the previous exercise.

1. In your text editor, create a main frameset page. Use a frameset with a side frame and a main frame. Save the page as C12frames2.htm.

```html
<html>
<head>
<title>Welcome to our site!</title>
</head>

<frameset cols="20%,80%" border=0>
 <frame name="side" src="side.htm">
 <frame name="main" src="main2.htm">
</frameset>
</html>
```

2. Add the following header-defined script to the frameset page. This script creates a custom-formatted date entry that details the day of the week, the month, and the date (e.g., Monday, December 25).

```javascript
<script type="text/javascript">

currMonth = new Array(12);
currMonth[1] = "January";
currMonth[2] = "February";
currMonth[3] = "March";
currMonth[4] = "April";
currMonth[5] = "May";
currMonth[6] = "June";
currMonth[7] = "July";
currMonth[8] = "August";
currMonth[9] = "September";
currMonth[10] = "October";
currMonth[11] = "November";
currMonth[12] = "December";

currDays = new Array(7);
currDays[1] = "Sunday";
currDays[2] = "Monday";
currDays[3] = "Tuesday";
currDays[4] = "Wednesday";
```

```
currDays[5] = "Thursday";
currDays[6] = "Friday";
currDays[7] = "Saturday";

function customDate(aDate) {
  var currentDay = currDays[aDate.getDay() + 1];
  var currentMonth = currMonth[aDate.getMonth() + 1];
  return currentDay + ", " + currentMonth + " " +
      aDate.getDate();
}
</script>
```

3. In your text editor, open the main frame page created in the previous example (main.htm). Insert the following script after the open body tag (<body>) and save the modified page as main2.htm. This body-defined script inserts the custom date entry into a right-aligned paragraph by calling the customDate() function in the parent document (the frameset page). The font size is enlarged using the FONT element, and the date text is displayed in bold using the bold() method of the String object.

```
<script type="text/javascript">
today = new Date();
display = "";
display += "<p align='right'><font size=+1>";
display += parent.customDate(today).bold();
display += "</font></p>";
document.write(display);
</script>
```

4. Load C12frames2.htm into Internet Explorer 5.0 or later. If you have made the edits correctly, the page should display as shown in Figure 12.6. As you can see from this example, body-defined scripts can be used to write custom content to the page.

MULTIPLE-CHOICE QUESTIONS

1. What property of the document object do you use to set the color of text on a page?

   A. text
   B. bgColor
   C. color
   D. fgColor

2. If you want to write content to a page or window, what method of the document object do you use?

   A. open()
   B. write()

12

FIGURE 12.6 Updating the body of the page can be accomplished with writes as well.

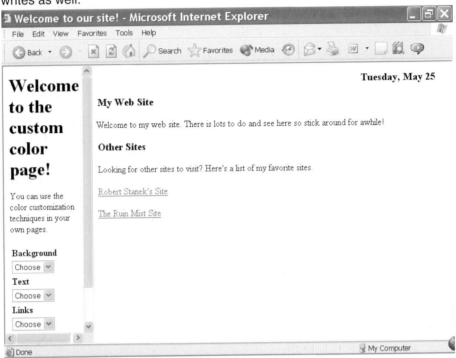

C. writeln()

D. writeit()

E. Either B or C

3. How are values set for color-related properties?

A. As 16-bit colors

B. As 24-bit colors

C. As hexadecimal triplet values

D. As Netscape color names

E. C and D only

4. Which method of the document object closes the write stream?

A. clear()

B. close()

C. done()

D. finish()

E. load()

5. If a page has several forms, to which form does `document.forms[1]` refer to?

    A. The first form on the page

    B. The form on the page named "1"

    C. The form on the page with one element

    D. The form in the index array

    E. The second form on the page

FILL-IN-THE-BLANK QUESTIONS

1. The _____ method is used to write a string to a page or window without inserting a carriage return.

2. _____ refers to the first frame in a frameset by its index position.

3. The _____ method is used to write a line to a page or window.

4. The _____ property sets the color for active links in a page.

5. The _____ property sets the color for visited links in a page.

6. The _____ property sets the color for unvisited links in a page.

7. If you want to determine the number of elements in a form, you can use the length property of the _____ array.

8. If you want to create a new window and write content to it, you'll use the _____, _____, and _____ methods.

9. You can determine when a document was last modified using the _____ property of the `document` object.

10. The _____ and _____ properties return the pixel dimensions of the content in the current window.

DEFINITIONS QUESTIONS

1. When you want to set the background color of the page, which property of the `document` object do you use?

2. When you want to set the color of text on the page, which property of the `document` object do you use?

3. Through which array do you reference forms by their index position?

4. Through which array do you reference frames by their index position?

5. What method of the `document` object do you need to call before you can write content to a new window?

12

INTERMEDIATE PROJECTS

The following short projects provide you with the opportunity to work with and create custom windows.

Project 12.1 – Customizing Pages for Users

This project will require you to create a frame-enhanced page that is split 30/70 between a top frame and a bottom frame. The top frame should contain a form whose elements, when updated, are used to customize the elements in the bottom frame.

As a starting point, the main frameset page should have the following source and be saved as C12project1.htm:

```
<html>
<head>
<title>Welcome to our site!</title>
</head>

<frameset rows="30%,70%" border=0>
  <frame name="Top" src="top.htm">
  <frame name="Bottom" src="bottom.htm">
</frameset>
</html>
```

The form should collect the user's name in an input field, and a set of radio buttons should be used to determine if the visitor is a child, a teen, or an adult. The initial content of the bottom frame can be empty, as shown in this example:

```
<html>
<head>
<title>Welcome to our site!</title>
</head>
</html>
```

Once a user enters information in the form and clicks a button labeled "Customize," the `customizeIt()` function should be called and the bottom frame should display customized information for the current visitor using the visitor's name and age information.

In a script, you can determine the value of an input field using the value property. For example if an input field is named `firstName`, you can obtain the value set using:

```
form.firstName.value
```

The way you determine the radio button that has been selected is to iterate through the list of available radio buttons and see which radio button has the checked property set to true. You could then read the value of this checked property and break out of the `for` loop. Here is an example:

```
for (var i = 0; i < form.age.length; i++) {
  if (form.age[i].checked) {
    //read the value
    //break out of the loop
    }
}
```

Once you have created the required pages, load the frameset page into Internet Explorer and Netscape Navigator to see if it displays correctly. The page should look similar to Figure 12.7. When you type your name and make an age selection, the page should update as shown in Figure 12.8.

FIGURE 12.7 Collecting user information in a form.

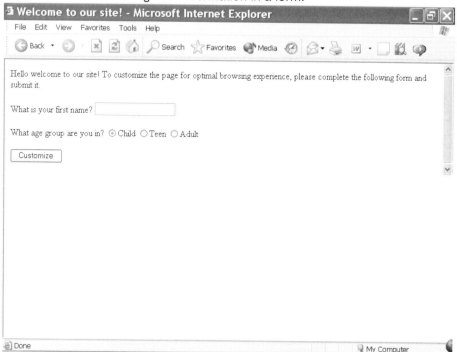

Project 12.2 – Customizing a Page On-the-Fly

This project will require you to modify Project 12.1 so that the page can be updated on-the-fly without the user having to click the Customize button. To help differentiate the projects, you will use the following frameset page:

```
<html>
<head>
<title>Welcome to our site!</title>
</head>

<frameset rows="30%,70%" border=0>
  <frame name="Upper" src="upper.htm">
  <frame name="Lower" src="lower.htm">
</frameset>
</html>
```

The form elements should collect the same information as before, but each should have its own event handler rather than a button. Because you want to be sure that no

FIGURE 12.8 Customizing the page based on user input.

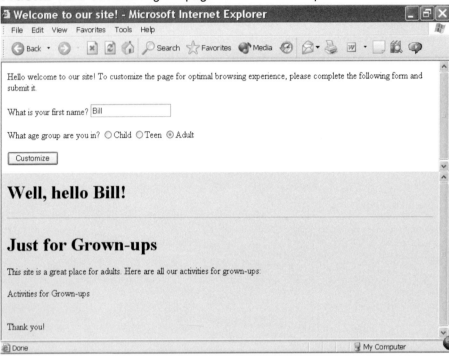

content is displayed unless it is appropriate, there should not be a default selection for content type. The initial content of the lower frame can be empty, as shown in this example:

```
<html>
<head>
<title>Welcome to our site!</title>
</head>
</html>
```

When you are finished, load the page into Internet Explorer and Netscape Navigator and test the window management functions you have defined. When you type your name in the input field and press Tab⇆, the page should look similar to Figure 12.9. Notice that there is no age-based content because no radio button selection has been made.

FIGURE 12.9 A customized page with on-the-fly updates.

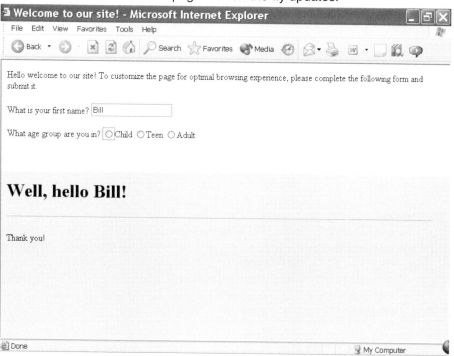

Career Builder

In this chapter, you have learned many useful skills for customizing documents. After following this chapter, you should have a number of ideas on how you can customize pages and manage content with utility functions. You should be able to easily modify the functions shown in this chapter so that you can use them in your real-world scripts.

The Career Builder exercise for this chapter is to use the skills you have learned to create a help and customization system for a JavaScript-based application. This application will use a frame-enhanced page divided into two columns. The smaller left column will contain the menu. The larger right column will contain the main application elements.

1. This example is all about putting the `document` object to use in a real-world project. Some sites on the Web offer help or tips to users via hypertext links in their pages. Using JavaScript, you can provide a more complete set of options for an application using a frame-enhanced page. The frameset page for the application has the source as shown in

(continued)

12

the following statements. Add the `customDate()` function to the header so that a custom date can be displayed in the side frame.

```html
<html>
<head>
<title>JavaScript Application</title>
<script type="text/javascript">

currMonth = new Array(12);
currMonth[1] = "January";
currMonth[2] = "February";
currMonth[3] = "March";
currMonth[4] = "April";
currMonth[5] = "May";
currMonth[6] = "June";
currMonth[7] = "July";
currMonth[8] = "August";
currMonth[9] = "September";
currMonth[10] = "October";
currMonth[11] = "November";
currMonth[12] = "December";

currDays = new Array(7);
currDays[1] = "Sunday";
currDays[2] = "Monday";
currDays[3] = "Tuesday";
currDays[4] = "Wednesday";
currDays[5] = "Thursday";
currDays[6] = "Friday";
currDays[7] = "Saturday";

function customDate(aDate) {
  var currentDay = currDays[aDate.getDay() + 1];
  var currentMonth = currMonth[aDate.getMonth() + 1];
  return currentDay + ", " + currentMonth + " " +
    aDate.getDate();
}

</script>
</head>

<frameset cols="15%,85%" border=0>
  <frame name="side" src="cb-side.htm">
  <frame name="main" src="cb-main.htm">
</frameset>
</html>
```

2. Next you will need to define the source for the side frame. In this frame, add the body-defined script that displays the custom date as well as the color selection script created earlier in the chapter. You need to

(continued)

make a fundamental change to the color-selection script so that it changes the colors in the main frame as well as the side frame, as shown in the following statements.

```html
<html>
<head>
<title>Menu Page</title>
<script type="text/javascript">

function setBColor(form,index) {
  var userColor = "";
  for (var i = 0; i < form.backColor.length; i++) {
    if (form.backColor.options[i].selected)
        userColor = form.backColor.options[i].text;
  }
  parent.frames[0].document.bgColor = userColor;
  parent.frames[1].document.bgColor = userColor;
}

function setTColor(form,index) {
  var userColor = "";
  for (var i = 0; i < form.textColor.length; i++) {
    if (form.textColor.options[i].selected)
        userColor = form.textColor.options[i].text;
  }
  parent.frames[0].document.fgColor = userColor;
  parent.frames[1].document.fgColor = userColor;
}

function setLColor(form,index) {
  var userColor = "";
  for (var i = 0; i < form.linkColor.length; i++) {
    if (form.linkColor.options[i].selected)
        userColor = form.linkColor.options[i].text;
  }
  parent.frames[0].document.linkColor = userColor;
  parent.frames[0].document.vlinkColor = userColor;
  parent.frames[0].document.alinkColor = userColor;

  parent.frames[1].document.linkColor = userColor;
  parent.frames[1].document.vlinkColor = userColor;
  parent.frames[1].document.alinkColor = userColor;
}
</script>
</head>
<body bgcolor="#FFFFFF">
<script type="text/javascript">
today = new Date();
display = "";
```

12

(continued)

```
display += "<p align='right'><font size=+1>";
display += parent.customDate(today).bold();
display += "</font></p>";
document.write(display);
</script>
<form>
<table>
<tr><th align=left>Background</th></tr>
<tr><td><select name="backColor" size=1
onChange="setBColor(this.form,'bgColor')">
<option>Choose</option>
<option>Aqua</option>
<option>Black</option>
<option>Blue</option>
<option>Fuchsia</option>
<option>Gray</option>
<option>Green</option>
<option>Lime</option>
<option>Maroon</option>
<option>Navy</option>
<option>Olive</option>
<option>Purple</option>
<option>Red</option>
<option>Silver</option>
<option>Teal</option>
<option>White</option>
<option>Yellow</option>
</select></td></tr>
<tr><th align=left>Text</th></tr>
<tr>
<td><select name="textColor" size=1 onChange=
    "setTColor(this.form,'textColor')">
<option>Choose</option>
<option>Aqua</option>
<option>Black</option>
<option>Blue</option>
<option>Fuchsia</option>
<option>Gray</option>
<option>Green</option>
<option>Lime</option>
<option>Maroon</option>
<option>Navy</option>
<option>Olive</option>
<option>Purple</option>
<option>Red</option>
<option>Silver</option>
<option>Teal</option>
```

(continued)

```
<option>White</option>
<option>Yellow</option>
</select></td></tr>
<tr><th align=left>Links</th></tr>
<tr>
<td><select name="linkColor" size=1 onChange=
    "setLColor(this.form,'linkColor')">
<option>Choose</option>
<option>Aqua</option>
<option>Black</option>
<option>Blue</option>
<option>Fuchsia</option>
<option>Gray</option>
<option>Green</option>
<option>Lime</option>
<option>Maroon</option>
<option>Navy</option>
<option>Olive</option>
<option>Purple</option>
<option>Red</option>
<option>Silver</option>
<option>Teal</option>
<option>White</option>
<option>Yellow</option>
</select></td></tr>
</table>
</form>
</body>
</html>
```

3. To complete this part of the Career Builder exercise, define the main page for the application. When you are finished, save all of the pages and then load the frameset page in Internet Explorer 5.0 or later. Test the application to make sure everything is working as expected.

   In the next chapter, we will extend this Career Builder to add help functionality.

12

Chapter | 13

Scripting Embedded Objects

In this chapter, you will learn techniques for scripting embedded objects. In addition to typical text and images, you can embed other kinds of content in Web pages. You can use hypertext links to create links between and within pages. You can use applets or ActiveX controls to provide additional functionality. Although these applets, controls, and other types of embedded content usually require browser extensions or plug-ins to load and display, all types of embedded content are accessed in scripts in much the same way and typically through one of several types of special arrays. You use the links[] array to work with hypertext links between pages, the anchors[] array to work with named anchors within pages, and the applets[] array to work with applets. Because the applet element has been deprecated in favor of the object element in HTML 4.0, this chapter also examines how you can work with the object element. The object element can be used to represent any type of embedded content and also replaces the rarely used embed element.

For Your Career

This chapter's primary focus is on the special arrays accessible via the document object and the object element. It does not cover the embeds[] array, because the embed element is rarely used and has been deprecated in favor of the object element. The chapter does go into detail on scripting the applets[] array, because the applet element continues to be used.

Chapter Exercises

This unit's exercises will teach you how to:

- Work with hypertext links in documents
- Examine and navigate anchors in documents
- Use scripts to work with applets
- Obtain information about embedded objects
- Reference embedded objects between frames

By working through the exercises, not only will you learn many things about links, anchors, embedded objects, and frames, you will also learn how these elements can be accessed in scripts.

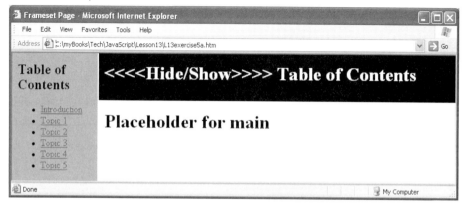

**Use the links[]
Array Carefully**

The following link ob-
ject event handlers are
available only in
Netscape Navigator 4.0,
Internet Explorer 4.0, or
later versions of these
browsers: ondblclick,
onmousedown,
onmouseout, and
onmouseup.

Exercise 13.1 – Examining the link Object

When you load a page into your browser, the browser uses arrays to track all links, anchors, forms, images, frames, and embedded objects. Each object has an index in the
array that is set according to the object's location in the page. The link object has ties
to all of the hypertext links in your pages. For example, properties of the first link on
the page are created with a <a href=""> tag and stored in the links[] array at
index 0.

Table 13.1 provides an overview of the properties, methods, and events of the
link object. In fact, link objects are a special type of location object whose
properties are, for the most part, extracted from the <a href="" assignment of a
specific link. This means that link objects support all of the properties of the
window.location object, which is discussed in Chapter 14, and the target property. Using the target property, you can get and set the target of a link, which is useful in frame-enhanced pages.

TABLE 13.1 The link object

Properties	Methods	Event Handlers
links[i].target	(none)	onclick=
links[i].hash		ondblclick
links[i].host		onmousedown
links[i].hostname		onmouseout
links[i].href		onmouseover
links[i].pathname		onmouseup
links[i].port		
links[i].protocol		
links[i].search		

As shown in Table 13.1, the link object uses several event handlers, including
onmouseover and onmouseout. These event handlers are inherited from the
location object. The onmouseover event executes automatically when the mouse
is moved over a hypertext link; the onmouseout event executes when you move the
mouse away from a link.

You set a message to display when the mouse is over a link as follows:

```
<a href="home.htm" onmouseover="window.status = 'Visit
    Our Home Page'" > Home Page </a>
```

You are using a location object to do this.

Table 13.2 describes the properties of the link object. As you study the table, keep
in mind that the properties are specific to a particular <a href=""> or <a

TABLE 13.2 The `link` object properties summary.

Property	Value	Type	Description
hash	String	Read/Write	Allows you to check or set an internal page link, designated with the hash mark (#). An example value is <u>#ruinmist</u>. Supported by NN2, IE3 and later as well as Mozilla and Safari.
host	String	Read/Write	Allows you to check or set the current hostname and port information in the designated link. An example value is <u>www. robertstanek.com:80</u>. Supported by NN2, IE3 and later as well as Mozilla and Safari.
hostname	String	Read/Write	Allows you to check or set the current hostname in the designated link. An example value is <u>www.robertstanek.com</u>. Supported by NN2, IE3 and later as well as Mozilla and Safari.
href	String	Read/Write	Provides the complete URL of the link; can be used to set the URL as well. An example value is <u>http://www.robertstanek. com:80/curr/books.html</u>. Supported by NN2, IE3 and later as well as Mozilla and Safari.
pathname	String	Read/Write	Allows you to check or set the URL path information in the designated link, which is relative to the current directory on the server. An example value is <u>/curr/books.html</u>. Supported by NN2, IE3 and later as well as Mozilla and Safari.
port	String	Read/Write	Allows you to check or set the current server port in the designated link. An example value is 80. Supported by NN2, IE3 and later as well as Mozilla and Safari.

13

TABLE 13.2 (*Continued*)

Property	Value	Type	Description
protocol	String	Read/Write	Allows you to check or set the protocol in the designated link. An example value is http:. Supported by NN2, IE3 and later as well as Mozilla and Safari.
search	String	Read/Write	Allows you to check or set the search query/form post information in the designated link. Basically, this is everything appended after the URL and starting with the question mark added for queries. An example value is ?books+ruin+mist. Supported by NN2, IE3 and later as well as Mozilla and Safari.
target	String	Read/Write	Allows you to check or set the target of the designated link. An example value is main. Supported by NN2, IE3 and later as well as Mozilla and Safari.

href="" target=""> assignment. As you study the table, consider the following assignment:

```
<a href="http://www.robertstanek.com:80/curr/books.html#
  ruinmist" target="main">
```

You can set and get properties of links by referencing the links[] array and the index of the link you want to work with. For example, if you want to get the value of the target for the first link in the page, you would use the following code:

```
targetName = document.links[0].target;
```

If you wanted to set the target name, you could do this as well. The following example sets the target name to main:

```
document.links[0].target = "main";
```

In this exercise, you will create a Web page with several links and display information about those links using the links[] array.

STEP 1 – CREATING A PAGE WITH LINKS

In your text editor, create a new Web page using the markup shown in Exhibit 13.1. Note that the page contains several links. You can use the links shown or add your own.

EXHIBIT 13.1

```
<html>
<head>
<title>Working with Links</title>
</head>
<body>
<h1>My Links</h1>
<p><a href="http://www.robertstanek.com/">Robert Stanek
  Page</a></p>
<p><a href="http://www.ruinmist.com/">Ruin Mist
  Page</a></p>
<p><a href="http://ruinmist.proboards23.com/">Ruin Mist
  Discussion</a></p>
</body>
</html>
```

STEP 2 – ADDING A FUNCTION TO EXAMINE LINKS

In your text editor, edit the page created in the previous step. Using the source shown in Exhibit 13.2, add a body-defined script that uses the `links[]` array to display information about the links in the page.

EXHIBIT 13.2

```
<script type="text/javascript">
document.write("<p>I hope you'll visit " + document.
  links[0].href + ". You might also like to visit "
  + document.links[1].href + ". And if you are
  interested in discussion, stop by " +
  document.links[2].href + ".</p>");
</script>
```

STEP 3 – DISPLAYING THE PAGE

In Internet Explorer, open the page you created in Steps 1 and 2. If you have edited the page correctly, you should see a list of links followed by a summary paragraph providing more information about the links. Note that if you were to change the links in the page, the rest of the text in the string you have passed to `document.write` would still be accurate. The reason for this is that the `links[i].href` property would be updated to reflect the current value of the `<a href="">` tag.

13

Exercise 13.2 – Examining the `anchor` Object

You use the `document.anchors` property to access the anchors in your pages according to their index. In HTML, you label anchors with the `name` attribute, as in the following example:

```
<h1><a name="Intro"> Introduction</a></h1>
```

If this was the first anchor on the page, you could reference this anchor as follows:

```
document.anchors[0]
```

The `anchor` object has no properties, methods, or events you can access directly. Like `link` objects, `anchor` objects are created when you access a Web page in a browser.

To track the number of entries in the `anchors[]` array, and thereby the number of anchors in a Web page, you can use the length property of the `array` object. You may want to assign the value returned by this property to a variable such as:

```
numAnchors = document.anchors.length;
```

In this exercise, you will create a Web page with several anchors and then navigate to those anchors with a script.

STEP 1 – CREATING A PAGE WITH ANCHORS

In your text editor, create a new Web page. You will create a sample HTML page using the source shown in Exhibit 13.3. Your page should contain the anchors as shown. Note that each anchor has a unique name. Note that the page has a body-defined script that displays the number of anchors in the page.

EXHIBIT 13.3

```
<html>
<head>
<title>Using the Anchor Object</title>
</head>
<body>
<h1><a id="intro" name="intro">Introduction</a></h1>
<p>This is the introduction.</p>
<hr size="2"/>
<h1><a id="section1" name="section1">Section 1</a></h1>
<p>This is section 1.</p>
<hr size="2"/>
<h1><a id="section2" name="section2">Section 2</a></h1>
<p>This is section 2.</p>
<hr size="2"/>
<h1><a id="section3" name="section3">Section 3</a></h1>
<p>This is section 3.</p>
```

```
<hr size="2"/>
<h1><a id="section4" name="section4">Section 4</a></h1>
<p>This is section 4.</p>
<hr size="2"/>
<p>
<script type="text/javascript">
document.write("<p>This page has " + document.anchors.
  length + " anchors defined</p>")
</script>
</p>
</body>
</html>
```

STEP 2 – ADDING NAVIGATION FUNCTIONALITY

In your text editor, edit the page created in the previous step. Add forms to the Introduction and Sections 1, 2, and 3. Each form should have a button that when clicked passes the name of the section to a function called nextAnchor(), as shown in the following example. In Section 4, add a form with a button, as in the preceding sections, but modify the button so that its label is "Back To Top" and it refers to "Introduction."

```
<form>
 <input type="button" name="next" value="Next Section"
 onclick="nextAnchor('section1')" />
</form>
```

STEP 3 – DEFINING THE NEXTANCHOR() FUNCTION

In your text editor, add a header-defined script that provides the navigation functionality. You script navigation to a particular anchor by assigning a value to the window.location.hash property as shown in the following example:

```
<script type="text/javascript">
function nextAnchor(theAnchor) {
window.location.hash = theAnchor;
}
</script>
```

13

STEP 4 – LOADING AND TESTING THE PAGE

In Internet Explorer, open the page you created as shown in Figure 13.1. Click the buttons to navigate through the document. If you have edited the page correctly, you should be able to navigate through each section of the document and then go back to the top of the document by clicking the button in Section 4.

FIGURE 13.1 Using a script to navigate a document's anchor tags.

Exercise 13.3 – Examining the `applet` Object

Check Property and Event Handler Support for the `applet` Object

The following `applet` object event handlers are available only in the Windows versions of Internet Explorer 5.0 or later: `oncellchange`, `ondataavailable`, `ondatasetchanged`, `onrowenter`, `onrowexit`, `onrowsdelete`, and `onrowsinserted`. The `archive` attribute is only available in Windows versions of Internet Explorer 6.0 or later.

`Applet` objects are created when you use the `<applet>` tag in a Web page. As soon as an applet is loaded into your page, you can read and write all the properties and methods of the applet just as you would read and write properties and methods for other JavaScript objects.

Table 13.3 provides an overview of the properties, methods, and events of the `applet` object.

Although `applet` objects have many properties and event handlers, in practice these properties and event handlers are rarely used except perhaps to set initial values for an applet. More commonly, scripts work with the properties and methods defined in the code of the applet itself.

As with the `anchor` object, you cannot access applet objects directly. Instead, you will access applets via the `document` object, either by name or by their index in the `applets[]` array. The name you use to reference an applet is the one assigned in the name attribute of the `<applet>` tag. If the following applet definition is in your Web page:

```
<applet code="myApp.class" name="applet1"></applet>
```

you would access the applet using this:

```
document.applet1.property
```

TABLE 13.3 The applet object.

Properties	Methods	Event Handlers
align	(Applet methods)	oncellchange
alt		ondataavailable
altHTML		ondatasetchanged
archive		ondatasetcomplete
code		onload
height		onrowenter
hspace		onrowexit
name		onrowsdelete
object		onrowsinserted
vspace		onscroll
width		
(Applet variables)		

or this:

```
document.applet1.method(parameters)
```

The general syntax for accessing applets by index is this:

```
document.applets[index].property
```

or this:

```
document.applets[index].method(parameters)
```

In this exercise, you will create a Web page with an applet and then display information about the applet.

STEP 1 – CREATING A PAGE WITH APPLETS

In your text editor, create a new Web page. You will create a sample HTML page as shown in Exhibit 13.4. Your page should contain the <applet> tags as shown. Note that you set the code attribute to an empty string so that your browser does not attempt to load actual applets.

EXHIBIT 13.4

```
<html>
<head>
<title>Using the Applet Object</title>
</head>
<body>
```

13

```
<h1>Applet Example</h1>
<applet code="" name="circles" height="200"
   width="400"></applet>
<applet code="" name="squares" height="200"
   width="400"></applet>
</body>
</html>
```

STEP 2 – GETTING INFORMATION ABOUT THE APPLET

In your text editor, edit the page you created in the previous step. Using the source shown in Exhibit 13.5, add a body-defined script that displays the number of applets defined in the page and the names of the applets. To display the names of the applets, you can use a `for` loop. To do this, use the `length` property of the `document.applets[]` array to control the number of iterations through the `for` loop.

EXHIBIT 13.5

```
<script type="text/javascript">
document.write("<p>There are " + document.applets.
   length + " applets defined for this document<\p>")
for (x = 0; x < document.applets.length; x++) {
document.write("<p>Applet " + x + " is " +
   document.applets[x].name + "</p>")
}
</script>
```

STEP 3 – LOADING AND TESTING THE PAGE

In Internet Explorer, open the page you created. If you have edited the page correctly, you should see the page as shown in Figure 13.2.

Exercise 13.4 – Examining Embedded Objects

The `<applet>` tag was defined for use with applets only. With the introduction of other types of embedded objects, including Flash and ActiveX Controls, the `<applet>` tag was deprecated in favor of the `<object>` tag in HTML 4.0. As Table 13.4 shows, `object` shares many of the same properties and event handlers with `applet`.

As with the `applet` object, the properties and methods of the `object` object are rarely used except perhaps to set initial values for an object. More commonly, scripts work with the properties and methods defined in the code of the object itself. Let's say

FIGURE 13.2 Examining applet information in scripts.

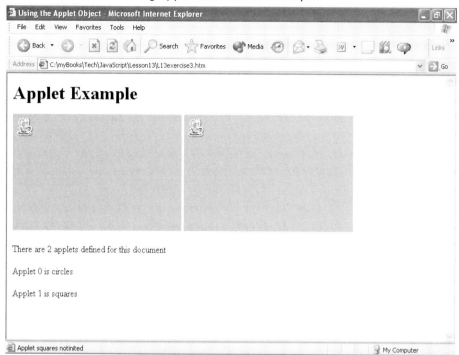

you defined an applet with the `<object>` tag as follows:

```
<object code="myApplet" id="theApp">
```

If the applet had a public variable called `numQuestions`, you could access the variable using the `getElementByID()` method of the `document` object as shown in this example:

```
document.getElementByID("theApp").numQuestions = 10;
```

Here, you access an element by its ID, which in this case is "theApp," and set the `numQuestions` property of the related object to 10. It is important to note that an object related to any element with an `ID` attribute can be obtained using the `document.getElementByID()` method. Once you have the associated object, you can work with it just as you would normally.

It is possible for an object to have properties with the same name as those of the `object` element itself. In this case, however, an attempt to read or write the property through the `object` element itself would read or write the `element` property and not the property of the object. Consider the following example:

```
document.getElementByID("theApp").form = 3;
```

Here, the applet has a property called `form`, which determines the type of questions, and you meant to specify that form 3 should be used. However, the `object` element

---

T I P

The Case of No Ambiguity Is Different

Under normal circumstances, when there is no ambiguity, the browser will check the element first and then the object to find a match. It is also important to note that there is not a `document.objects[]` array. This means that the `getElementByID()` and `getElementsByName()` functions provide the only way to script objects defined with the `object` element.

13

TABLE 13.4 The `object` object.

Properties	Methods	Event Handlers
align	(Object methods)	oncellchange
alt		ondatavailable
altHTML		ondatasetchanged
archive		ondatasetcomplete
BaseHref		onload
baseURI		onrowenter
border		onrowexit
classid		onrowsdelete
code		onrowsinserted
codeBase		onscroll
codeType		
contentDocument		
data		
form		
height		
hspace		
name		
object		
type		
useMap		
vspace		
width		
(Object variables)		

has a `form` property (which is read-only) and in this case, you attempted to set it, which causes an error. To ensure that you set the property of the applet and not the `object` element, you must insert the `object` property in the reference as shown in this example:

```
document.getElementByID("theApp").object.form = 3;
```

Another way to work with objects is to use the `getElementsByName()` method of the `document` object. If an `object` tag has a `name` attribute, you can use `getElementsByName()` to work with it in much the same way that you can use the `getElementByID()` method.

In this exercise, you will create a Web page with several embedded objects and then display information about those objects.

STEP 1 – CREATING A PAGE WITH AN EMBEDDED OBJECT

In your text editor, create a new Web page. You will create a sample HTML page as shown in Exhibit 13.6. Your page should contain the `<object>` tag as shown. Keep in mind that the `classid` property represents the `classid` attribute of the `object` element. Internet Explorer uses this attribute to assign the globally unique ID (GUID) of an ActiveX control. In this example, the GUID is for the Windows Media Player control. The `codebase` attribute is used to specify the minimum version of a control that is to load. In this case, the minimum version is version 1.0.

EXHIBIT 13.6

```
<html>
<head>
<title>Using Embedded Objects</title>
</head>
<body>
<h1>Media Player</h1>
<object id="mediaPlayer" width="300" height="200"
classid="CLSID:22d6f312-b0f6-11d0-94ab-0080c74c7e95"
codebase="#Version=1,0,0,0"></object>

<h1>Details</h1>

</body>
</html>
```

STEP 2 – GETTING INFORMATION ABOUT THE EMBEDDED OBJECT

In your text editor, edit the page you created in the previous step. Using the source shown in Exhibit 13.7, add a body-defined script that examines the embedded object and displays information about the object under the Details heading. Be sure to place the code block after the media player object.

EXHIBIT 13.7

```
<script type="text/javascript">
document.write("<p>Classid : " +
  document.getElementById
  ('mediaPlayer').classid + "</p>");
document.write("<p>Codebase : " +
  document.getElementById
  ('mediaPlayer').codeBase + "</p>");
document.write("<p>Height : " + document.getElementById
  ('mediaPlayer').height + "</p>");
document.write("<p>Width : " + document.getElementById
  ('mediaPlayer').width + "</p>");
</script>
```

13

STEP 3 – LOADING AND TESTING THE PAGE

In Internet Explorer, open the page you created. If you have edited the page correctly, you should see the page as shown in Figure 13.3. The value returned for the `classid` is the complete string assigned to the attribute. It is also important to note that the `CLSID:` prefix is part of the value returned.

FIGURE 13.3 Examining embedded objects in a page.

Exercise 13.5 – Working with the `frame` Object

In previous chapters, you learned some basic frame-handling techniques. As you have seen, you can use frames to create a document with multiple window frames. One frame can contain a menu, another frame can hold the main document, and yet another frame can showcase the banners of advertisers. When you combine the versatility of frames with the power of JavaScript, you have all the ingredients necessary for advanced applications.

In HTML, you use the `<frameset>` tag to divide the browser window into rows and columns of frames. With the `src` attribute of the `<frame>` tag, a source document is associated with each frame. Here is a sample frameset that divides a window into two columns with two frames:

```
<frameset cols="20%,80%">
<frame name="Side" src="menu.htm">
<frame name="Main" src="main.htm">
</frameset>
```

If you precisely size the side frames so that all content is showing and set the `border` attribute to zero, most current browsers will create borderless frames. **_Borderless frames_** give your page a more cohesive appearance because they do not display scrollbars:

```
<frameset rows="25%,75%" border="0">
<frame name="Upper" src="banner.htm">
<frame name="Lower" src="main.htm">
</frameset>
```

JavaScript's `frame` object has all of the properties, methods, and event handlers of the `window` object. When you access the methods, properties, or event handlers, you must do so via the object hierarchy. With frames, this hierarchy is slightly different from the hierarchy you have followed thus far. Any document that contains a frameset definition is a **_parent document_**. Frames created by the parent document are referred to as **_children_**. If a script in a child frame needs to access the functions, methods, or properties of the parent document, the script must follow the hierarchy from the parent document, such as this:

```
parent.displayPage()
```

or this:

```
parent.document.myform.mybutton.click()
```

Beyond references to the parent document, you can also refer to `self` and `top`. The `self` reference is used to refer to the current window or frame. The `top` reference is used to refer to the top-most document, which is the document that contains the original frameset definition. You will use the `top` reference if your pages have multiple framesets.

When you need to reference from a parent document to a **_child document_** in a frameset, you can reference the child document according to its index position in the `frames[]` array, such as:

```
[window.]frames[1].myform.address.value
```

according to its name, also within the `frames[]` array, such as:

```
[window.]frames["Side"].myform.address.value
```

or directly by name, such as:

```
[window.]Side.myform.address.value
```

When you want to reference from a child document to another child document, you must start with a reference to the parent. Once the reference is at the parent level, you can continue the reference as you would if you were starting from the parent document. Thus, to access a form field in a frame called "Side," you could use any of these references:

```
parent.frames[1].myform.address.value
parent.frames["Side"].myform.address.value
parent.Side.myform.address.value
```

Reference Frames by Index or Name

The numeric index values for frames are based on the order in which the `<frame>` tags appear in the frameset document. You can access the frame as long as it is in the ordinal position referenced in the `frames[]` array. The simplest way, however, to access frames is to reference the frame's name. When clarity in your code is important, you should reference the frame by its defined name.

13

Knowing this, you should now be able to reference between any frame documents from parent to child, from child to parent, or from child to child.

In this exercise, you will create a Web page that uses nested framesets. You will then modify these framesets on-the-fly to either show or hide a table of contents frame.

STEP 1 – CREATING THE FRAMESET PAGE

In your text editor, create a new frameset page using the HTML shown in Exhibit 13.8. Save the page as C13exercise5a.htm. This frameset page nests one frameset within another frameset. When framesets are nested within one another, a parent-child relationship exists between containing and contained framesets. Here, `toggleFrame` and `mainFrame` are child frames of `innerFrameset`. Both `innerFrameset` and `contentsFrame` are child frames of `outerFrameset`. The best way to reference elements between these frames is to make a reference to `parent.document.getElementByID("FrameName")`.

EXHIBIT 13.8

```html
<html>
<head>
<title>Frameset Page</title>
</head>
<frameset id="outerFrameset" frameborder="no" cols=
    "150,*">
<frame id="TOC" name="contentsFrame" src=
    "C13exercise5b.htm" />
<frameset id="innerFrameset" rows="80,*">
<frame id="toggle" name="toggleFrame" src=
    "C13exercise5c.htm" />
<frame id="main" name="mainFrame" src="main.htm" />
</frameset>
</frameset>
</html>
```

STEP 2 – DEFINING THE CONTENTS FRAME

In your text editor, create a new Web page using the HTML shown in Exhibit 13.9. Save this page as C13exercise5b.htm. This page defines the contents frame and has links that target the main frame.

EXHIBIT 13.9

```html
<html>
<head>
<title>Table of Contents</title>
</head>
<body bgcolor="#A9A9A9">
```

```
<h2>Table of Contents</h2>
<ul>
<li><a href="main.htm#intro"
  target="mainFrame">Introduction</a></li>
<li><a href="main.htm#topic1" target="mainFrame">Topic
  1</a></li>
<li><a href="main.htm#topic2" target="mainFrame">Topic
  2</a></li>
<li><a href="main.htm#topic3" target="mainFrame">Topic
  3</a></li>
<li><a href="main.htm#topic4" target="mainFrame">Topic
  4</a></li>
<li><a href="main.htm#topic5" target="mainFrame">Topic
  5</a></li>
</ul>
</body>
</html>
```

STEP 3 – DEFINING THE TOGGLE FRAME

In your text editor, create a new Web page using the HTML shown in Exhibit 13.10. Save this page as C13exercise5c.htm. This page defines the toggle frame. When a user clicks the hotspot labeled Hide/Show, the `toggleContents()` function in the frameset page is called to either hide or show the contents frame as appropriate.

EXHIBIT 13.10

```
<html>
<head>
<title>Toggle</title>
</head>
<body bgcolor="#000000" text="#FFFFFF">
<h1><span id="tocToggle"
onclick="parent.toggleContents()"><<<<Hide/Show>>>></sp
  an> Table of Contents</h1>
</body>
</html>
```

13

STEP 4 – DEFINING THE TOGGLE FRAME

In your text editor, create the main frame using the HTML shown in Exhibit 13.11. Save this page as main.htm. This page defines the contents of the main page. Although the HTML shown is meant as a placeholder, you can add headings and anchors so that the links in the contents frame work when clicked, if desired.

EXHIBIT 13.11

```
<html>
<head>
<title>Main</title>
</head>
<body>
<h1><a name="intro">Introduction</a></h1>
<p> </p>
<h1><a name="topic1">Topic 1</a></h1>
<p> </p>
<h1><a name="topic1">Topic 2</a></h1>
<p> </p>
<h1><a name="topic1">Topic 3</a></h1>
<p> </p>
<h1><a name="topic1">Topic 4</a></h1>
<p> </p>
<h1><a name="topic1">Topic 5</a></h1>
<p> </p>
</body>
</html>
```

STEP 5 – DEFINING THE FRAMESET FUNCTIONS

In your text editor, open the main frameset page, C13exercise5a.htm, and add the header-defined script shown in Exhibit 13.12. Now that you have defined all the frame documents, you can define the main script that provides the hide/show contents functionality. To do this, you need a `hideTOC()` function that copies the original `cols` property settings for the `outerFrameset` to a global variable and then resizes the `cols` property so that the contents frame is hidden. The same global variable is then used in the `showTOC()` function to restore the `outerFrameset` to its original configuration. Now when the `toggleContents()` function is called, you simply test whether the global variable exists. If it exists, it means the variable has been set, and you must call `showTOC()` to restore the hidden contents frame. If it does not exist, the variable has not been set, and you must call the `hideTOC()` function to resize and hide the contents frame.

EXHIBIT 13.12

```
<script type="text/javascript">
var currCols;
function toggleContents(item, frms) {
  if (currCols) {
  showTOC(item);
```

```
  } else {
 hideTOC(item, frms);
  }
}

function hideTOC(item, frms) {
 var frameset = document.
   getElementById("outerFrameset");
 currCols = frameset.cols;
 frameset.cols = "0,*";
}

function showTOC(item) {
 if (currCols) {
 document.getElementById("outerFrameset").cols
   = currCols;
 currCols = null;
 }
}
</script>
```

STEP 6 – LOADING AND TESTING THE PAGE

In Internet Explorer, open the frameset page, C13exercise5a.htm. If you have edited the page correctly, you should see the page as shown in Figure 13.4. When you click Hide/Show, the contents frame should disappear. When you click Hide/Show again, the contents frame should be restored.

FIGURE 13.4 Showing or hiding a frame.

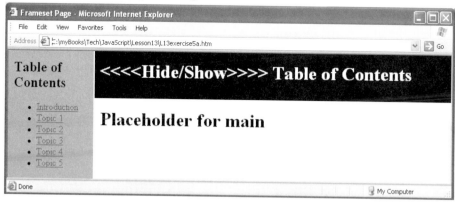

13

Summary

Most Web pages have text and images as well as other types of embedded elements. These embedded elements can include links, anchors, applets, ActiveX controls, and more—all of which can be manipulated in scripts. You can use the `links[]` array to examine a document's links, the `anchors[]` array to work with a document's anchors, and the `applets[]` array to work with a document's applets. Other types of objects, such as ActiveX controls, can be manipulated using the `object` element with which they are defined. If you create a superset of documents using a frameset document, you can create pages with multiple frames. To reference elements from one frame to the next, you can use the `frames[]` array as well as the window hierarchy.

Test Your Skills

Practice Drill 13.1: Iterating Through the `links[]` Array

Previously, you learned how to access individual links in the `links[]` array. In some cases, you might want to iterate through all of the links in a page and either manipulate the links in some way or display information about the links.

The following example shows how you can iterate through all the links in a page:

1. In your text editor, create a HTML page with the appropriate HEAD and BODY elements. Use a TITLE element with the text "Examining Links in a Page."

```
<html>
 <head>
  <title>Examining Links in a Page</title>
 </head>
 <body>
 </body>
</html>
```

2. In the BODY element, insert a heading and several links. You can use the links shown or add your own as long as one or more of the links include specific paths within a site.

```
<h1>Links to Examine</h1>
<ul>
<li><a href="http://www.robertstanek.com/">
   Main</a></li>
<li><a href="http://www.robertstanek.com:80/
   curr/books.html#ruinmist">Current Books</a></li>
<li><a href="http://www.ruinmist.com/">
   Background</a></li>
<li><a href="http://www.ruinmist.com/history/
   log.html">Logs</a></li>
</ul>
<h1>Link Details</h1>
```

3. Insert the following JavaScript code block after the Link Details heading. This script displays detailed information about each link on the page.

```
<script type="text/javascript">
for (x = 0; x < document.links.length; x++) {
document.write("<p>Link " + x + " is <b>" +
  document.links[x].href + "</b> This links
  properties   follow:</p>");
document.write("<ul><li>Protocol " + document.
  links[x].protocol + "</li>");
document.write("<li>Host " + document.links[x].
  host + "</li>");
document.write("<ul><li>Hostname " + document.
  links[x].hostname + "</li>");
document.write("<li>Port " + document.links[x].
  port + "</li></ul>");
document.write("<li>Pathname " + document.links[x].
  pathname + "</li>");
document.write("<li>Hash " + document.links[x].hash +
  "</li></ul>");
}
</script>
```

4. Load the page into Internet Explorer 5.0 or later. You should see a list of each link in the page followed by details of a particular link's properties. This is handled with a `for` loop that uses the `length` property of the `links[]` array to determine the number of times to iterate through the `for` loop.

Practice Drill 13.2: Updating Links Dynamically

Sometimes you will want to update links in a page dynamically. For example, if a visitor to your site has indicated a preference for a certain type of content, you might want to customize links on a page based on the user's preference. As discussed previously in this chapter, you can change the value of a link using the properties of the related `link` object.

Try your hand at updating links dynamically by completing the following exercise.

1. In your text editor, create a HTML page with the elements as shown here. Use appropriate HEAD and BODY elements. Use a TITLE element with the text: "My Custom Links."

```
<html>
<head>
<title>My Custom Links</title>
</head>
<body>
</body>
</html>
```

13

2. In the BODY element, insert the elements to be displayed. Note that a form is used to display a button that when clicked changes the links on the page.

```html
<h1>Dynamic Links Example</h1>

<ul><li><a href="">Link 1</a></li>
<li><a href="">Link 2</a></li>
<li><a href="">Link 3</a></li>
</ul>

<hr size=5 noshade>
<form>
<p><input type="button" value="Change Links" onclick
  ="modLinks()"></p>
</form>
```

3. Insert the following JavaScript code block after the TITLE element but before the </head> tag. The modLinks() function updates the links on the page based on whether the current variable is null or not.

```html
<script type="text/javascript">
var current;

function modLinks() {

  if (current) {
  document.links[0].href = "http://www.amazon.com/";
  document.links[1].href = "http://www.bn.com/";
  document.links[2].href = "http://www.buy.com/";
  current = null;
  } else {
  document.links[0].href = "http://www.yahoo.com/";
  document.links[1].href = "http://www.excite.com/";
  document.links[2].href = "http://www.google.com/";
  current = 1;
  }
}
</script>
```

4. Load the page into a Web browser. Note that the initial value of the links is set to an empty string. When you click the Change Links button, the link values are set to www.yahoo.com, www.excite.com, and www.google.com, respectively. If you click the Change Links button again, the link values are set to www.amazon.com, www.bn.com, and www.buy.com, respectively.

5. Modify the page so that the links are set to an initial value by adding a script block that calls the modLinks() function to the BODY element. Insert the following script block after the link definitions and before the end body tag </body>.

```html
<script type="text/javascript">
modLinks()
</script>
```

6. Load the page into a Web browser. The links should now have an initial value, and you can toggle between the sets of link values by clicking the Change Links button. Move the pointer over a link to see its new value on the status bar.

MULTIPLE-CHOICE QUESTIONS

1. Which property of the `link` object provides the complete URL of a link?

    A. `target`

    B. `hash`

    C. `pathname`

    D. `href`

2. Which property of the `link` object provides the target of a link?

    A. `target`

    B. `hash`

    C. `pathname`

    D. `href`

3. What special array do you use to access named locations in a page?

    A. `links[]`

    B. `objects[]`

    C. `anchors[]`

    D. `applets[]`

4. Which index position in the `links[]` array references the third link in a page?

    A. 0

    B. 1

    C. 2

    D. 3

    E. 4

5. Which snippet of code could you use if you wanted to determine the number of links in a page?

    A. `numLinks = document.links[].length;`

    B. `numLinks = document.links.length;`

    C. `numLinks = document.links[];`

    D. `numLinks = document.links;`

6. Which snippet of code could you use to store the value of the `numTurns` property of an applet?

    A. `value = document.applet1.numTurns;`

    B. `value = document.applets[0].numTurns;`

13

   C. Either A or B if the applet is named `applet1` and is the first applet on the page

   D. None of the above

7. In HTML 4.0, what is the preferred tag to use when working with embedded objects?

   A. `<object>`

   B. `<applet>`

   C. `<embed>`

   D. `<control>`

8. If an ActiveX control with an ID of *"quizMaker"* was the only embedded object on a page, how would you access its `currOptions` property in a script?

   A. `document.objects[0].currOptions`

   B. `document.objects["quizMaker"].currOptions`

   C. `document.getElement("quizMaker").currOptions`

   D. `document.getElementByID("quizMaker").currOptions`

9. In a script in another frame, which of the following references could you use to access a form field in a frame called "`Main`"?

   A. `parent.frames[1].myform.address.value`

   B. `parent.frames["Main"].myform.address.value`

   C. `parent.Main.myform.address.value`

   D. All of the above if the frame is the first frame defined in the frameset document.

   E. Only B and C if the frame is the first frame defined in the frameset document.

10. Which object discussed in this chapter is a special type of `location` object?

   A. `link`

   B. `anchor`

   C. `applet`

   D. `object`

   E. None of the above

FILL-IN-THE-BLANK QUESTIONS

1. The _____ property allows you to check or set an internal page link.

2. The _____ array is a special array that allows you to work with the links in a page.

3. The _____ array is a special array that allows you to work with the anchors in a page.

4. To determine the number of links in a page, you can use the _____ property of the `links[]` array.

5. The _____ method of the `document` object is used to access an element according to its `name` attribute.

6. The _____ method of the `document` object is used to access an element according to its `ID` attribute.

7. You use the _____ tag to divide the browser windows into rows and columns of frames.

8. The source of a frame is defined with the _____ tag.

9. When you want to reference from a child document to another child document, you must start with a reference to the _____.

10. You label anchors with the _____ attribute of the `<a>` tag.

DEFINITIONS QUESTIONS

1. When working with links, what does `links[1]` refer to?

2. When working with anchors, what does `anchor[0]` refer to?

3. What is the preferred tag to use when defining an embedded object?

4. What object shares many of the same properties with the `applet` object?

5. What special array tracks the frames used in a page?

INTERMEDIATE PROJECTS

The following projects provide you with additional opportunities to script embedded objects in Web pages.

Project 13.1 – Navigating Anchors in a Page

This project will require you to create a page where users can navigate back and forth between anchors in a page. Although you can use the page created in Exercise 13.2 as a starting point, you should change the function so that it is called `goAnchor()` rather than `nextAnchor()`.

The page should have buttons labeled Previous, Next, and Back To Top to be used as appropriate and necessary for navigating between sections.

Once you have created the HTML page, load it into Internet Explorer and Netscape Navigator to see if it displays correctly. The page should look similar to Figure 13.5.

13

FIGURE 13.5 Navigating anchors.

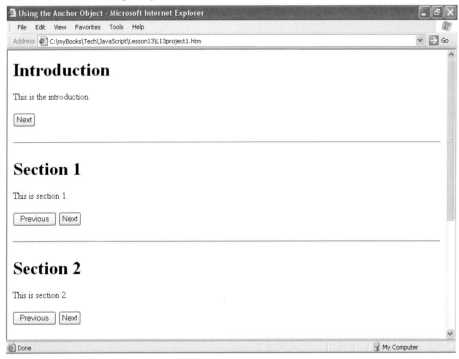

Project 13.2 – Displaying Applet Details Using the object **Element**

This project will require you to create a page with two applets. The applets must be defined with <object> tags rather than <applet> tags and have id, height, and width properties. In a script, you must then use these properties to display information about embedded objects. Set the applet IDs to circles and squares, respectively.

Rather than hard-coding the name of the objects, create a new array to store the names of the objects and then use a for loop to iterate through the items in the array and display the values of the id, height, and width properties. Hint: You can initialize the array as follows:

```
var currObject = new Array("circles", "squares");
```

When you are finished, load the page into Internet Explorer and Netscape Navigator and test the window management functions you have defined. The page should look similar to Figure 13.6. When you are finished, look at the source for C13project2b.htm for an alternate solution. Be sure to study how this alternate solution works.

FIGURE 13.6 Working with embedded objects.

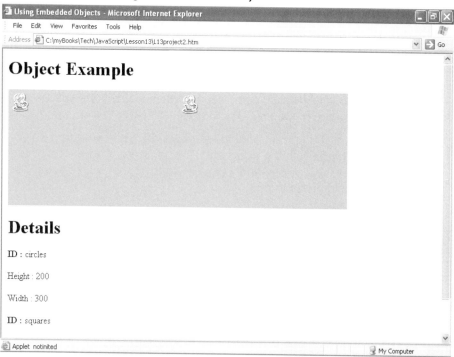

Career Builder

In this chapter, you have learned more about the special arrays that are available for scripting and how to manipulate embedded objects. A key part of the chapter provided a more extended discussion on frames, which you have been working with for several chapters.

The Career Builder exercise for this chapter extends the JavaScript-based application you have been developing. Here, you will add to the help and customization system so that users can get more information about the application when they need it.

- Before you create the help features for any site or application, you should consider the types of problems users may experience. Many new users do not understand the basics, such as how links in text and graphics work, how to navigate from page to page, or how to get back to the main or front page at the site. Other new user problems deal with browser problems, such as caching.

(continued)

13

- After considering the various subject areas for the help system, you should address the questions you feel will be of concern at your Web site. For the purposes of this Career Builder, you will assume that most of the users will have questions about the application itself, usage in general, and customizing colors. As users become more experienced, they may also want helpful tips for increasing productivity and such. In the help system, each of these questions will be answered with a help option.

- To implement the corresponding help options, you can add a selection list to the form in the application's side frame. Add the following markup after the `<form>` and `<table>` tags so that the selection list is the first field of the form:

```
<tr><th align=left>Help System</th></tr>
<tr>
<td><select name="helpSel" size=1 onChange=
  "userHelp(this.form)">
<option>Choose
<option>About
<option>Help
<option>Colors
<option>Tips
</select></td>
</tr>
```

- The main feature for the help system is a selection list that calls the `userHelp()` function. The markup for this function is shown next. As you can see, a `for` loop is used to determine which help option was selected and then an appropriate function is called.

```
function userHelp(form) {
var helpOption = "";
  for (var i = 0; i < form.helpSel.length; i++) {
   if (form.helpSel.options[i].selected) helpOption
     = form.helpSel.options[i].text;
  }
  if (helpOption == "About") aboutWindow();
  if (helpOption == "Help") helpWindow();
  if (helpOption == "Colors") colorsWindow();
  if (helpOption == "Tips") tipsWindow();
  }
```

- Create placeholder functions for each of the help functions you need as shown in the following code example.

```
function aboutWindow() {
  window.alert("About");
  }
function helpWindow() {
```

(continued)

```
 window.alert("Help");
}
function colorsWindow() {
 window.alert("Colors");
}
function tipsWindow() {
 window.alert("Tips");
}
```

- When you are finished modifying the side frame, save the changes and then load the frameset page in Internet Explorer 5.0 or later. Test the application to make sure everything is working as expected. The new selection list should display. You should be able to make selections and display a related alert dialog box. In the next chapter, we will extend this Career Builder to develop the help windows.

13

Chapter | 14

Working with the Browser History List and Locations

Browsers maintain information about the page you are currently visiting—the *browser location*—as well as pages you have visited previously—the browser's *history list*. In this chapter, you will learn techniques for accessing and working with browser locations and history lists. Before you get started though, it is important to note that security restrictions in most browsers restrict access to some browser history and location information. One workaround with Netscape Navigator 4 or later browsers is to use signed scripts. Otherwise, the information simply is not accessible to a script.

For Your Career

In the Career Builder at the end of the chapter, you will learn a technique for working around some of the security restrictions in Netscape Navigator 4 and later versions of the browser. This technique uses the `netscape.security.PrivilegeManager.enablePrivilege()` method. Note how this method is used to allow the script to be used with both Internet Explorer and Netscape Navigator.

Chapter Exercises

This unit's exercises will teach you how to:

- Work with the browser's history list
- Navigate forward or backward through the history list
- Jump around the history list
- Use the `location` object to load pages
- Assign, reload, and replace locations
- Examine URL components

By working through the exercises, you will learn many things about the browser history list and locations.

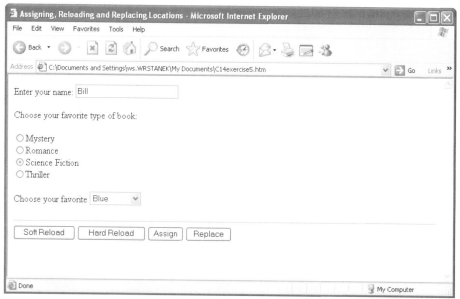

Exercise 14.1 – Examining the `history` Object

When you surf the Web, your browser keeps a list of the places you have visited. This list of visited sites, called the *history list,* is accessible to your scripts via the `history` object. However, unless you use signed scripts and the user grants explicit permission, you cannot extract the URLs of sites users have visited. Instead, you can only move back and forth to different elements in the list.

The components of the `history` object are summarized in Table 14.1. Although the list is fairly short, you can use these properties and methods to manipulate the history list in many ways.

TABLE 14.1 The `history` object.

Properties	Methods	Event Handlers
`current`	`back()`	(none)
`length`	`forward()`	
`next`	`go(int|"URLorTitleSubstring")`	
`previous`		

To safeguard users' privacy, three of the four properties summarized in Table 14.1 can only be used with signed scripts and when a user gives permission. These properties are `current`, `next`, and `previous`—all of which are read-only strings:

- `current`—Gets the URL of the current page from the history list.
- `next`—Gets the URL of the next page in the history list. This generally assumes you have used `back` or `previous` first.
- `previous`—Gets the URL of the previous page in the history list.

The final property, `length`, is accessible in any script and is a read-only numeric value. The `length` property counts the number of items in the history list, which is used in conjunction with other properties or methods of the `history` object.

The history list itself is useful. The most recently loaded document is at the top of the history list. A document's position in the history list does not change if users use the Back button or the Go/View menu to jump to an item in the history list. A `history.length` value of 1 indicates that the current document is the first one the user loaded since starting the browser.

In this exercise, you will create a page that lets users check how many pages they have visited since starting their browser.

STEP 1 – CREATING A PAGE

In your text editor, create a new Web page. You will create a sample HTML page as shown in Exhibit 14.1. Your page should contain the form as shown. Note that when clicked, the button calls the pageVisits() function.

EXHIBIT 14.1

```
<html>
<head>
<title>Using the History.length Property</title>
</head>
<body>
<form>
<input type="button" name="historylist" value="Check
   number of Pages browsed" onclick="pageVisits()" />
</form>
</body>
</html>
```

STEP 2 – ADDING A FUNCTION TO EXAMINE THE HISTORY LIST

In your text editor, edit the page created in the previous step. After the TITLE element, add Exhibit 14.2 as a header-defined script. This script uses the history.length property to display information about the number of pages the user has visited.

EXHIBIT 14.2

```
<script type="text/javascript">
function pageVisits() {
var numPages = window.history.length;
if (numPages == 1) {
alert("This is the first Web page you've visited since
   starting your browser.");
} else {
alert("You've visited " + numPages + " Web pages since
   starting your browser.");
}
}
</script>
```

14

STEP 3 – DISPLAYING THE PAGE

In Internet Explorer, open the page you created in Steps 1 and 2. Figure 14.1 shows the page. If you click the button, you should see an alert telling you how many items are in the history list, which is essentially the number of pages you have visited since starting your browser.

FIGURE 14.1 Using the history list.

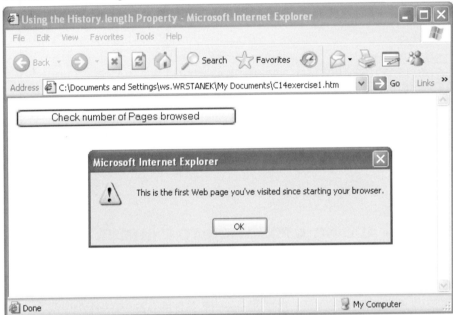

Exercise 14.2 – Navigating the History List

Because you do not need to worry about signed scripts and permissions, the `history` object's methods are more useful than its properties. You can use the methods to move to any item in the history list. The only problem is that you typically cannot read the list to see what is in it. Therefore, you should only use these methods when you are certain about the path the user has taken to the current page. Otherwise, simply set the `window.location` object to the URL you want to access.

The `history` object's methods are used as follows:

- `history.back()` goes back one page in the history list. It performs the same action as the Back button on the toolbar. This method could be used in a page as follows:

```
<input type="button" value="Go Back" onclick=
   "history.back()" />
```

- `history.forward()` goes forward one page in the history list. It is rarely used unless you have previously moved back in the history list. This method could be used in a page as follows:

```
<input type="button" value="Go Forward" onclick=
  "history.forward()" />
```

- `history.go()` moves to the relative index specified in the history list. Alternately, you can specify an exact string for a title or URL in the history list. This method could be used in a page as follows:

```
<input type="button" value="Go Back 2" onclick=
  "history.go(-2)" />
```

With the `go()` method, any positive integer moves to the page that number of items forward in the history list. A negative integer moves to the page that number of items back in the history list. Following this, `history.go(1)` is the same as `history.forward()`, and `history.go(-1)` is the same as `history.back()`. In practice, these are the methods/values of the `history` object that you will use most often.

It is also useful to use a value of zero for the `go()` method, as in `history.go(0)`. This tells the browser to perform a soft reload of the current window, which allows the window to be reloaded from cache. Note, however, that with Internet Explorer 4.0 and later, the browser may actually reload by going back to the server and requesting the page again.

Using the `history` properties is a good way to navigate about your site when you disable or do not show the Back and Forward buttons. In this exercise, you are going to work with the `history.back()` and `history.forward()` methods. To implement a Back or Next Page button, you simply assign the `back()` or `forward()` methods to the `onClick` event of a button. Whenever you use the `back()` and `forward()` methods, you want to be sure these options are actually available to the user. The way to do this is to track the user's progress through your Web site.

STEP 1 – CREATING A FRAMESET

In your text editor, create a new Web page. You will create a frameset page as shown in Exhibit 14.3. Save the page as C14exercise2.htm.

EXHIBIT 14.3

```
<html>
<head>
<title>Using the Back and Forward Methods of the
  History Object</title>
</head>
<frameset cols="25%,75%">
<frame name="menu" src="exhibit14-7.htm" />
<frame name="main" src="exhibit14-8.htm" />
</frameset>
</html>
```

14

STEP 2 – DEFINING THE CONTROL PAGES

In your text editor, you will create a series of Web pages using Exhibits 14.4, 14.5, and 14.6. Save the pages as exhibit14-4.htm, exhibit14-5.htm, and exhibit14-6.htm.

EXHIBIT 14.4

```html
<html>
<head>
<title>Control Page 1</title>
</head>
<body bgcolor="#FFFFFF" text="#000000">
<h1>Control Page 1</h1>
</body>
</html>
```

EXHIBIT 14.5

```html
<html>
<head>
<title>Control Page 2</title>
</head>
<body bgcolor="#000000" text="#FFFFFF">
<h1>Control Page 2</h1>
</body>
</html>
```

EXHIBIT 14.6

```html
<html>
<head>
<title>Control Page 3</title>
</head>
<body bgcolor="#FFFF00" text="#000000">
<h1>Control Page 3</h1>
</body>
</html>
```

STEP 3 – DEFINING THE MENU PAGE

In your text editor, create the menu page as shown in Exhibit 14.7. Save the page as exhibit14-7.htm. This page provides controls for displaying the control pages and then navigating back and forth through the history list.

EXHIBIT 14.7

```
<html>
<head>
<title>Menu Page</title>
</head>
<body>
<b>Load pages into the right frame by clicking on each
  of these links. Keep track of the order of your
  clicks.</b>
<ul><li><a href="exhibit14-4.htm" target="main">Exhibit
  14-4</a></li>
<li><a href="exhibit14-5.htm" target="main">Exhibit
  14-5</a></li>
<li><a href="exhibit14-6.htm" target="main">Exhibit
  14-6</a></li></ul>
<hr size=5 />
<form name="nav">
<b>Navigate the history list using the buttons
  provided.</b>
<ul><li><input type="button" value="Go Back" onclick=
  "history.back()" /></li>
<li><input type="button" value="Go Forward" onclick=
  "history.forward()" /></li></ul>
</form>
</body>
</html>
```

STEP 4 – DEFINING THE MAIN PAGE

In your text editor, create the main page as shown in Exhibit 14.8. Save the page as exhibit14-8.htm. This page provides the right frame defined in the frameset page.

EXHIBIT 14.8

```
<html>
<head>
<title>Main Page</title>
</head>
<body bgcolor="#00FF00" text="#000000">
<h1>Welcome to the Navigation test page!</h1>
</body>
</html>
```

14

STEP 5 – DISPLAYING THE FRAME-ENHANCED PAGE

In Internet Explorer, open the page you created in Step 1. Figure 14.2 shows the page. Click the links provided and then navigate the history list using the Go Back and Go Forward buttons.

FIGURE 14.2 Testing the navigation functions of the `history` object.

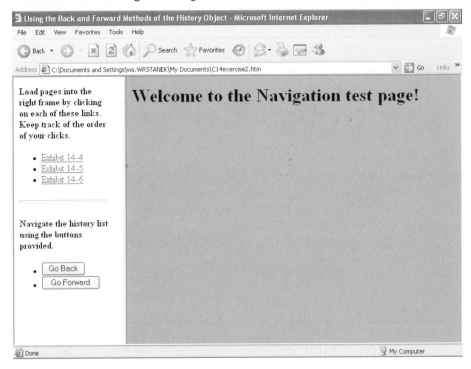

Exercise 14.3 – Going to a Page in the History List

You can use the `go()` method to jump around the history list. The `go()` method accepts an integer value that describes where you want to move in the history list as well as a URL or title string to search for in the history list.

When you enter a number, you always reference the position in the history list you want to jump to in relation to the current position in the history list. A reference of +2 would move you forward two steps in the list. A reference of -2 would move you backward two steps in the list.

The real power of the `go()` method is the ability to pattern match strings from titles or URLs of pages in the history list. If you use a value of `history.go("Home Page")`, the `go()` method compares the string to all entries in the history list and returns the first page whose title matches the specified string.

In this exercise, you use the `go()` method to let users search through their history list.

STEP 1 – CREATING A PAGE

In your text editor, create a new Web page. You will create a sample HTML page as shown in Exhibit 14.9. You implement the search functionality with text fields and buttons. The first text field and button are used to go to a position in the history list relative to the current position. The second text field and button are used to search for a matching URL or title string—both of which must be specified exactly. Keep in mind that the history list builds as you browse pages. If you clear out the cache or restart the browser, you effectively clear out the history list.

EXHIBIT 14.9

```
<html>
<head>
<title>Searching the history list</title>
</head>
<body>
<h1>Searching the history list</h1>
<form>
<p>Enter a the number of pages to go back or forward
  (+/-):</p>
<input type="text" name="searchfield1" size=25>
<input type="button" value="search" onclick=
  "searchNum(this.form)">
<p>Enter a search string:</p>
<input type="text" name="searchfield2" size=25>
<input type="button" value="search" onclick=
  "searchWord(this.form)">
</form>
<hr size=5>
</body>
</html>
```

STEP 2 – ADDING THE NAVIGATION FUNCTIONS

In your text editor, edit the page you created in the previous step. After the TITLE element, add Exhibit 14.10 as a header-defined script. This script uses the history.go() method to navigate the history list. Two functions are needed, as shown.

EXHIBIT 14.10

```
<script type="text/javascript">
function searchNum(form) {
window.history.go(parseInt(form.searchfield1.value));
}
```

T I P

Use go() When It Makes Sense

You can easily insert buttons that use the go() method. The difficult part is ensuring that the buttons work. As with back() and forward(), the best time to implement this method is when you know the path the user has taken through your Web site. For example, if you can only access a product demo page from a product summary page, then you could be certain of the user's path through the site (but not the rest of the URLs in the user's history list).

14

```
function searchWord(form) {
window.history.go(form.searchfield2.value);
}
</script>
```

STEP 3 – DISPLAYING THE PAGE

In Internet Explorer, open the page you created in Steps 1 and 2. Try navigating the history list by entering appropriate values in the text fields provided. Enter a value of -2 to go back in the history list two positions then click the Forward button twice to get back to the page. Enter a value of 0 to perform a soft reload of the page.

Exercise 14.4 – Working with Locations and the `location` Object

Browsers maintain information about the current page you are visiting. The URL of the current page is referred to as the *browser location* and is stored in the `location` object.

You can use the `location` object to examine information pertaining to the current URL, which is tracked as the absolute or complete URL of the current document, such as:

```
http://www.robertstanek.com/index.html
```

Table 14.2 shows the properties and methods of the `location` object.

In this exercise, you are going to use the `location` object to load a new page in the browser window based on the user's selection. To do this, you will set `window. location` equal to the URL of the page you want to load into the browser window. Consider the following example:

```
window.location = "index.htm"
```

TABLE 14.2 The `location` object.

Properties	Methods	Event Handlers
hash	assign()	(none)
host	reload()	
hostname	replace()	
href		
pathname		
port		
protocol		
search		

Here, you load the page relative to the current location. If you were visiting http://www.robertstanek.com/current.htm, you would then access http://www.robertstanek.com/index.htm.

You can also specify the complete URL, such as:

```
window.location = "http://www.robertstanek.com/"
```

STEP 1 – CREATING A FRAMESET

In your text editor, create a new Web page. You will create a frameset page as shown in Exhibit 14.11. Save the page as C14exercise4.htm.

EXHIBIT 14.11

```
<html>
<head>
<title>Loading a new page into the browser
  window</title>
</head>
<frameset cols="25%,75%">
<frame name="menu" src="exhibit14-12.htm" />
<frame name="main" src="exhibit14-8.htm" />
</frameset>
</html>
```

STEP 2 – DEFINING THE MENU PAGE

In your text editor, create the menu page as shown in Exhibit 14.12. Save the page as exhibit14-12.htm. As you can see, you are reusing the control pages created in Exercise 14.2. However, rather than providing direct links, you use buttons and configure each so that when you make a selection the related page is loaded into the browser window.

EXHIBIT 14.12

```
<html>
<head>
<title>Menu Page</title>
</head>
<body>
<p><b>Click a button to load a page into the main
  frame.</b></p>
<form>
<ul><li><input type="button" name="button1" value=
  "Control Page 1" onclick="parent.main.location=
  'exhibit14-4.htm'" /></li>
```

14

```
<li><input type="button" name="button1" value="Control
  Page 2" onclick="parent.main.location='exhibit14-5.
  htm'" /></li>
<li><input type="button" name="button1" value="Control
  Page 3" onclick="parent.main.location='exhibit14-
  6.htm'" /></li></ul>
</form>
<hr size=5 />
</body>
</html>
```

STEP 3 – DISPLAYING THE FRAME-ENHANCED PAGE

In Internet Explorer, open the page you created in Step 1. Figure 14.3 shows the page. Click the buttons provided to load one of the control pages into the main frame. Note that you set the location for the main frame by referencing `parent.main. location`. If you were to specify `window.location` instead, you would be referencing the current window/frame, and the control pages would be loaded into the menu frame itself rather than the main frame.

FIGURE 14.3 Loading pages using the `window.location` object.

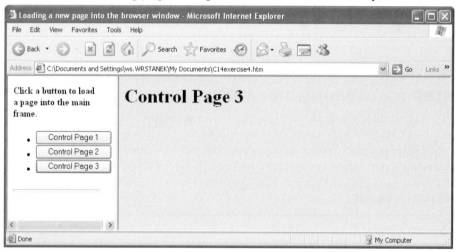

Exercise 14.5 – Assigning, Reloading, and Replacing Locations

The methods of the `location` object are really quite useful, as shown in the following list.

- `location.assign("URL")`—Navigates to a new page by assigning a new URL to the `location` object.

- `location.reload(GETBoolean)`—Reloads the page in its initial state without updates or form entries. This has the same effect as choosing Open Location from the File menu and entering the URL to the current page.

- `location.replace("URL")`—Loads the specified page and replaces the current history entry with the entry for the new page.

Use a Relative or Absolute URL

With `location.assign()` and `location.replace()`, the URL must be specified relative to the current directory in which the page is located or specified absolutely. Following this, you could access a file name located in the current directory using its name, such as C14exercise5.htm, but to access a page on a different site you would need to use a complete URL, including the `http://`, such as http://www.robertstanek.com/index.htm.

If you want to explicitly show a URL assignment, you can use the `location.assign()` method to do so. Using `location.assign()` is the same as assigning a URL to the `window.location` object, as discussed in the previous exercise. In fact, when you assign a URL to the `window.location` object, JavaScript calls `window.location.assign()` for you. Using `window.location.assign()` offers no speed, performance, or other benefit except perhaps that it explicitly shows the URL assignment and is perhaps clearer to a novice scripter.

You will use the `reload()` method whenever you want a page to go back to its original state. A reload is more powerful than the browser's Refresh/Reload functionality because it clears form control values that might otherwise remain after a refresh/reload. When you use `location.reload()`, a browser should obtain the original page from cache and reload it. This is different from using `history.go(0)`, which performs a soft reload of the page and should preserve form control settings.

The `location.reload()` method accepts a single parameter, which by default is set to false. If you set this parameter to true, you tell the browser to perform an unconditional GET to the server and ignore the cached version of the page.

You will use the `replace()` method to ensure that certain pages do not show up in the user's history list. By calling `replace()` rather than loading the next location through an assignment, you replace the current history list entry with that of the referenced page. This ensures that the user has no means of using the Back button to go back to the previous page.

Watch Out for Browser Variances

Results may vary between browser types and/or versions. If you want to be sure of behavior, test thoroughly and try different techniques until you achieve the desired effect.

Why is this useful? Consider, for example, the case of a user who is registering to access your site. You have a specific sequence of pages that must be followed, but the pages do not make sense out of order and should not be accessible after registration. In this case, you may not want a user to be able to go back to a previous page in the registration process using the Back button. For this reason, you use the `location.replace()` method to navigate to another page but not let the current page stay in the history list. Thus, the page to which the user is navigating always replaces the current page in the history list, and the user cannot use the Back button to navigate to a previous page.

In this exercise, you try different methods of accessing and reloading pages to test browser behavior.

STEP 1 – CREATING A PAGE

In your text editor, create a new Web page. You will create a sample HTML page as shown in Exhibit 14.13. You are going to use the input fields on the page to test what happens when you use various methods of reloading the page. You are going to use buttons to provide the reload, replace, and assign functionality.

14

EXHIBIT 14.13

```
<html>
<head>
<title>Assigning, Reloading and Replacing
  Locations</title>
</head>
<body>
<form name="testForm">
<p>Enter your name: <input type="text" name="text1"
  SIZE=25></p>
<p>Choose your favorite type of book:</p>
<input type="radio" name="radio1" value="1" />
  Mystery<br />
<input type="radio" name="radio1" value="2" />
  Romance<br />
<input type="radio" name="radio1" value="2" />
  Science Fiction<br />
<input type="radio" name="radio1" value="3" />
  Thriller<br />
<p>Choose your favorite <select name="theList">
<option>>Choose<</option>
<option>Blue</option>
<option>Green</option>
<option>Red</option>
<option>Yellow</option>
</select></p>
<hr />
<input type="button" value="Soft Reload" onclick=
  "goReload()" />
<input type="button" value="Hard Reload" onclick=
  "locReload()" />
<input type="button" value="Assign" onclick=
  "locAssign()" />
<input type="button" value="Replace" onclick=
  "locReplace()" />
</form>
</body>
</html>
```

STEP 2 – ADDING THE CHANGE FUNCTIONS

In your text editor, edit the page created in the previous step. After the TITLE element, add Exhibit 14.14 as a header-defined script. This script provides the reload, replace, and assign functionality. Four functions are needed, as shown.

EXHIBIT 14.14

```
<script type="text/javascript">
function locReload() {
location.reload(true);
}

function goReload() {
history.go(0);
}

function locReplace() {
location.replace("exhibit14-5.htm");
}

function locAssign() {
location.assign("exhibit14-6.htm");
}
</script>
```

STEP 3 – DISPLAYING THE PAGE

In Internet Explorer, open the page you created in Steps 1 and 2. As shown in Figure 14.4, complete the fields by typing your name and making selections. Afterward, click each of the buttons in turn and note what happens. Note that when you click the Assign button, you can use the browser's back button to return to the page. However, when you

FIGURE 14.4 Manipulating the page location.

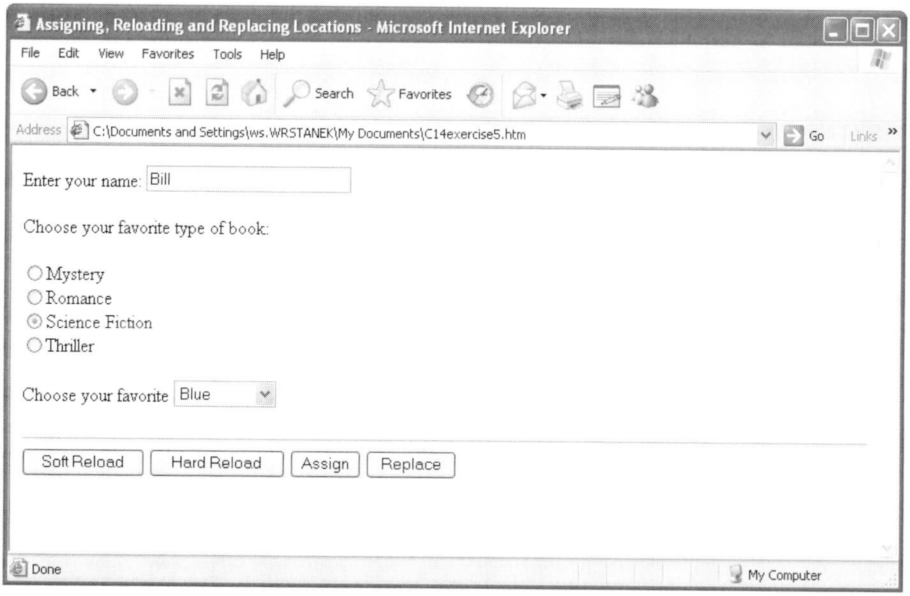

14

click the Replace button, you cannot use the Back button to return to the page—the page entry no longer exists in the browser's history list.

Exercise 14.6 – Examining URL Components

You can use the properties of the `location` object to work with the components of a URL. In addition to providing access to the complete URL of the current page, the properties of the `location` object allow you to set the URL either in whole or in part. Because you can set the individual components of a URL, you can build URLs to pages based on user input. You can even build queries to search engines.

Table 14.3 describes the properties of the `location` object. As you study the table, consider the following URL:

`http://www.robertstanek.com:80/current/books.html#ruinmist`

In this exercise, you work with the URL components of the current page.

TABLE 14.3 Properties of the `location` object.

Property	Value	Type	Description
hash	String	Read/Write	Provides access to internal page links, designated by the hash mark (#). By setting the hash property, you can jump to the various internal links of a page. An example value is #ruinmist. Supported by NN2, IE3 and later as well as Mozilla and Safari.
host	String	Read/Write	Allows you to check or set the current hostname and port information. An example value is www.robertstanek.com:80. Supported by NN2, IE3 and later as well as Mozilla and Safari.
hostname	String	Read/Write	Allows you to check or set the current hostname. An example value is www.robertstanek.com. Supported by NN2, IE3 and later as well as Mozilla and Safari.
href	String	Read/Write	Provides the complete URL to the current page; can be used to set the URL as well. An example value is http://www.robertstanek.com:80/current/books.html. Supported by NN2, IE3 and later as well as Mozilla and Safari.

TABLE 14.3 (*Continued*)

Property	Value	Type	Description
pathname	String	Read/Write	Allows you to check or set the URL path information, which is relative to the current directory on the server. An example value is `/current/books.html`. Supported by NN2, IE3 and later as well as Mozilla and Safari.
port	String	Read/Write	Allows you to check or set the current server port. An example value is `80`. Supported by NN2, IE3 and later as well as Mozilla and Safari.
protocol	String	Read/Write	Allows you to check or set the protocol used to access the current page. An example value is `http:`. Supported by NN2, IE3 and later as well as Mozilla and Safari.
search	String	Read/Write	Allows you to check or set the search query/form post information from the URL. Basically, this is everything appended after the URL and starting with the question mark added for queries. An example value is `?books+ruin+mist`. Supported by NN2, IE3 and later as well as Mozilla and Safari.

STEP 1 – CREATING A PAGE

In your text editor, create a new Web page. You will create a sample HTML page as shown in Exhibit 14.15.

EXHIBIT 14.15

```
<html>
<head>
<title>Examining URL Components</title>
</head>
<body>
<h1>Components of the Current URL</h1>
</body>
</html>
```

14

STEP 2 – ADDING THE CHANGE FUNCTIONS

In your text editor, edit the page created in the previous step. After the H1 element, add Exhibit 14.16 as a body-defined script. This script displays the URL component details.

EXHIBIT 14.16

```
<script type="text/javascript">
document.write("<ul><li>Protocol <b>" +
  window.location.protocol + "</b></li>");
document.write("<li>Host <b>" + window.location.host +
  "</b></li>");
document.write("<ul><li>Hostname <b>" +
  window.location.hostname + "</b></li>");
document.write("<li>Port <b>" + window.location.port +
  "</b></li></ul>");
document.write("<li>Pathname <b>" + window.location.
  pathname + "</b></li>");
document.write("<li>Hash <b>" + window.location.hash +
  "</b></li>");
document.write("<li>Href <b>" + window.location.href +
  "</b></li></ul>");
</script>
```

STEP 3 – DISPLAYING THE PAGE

In Internet Explorer, open the page you created in Steps 1 and 2. If you loaded the page from a file on the local computer, you should see that only the protocol, pathname, and href information are available.

Summary

Browser history lists and related locations are maintained automatically by browsers. As you have seen in this chapter, you access this information through the `history` and `location` objects. The `history` object has properties and methods that can be used to navigate through pages that have been accessed by the browser. The `location` object has properties and methods that can be used to examine URL components of the current page you are visiting and to assign, replace, and reload pages.

Test Your Skills

Practice Drill 14.1: Creating a Navigation Window

Previously, you learned how to use the `history` object to navigate backward or forward through the history list. You also learned how to use `window.location` to load a new page in the browser window. In this exercise, you build on the earlier discussions and see how these techniques can be applied to multiple windows.

The following example shows how you can navigate between windows using the `history` and `location` objects.

1. In your text editor, create a HTML page with the appropriate HEAD and BODY elements. Use a TITLE element with the text: "Navigating with history and location Objects."

```
<html>
<head>
<title>Navigating with history and location
  Objects</title>
</head>
<body>
</body>
</html>
```

2. In the BODY element, insert a heading and form that has a button control you can use to open a custom window.

```
<h1>Navigating between Windows</h1>
<form><input type="button" Value="Open Nav Window"
  onClick="createNavWindow()" />
</form>
```

3. Insert the following header-defined code block after the TITLE element. This script creates the navigation window. Note the reference to `opener` rather than `window` or `parent`. This reference allows scripts in new windows to refer back to the window that opened them.

```
<script type="text/javascript">
var navWindow;
function createNavWindow() {
```

14

```
if (!navWindow || navWindow.closed) {
 navWindow = window.open("","NavigationHelper",
   "resizable,height=100,width=400");
 navWindow.document.write("<html><head><title>
   Navigation Helper...</title></head>");
 navWindow.document.write("<body bgcolor=
   '#FFFFFF'>");
 navWindow.document.write("<form name='nav'>");
 navWindow.document.write("<p><input type='text'
   name='goto' size=25>");
 navWindow.document.write("<input type='button'
   value='Open Page' onclick='opener.location.
   assign(form.goto.value)'>");
 navWindow.document.write("<p><input type='button'
   value='Go Back' onclick='opener.history.back()'
   />");
 navWindow.document.write("<input type='button'
   value='Go Forward' onclick='opener.history.
   forward()' />");
 navWindow.document.write("</form>");
 navWindow.document.write("</body></html>");
 navWindow.document.close();
 }
}
</script>
```

4. Save the finished page as C14practice1.htm. Load the page into Internet Explorer 5.0 or later and then click the Open Nav Window button. You should see the Navigation Helper window, which has a text field and three button controls.

5. Type a valid URL in the text field. The URL must be a file name located in the current directory, such as C14exercise3.htm, or a complete URL that includes http://, such as http://www.robertstanek.com/index.htm. Click the Open Page button after you type the URL. The specified page should load in the main browser window. If you click the Go Back button, you should see the main page for this exercise. If you click Go Forward, you should see the previously specified page.

Practice Drill 14.2: More Work with History Lists and Locations

In scripting, you will find that there are often many solutions to a problem. For example, if you want to reset a page to refresh or reload a page, you have many options. You can use history.go(0) to perform a soft reload or location.reload() to perform a hard reload.

Another way to reload the page is to use location.assign() and assign the current URL as the method parameter. The following example shows you how to do this.

1. In your text editor, create a HTML page with the elements as shown here. Use appropriate HEAD and BODY elements. Use a TITLE element with the text: "History and Location Info."

```
<html>
<head>
<title>History and Location Info</title>
</head>
<body>
</body>
</html>
```

2. In the BODY element, insert the elements to be displayed. You will use document.write() method calls to write information to the page and provide a button control to reload the page. Note that by setting the location.assign() method's parameter to the URL of the current page, you reload the page.

```
<h1>Display History and Location Info</h1>
<script type="text/javascript">
document.write("<p>You've visited " +
window.history.length + " pages since starting your
  browser</p>");
document.write("<p>The current page is <b>" +
  window.location.href + "</b></p>");
</script>
<form>
<input type="button" name="relPage" value="Reload
  Page" onclick="window.location.assign(window.
  location.href)" />
</form>
```

3. Load the page into a Web browser. When you click the Reload Page button, the page is reloaded in much the same way as if you had performed a refresh/reload.

4. Modify the page so that the button control calls the cont() function when clicked rather than directly assigning the URL. Then insert the following JavaScript code block after the TITLE element but before the </head> tag. The cont() function displays a confirmation dialog box when called.

```
<script type="text/javascript">
var response;
function cont() {
 var response = confirm("Do you want to reload the
  page?");
 if (response) {
  window.location.assign(window.location.href);
 }
```

14

```
      else {
       alert("Action cancelled.");
      }
     }
    }
    </script>
```

5. Load the page into a Web browser. Click the Reload Page button. Test what happens when you click Yes or Cancel. If you click Yes, the page should reload. If you click Cancel, an alert should be displayed.

MULTIPLE-CHOICE QUESTIONS

1. Which properties of the `history` object require a signed script and user permission?

   A. `current`

   B. `length`

   C. `next`

   D. `previous`

   E. A, C, and D only

2. Which property of the `history` object counts the number of items in the history list?

   A. `current`

   B. `length`

   C. `total`

   D. `span`

3. Which of the following is true?

   A. `history.back()` is the same as `history.go(1)`.

   B. `history.forward()` is the same as `history.go(-1)`.

   C. `history.back()` is the same as clicking the browser's Back button.

   D. `history.forward()` is the same as clicking the browser's Forward button.

   E. Both C and D

4. What does a call to `history.go(0)` do?

   A. Performs a soft reload, which allows the browser to get the page from cache

   B. Performs a hard reload, which forces the browser to get the page from the server

   C. Gets the first page in the history list

   D. Closes the browser window

5. Which snippet of code could you use if you wanted to determine the number of pages a user has visited?

   A. `numPages = window.history.length;`

   B. `numPages = document.links.length;`

```
    C. numPages = window.history[];
    D. numPages = window.history;
```

6. Which snippet of code could you use to load a new page in the browser window?

    A. `window.location = "index.html";`

    B. `window.location.assign("index.html");`

    C. Either A or B

    D. None of the above

7. What property of the `location` object do you use to list the complete URL?

    A. `hash`

    B. `host`

    C. `href`

    D. `pathname`

8. What method of the `location` object do you use to load a page in such a way that it takes the place of the current page in the history list?

    A. `location.assign()`

    B. `location.reload()`

    C. `location.place()`

    D. `location.replace()`

9. What property of the `location` object would you use to examine the internal link associated with the current URL?

    A. `hash`

    B. `host`

    C. `link`

    D. `anchor`

10. What property of the `location` object would you use to check the host name associated with the current URL?

    A. `host`

    B. `hostname`

    C. Either, but A is preferable because it does not include port information

    D. Either, but B is preferable because it does not include port information

    E. None of the above

FILL-IN-THE-BLANK QUESTIONS

14

1. The _____ object maintains information on visited sites and pages.

2. The _____ object maintains information about the current page.

3. In the history list, you use _____ to reload the current page.

4. In the history list, you use _____ to go back two pages in the history list.

5. In the history list, you use _____ to go forward two pages in the history list.

6. If the current page is the first page you have visited since starting the browser, `history.length` has a value of _____.

7. You can use the _____ and _____ methods to load a new page in the browser window.

8. You can use the _____ property to determine the Internet protocol used to access the current page.

9. In a signed script, you can use the _____ property to determine the URL of the previous page in the history list.

10. In a signed script, you can use the _____ property to determine the URL of the next page in the history list.

DEFINITIONS QUESTIONS

1. What is the history list?

2. When working with the history list, what does `history.go(-1)` refer to?

3. When working with the history list, what does `history.go(1)` refer to?

4. Name two techniques that you can use to reload the current page.

5. Name two techniques that you can use to load a new page in the browser.

INTERMEDIATE PROJECTS

The following projects provide you with additional opportunities to work with history lists and locations.

Project 14.1 – Creating an Analysis Page

This project will require you to create a frame-enhanced page with a main frame and a side frame, defined as follows:

```
<frameset cols="65%,35%" border=0>
<frame name="main" src="C14project-main.htm">
<frame name="side" src="C14project-side.htm">
</frameset>
```

The main frame should have two forms. The first form should have a text field that can be used to enter a URL and a button control that calls the `getdoc()` function when clicked and passes the form object, as shown here:

```
<form>
<p>Enter the URL of the document you want to open:</p>
<p><input type="text" name="urlfield" size=25>
<input type="button" value="open" onclick="getdoc
  (this.form)"></p>
</form>
```

The second form should have three radio buttons and a series of input fields for displaying the window name and the following components of a particular URL: `hash`, `host`, `hostname`, `href`, `pathname`, `port`, `protocol`, and `search`. The radio buttons are used to determine the window or frame whose URL you want to examine, as shown here:

```
<input type="radio" name="checkframe" value="parent"
  checked>parent window
<input type="radio" name="checkframe" value="parent.
  frames[0]">current frame
<input type="radio" name="checkframe" value="parent.
  frames[1]">right frame
```

Follow the radio buttons with button controls for viewing the URL components and clearing out the form fields, as shown here:

```
<input type="button" name="checkproperties" value="view"
  onclick="viewlocprops(this.form)">
<input type="reset" value="clear"><p>
```

The text fields for displaying the Window name and URL components should all have unique names, such as:

```
<input type="text" name="windowname" size=25>
```

Once you have created the HTML page, load it into Internet Explorer and Netscape Navigator to see if it displays correctly. The page should look similar to Figure 14.5. You will create the necessary scripts in the second project.

Project 14.2 – Defining the Property Analysis Scripts

This project will require you to write the required functions for the property analysis utility. Two functions are needed, both of which should be added to the main frame.

The first function, called `getdoc()`, is used to load a user-specified page into the side frame. Ideally, this function ensures that only valid and accessible page URLs are loaded. In this way, the user does not see unnecessary error dialogs. This can be handled in many ways, one solution is as follows:

```
function getdoc(form) {
currurl = form.urlfield.value;
if (currurl != null && currurl != "") {
parent.frames[1].location = currurl;
}
}
```

14

FIGURE 14.5 Creating a property analysis utility.

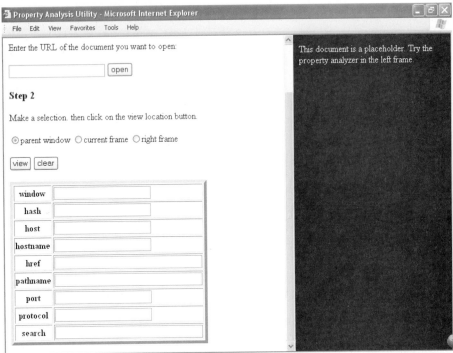

The second function, `viewlocprops()`, is used to view location properties. Although you could build the view mechanism with a single button, you enhance the functionality of the utility by allowing users to check properties of all open windows, which includes the parent window, the left frame, and the right frame. You handle this with a group of radio buttons that allow you to read values that identify the window or frame of choice. To create a function that examines the location properties of the target window or frame, you need to check which window or frame you selected and then send output to the text fields. One way to handle this is as follows:

```
function viewlocprops(form) {
for (var i = 0; i <3; i++) {
if (form.checkframe[i].checked) {
var windowname = form.checkframe[i].value;
break;
}
}
var currwind = "" + windowname + ".location";
var currobj = eval(currwind);
//set window name
form.windowname.value = windowname;
form.windowhash.value = currobj.hash;
form.windowhost.value = currobj.host;
form.windowhostname.value = currobj.hostname;
```

```
form.windowhref.value = currobj.href;
form.windowpath.value = currobj.pathname;
form.windowport.value = currobj.port;
form.windowprotocol.value = currobj.protocol;
form.windowsearch.value = currobj.search;
}
```

When you are finished, load the page into Internet Explorer and Netscape Navigator and test the property analysis functions you have defined. The page should look similar to Figure 14.6. Note that in Internet Explorer 6.0 or later, you may get a permission error regarding the hash property. This occurs because the hash property is not accessible.

FIGURE 14.6 Analyzing URL components of selected windows.

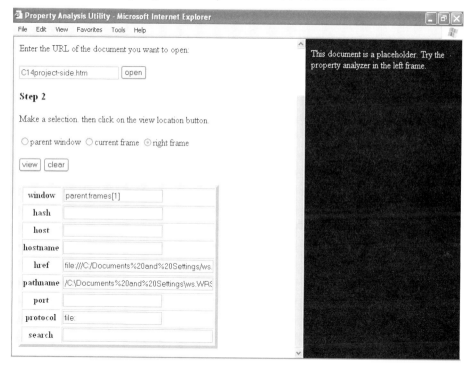

Career Builder

In Netscape Navigator, you may have problems with security when you try to access URL components. In some cases, you can work around this using the `UniversalBrowserRead` privilege. Because this privilege is unique to Netscape Navigator 4 and later, you must use it very carefully.

The Career Builder exercise for this chapter extends the property analysis utility so that it works with Netscape security. Updating the utility so that it is compatible with Netscape Navigator requires several important steps:

- Before you try to enable the `UniversalBrowserRead` privilege, you must first determine that you are working with Netscape Navigator. You do this by checking the browser version:

```
var isNav = (typeof netscape != "undefined") ? true
  : false;
```

- You now have a Boolean value called `isNav`, which is set to true if the browser is Netscape Navigator or false otherwise. You use the Boolean value to set the `UniversalBrowserRead` privilege as appropriate:

```
if (isNav) {
netscape.security.PrivilegeManager.enablePrivilege
  ("UniversalBrowserRead");
}
```

- When you are done using the `UniversalBrowserRead` privilege, you should disable it to restore proper security restrictions. Here is how you could do this:

```
if (isNav) {
netscape.security.PrivilegeManager.disablePrivilege
  ("UniversalBrowserRead");
}
```

- When you put all of this together, the source for the revised script should be similar to the following:

```
<script type="text/javascript">
var isNav = (typeof netscape != "undefined") ? true
  : false;
//get the url of document entered into text field
function getdoc(form) {
currurl = form.urlfield.value;
if (currurl != null && currurl != "") {
```

(continued)

```
parent.frames[1].location = currurl;
}
}
//access location properties for viewing
function viewlocprops(form) {
for (var i = 0; i <3; i++) {
if (form.checkframe[i].checked) {
var windowname = form.checkframe[i].value;
break;
}
}
var currwind = "" + windowname + ".location";
var currobj = eval(currwind);
//set window name
form.windowname.value = windowname;
if (isNav) {
netscape.security.PrivilegeManager.enablePrivilege
  ("UniversalBrowserRead");
}
form.windowhash.value = currobj.hash;
form.windowhost.value = currobj.host;
form.windowhostname.value = currobj.hostname;
form.windowhref.value = currobj.href;
form.windowpath.value = currobj.pathname;
form.windowport.value = currobj.port;
form.windowprotocol.value = currobj.protocol;
form.windowsearch.value = currobj.search;
if (isNav) {
netscape.security.PrivilegeManager.disablePrivilege
  ("UniversalBrowserRead");
}
}
</script>
```

14

Chapter 15

Accessing Browser and Operating System Version Information

Scripts often need to know more about the browser and computer environment in which they are running so that they can tailor content based on that information. For example, you may want to display different content to Macintosh users than Windows users. Or, you may want to use code that is compatible with one particular browser version but incompatible with other browser versions. For example, an object property may be compatible with Internet Explorer 4.0 or later but not with Netscape Navigator or other browsers. In this case, you would want to ensure that the code referencing this object property is only executed when Internet Explorer 4.0 or later is being used, and ignored otherwise.

JavaScript provides objects to help you determine which browser and operating system are being used, including `navigator` and `clientInformation`.

The `navigator` object was first implemented in Netscape Navigator 2. It is supported by just about every current browser, including Netscape Navigator 2 and later, Internet Explorer 3 and later, Mozilla, and Safari. Internet Explorer 4 and later support the `clientInformation` object as an alternative to the `navigator` object. All properties and methods of the `navigator` and `clientInformation` objects are identical. Although `navigator` is the focus of the discussion in this chapter, all references to the `navigator` object also apply to the `clientInformation` object.

For Your Career

Because Internet Explorer 3 and later support the `navigator` object, there is little reason to use the `clientInformation` object. If you are developing JavaScript applications strictly for Internet Explorer, you may want to use the Internet Explorer-specific `clientInformation` object. However, only do this when you are certain that all users will have Internet Explorer 4.0 or later.

Chapter Exercises

This unit's exercises will teach you how to:

- Determine which browser the user has
- Control script execution according to the user's browser or operating system version
- Tailor pages for users based on the browser or operating system version

By working through the exercises, you will learn how to read the brand and version of browser that holds the current document as well as the operating system being used. You can then use this information to tailor pages for users.

Exercise 15.1 – Getting Started with the `navigator` Object

A good Web site makes you feel welcome. A truly powerful way to make users feel welcome is to customize pages for their individual needs. When you customize pages, you create pages with features designed specifically for the user's browser. The key to customizing pages for individual browsers is the `navigator` object.

Table 15.1 summarizes the properties, methods, and events of this object. Although you will primarily use properties of the `navigator` object to customize pages, the methods of the `navigator` object are also useful.

TABLE 15.1 The `navigator` object.

Properties	Methods	Event Handlers
appCodeName	javaEnabled()	(none)
appMinorVersion	preference()	
appName	taintEnabled()	
browserLanguage		
cookieEnabled		
cpuClass		
language		
mimeTypes[i]		
online		
oscpu		
platform		
plugins[i]		
product		
productSub		
securityPolicy		
systemLanguage		
userAgent		
userLanguage		
userProfile		
vendor		
vendorSub		

Current browsers from Internet Explorer 4, Netscape Navigator 6, and later allow you to access the `navigator` object via the `window` object. This means that you can access `navigator` properties and methods in the form:

```
window.navigator.propertyName
```

or

```
window.navigator.methodName
```

Although current browsers treat the `navigator` object as part of the `window` object, this is not how the `navigator` object was originally handled. Originally, `navigator` was created as a stand-alone object, and you accessed its properties and methods in the form:

```
navigator.propertyName
```

or

```
navigator.methodName
```

Because you can omit a reference to the `window` object when working with the current browser window, you can use this method to access the `navigator` object in any browser. For example, if you wanted to assign the value of the `appName` property to a variable, you could use:

```
var currBrowser = navigator.appName;
```

And this assignment would work in any JavaScript-compatible browser.

As shown in Table 15.2, methods of the `navigator` object let you check settings in the user's browser. Generally, the methods return true if the setting is enabled and false if it is not enabled.

In this exercise, you will create a page that checks to see if Java is enabled before displaying Java applets. If Java is not enabled, images are displayed instead.

STEP 1 – CREATING A PAGE

In your text editor, create a new Web page. You will create a sample HTML page as shown in Exhibit 15.1.

EXHIBIT 15.1

```
<html>
<head>
<title>Testing for Java support</title>
</head>
<body>
</body>
</html>
```

15

TABLE 15.2 The `navigator` object methods.

Method	Example	Description
`javaEnabled()`	`navigator.` `javaEnabled()`	Checks browser settings to see if the user has enabled the use of Java applets in the browser. Supported by NN3, IE4 and later as well as Mozilla and Safari.

`preference()`	`navigator.`
	`preference`
	`(name[,val])`
		Allows signed scripts to view or change user preferences in Netscape Navigator 4 or later. These preferences include whether Java, JavaScript, and AutoInstall are enabled as well as whether cookies are accepted. Only supported by NN4 and later.

`taintEnabled()`	`navigator.` `taintEnabled()`	Checks browser settings to see if the user has enabled data tainting. Data tainting was implemented in Netscape Navigator 3 to allow authorized scripts to read secure properties of the `history` object. This capability is replaced by signed scripts in later browser versions and should not be used.

STEP 2 – TESTING A CONDITION

In your text editor, edit the page you created in the previous step. Add Exhibit 15.2 as a body-defined script. This script uses the `navigator.javaEnabled()` method in a conditional expression. When Java is enabled, the `if` code block is executed. Otherwise, the `else` code block is executed, because Java is disabled.

EXHIBIT 15.2

```
<script type="text/javascript">
if (navigator.javaEnabled()) {
 //Java is enabled
} else {
 //Java is disabled
}
</script>
```

STEP 3 – DEFINING THE `if` AND `else` CODE BLOCKS

In your text editor, define the `if` and `else` code blocks. If Java is enabled, two applets should be displayed along with information about the applets. If Java is disabled, two images should be displayed along with information about the images. The code within the `if` construct is defined as shown in Exhibit 15.3.

EXHIBIT 15.3

```
document.write("<h1>Applet Example</h1>");
document.write("<applet code='' name='circles' height=
  '200' width='300'></applet>");
document.write("<applet code='' name='squares' height=
  '200' width='300'></applet>");
document.write("<p>There are " + document.
  applets.length  + " applets defined for this
  document<\p>");
for (x = 0; x < document.applets.length; x++) {
document.write("<p>Applet " + x + " is " + document.
  applets[x].name + "</p>");
}
```

The code within the `else` construct is defined as shown in Exhibit 15.4.

EXHIBIT 15.4

```
document.write("<h1>Image Example</h1>");
document.write("<img src='image1.gif' alt='Circles'
  height='200' width='300' />");
document.write("<img src='image2.gif' alt='Squares'
  height='200' width='300' />");
document.write("<p>There are " + document.images.
  length + " images defined for this document<\p>");
for (x = 0; x < document.images.length; x++) {
document.write("<p>Image " + x + " is " +
  document.images[x].alt + "</p>");
}
```

STEP 4 – LOADING AND TESTING THE PAGE

Open the page in Internet Explorer. If you have edited the page correctly, you should see Java applets if Java is enabled and images if Java is disabled. Figure 15.1 shows an example.

15

FIGURE 15.1 Testing compatibility.

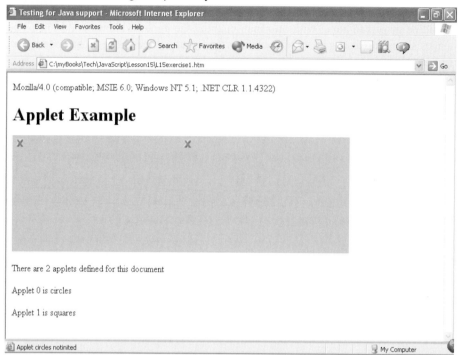

Exercise 15.2 – Examining Browser and OS-Related Properties

Mozilla Was the First Graphics-Capable Browser Engine

The history of Mozilla goes all the way back to the early days of the Web. In those days, NCSA Mosaic was the only browser available that displayed both text and graphics. Because the browser engine was available as open source, first Netscape and then Microsoft chose to use the browser engine as the basis of their browsers. The only browser that we know of that does not report the appCodeName as Mozilla is Opera, which identifies itself as Opera.

Practically every new browser version since Netscape Navigator 2 and Internet Explorer 3 has introduced new features for the navigator object. This can introduce compatibility problems if you want to work with some of the more advanced properties of the navigator object. To help you steer around these problems, Table 15.3 provides a brief description of each property and a list of the browsers that support the property.

As you can see, these properties provide many ways to examine the client browser. By using conditional constructs and looping, you can use these properties to customize pages based on client type. The properties supported by the most browsers are the ones you will most likely want to work with. These include appCodeName, appName, appVersion, and userAgent.

When you start working with the navigator properties, you will find that you can narrow the useful properties list quickly. The appCodeName property, for example, reports the internal code name of the client browser, and just about every browser has an internal code name of Mozilla, because most browsers are based on the NCSA browser engine created originally for the NCSA Mosaic browser. This means that appCodeName is not very useful.

The appName property reports the official name of the browser. The appName reported by Netscape Navigator is Netscape. Internet Explorer reports the appName as Microsoft Internet Explorer. Knowing the official browser name is useful

TABLE 15.3 The `navigator` object properties.

Property	Value	Type	Description
appCodeName	String	Read-only	Returns the internal code name of the client browser. Most browsers are based on the first browser engine created by NCSA and return the codename `Mozilla`. Supported by NN2, IE3 and later as well as Mozilla and Safari.
appName	String	Read-only	Returns the official name of the client browser. For Netscape Navigator, the `appName` is `Netscape`. For Internet Explorer, the `appName` is `Microsoft Internet Explorer`. Opera can be configured to state that it is Netscape, Internet Explorer, or Opera. Safari states that it is `Netscape`. Supported by NN2, IE3 and later as well as Mozilla and Safari.
appVersion	String	Read-only	Returns version information that includes the version number, platform, and country code, such as `5.0 (Windows; en-US)`. Supported by NN2, IE3 and later as well as Mozilla and Safari.
browserLanguage	String	Read-only	Returns the identifier for the localized language version of the browser: `en` for English, `de` for German, `es` for Spanish, `fr` for French, and so on. Only supported by Internet Explorer 4 and later.
cookieEnabled	Boolean	Read-only	Returns `true` if the browser has cookies enabled, `false` otherwise. Supported by NN6, IE4 and later, Mozilla, and Safari.

15

TABLE 15.3 (*Continued*)

Property	Value	Type	Description
`cpuClass`	String	Read-only	Returns a string that identifies the family of CPU the computer is running: `x86` for Intel x86-based processors, `PPC` for Mac PPC, `68K` for Motorola 68000 (Macintosh), `Alpha` for DEC Alpha processors, and so on. There is also `Other` for other processors, such as Sun SPARC. Only supported by Internet Explorer 4 and later.
`language`	String	Read-only	Returns a string that identifies the language for which the browser was written. It is similar to the `navigator.browserLanguage` property used by Internet Explorer but exclusive to Netscape Navigator 4 and later.
`mimeTypes[i]`	Array	Read-only	Allows you to access the array of MIME types known by your browser. Supported by Mac Internet Explorer 5, Netscape Navigator 4 and later, Mozilla, and Safari.
`onLine`	Boolean	Read-only	Returns a Boolean value that indicates whether the browser is set to browse offline. If `navigator.onLine` returns `true`, the browser is in online mode, which does not necessarily mean that the user is on the Internet—only that the browser is in online mode. The user could be accessing a local file from the hard drive as well. Supported by Internet Explorer 4 and later.

TABLE 15.3 (*Continued*)

Property	Value	Type	Description
oscpu	String	Read-only	Returns a string that identifies the operating system and sometimes the CPU as well. For Mac OS X, you get a value of `PPC Mac OS X Mach-0`. With Windows NT 4.0, you get a value of `WinNT4.0`. With Windows 2000, you get a value of `Windows NT 5.0`. With Windows XP, you get a value of `Windows NT 5.1`. With Windows Server 2003, you get a value of `Windows NT 5.2`. Only supported by Netscape Navigator 6 and later.
platform	String	Read-only	Returns a string that identifies the operating system platform: `Win16` for Windows 3.x, `WinNT` for Windows NT, `Win98` for Windows 98, `Win32` for Windows XP/Windows 2000/Windows Server 2003, `Mac68k` for Mac 680000 CPU, `MacPPC` for Mac PPC CPU, `SunOS` for Sun Solaris, and so on. Supported by NN4, IE4 and later as well as Mozilla and Safari.
plugins[i]	Array	Read-only	Allows you to check which plug-ins are installed for use with the browser. Supported by Mac, Internet Explorer 5, and Netscape Navigator 3 and later as well as Mozilla and Safari. Plug-ins are similar to ActiveX controls in that they add functionality to the browser.

15

TABLE 15.3 (*Continued*)

Property	Value	Type	Description
product	String	Read-only	Returns a product code; meant to be used if a vendor adapts the browser engine to a specific use or distribution. Supported by Netscape Navigator 6 and later, Mozilla, and Safari.
productSub	String	Read-only	Returns a product sub code; meant to be used if a vendor adapts the browser engine to a specific use or distribution. Supported by Netscape Navigator 6 and later, Mozilla, and Safari.
securityPolicy	String	Read-only	Returns a string that indicates the cryptographic scheme implemented in the browser. Typically, the value is either US and CA domestic policy or export policy. Supported by Netscape Navigator 4 and later, Mozilla, and Safari.
systemLanguage	String	Read-only	Returns a string that indicates the localized language version of the operating system. Only supported by Internet Explorer 4 and later.
userLanguage	String	Read-only	Returns a string that indicates the localized language version for the user's OS, which in some cases may be different from that of the user. Only supported by Internet Explorer 4 and later.
userAgent	String	Read-only	Returns a combination of the appCodeName and appVersion data. This is the same as the data returned by USER_AGENT

TABLE 15.3 (*Continued*)

Property	Value	Type	Description
			in HTTP headers, such as `Mozilla/4.0 (compatible; MSIE 6.0; Windows NT 5.1; .NET CLR 1.1.4322)` for Internet Explorer 6.0 running on Windows XP. Supported by NN2, IE3 and later as well as Mozilla and Safari.
userProfile	String	Read-only	Returns a `userProfile` object that provides access to some of the user profile settings in Internet Explorer. Only supported by Internet Explorer 4 and later.
vendor	String	Read-only	Returns a vendor code; meant to be used if a vendor adapts the browser engine to a specific use or distribution. Supported by Netscape Navigator 6 and later, Mozilla, and Safari.
vendorSub	String	Read-only	Returns a vendor sub code; meant to be used if a vendor adapts the browser engine to a specific use or distribution. Supported by Netscape Navigator 6 and later, Mozilla, and Safari.

if you want to know the general category of browser and make some basic decision based on whether the user has Internet Explorer, Netscape Navigator, or some other browser. Consider the following example:

```
if (navigator.appName == "Microsoft Internet Explorer") {
//do this
} else if (navigator.appName == "Netscape") {
//do something else
}
```

In this exercise, you will create a page that checks to see what browser is being used and displays information tailored to that browser.

15

STEP 1 – CREATING A PAGE

In your text editor, create a new Web page. You will create a sample HTML page as shown in Exhibit 15.5.

EXHIBIT 15.5

```
<html>
<head>
<title>Browser Test Page</title>
</head>
<body>
</body>
</html>
```

STEP 2 – DEFINING THE CODE BLOCK

In your text editor, edit the page you created in the previous step. Add the body-defined script shown in Exhibit 15.6 that uses the `navigator.appName` property to determine what browser is being used and to display unique content for that browser.

EXHIBIT 15.6

```
<script type="text/javascript">
if (navigator.appName == "Microsoft Internet
  Explorer") {
document.write("<h1>Welcome to the custom page for
  Internet Explorer!</h1>");
document.write("<p>We've customized our site for
  Internet Explorer. This should improve your
  browsing experience.</p>");
} else if (navigator.appName == "Netscape") {
document.write("<h1>Welcome to the custom page for
  Netscape Navigator!</h1>");
document.write("<p>We've customized our site for
  Netscape Navigator. This should improve your
  browsing experience.</p>");
} else {
document.write("<h1>Unrecognized</h1>");
document.write("You are using a browser we don't
  recognize so we can't customize the site for
  you.</p>");
document.write("Download <a href='http://www.microsoft.
  com/ie'>IE</a> or <a href='http://www.netscape.
  com/'>NN</a>.</p>");
}
</script>
```

STEP 3 – LOADING AND TESTING THE PAGE

Open the page in Internet Explorer or Netscape Navigator. If you have edited the page correctly, you should see a custom page for the specific browser you are using, as shown in Figure 15.2.

FIGURE 15.2 Checking the official browser name.

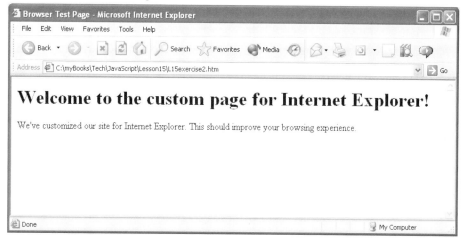

Exercise 15.3 – Customizing Content for Browser Compatibility

Most pages that use client-side scripts to customize content for users based on browser type use the `appVersion` property, the `userAgent` property, or a combination of the two to determine the specific browser version being used. The `appVersion` and `userAgent` properties are similar. The `appVersion` property reports version information, including the version number, platform, and country code. The `userAgent` property reports a combination of the `appCodeName` and `appVersion` properties.

If `appVersion` reported the browser information as `4.0  (compatible; MSIE 6.0; Windows NT 5.1; .NET CLR 1.1.4322)`, the `userAgent` property would report the browser information as `Mozilla/4.0 (compatible; MSIE 6.0; Windows NT 5.1; .NET CLR 1.1.4322)`. In this case, the only difference between `appVersion` and `userAgent` is that `userAgent` includes the string `Mozilla/`.

You can learn a lot about a browser by examining the `appVersion` string given previously:

- `4.0`—Indicates browser engine compatibility. In this case, the browser's base compatibility is that of version 4.0 of this particular browser. This means that the browser can use all of the features of the 4.0 browser object model.

- `Compatible`—Indicates that the browser is running in compatibility mode (meaning it is running so it is compatible with the indicated Netscape Navigator version). Internet Explorer always runs in compatibility mode.

15

Internet Explorer Browser Version Is Hidden

Many times you will want to use a specific browser property but need to confirm that the user's browser supports this property by checking the actual browser version. When working with Internet Explorer, it is important to note that the actual browser version is buried within the string value returned by `appVersion` and `userAgent`. This presents a special problem when you want to determine the actual browser version being used, and you'll learn a solution for resolving this shortly.

- `MSIE 6.0`—Indicates the actual version number of the browser. In this case, the browser is Internet Explorer 6.0.

- `Windows NT 5.1`—Indicates the operating system on which the browser is running. In this case, the browser is running on Windows XP.

- `.NET CLR 1.1.4322`—Additional information that indicates the computer has the .NET client runtime version 1.1 installed.

Netscape Navigator reports a similar string. However, unlike Internet Explorer, the first part of the string contains the only browser compatibility information available. For example, Netscape Navigator might return an `appVersion` string of `5.0 (Macintosh; U; PPC Mac OS X Mach-0; en-US; rv:1.4)`, `4.73 (Macintosh; U; PPC)`, or a similar value. In all cases, the browser compatibility level is given first.

On some systems, Netscape Navigator provides information that identifies the CPU architecture, such as whether the browser is running on a PowerPC or a 68K Mac. The extra field is inserted as follows:

```
5.0 (Macintosh; U; PPC)
```

For international versions of Netscape Navigator, you may also see a field that indicates the specific language version of the browser, such as German. Here is an example for a German-language version of Netscape:

```
5.0 [de] (Win98; I)
```

When you want to customize content, oftentimes you will simply want to know the minimum browser object model supported—its compatibility level, so to speak. The easiest way to do this is to perform a numeric comparison using the `appVersion` property and the `parseInt()` or `parseFloat()` methods. For example, you might want to know if the browser version is at least 4.0 compatible, because the features you are using are supported by 4.0 browser versions and later.

If you want to determine the browser compatibility level, you can use:

```
parseInt(navigator.appVersion);
```

This gives you the whole number to the left of the decimal, such as 4 or 5, and all the other characters after this value are ignored. If you want to determine the complete browser compatibility level, including any decimal values, you can use:

```
parseFloat(navigator.appVersion);
```

This gives you the floating-point value, such as 5.0 or 4.74. Again, all the other characters after this value are ignored.

Once you have obtained the compatibility level for Internet Explorer, you can dig a little deeper and determine the actual browser version being used. The most common way to do this is to use the string method `indexOf()` to determine if the `appVersion` contains a specific string. Consider the following examples:

```
var isIE4x = navigator.appVersion.indexOf("MSIE 4") != -1;
var isIE5x = navigator.appVersion.indexOf("MSIE 5") != -1;
var isIE6x = navigator.appVersion.indexOf("MSIE 6") != -1;
```

Here you test for the major browser version. If the browser version is 4.x, `isIE4x` is set to `true`. If the browser version is 5.x, `isIE5x` is set to `true`. If the browser version is 6.x, `isIE6x` is set to `true`.

However, testing for specific browser versions presents a problem. What happens when the next generation of Internet Explorer becomes available? Do you have to go back and update all of your scripts? Would you want to? Probably not. Don't worry, you will find a workaround later in this exercise.

With Netscape Navigator, `parseInt()` and `parseFloat()` give you a specific browser compatibility level. You do not have to dig deeper—mostly because you can't. This is unfortunate, however, because it is useful to be able to determine the exact browser version, not just a compatibility level. For example, Navigator versions 6 and 7 report a compatibility level of 5. Netscape Navigator 6 and later have significant changes to their browser object model that make them incompatible in some ways with the Netscape Navigator 4 browser object model. This means that Navigator 4 code may break in Navigator 6 and 7 browsers.

In this exercise, you will create a page that checks the browser type and browser version so that the page can be tailored to specific browsers and browser versions.

STEP 1 – CREATING A PAGE

In your text editor, create a new Web page. You will create a sample HTML page as shown in Exhibit 15.7. Note the code block for a body-defined script has already been added.

EXHIBIT 15.7

```
<html>
<head>
<title>Custom Content Page</title>
</head>
<body>
<h1>Welcome to the custom content page!</h1>
<script type="text/javascript">
</script>
</body>
</html>
```

STEP 2 – CHECKING THE BROWSER NAME

In your text editor, edit the page you created in the previous step. Within the body-defined script, define two variables: `isIE` and `isNN`. Use the `navigator.appName` property to determine whether the browser is in fact Internet Explorer or Netscape Navigator. Although there are many ways to do this, the easiest way is to make a simple comparison after the variable assignment, as shown in Exhibit 15.8. In this way, `isIE` is `true` when you are using Internet Explorer, and `false` otherwise. Similarly, `isNN` is `true` when you are using Netscape Navigator, and `false` otherwise.

15

EXHIBIT 15.8

```
var isIE = navigator.appName == "Microsoft Internet
  Explorer";
var isNN = navigator.appName == "Netscape";
```

STEP 3 – DETERMINING THE NETSCAPE VERSION BEING USED

In your text editor, define a code block that determines which version of Netscape Navigator is being used. Again, although there are many ways to do this, the easiest way is to check to see if the browser is Netscape Navigator and then perform a comparison on the browser version. Netscape Navigator has three significant families of browsers: Netscape Navigator 6, Netscape Navigator 4 and Navigator 4.7. Netscape Navigator 6 and later support a browser model that is slightly incompatible with the Navigator 4 model and includes additional features. Navigator 4.7x supports HTML 4 and earlier versions, including Navigator 2, 3, and 4. The code to determine the Navigator version is shown as Exhibit 15.9.

EXHIBIT 15.9

```
if (isNN && parseInt(navigator.appVersion) >= 5) {
  //Customize for Netscape Navigator 6 or later
  alert("You are using Netscape Navigator 6 or later");
} else if (isNN && parseFloat(navigator.appVersion) >=
  4.7) {
  //Customize for Netscape Navigator 4.7x or later
  alert("You are using Netscape Navigator 4.7x");
} else if (isNN) {
  //Customize for Netscape Navigator 2, 3 or 4
  alert("You are using an older Netscape browser");
}
```

STEP 4 – DETERMINING THE VERSION OF INTERNET EXPLORER BEING USED

In your text editor, define a code block that determines which version of Internet Explorer is being used. Internet Explorer has four significant families of browsers: Internet Explorer 6 and later, Internet Explorer 5, Internet Explorer 4, and earlier versions, including Internet Explorer 2 and 3. One way to determine which version of Internet Explorer is being used is shown as Exhibit 15.10. This process is more complex than with Navigator, because you need to examine substrings.

EXHIBIT 15.10

```
var currUA = navigator.userAgent;
function getIEVersion() {
var IEstr = currUA.indexOf("MSIE ");
return parseFloat(currUA.substring(IEstr + 5, currUA.
  indexOf(";", IEstr)));
}

if (isIE && parseInt(getIEVersion()) >= 6) {
  //Customize for Internet Explorer 6 or later
  alert("You are using Internet Explorer 6 or later");
} else if (isIE && parseInt(getIEVersion()) >= 5) {
  //Customize for Internet Explorer 5
  alert("You are using Internet Explorer 5.X");
} else if (isIE && parseInt(getIEVersion()) >= 4) {
  //Customize for Internet Explorer 4
  alert("You are using Internet Explorer 4.X");
} else if (isIE) {
  //Customize for Internet Explorer 2 or 3
  alert("You are using an older Internet Explorer
    browser");
}
```

STEP 5 – LOADING AND TESTING THE PAGE

Open the page in Internet Explorer. If you have edited the page correctly, you should see an alert telling you what browser version you are using, as shown in Figure 15.3.

FIGURE 15.3 Determining the exact browser version.

In this chapter, you have learned techniques for working with the navigator object. Although the object has been expanded with the introduction of various browser versions, the most significant features remain those that were initially introduced with Netscape Navigator 2, including the appName, appVersion, and userAgent properties. These properties can be used with practically all browsers that are in use today.

Many important concepts were introduced in this chapter, including the use of a single line of code to determine the appName, such as:

```
var isIE = navigator.appName == "Microsoft Internet
Explorer";
```

and a single line of code to determine a specific appVersion substring, such as:

```
var isIE4x = navigator.appVersion.indexOf("MSIE 4") != -1;
```

In the first example, you assign a variable equal to the navigator.appName string and then compare the string value with another string. If the second string is "Microsoft Internet Explorer", the isIE variable is then set to true; otherwise, it is set to false.

In the second example, you check for a substring in the navigator.appVersion string. This value is either the index position of the character in the string (indicating a match) or -1 (indicating no match). You then test to determine if the value is something other than -1. If it is, the isIE4x variable is set to true; otherwise, it is set to false.

Summary

Some of the most important utility functions in your JavaScript toolkit are those that you use to determine the browser and operating system version being used. Although the clientInformation object is available as an option for Internet Explorer-only environments, in the real world you will usually want to rely on the navigator object when creating these utility functions. The appName, appVersion, and userAgent properties are the most useful features of the navigator object, because they can be read in just about any browser. Once you have used these properties to narrow the browser version, you can then use some of the more specific properties to extract additional information about the browser and operating system. However, most of this information is provided as part of the appVersion and userAgent strings anyway. Because of this, it is often easier just to use the indexOf() method of the string object to check for a substring within the appVersion or userAgent string.

Test Your Skills

Practice Drill 15.1: Determining the Operating System

In this chapter, you learned the basic skills needed to extract information from the navigator object. You can extend this discussion to just about any type of information that can be obtained from this object. As you may remember, the operating system version is included as part of the userAgent string.

The following exercise shows how you can determine which operating system is being used and tailor content for the operating system.

1. In your text editor, create a HTML page with the appropriate HEAD and BODY elements. Use a TITLE element with the text: "Customizing Content for Operating Systems."

```
<html>
<head>
<title>Customizing Content for Operating
  Systems</title>
</head>
<body>
<h1>An OS-tailored page!</h1>
<script type="text/javascript">
</script>
</body>
</html>
```

2. Within the body-defined script, define two variables: isMac and isWin. Use the navigator.appName property to determine whether the Macintosh or

15

Windows operating system is being used. The easiest way to do this is to make a simple comparison after the variable assignment. You could, of course, add checks for other operating systems, such as Linux or SunOS, as well.

```
var isMac = navigator.appVersion.indexOf("Mac")
   != -1;
var isWin = navigator.appVersion.indexOf("Win")
   != -1;
```

3. Define a code block that determines which Macintosh version is being used. Macintosh has several major variants, including those based on the Motorola 68000 family of processors and those based on Motorola PowerPC processors.

```
if (isMac && (navigator.appVersion.indexOf("PPC")
   != -1 || navigator.appVersion.indexOf("PowerPC")
   != -1)) {
   //Mac PPC
   alert("You are using a Mac with a Motorola Power
     PC processor");
} else if (isMac &&
navigator.appVersion.indexOf("68k")) {
   //Mac with Motorola 68000-processor family
   alert("You are using a Mac with a Motorola 68000-
     processor family");
} else if (isMac) {
   //Other Mac
   alert("You are using a Mac");
}
```

4. Define a code block that determines which version of Windows is being used. Windows has many major variants, including Windows 2000, Windows XP, and Windows Server 2003.

```
if (isWin && navigator.appVersion.indexOf("Windows
   NT 5.2") !=-1) {
   //Windows Server 2003
   alert("You are using Windows Server 2003");
} else if (isWin && navigator.appVersion.indexOf
   ("Windows NT 5.1") !=-1) {
   //Windows XP
   alert("You are using Windows XP");
} else if (isWin &&
navigator.appVersion.indexOf("Windows NT 5.0")
   !=-1) {
   //Windows 2000
   alert("You are using Windows 2000");
} else if (isWin && navigator.appVersion.indexOf
   ("Windows 98") !=-1) {
   //Windows 98
   alert("You are using Windows 98");
```

```
  } else if (isWin && navigator.appVersion.indexOf
    ("Windows 95") !=-1) {
    //Windows 95
    alert("You are using Windows 95");
  } else if (isWin) {
    //Other Win
    alert("You are using a Windows computer");
  }
```

5. Load the page into a Web browser. You should see an alert that tells you what operating system you are running. You can easily replace the alert statements with custom content for that specific operating system and version.

Practice Drill 15.2: Using Browser-Specific Code

Often you will want to use code that is compatible in one browser version but incompatible in others. For example, an object property may be compatible with Internet Explorer 4 and later, but not with Netscape Navigator or other browsers. In this case, you would want to ensure that the code referencing this object property was only executed when Internet Explorer 4 or later is being used, and ignored otherwise.

To see how this could be handled using the techniques you have learned in this chapter, complete the following exercise.

1. In your text editor, create a HTML page with the elements shown. Use a TITLE element with the text: "Using browser-specific code!"

```
<html>
<head>
<title>Using browser-specific code!</title>
</head>
<body>
<h1>A browser-tailored page!</h1>
</body>
</html>
```

2. Insert the following JavaScript code into the body of the document. This code determines whether the browser being used is Internet Explorer 4 or later or an earlier version. You could extend this to check Navigator versions as well.

```
<script type="text/javascript">
var isIE = navigator.appName == "Microsoft Internet
  Explorer";

var currUA = navigator.userAgent;
function getIEVersion() {
var IEstr = currUA.indexOf("MSIE ");
return parseFloat(currUA.substring(IEstr + 5,
  currUA.indexOf(";", IEstr)));
}

if (isIE && parseInt(getIEVersion()) >= 4) {
  //Customize for Internet Explorer 4 or later
```

15

```
} else if (isIE) {
  //Customize for Internet Explorer 2 or 3
}
</script>
```

3. Add the custom content for Internet Explorer 4 or later. Here, you are using properties of the `navigator` object, which are only valid with Internet Explorer 4 or later.

```
document.write("<p>You have IE 4 or later. ");
document.write("Your browser language is " +
  window.navigator.browserLanguage + ". ");
document.write("This might be different from the
  system language, which is currently set to " +
  window.navigator.systemLanguage + ". ");
document.write("It might also be different from the
  default language for your login, which is currently
  set to " + window.navigator.userLanguage + ". ");
document.write("The CPU class of your computer is "
  + window.navigator.cpuClass + " and ");
document.write("you are using a " + window.
  navigator.platform + " platform.");
```

4. Add the custom content for earlier versions of Internet Explorer. In this case, you may want to display a warning that certain features of the site will not work. Here, you simply display an alert.

```
alert("You are using an older Internet Explorer
  browser");
```

5. Load the page into Internet Explorer 4.0 or later. You should see the custom content.

MULTIPLE-CHOICE QUESTIONS

1. With which browser versions might you consider using the `navigator` object?

   A. Only Internet Explorer

   B. Only Netscape Navigator

   C. Either Internet Explorer or Netscape Navigator

   D. None of the above

2. What is the proper way to reference the `navigator` object?

   A. Via the `window` object in any browser

   B. Via the `window` object only with Internet Explorer 4, Netscape Navigator 6 and later

   C. Via the `frame` object

   D. Via the `frame` object only with Internet Explorer 4, Netscape Navigator 6 and later

3. What feature of the `navigator` object do you use to determine whether Java is enabled?

   A. The `javaOn` property

   B. The `javaOn()` method

   C. The `javaEnabled` property

   D. The `javaEnabled()` method

4. What feature of the `navigator` object do you use to determine if cookies are enabled?

   A. The `cookieOn` property

   B. The `cookieOn()` method

   C. The `cookieEnabled` property

   D. The `cookieEnabled()` method

5. What feature of Netscape Navigator has replaced the data-tainting technique?

   A. Signed scripts

   B. User preferences

   C. Auto install

   D. Java

FILL-IN-THE-BLANK QUESTIONS

1. _____ is an alternative object to `navigator` that is used with Internet Explorer 4 or later.

2. In most browsers, the value of the `appCodeName` property is usually _____.

3. In newer browsers, you can reference the `navigator` object via the _____ object.

4. The _____ property returns the official browser name.

5. When using Internet Explorer, the official name returned by the `navigator.appname` property is _____.

6. When using Netscape Navigator, the official name returned by the `navigator.appname` property is _____.

7. You can use the _____ or the _____ property to determine the browser compatibility level and other information about the browser and the operating system.

8. The `userAgent` property returns a combination of the _____ and _____ properties.

15

9. The _____ property can help identify the operating system platform.

10. The _____ property represents the state of the offline browser setting.

DEFINITIONS QUESTIONS

1. What technique would you use to determine if Internet Explorer is being used?

2. What property or method would you use to determine the exact Internet Explorer version being used?

3. What is the difference between the `appVersion` and `userAgent` properties?

4. What is the difference between the `navigator` and `clientInformation` objects?

5. What technique would you use to determine the operating system platform if you want the widest compatibility with current and older browsers?

INTERMEDIATE PROJECTS

The following short projects provide you with additional opportunities to work with the `navigator` object.

Project 15.1 – Limiting Execution Scope by Browser and Operating System

Sometimes a feature is only available with a particular browser version running on either Windows or Mac, but not both. In this case, you must ensure that a feature is only used when the correct operating system and browser versions are present, and ignored otherwise.

In this project, you must create a script that determines if the user has Internet Explorer 4 or later and whether Windows or Mac is being used. If Windows is being used, the script should display custom content for Internet Explorer running on Windows. If Mac is being used, the script should display custom content for Internet Explorer running on Mac. You can use Practice Drill 15.1 to get started if you need some help, but first try to write the script on your own.

Once you have created the HTML page, load it into Internet Explorer and Netscape Navigator to see if it displays correctly. In Internet Explorer, the page should look similar to Figure 15.4.

Project 15.2 – Directing Users with Platform-Specific Content

This project will require you to create a script using the `platform` property that determines the general operating system platform being used and directs users to an appropriate download for their platform automatically. Your script should check for the following platforms: Mac 68000 CPU, Mac PPC CPU, 16-bit Windows, and 32-bit Windows.

The script should test for all the appropriate conditions before trying to direct the user to a specific download. Hint: `platform` can only be used with certain browsers.

When you are finished, load the page into Internet Explorer and Netscape Navigator and test the script you have defined. The page should look similar to Figure 15.5.

FIGURE 15.4 Handling browser- and OS-specific features.

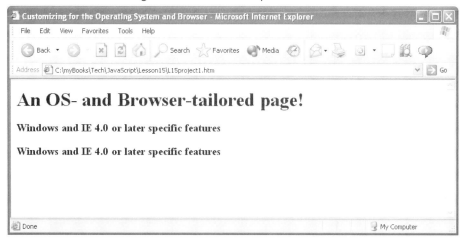

FIGURE 15.5 Customizing content for specific platforms.

Career Builder

In this Career Builder exercise, you finish the help system for the JavaScript-based application developed in Chapters 10 through 13. As you may recall, the application uses a frame-enhanced page, with a side frame used as a menu and the main frame used to display the main contents.

Previously, you defined the help function, which gave users five help options: Choose (the default), About, Help, Colors, and Tips. Now it is time to define the related windows and their contents.

- Before you begin, create a copy of the existing Career Builder files in a working directory and then open cb-side.htm in your text editor. You

(continued)

15

should see four placeholder functions—one for each of the windows needed—that look like this:

```
function aboutWindow() {
 window.alert("About");
}
function helpWindow() {
 window.alert("Help");
}
function colorsWindow() {
 window.alert("Colors");
}
function tipsWindow() {
 window.alert("Tips");
}
```

- Think about the type of help windows you need to create and the related content that is needed. You need an About window that displays information about the Web site, a Help window that provides answers to common problems users at the site encounter, a Colors window that explains how to use the custom color features, and a Tips windows that provides helpful tips for the site's more advanced users.
- Think about how the windows will be created and used. You only want the related window to be created if it does not already exist. This means that you should test for the window before you try to create it. Additionally, you will probably want users to be able to open each of the windows separately. If this is the case, each window needs a unique name and is worked with separately, such as:

```
if (!helpWindow || helpWindow.closed) {
 var helpWindow = window.open("","Help","height=300,
   width=400");
//define and write the window content, then close
//the window.

}
```

- One way to create a window is with a series of write statements. A better way to build a window is to create a string object to hold the text and markup and then use a single write statement to output the contents of the object. You can then use the close() method to close the write stream. In addition to being a sign of a skilled programmer, the use of the string object makes it easier to enter long series of text and markup. Here is an example:

```
var helpPage = "";
helpPage += "<html><head><title>Help
  Page</title></head>";
helpPage += "<body bgcolor='#ffffff'>";
helpPage += "<h2 align=center>Web Site Help
  Page</h2>";
```

(continued)

```
helpPage += "<p>Using our site is really easy as
  long as you have";
helpPage += " IE 4, NN 4 or later with Javascript
  and cookies enabled.";
helpPage += " If you don't have these features
  enabled, turn them on";
helpPage += " then access our site again. You will
  then be able to create";
helpPage += " a user account and password.</p>";
helpPage += "</body></html>";
helpWindow.document.write(helpPage);
helpWindow.document.close();
```

- The complete code for the `helpWindow()` function follows. Use this code as an example to help you create the other help windows that are needed. When you are finished modifying the side frame, save the changes and then load the frameset page in Internet Explorer 5.0 or later. Test the application to make sure everything is working as expected. The selection list should display and you should be able to display each of the help windows.

```
function helpWindow() {
  if (!helpWindow || helpWindow.closed) {
     var helpWindow = window.open("","Help","height=
        300,width=400");
     var helpPage = "";
     helpPage += "<html><head><title>Help
        Page</title></head>";
     helpPage += "<body bgcolor='#ffffff'>";
     helpPage += "<h2 align=center>Web Site Help
        Page</h2>";
     helpPage += "<p>Using our site is really easy
        as long as you have";
     helpPage += " IE 4, NN 4 or later with
        Javascript and cookies enabled.";
     helpPage += " If you don't have these features
        enabled, turn them on";
     helpPage += " then access our site again. You
        will then be able to create";
     helpPage += " a user account and password.</p>";
     helpPage += "</body></html>";

     helpWindow.document.write(helpPage);
     helpWindow.document.close();
   }
}
```

15

Chapter | 16

Creating Client-Side Cookies

Every browser since Netscape Navigator 2.0 and Internet Explorer 3.0 has supported cookies. *Cookies* are used to store information on the client computer so that it can be retrieved in other pages or in other browser sessions. Cookies are commonly used to store user names and encrypted passwords for protected Web sites, items selected for purchase at online stores, and user preferences. Many Web sites store user information to customize their pages for individual users. By storing user names and passwords, a site does not have to prompt users for login information each time they visit and can instead read this information from the cookies stored on users' computer. By tracking the items a user has looked at, an online store can guess the user's shopping preferences and suggest related items.

With cookies, you can also customize the appearance of the page, including the color of text, backgrounds, foregrounds, and links. You can create different levels in the help system for novice, intermediate, and advanced users. You can let users set their preferred level of graphics and extras with categories such as feature rich, average, and basic. You can allow the user to select a preferred language, such as English, Spanish, French, or German. Enabling these options is a matter of determining which option the user has selected, setting a cookie with the matching value, and creating a page that takes advantage of the preferred option. You can use these concepts to make any area of your Web site customizable. If you place preference selection menus on your home page, you could even make your entire site customizable.

For Your Career

The techniques discussed in this chapter are an essential part of every Web programmer's toolkit. Just about every commercial site on the Internet uses cookies in one way or another, as do hobbyist sites. Browsers limit the number of cookies you can use to 20 cookies per domain. Netscape adds another limit by setting the total number of allowed cookies for all domains to 300.

Chapter Exercises

This unit's exercises will teach you how to:

- Create cookies to store bits of information
- Create cookies with multiple parameters
- Read cookies and use their values
- Delete cookies when you are finished with them

By working through the exercises, you will learn to how to use cookies in your Web pages. Not only will you learn how to create cookies, you will also learn how to use their values to store information between browser sessions.

Exercise 16.1 – Creating Your First Cookie

The mechanics of how cookies work is fairly straightforward. Cookies are written to and read from a text file on the user's computer using the `cookie` property of the `document` object.

Mozilla-based browsers store cookies in a file called cookies.txt, which is stored in the browser's profiles folder. On Windows systems, this folder is found under `C:\Windows\Application Data\Mozilla\Profiles\`*`ProfileName`*, where `ProfileName` is the name of the profile for the currently logged on user. On Macintosh systems, this folder is found under `UserName/Library/Mozilla/Profiles/`*`ProfileName`*, where `UserName` is the name of the currently logged on user and `ProfileName` is the current profile for this user.

Internet Explorer browsers save cookies in a domain-specific text file, which is stored in the `%UserProfile%\Cookies` folder on Windows XP. With earlier versions of Windows, the cookies folder typically is located in a subdirectory of the C:\Windows directory. Internet Explorer stores cookie files in a domain-specific manner to aid the task of restricting access to cookies on a per domain basis—something that all browsers do.

Cookies are read from and written to cookie files as records. Fields in a cookie record detail:

- The domain of the server that created the cookie

- The name of the cookie

- The string of data being stored in the cookie

- The expiration date for the cookie

- A Boolean value indicating whether you need a secure HTTP connect to access the cookie

- A path indicating the URL path(s) that can access the cookie

The first thing you should notice is that cookies are tracked by domain. If you visit www.amazon.com, your browser will have a related cookie file for the domain amazon.com. When you access www.amazon.com, www is the computer name and amazon.com is the domain name. If you later access secure.amazon.com as part of the purchase process, the Web server has access to any cookies previously created in the amazon.com domain. A computer in another domain would not be able to access these cookies, however. If a computer in one domain creates a cookie, a computer in another domain cannot access it.

Cookies can also have an expiration date. When you set an expiration date, you create what is called a **_stored_** (persistent) **_cookie_**. At any time before the expiration date, you can read the stored cookie. When you set a cookie without an expiration date, you create a **_temporary cookie_** that is only valid for the current session. If the user exits the browser window, this temporary cookie is deleted.

Because security is a major concern when using cookies, there are two additional security mechanisms beyond the domain access restriction. The first restriction requires that the cookie be accessed with a secure HTTP connection. If you are creating e-commerce sites, you will find that this is a useful restriction that helps ensure that a user's logon or purchase information is protected if you use temporary cookies to take orders. You can also restrict access to a cookie to a specific URL path. For example, a cookie set for the path www.amazon.com/purchase could only be accessed by pages in the `purchase` directory.

You create cookies using a JavaScript assignment operator with the `document.cookie` property. Six parameters can be used, and the general syntax follows, with optional parameters shown in brackets:

```
document.cookie = "cookieName=cookieData"
[; expires=timeString]
[; path=pathString]
[; domain=domainString]
[; secureBoolean];
```

Table 16.1 summarizes the usage of each parameter. As you can see, the only mandatory parameters are the cookie name and the cookie data. The remaining parameters are optional.

TABLE 16.1 Using the `cookie` parameters.

Parameter	Type	Description
cookieName	Mandatory	Generally a one-word descriptor for the cookie, such as `selectedItems` for a cookie that stores the names of the items a user has in his or her shopping cart. Cookie names must be unique on a per domain basis. When you create a cookie, the browser first looks to see if a cookie with this name exists. If no cookie with this name exists, the browser creates the cookie. If a cookie with this name exists, the browser replaces the old data with the new data.
cookieData	Mandatory	The data the cookie is storing. Because the combined name/data string cannot contain spaces, semicolons, or commas, the cookie data is usually URL-encoded (escaped) using the global `escape()` function. This ensures that cookie data is always stored properly. Additionally, although you cannot save an array or object to a cookie, you could use the `Array.join()` method to convert an array to a string. If you needed to recreate the array, you could use the `String.split()` method after reading the cookie.
expiration date	Optional	The expiration date for the cookie. Although the expiration date and time is stored as a numeric value (in seconds elapsed since

16

TABLE 16.1 (*Continued*)

Parameter	Type	Description
		00:00:00 January 1, 1970), it must be set as a GMT date string. If no expiration date is set, the cookie is created as a temporary cookie. If you want to delete a cookie before its expiration date, you can set the cookie's expiration date to an earlier time than the current time.
path	Optional	The path within the domain the cookie is valid for. The default path setting is the current directory. If you want a cookie to be available under a different path, you could create a duplicate cookie with this path. If you want a cookie to be available along any path in a site, you can set the path to /.
domain	Optional	The domain for the cookie. The default is the current domain. If you need to ensure that a cookie can be accessed across all servers in a domain, you should explicitly set the base domain in which access to the cookie should be granted. The easiest way to set the domain string is to use two periods, where the first period is used to match all subdomains of a domain. For example, if you wanted to ensure domain-wide access, you could use .amazon.com as the domain string.
secure	Optional	A Boolean value that indicates whether a secure connection is required. Set this parameter to true if a secure connection (using HTTPS) is required. The default is false, meaning that a secure connection is not required and a standard HTTP connection can be used.

In this exercise, you are going to create your first cookie. By following this exercise, you will learn how create a cookie and then read the stored cookie.

STEP 1 – CREATING A PAGE

In your text editor, create a new Web page using the markup shown in Exhibit 16.1 and then save it as C16exercise1.htm. Note that the form has a single text field named "field1" and a button. When the button is clicked, the createLogon() function is called. The parameter passed to the function is the current form object (this.form).

EXHIBIT 16.1

```
<html>
<head>
<title>Getting Started: Page 1</title>
</head>
<body>
<form>
<p>Please type in a user name: <input type="text"
   name="field1" /></p>
<p><input type="button" name="go" value="Get Started"
   onclick="createLogin(this.form)"/></p>
</form>
</body>
</html>
```

STEP 2 – SETTING THE COOKIE NAME AND DATA

In your text editor, edit the page you created in the previous step. Add Exhibit 16.2 as a header-defined script. This script creates a cookie named `userName` and uses the value of field1 as its data. Note that no other cookie parameters are used, so the browser will use any applicable default values. After setting the cookie, the script tells the browser to open page2.htm.

EXHIBIT 16.2

```
<script type="text/javascript">
function createLogin(form) {
document.cookie = "userName=" + form.field1.value;
document.location='page2.htm';
}
</script>
```

STEP 3 – CREATING THE SECOND PAGE

In your text editor, create a new Web page as shown in Exhibit 16.3 and save it as page2.htm. This is the page that is accessed after you enter a user name to use for the current session. The page also writes the current value of the `document.cookie` property as an example of how cookie data can be accessed once it is written.

EXHIBIT 16.3

```
<html>
<head>
<title>Page 2: Welcome to our site!</title>
</head>
<body>
```

```
<h1>You're Ready To Go</h1>
<script type="text/javascript">
document.write("<p>" + document.cookie + "</p>")
</script>
</body>
</html>
```

STEP 4 – LOADING AND TESTING THE EXERCISE

Open the C16exercise1.htm page in Internet Explorer. If you have edited the page correctly, you should be able to enter a user name and then click the "Getting Started" button to access page2.htm. Figure 16.1 shows an example of both pages.

FIGURE 16.1 Reading and writing cookie data.

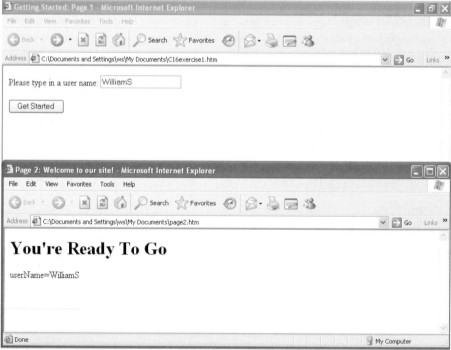

Exercise 16.2 – Creating Cookies with Multiple Parameters

Now that you know the basics of creating cookies and obtaining their values, let's look at programming techniques you can use to create cookies with multiple parameters. Because cookie data cannot be stored with spaces, semicolons, or commas, you should URL encode data `escape()` function, encoding cookie data URL encode the data to ensure that it can be stored properly. To do this, you can use a built-in function called `escape()`. As an example, this function would URL encode the space in the user name `William Stanek` as `%20`, making the string `William%20Stanek`. To retrieve encoded cookie data, you need to use the global `unescape()` function.

A cookie without an expiration date is a temporary cookie. If you want to create a stored cookie, you must set an expiration date. This date must be in GMT date format, such as `Wed, 16-Aug-06 23:59:59 GMT`. Rather than writing out the date yourself, you can simply convert a date you pass when setting a cookie using the `toGMTString()` method. This ensures that the date is precisely formatted and allows you to pass `Date` objects in other formats.

Although you should rarely set the domain parameter to anything but the default, you may want to set the path parameter. One reason to do this would be to allow wider access to the cookie within the site. For example, if a page in the `products/software` directory of your site sets the cookie, you might want pages in `products/docs` and `products/info` to be able to access the cookie. You would do this by setting the path to `products`. If you want any page at the site to be able to access the cookie, set the path to `/`.

In this exercise, you are going to practice setting multiple parameters for cookies. As you will see, one of the most important things to remember when using multiple cookie parameters is that each parameter must be separated by a semicolon.

TIP

Update Cookies in the Same Way You Create Them

16

In JavaScript, you can update the value of a cookie in the same way that you created the cookie in the first place. You simply set the cookie to the desired value. Watch out for the path and domain parameters. If you use these parameters, you may end up with two like-named cookies. For example, you might have a userName cookie for the products/doc path and a userName cookie for the products/software path. To update the right cookie in this case, you would need to specify that path when setting the cookie data.

STEP 1 – CREATING A PAGE

In your text editor, create a new Web page using the markup shown in Exhibit 16.4 and then save it as C16exercise2.htm. The form has a single text field and button. When clicked, this button calls the `getName()` function and passes the current `form` object (`this.form`) as a parameter.

EXHIBIT 16.4

```
<html>
<head>
<title>Enter A User Name</title>
</head>
<body>
<form>
<p>Please type in a user name: <input type="text"
   name="field1" /></p>
<p><input type="button" name="go" value="Enter Your
   User Name"
onclick="getName(this.form)"/></p>
</form>
</body>
</html>
```

STEP 2 – SETTING THE COOKIE NAME AND DATA

In your text editor, edit the page you created in the previous step. Add Exhibit 16.5 as a header-defined script. This script defines the getName() function. This function instantiates a Date object and uses the Date object to set the cookie expiration to a date one year from today. Rather than writing out the date yourself, you can simply convert a date you pass when setting a cookie using the toGMTString() method. This ensures that the date is precisely formatted and allows you to pass Date objects that were originally in other formats.

The function also uses the global escape() function to URL encode the user name. This ensures that if the user name contains a space, semicolon, or comma, it is saved properly. Note also how cookie parameters are concatenated. You enter a semicolon to separate parameters. After setting the cookie, the script tells the browser to open nextpage.htm .

EXHIBIT 16.5

```
<script type="text/javascript">
function getName(form) {
var cookieExp = new Date();
var year = cookieExp.getTime() + (365 * 24 * 60 *
   60 * 1000);
cookieExp.setTime(year);
var name = escape(form.field1.value);
document.cookie = "userName=" + name + "; expires=" +
   cookieExp.toGMTString()+ "; path=/";
document.location='nextpage.htm';
}
</script>
```

STEP 3 – CREATING THE SECOND PAGE

In your text editor, create a new Web page as shown in Exhibit 16.6 and save it as nextpage.htm. This is the page that is accessed after you enter a user name for the current session. The page also writes the current value of the document.cookie property, making sure to unescape the URL-coded value.

EXHIBIT 16.6

```
<html>
<head>
<title>Continue Your Visit</title>
</head>
```

```
<body>
<h1>Thank you!</h1>
<script type="text/javascript">
document.write("<p>" + unescape(document.cookie)
    + "</p>")
</script>
</body>
</html>
```

STEP 4 – LOADING AND TESTING THE EXERCISE

Open the C16exercise2.htm page in Internet Explorer. If you have edited the page correctly, you should be able to enter a user name and then click the "Enter Your User Name" button to access nextpage.htm. Figure 16.2 shows an example of both pages. It is important to note that when you retrieve the cookie only the cookie data is obtained. The expiration date, the path, or other optional parameters are used only by the browser.

FIGURE 16.2 Setting a cookie expiration date and encoding data.

Exercise 16.3 – Extracting Cookie Data

After you set a cookie—even a temporary cookie—you can retrieve the stored data. Although temporary cookies are retrieved from the browser's memory and stored cookies are retrieved from the cookie file on the user's file system, the method to retrieve cookie data is the same:

1. Call `document.cookie`.
2. Find where the cookie you want to work with is located in the list of stored cookies.
3. Extract the cookie by name.
4. Extract and decode the associated data for that cookie.

Cookie data retrieved using JavaScript is returned as a single string, which contains the name/data pairs of all of the cookies set for the current domain. Although JavaScript stores additional parameters for cookies, you can only get the data associated with a named cookie. You cannot examine the other parameters. These parameters are used by and only available to the browser.

Like the cookie parameters themselves, cookie name/data pairs are separated with a semicolon and a space, as shown in the following example:

```
userName=WilliamS; currentItems=A5557324B5558902
```

JavaScript does not have a built-in function to parse the cookie data string and break it down into name/data pairs. This means that you will need to perform a fairly complex manipulation of the cookie data string to get at the actual name/data pair you want to work with. Rather than trying to code a new function every time you work with cookies, you should create a general-purpose cookie retrieval function and then use this function whenever you need to extract cookie data.

Exhibit 16.7 provides a function called `getCookie()`. If you follow the logic of this function, you can see how cookie data are extracted. As you can see, there are actually two functions. The second function, `cookieValue()`, is used by `getCookie()`. These functions are used together to parse the entire cookie string; they look for an instance of the string you specified as the cookie name. Once the name is found, the function determines where the data for this cookie starts and then looks for an instance of the semicolon character to determine where the cookie ends. If no semicolon is found, the function considers everything after the cookie name and the equal sign to be the cookie data.

EXHIBIT 16.7

```
//cookieValue() is used with getCookie(); don't call
   directly
function cookieValue(index) {
var stringEnd = document.cookie.indexOf (";", index);
if (stringEnd == -1)
stringEnd = document.cookie.length;
return unescape(document.cookie.substring(index,
   stringEnd));
}
```

```
//Call getCookie() with name of cookie
function getCookie(name) {
var checkString = name + "=";
var lengthCheckString = checkString.length;
var lengthCookie = document.cookie.length;
var position1 = 0;
while (position1 < lengthCookie) {
var position2 = position1 + lengthCheckString;
if (document.cookie.substring(position1, position2)
   == checkString) {
return cookieValue (position2);
}
position1 = document.cookie.indexOf(" ", position1)
   + 1;
if (position1 == 0) {
break;
}
}
return null;
}
```

With this function, you can retrieve the data associated with a cookie simply by calling `getCookie()` with the name of the cookie. Consider the following example:

```
var name = getCookie("userName");
```

In this example, you call `getCookie()` to obtain the value set for the `userName` cookie and assign this value to the name variable.

In this exercise, you are going to create a miniature shopping cart that uses the `getCookie()` function. By following this exercise, you will learn more about working with cookies in general and how to work with this function.

STEP 1 – CREATING PAGE 1

In your text editor, create a new Web page using the markup shown in Exhibit 16.8 and then save it as C16exercise3.htm. In your browser, the page should look similar to Figure 16.3. Here you create a form that allows you to add a selected item to a shopping cart and access the next page in the shopping/checkout process (shopping2.htm). The `addToCart()` function is very similar to other cookie-setting functions you have used previously. For convenience, you hard code the item value. You will learn how to read the values associated with radio buttons in the next chapter.

Find the Images for This Exercise on the Web

This exercise uses several image files. These files can be found on the Companion Web site for this book (www.prenhall.com/webguru). Before you begin, you should copy these images to your current working folder (the one in which you have saved the document for this exercise).

EXHIBIT 16.8

```
<html>
<head>
<title>Shopping Plaza: Choose Your Free Members-only
   Tote Bag</title>
```

```
<script type="text/javascript">
function addToCart(form) {
var cookieExp = new Date();
var year = cookieExp.getTime() + (365 * 24 * 60 *
    60 * 1000);
cookieExp.setTime(year);
var item = "A5557234";
document.cookie = "totebag=" + item + "; expires="
    + cookieExp.toGMTString()+ "; path=/";
document.location='shopping2.htm';
}
</script>
</head>
<body>
<h1>Choose the Color of Your Tote Bag</h1>
<p>
<img border="0" src="totebag.jpg" width="150"
    height="150"></p>
<form>
<p>A tote bag comes free with your membership.
    Choose the color you want and then
click the button.</p>
<p><input type="radio" name="A5557234" value=
    "A5557234Red-Gold" >Red/gold</p>
<p><input type="radio" name="A5557234"
    value="A5557234Blue-White">Blue/white</p>
<p><input type="radio" name="A5557234"
    value="A5557234Silver-Yellow">Silver/yellow</p>
<p> </p>
<p><input type="button" value="Save to Cart &
    Continue" name="saveItem"
    onclick="addToCart()" /></p>
</form>
</body>
</html>
```

STEP 2 – CREATING PAGE 2

In your text editor, create a new Web page using the markup shown in Exhibit 16.9 and then save it as shopping2.htm. As Figure 16.4 shows, this page is very similar to the first shopping page you created. This time, however, after addToCart() creates the necessary cookie, the shopping3.htm page is loaded into the browser. As stated previously, you will learn how to read the values associated with radio buttons in the next chapter.

FIGURE 16.3 Shopping plaza page 1.

EXHIBIT 16.9

```
<html>
<head>
<title>Shopping Plaza: Choose Your Free Members-only
   T-Shirt</title>
<script type="text/javascript">
function addToCart(form) {
var cookieExp = new Date();
var year = cookieExp.getTime() + (365 * 24 * 60 *
   60 * 1000);
cookieExp.setTime(year);
var item = "B555823";
document.cookie = "tshirt=" + item + "; expires="
   + cookieExp.toGMTString()+ "; path=/";
document.location='shopping3.htm';
}
</script>
</head>
<body>
<h1>Choose the Color of Your T-Shirt</h1>
<p>
<img border="0" src="tshirt.jpg" width="150"
   height="150"></p>
```

```
<form>
<p>This stylish t-shirt comes in a variety of colors.
   Choose the color you want to and then click the
   button.</p>
<p><input type="radio" name="B555823" value=
   "B555823White" >White</p>
<p><input type="radio" name="B555823"
   value="B555823Blue">Blue</p>
<p><input type="radio" name="B555823"
   value="B555823Yellow">Yellow</p>
<p><input type="radio" name="B555823"
   value="B555823Red">Red</p>
<p> </p>
<p><input type="button" value="Save to Cart & Finish"
   name="saveItem" onclick="addToCart()" /></p>
</form>
</body>
</html>
```

FIGURE 16.4 Shopping plaza page 2.

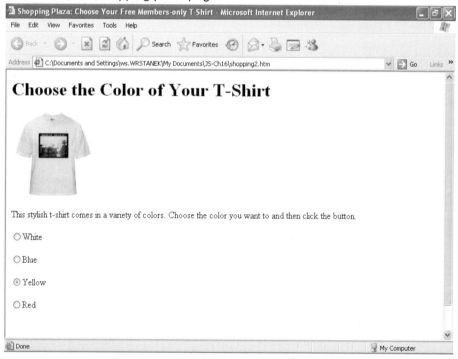

STEP 3 – CREATING THE FINAL PAGE

In your text editor, create a new Web page. As Exhibit 16.10 shows, add the `getCookie()` and `cookieValue()` functions to this page as part of a header-defined script and then save this page as shopping3.htm.

EXHIBIT 16.10

```
<html>
<head>
<title>Shopping Plaza: Almost Finished!</title>
<script type="text/javascript">
//cookieValue() is used with getCookie()
//don't call directly
function cookieValue(index) {
var stringEnd = document.cookie.indexOf (";", index);
if (stringEnd == -1)
stringEnd = document.cookie.length;
return unescape(document.cookie.substring(index,
    stringEnd));
}
// Call getCookie() with name of cookie
function getCookie(name) {
var checkString = name + "=";
var lengthCheckString = checkString.length;
var lengthCookie = document.cookie.length;
var position1 = 0;
while (position1 < lengthCookie) {
var position2 = position1 + lengthCheckString;
if (document.cookie.substring(position1, position2)
   == checkString) {
return cookieValue (position2);
}
position1 = document.cookie.indexOf(" ",
   position1) + 1;
if (position1 == 0) {
break;
}
}
return null;
}
</script>
</head>
<body>
</body>
</html>
```

STEP 4 – DEFINING THE BODY OF THE FINAL PAGE

In your text editor, edit the page created in the previous step (shopping3.htm) and insert the body-defined scripts shown in Exhibit 16.11. If you examine the source of this exhibit closely, you will see several different ways of using cookie data. In the first example, you simply write the value of the cookie data as part of a text paragraph. In the second example, you use the value of the cookie data as part of the file name for an image. Here, note the syntax—this syntax must be followed exactly for this technique to work.

EXHIBIT 16.11

```
<script type="text/javascript">
var summary = "<h1>Summary</h1>";
summary += "<p>You selected tote bag: " +
    getCookie('totebag') + "</p>";
summary += "<p><img src='" + getCookie('totebag')
    + ".jpg'></p>";
summary += "<p>You selected t-shirt: "
    + getCookie('tshirt') + "</p>";
summary += "<p><img src='" + getCookie('tshirt')
    + ".jpg'></p>";
summary += "<p><b>Thank you for becoming a
    member!</b></p>";
document.write(summary);
</script>
```

STEP 5 – LOADING AND TESTING THE EXERCISE

Open the C16exercise3.htm page in Internet Explorer. If you have edited the page correctly, you should be able to make a tote bag selection and then click the button to get to the second page (shopping2.htm). On this page, you should be able to make a t-shirt selection and click the button to display the summary page shown in Figure 16.5.

> ### TIP
>
> **Provide the Path and Domain If Necessary**
>
> Cookies must be deleted according to the path and domain set when they were created. Although you can delete a cookie created in any path within the current domain, you can only delete cookies from the current domain or the subdomains of the current domain. For example, if the current domain is pearson.edu, in most cases you could delete a cookie from the tech.pearson.edu domain.

Exercise 16.4 – Deleting Cookies

Temporary cookies are removed automatically when the user closes his or her browser. Stored cookies remain until they expire or are removed. You can remove a cookie programmatically in JavaScript by setting the cookie's expiration date to a time earlier than the current time. The best date to use is:

```
Thu, 01-Jan-70 00:00:01 GMT
```

This date is the earliest date possible in JavaScript. You could set the cookie expiration to this date and time, as shown in the following example:

```
document.cookie = "userName=; expires=Thu, 01-Jan-70
    00:00:01 GMT ";
```

In this exercise, you will practice techniques for creating and deleting cookies. By following this exercise, you will learn how delete a stored cookie.

STEP 1 – CREATING A PAGE

In your text editor, create a new Web page using the markup shown in Exhibit 16.12 and then save it as C16exercise4.htm. This page creates the visual side of e-commerce

FIGURE 16.5 The summary page for the shopping plaza example.

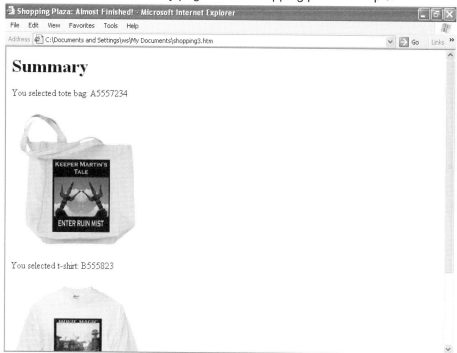

shopping functionality using forms that contain buttons and hidden fields. As with many shopping carts used on the Web, each item has its own form, which contains buttons used to add or remove the item, and a hidden field that tracks the item identifier. Another form provides the checkout functionality, which is simply a button that when clicked takes you to a checkout page. Note also that the page includes a body-defined script with a function call to `cartStatus()`. This function call is used to display the status of the shopping cart when the page is first accessed.

EXHIBIT 16.12

```
<html>
<head>
<title>Shopping Plaza: T-Shirts</title>
</head>
<body>
<h1>T-Shirts at the Shopping Plaza</h1>
<p>
<form>
<img border="0" src="raglant.jpg" width="150"
    height="150"><input type="button" value="Add to
    Cart" onclick="addToCart(this.form)" /><input
```

```
     type="button" value="Remove from Cart"
     onclick="removeFromCart(this.form)" /><input
     type="hidden" name="item" value="TShirtLtBlue005" />
</form>
<form>
<img border="0" src="greyt.jpg" width="150"
     height="150"><input type="button" value="Add to
     Cart" onclick="addToCart(this.form)" /><input
     type="button" value="Remove from Cart"
     onclick="removeFromCart(this.form)" /><input
     type="hidden" name="item" value=
     "TShirtAshGrey005" />
</form>
</p>
<h1>Item Currently In Your Shopping Cart</h1>
<script type="text/javascript">
cartStatus();
</script>
</body>
</html>
```

STEP 2 – ADDING THE UTILITY FUNCTIONS

In your text editor, edit the page you created in the previous step. Add Exhibit 16.13 as a header-defined script. This script uses the `cookieValue()` and `getCookie()` utility functions discussed previously. These functions will be needed when you work with the cookies.

EXHIBIT 16.13

```
<script type="text/javascript">
function cookieValue(index) {
var stringEnd = document.cookie.indexOf (";", index);
if (stringEnd == -1)
stringEnd = document.cookie.length;
return unescape(document.cookie.substring(index,
     stringEnd));
}
function getCookie(name) {
var checkString = name + "=";
var lengthCheckString = checkString.length;
var lengthCookie = document.cookie.length;
var position1 = 0;
while (position1 < lengthCookie) {
var position2 = position1 + lengthCheckString;
```

```
if (document.cookie.substring(position1, position2)
    == checkString) {
return cookieValue (position2);
}
position1 = document.cookie.indexOf(" ", position1)
    + 1;
if (position1 == 0) {
break;
}
}
return null;
}
</script>
```

STEP 3 – DEFINING THE ADD AND REMOVE ITEM FUNCTIONS

Next you need to define the functions for adding or removing shopping cart items. The "Add to Cart" buttons on the shopping page call the addToCart() function and pass the current form object (this.form) as the first parameter. Similarly, the "Remove from Cart" buttons on the shopping page call the removeFromCart() function and pass the current form object (this.form) as the first parameter. In your text editor, add the addToCart() and removeFromCart() functions to the page's header-defined script. The source for these functions is shown in Exhibit 16.14. Note that addToCart() reads the value of the hidden field "item" and uses this to set the tshirt cookie. removeFromCart() deletes the tshirt cookie by resetting its expiration date. Both functions reload the page using a call to document. location.reload(). This is important, as you will see in a moment, because this is how the cart status is updated on the page.

EXHIBIT 16.14

```
function addToCart(form) {
var cookieExp = new Date();
var year = cookieExp.getTime() + (365 * 24 * 60 *
    60 * 1000);
cookieExp.setTime(year);
document.cookie = "tshirt=" + form.item.value + ";
    expires=" + cookieExp.toGMTString()+ "; path=/";
document.location.reload();
}
function removeFromCart(form) {
document.cookie = "tshirt=; expires=Thu, 01-Jan-70
    00:00:01 GMT ";
document.location.reload();
}
```

STEP 4 – SETTING THE CART STATUS

In your text editor, add the `cartStatus()` function to the final element in the header-defined script using the source shown in Exhibit 16.15. This function serves to display the selected item in the shopping cart as applicable.

EXHIBIT 16.15

```
function cartStatus() {
var currItem = getCookie('tshirt');
if (currItem == "TShirtLtBlue005") {
document.write("<p>Jr. Ragland T-Shirt - Light
    Blue</p>");
} else if (currItem == "TShirtAshGrey005") {
document.write("<p>Ash Grey T-Shirt - Blue</p>");
} else {
document.write("<p>None</p>");
}
}
```

STEP 5 – LOADING AND TESTING THE PAGE

Open the C16exercise4.htm page in Internet Explorer. If you have edited the page correctly, you should see the page shown in Figure 16.6. Working with the page can show

FIGURE 16.6 Using cookies in a shopping cart.

you many things about working with cookies. Try adding and removing items to see what happens. Note also what happens if you add one item and then add the other item. You should see that the second item you selected replaces the first item. This occurs because you are setting the `tshirt` cookie to a specific value. If you wanted to allow both items to be in the cart, you would need to read the current cookie data, create a string containing the current data and the new value, and then set the cookie data. For an alternate solution that uses dynamic writes to create the page, take a look at the C16exercise4b.htm file on the Companion Web site, www.prenhall.com/webdevelopment

Summary

Knowing how to create and work with cookies is essential for any JavaScript programmer. Cookies are widely used on the Web. They help track everything from users' names to their preferences to the items they have selected for purchase. As you have seen in this chapter, two types of cookies can be created: temporary or stored. Temporary cookies are cookies that do not have expiration dates. Stored cookies are cookies that have valid future expiration dates. Although temporary cookies are only good for the current browser session, stored cookies are valid until their expiration date is reached or until the cookie is deleted, whichever comes first. In JavaScript, you delete a stored cookie by setting its expiration date to an earlier date.

Test Your Skills

Practice Drill 16.1: Setting Cookie Expiration Dates

A cookie's expiration date must always be set in proper date format. If it is not, the cookie will be invalid and may not be created or stored as expected. As you have seen in this chapter, it is not easy to set a cookie's expiration date. You must instantiate a `Date` object, get the current time, add this to the current time, and then set the cookie's expiration date accordingly, as shown in this example:

```
function getName(form) {
var cookieExp = new Date();
var year = cookieExp.getTime() + (365 * 24 * 60 * 60 *
    1000);
cookieExp.setTime(year);
var name = escape(form.field1.value);
document.cookie = "userName=" + name + "; expires=" +
    cookieExp.toGMTString()+ "; path=/";
}
```

It would be much better if you could set the expiration date to the period of time for which the cookie should be valid in terms of hours and days. Think for a moment about how this could be accomplished using a utility function and then consider the following example function call:

```
setCount(7,12);
```

Knowing that the first parameter is the number of days and the second parameter is the number of hours for which the cookie should be valid, consider what the function would look like and how would it be used and then complete the following exercise.

1. In your text editor, open the page created in Exercise 16.4 and save it as C16practice1.htm. Within the header-defined script, add the `setCount()` function.

```
function setCount(day,hour) {
var theCount = (day * 24 * 3600 * 1000) + (hour *
   3600 * 1000);
return theCount;
}
```

2. Next, update the `addToCart()` function so that `setCount()` is used to set a cookie's expiration date to a date 7 days and 12 hours from now, as shown in this example:

```
function addToCart(form) {
var cookieExp = new Date();
var theDate = cookieExp.getTime() + setCount(7,12);
cookieExp.setTime(theDate);
document.cookie = "tshirt=" + form.item.value + ";
   expires=" + cookieExp.toGMTString()+ "; path=/";
document.location.reload();
}
```

3. Load the page into a Web browser. You should be able to add and remove shopping cart items. If you have incorrectly edited the page, you will either see an error dialog or you may find that the cookie data are not being set. Make changes as appropriate to resolve the issue.

4. Modify the day and hour values to set different expiration dates for the cookie. As you can probably see, this technique is much easier to use and less error prone than setting time values manually.

Practice Drill 16.2: Adding Checkout Functionality

The shopping cart page you created in this chapter allows you to add and remove items. However, it does not allow you to check out and review the items you have purchased. To see how this functionality could be added to the shopping cart application, complete the following exercise.

1. In your text editor, create a HTML page with the elements shown here. Include appropriate HEAD and BODY elements. Use a TITLE element with the text: "Shopping Plaza: Check Out."

```
<html>
<head>
<title>Shopping Plaza: Check Out</title>
</head>
<body>
</body>
</html>
```

2. Insert the following `getcookie()` and `cookieVal()` functions into a header-defined script. This code will be used to get the value stored in the tshirt cookie.

```
<script type="text/javascript">
//cookieValue() is used with getCookie()
//don't call directly
function cookieValue(index) {
var stringEnd = document.cookie.indexOf (";",
    index);
if (stringEnd == -1)
stringEnd = document.cookie.length;
return unescape(document.cookie.substring(index,
    stringEnd));
}

// Call getCookie() with name of cookie
function getCookie(name) {
var checkString = name + "=";
var lengthCheckString = checkString.length;
var lengthCookie = document.cookie.length;
var position1 = 0;
while (position1 < lengthCookie) {
var position2 = position1 + lengthCheckString;
if (document.cookie.substring(position1, position2)
    == checkString) {
return cookieValue (position2);
}
position1 = document.cookie.indexOf(" ", position1)
    + 1;
if (position1 == 0) {
break;
}
}
return null;
}
</script>
```

3. Add the following body-defined script, which dynamically writes the content of the page based on the value of the `tshirt` cookie. Note that if the cookie is set, the item selected is displayed and there is a "Complete Your Purchase" button. On the other hand, if the `tshirt` cookie is not set, the page provides a link to go back to the previous page and continue shopping.

```
<script type="text/javascript">
var thePage = "<h1>Review Your Purchase</h1>";
var currItem = getCookie('tshirt');
if (currItem == "TShirtLtBlue005") {
thePage += "<p>Jr. Raglan T-Shirt - Light Blue</p>";
thePage += "<img border='0' src='raglant.jpg'
    width='150' height='150'>";
thePage += "<form><input type='button' value=
    'Complete Your Purchase' onclick='document.
    location=checkout2.htm' /></form>";
```

```
} else if (currItem == "TShirtAshGrey005") {
thePage += "<p>Ash Grey T-Shirt - Blue</p>";
thePage += "<img border='0' src='greyt.jpg'
   width='150' height='150'>";
thePage += "<form><input type='button' value=
   'Complete Your Purchase' onclick='
document.location=checkout2.htm' /></form>";
} else {
thePage += "<p>Oops you haven't selected an item
   for purchase!</p>";
thePage += "<p><a onclick='history.go(-1)'>Go back
   and continue shopping</a></p>";
}
document.write(thePage);
</script>
```

4. Save the page as checkout.htm. If you load the page created in Practice Drill 16.1, you should be able to click the Check Out button to access this page. You should also see customized content based on your item selection. If you click the Complete Your Purchase button, your browser will try to access the next page in the checkout process—checkout2.htm—which you have not defined.

MULTIPLE-CHOICE QUESTIONS

1. How are cookies created?

   A. By setting a value for the `document.cookie` property

   B. By setting a value for the `document.cookie.value` property

   C. By setting a value for the `document.cookie.text` property

   D. None of the above

2. What parameters are mandatory when setting a cookie?

   A. Cookie name and domain

   B. Cookie name and data

   C. Cookie name, data, and domain

   D. Cookie name, data, domain, and path

3. What are the optional parameters when setting a cookie?

   A. Domain

   B. Path

   C. Expiration date

   D. Secure Boolean

   E. All of the above

4. What parameter should you use when you want to require an HTTPS connection when working with a cookie?

A. Name

B. Data

C. Path

D. Secure Boolean

5. What path value would you use if you wanted a cookie to be accessible on any path?

A. /

B. *pathname/allowanypath*

C. *

A. ./.

FILL-IN-THE-BLANK QUESTIONS

1. The cookie _____ and _____ are the only cookie parameters that you can read in scripts.

2. The _____ character and a space are used to separate cookie parameters.

3. To ensure that cookie data are stored properly, you should _____ the data.

4. When you set an expiration date for a cookie, you should use the _____ function to ensure that the date is properly formatted.

5. If cookie data were read as William%20Stanek and you wanted it to display properly, you would need to use the _____ global function.

6. The default path for a cookie is the _____ directory.

7. You update a cookie's data in the same way that you _____ it.

8. You delete a cookie by resetting its _____ .

9. Mozilla-based browsers store cookies in a file called _____.

10. Temporary cookies do not have a(n) _____ set in the code.

DEFINITIONS QUESTIONS

1. What is the purpose of the cookie's domain parameter?

2. What is the default value of the cookie's domain parameter?

3. What is the purpose of the cookie's path parameter?

4. What is the path parameter's default value?

5. What type of values can you store in a cookie? Can you store an object or an array?

INTERMEDIATE PROJECTS

The following short projects provide you with additional opportunities to work with browser cookies.

Project 16.1 – Creating Cookies with a Utility Function

As a JavaScript programmer, you will spend a lot of time working with cookies. Because of this, you will find it handy to use a utility function for setting cookies. This project defines a utility function for this purpose called `createCookie()`, as shown here:

```
function createCookie(name,data,expires,path,domain,
   secure) {
 document.cookie = name + "=" + escape (data) +
   ((expires) ? "; expires=" + expires.toGMTString() : "")+
   ((path) ? "; path=" + path : "") +
   ((domain) ? "; domain=" + domain : "") +
   ((secure) ? "; secure" : "");
}
```

When you work with `createCookie()`, you must pass the parameters in the order listed. The cookie name and the cookie data are the only required parameters. This means that you could call `createCookie()` as shown in this example:

```
createCookie("selectedItem","A55774983");
```

If you use the other parameters, you must specify them in the order listed and enter null for any parameters you are not setting. Consider the following example:

```
createCookie("selectedItem","A55774983","Dec 31, 2009,
   23:59:59", "/", null, true);
```

Here, you set the cookie name, data, expiration date, path, and secure transfer parameters. Because you do not set the domain parameter, you must enter null as the value for this parameter.

For this project, open Exercise 16.4 and save it as C16project1.htm. Then update the file so that it uses the `createCookie()` function rather than setting the cookie directly. Next, use comments to add documentation that details how the function works and describes each of its parameters. When you finish this and have tested the page, you can update the other exercises created in this chapter if you want more practice.

Project 16.2 – Deleting Cookies with a Utility Function

Because deleting cookies can also be tricky, you may also want to have a utility function for this purpose. This project defines a cookie deletion function appropriately called `deleteCookie()`, as shown here:

```
function deleteCookie(name,path,domain) {
if (getCookie(name)) {
document.cookie = name + "=" +
((path) ? "; path=" + path : "") +
((domain) ? "; domain=" + domain : "") +
"; expires=Mon, 01-Jan-70 00:00:01 GMT";
}
}
```

To delete a cookie using `deleteCookie()`, simply call this function with the name of the cookie:

```
cookieDelete("selectedItem");
```

If you use the other parameters, you must specify them in the order listed and enter null only if you want to use the domain parameter. Consider the following examples:

```
cookieDelete("selectedItem","/");
cookieDelete("selectedItem",null,".amazon.com");
```

In the first example, you delete a cookie with a specific path. In the second example, you delete a cookie from a specific domain (providing, of course, that the page is running on a server in this domain).

For this project, open the file created in the previous project and save it as C16project2.htm. Then update the file so that it uses the `deleteCookie()` function. Next, use comments to add documentation that details how the function works. When you finish this and have tested the page, you can update the other exercises created in this chapter if you want more practice.

Career **Builder**

In this Career Builder exercise you are going to develop a cookie utility library that you can add to your pages any time you want to work with cookies. If you have followed all of the exercises thus far, you have the functions. Now you just need to put them together in a way that is useful.

- Get started by using comments to create a header section that specifies what the library is used for and what functions it contains. This library will contain the `createCookie()`, `deleteCookie()`, `getCookie()`, and `setCount()` functions developed in this chapter, so the header can look like this:

(continued)

```
/*
  The Making Cookies Utility
  By William R. Stanek (williamstanek
  Web Guru's Guide to JavaScript

  Notes: Utility functions to set, get and  cookie
     utility library delete cookies.
     createCookie() - sets a cookie
     deleteCookie() - deletes a named cookie
     getCookie() - gets a named cookie
     setCount() - sets a time string in days and hours
*/
```

- Add the `createCookie()` function and documentation on how to use the function.

```
/*
Setting cookies: call createCookie() with up to
    6 parameters
 1. The name of the cookie (mandatory)
 2. The data the cookie is storing (mandatory)
 3. The expiration date for cookie (optional)
  Do not set expiration date for temporary cookies
 4. The path within domain cookie is valid for
    (optional)
  Default is current path
 5. The domain for the cookie (optional)
  Default is current domain
 6. Set to true to require secure connection
    (optional)
  Default is false
*/
function createCookie(name,data,expires,path,domain,
    secure) {

  document.cookie = name + "=" + escape (data) +
  ((expires) ? "; expires=" + expires.toGMTString()
        : "") +
  ((path) ? "; path=" + path : "") +
  ((domain) ? "; domain=" + domain : "") +
  ((secure) ? "; secure" : "");
}
```

- Add the `deleteCookie()` function and cookie utility library documentation on how to use the function.

```
/*
Deleting cookies: call deleteCookie() with up to
    3 parameters
        1. The name of the cookie (mandatory)
```
(continued)

```
         2. The path within domain cookie is valid
            for (optional)
             Default is current path
         3. The domain for the cookie (optional)
            Default is current domain
    Note: makes a cookie invalid by setting to
       already expired date
*/

function deleteCookie(name,path,domain) {
if (getCookie(name)) {
document.cookie = name + "=" +
((path) ? "; path=" + path : "") +
((domain) ? "; domain=" + domain : "") +
"; expires=Mon, 01-Jan-70 00:00:01 GMT";
}
}
```

- Continue building the library by adding the `getCookie()` function and the related *cookieValue()* function:

```
//used with getCookie(); don't call directly
function cookieValue(index) {
var stringEnd = document.cookie.indexOf (";", index);
if (stringEnd == -1)
stringEnd = document.cookie.length;
return unescape(document.cookie.substring(index,
    stringEnd));
}

/*
Getting cookies: call  cookie utility library
    getCookie() with name of cookie
*/

function getCookie(name) {
var checkString = name + "=";
var lengthCheckString = checkString.length;
var lengthCookie = document.cookie.length;
var position1 = 0;
while (position1 < lengthCookie) {
var position2 = position1 + lengthCheckString;
if (document.cookie.substring(position1, position2)
    == checkString) {
return cookieValue (position2);
}
position1 = document.cookie.indexOf(" ", position1)
    + 1;
if (position1 == 0) {
```

(continued)

16

```
          break;
        }
      }
      return null;
    }
```

- Add the `setCount()` function cookie utility library and its documentation to the library file:

```
/*
Getting a time string in days and hours. Call
   setCount with up to two parameters:
        1. The number of days during which valid
        2. The number of hours during which valid
Used when setting the cookie expiration, as in
   this example:

var cookieExp = new Date();
var theDate = cookieExp.getTime() + setCount(7,12);
cookieExp.setTime(theDate);
createCookie(name,data, setCount(7,12));

*/

function setCount(day,hour) {
var theCount = (day * 24 * 3600 * 1000) + (hour *
3600 * 1000);
return theCount;
}
```

- Save the library file as C16careerbuilder.js. Note cookie utility library that it does not contain a begin or end script block statement (`<script></script>`). The reason for this is that you will use this file as a utility library and will not be inserting the contents of the file into your pages. Instead, in pages that need to use the utility functions, you will insert the following markup into the page header:

```
<script type="text/javascript"
src="C16careerbuilder.js">
</script>
```

- Once you reference the library file, you can call its functions in any of the scripts on the page in the same way you would if the functions were inserted directly into the page. The key thing to keep in mind is that the `src` attribute as shown assumes that the library file is in the current working directory. If the library file is not in the current working directory, you will need to include the appropriate path when you reference the file, cookie utility library such as `src="/utils/C16careerbuilder.js"`.

Chapter | 17

Scripting HTML Forms

Throughout this book, you have seen examples of how scripts can be used to examine form fields. You have used scripts to examine many types of form fields. Now it is time to take a closer look at how scripts can be used with forms. Forms can contain a wide variety of input fields, including push buttons, radio buttons, checkboxes, selection menus, and text fields.

For Your Career

This chapter focuses on scripting standard form elements, including push buttons, radio buttons, checkboxes, selection menus, and text-related input fields. These are the key form elements you will work with. As you read the chapter and follow the exercises, pay particular attention to the way form elements are validated. Whenever possible, you should try to examine and work with forms on the client—even if later submission to a server is required. Preprocessing forms in a user's browser is much faster and much more efficient than having to send a form to a server for validation.

Chapter Exercises

This unit's exercises will teach you how to:

- Examine form objects
- Script push buttons and form submissions
- Manipulate checkboxes
- Work with radio buttons
- Check the options on a selection menu
- Validate the contents of text-related input fields

By working through the exercises, you will learn to how to script form fields. The techniques you will learn will help you process and validate form contents in a user's browser without requiring submission to a server for initial processing. The preprocessed content can then be stored in cookies or used as otherwise necessary, such as to set user preferences. You can also pass the validated form contents to a server for final processing.

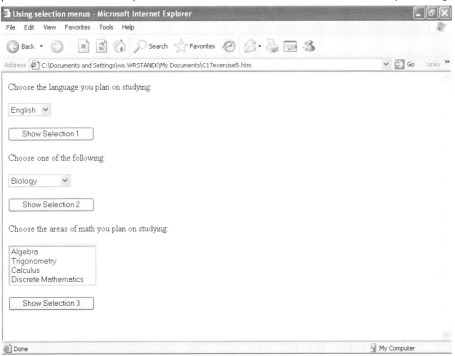

Exercise 17.1 – Examining the `form` Object

A HTML page can contain multiple forms. Each form's contents are enclosed within the `<form>` and `</form>` tags, and each has a related `form` object that can be referenced using the `document.forms[]` array. The first form on a page is referenced as `document.forms[0]`, the second as `document.forms[1]`, and so on. Forms can also be referred to by name. For example, if the `name` attribute of a form is set as `name="MyForm"`, you could reference the form using `document.forms["MyForm"]` or `document.MyForm`.

Before you can learn how to use scripts to examine forms, you first must learn more about the `form` object. The `form` object is used to access form element objects, which are also sometimes referred to as *form controls*. Table 17.1 summarizes the properties, methods, and events available to the `form` object.

As you can see in Table 17.2, most of the `form` object's properties are used to access the attributes of the `<form>` tag. The exception to this is the `elements[]` property, which allows you to access form elements according to their index position in the form. For example, you could use the `elements[]` array to access the value associated with the first form element, as shown in this example:

```
theValue = document.MyForm.elements[0].value;
```

You can also access the value of a field by name. Consider the following example:

```
theValue = document.theform.theinput.value;
```

Here you determine the value of a form field named `theinput` in a form named `theform`.

The methods and events of the `form` object have similar purposes. The `reset()` and `submit()` methods are used to programmatically reset or submit a form, respectively, rather than using the Reset or Submit buttons of a form. Resetting a form triggers the `onreset` event handler regardless of whether the `reset()` method is called or

TABLE 17.1 The `form` object.

Properties	Methods	Events
acceptCharset	handleEvent()	*onreset*
action	reset()	*onsubmit*
autocomplete	submit()	
elements[i]		
encoding		
enctype		
length		
method		
name		
target		

TABLE 17.2 The `form` object properties summary.

Property	Value	Type	Description
acceptCharset	String	Read/Write	The value assigned to the `acceptCharset` attribute of a form, which is used to specify a list of one or more character sets that the server supports. Supported by Netscape Navigator 6 and later, Internet Explorer 5 and later, Mozilla, and Safari.
action	URL String	Read/Write	The value assigned to the `action` attribute of a form; typically the URL to a CGI script or a `mailto:` reference. Supported by Netscape Navigator 2 and later, Internet Explorer 3 and later, Mozilla, and Safari.
autocomplete	String	Read/Write	A value that determines whether autocomplete text can be used to fill in the contents of form fields as users enter values. Only supported by Internet Explorer 5 and later on Windows systems.
elements[]	Array	Read-only	An array of all the form elements; can be used to access form elements by their index. Supported by Netscape Navigator 2 and later, Internet Explorer 3 and later, Mozilla, and Safari.
encoding	String	Read/Write	The value assigned to the `enctype` attribute of the form; the encoding type for the form data. Deprecated in the W3C Document Object Model (DOM). Supported by Netscape Navigator 2 and later, Internet Explorer 3 and later, Mozilla, and Safari.
enctype	String	Read/Write	Same as `encoding`. This property is defined in the W3C DOM and is meant to replace

TABLE 17.2 (*Continued*)

Property	Value	Type	Description
			the `encoding` property. Supported by Netscape Navigator 6 and later, Windows Internet Explorer 6 and later, Macintosh Internet Explorer 5 and later, Mozilla, and Safari.
`length`	Integer	Read-only	The number of elements in the form. Returns the same result as using the `length` property of the `elements[]` array. Supported by Netscape Navigator 2 and later, Internet Explorer 3 and later, Mozilla, and Safari.
`method`	String	Read/Write	The value assigned to the `method` attribute of the form; returns either GET or POST. Supported by Netscape Navigator 2 and later, Internet Explorer 3 and later, Mozilla, and Safari.
`name`	String	Read/Write	The value assigned to the `name` attribute of the form; the name of the form instance. Supported by Netscape Navigator 2 and later , Internet Explorer 3 and later, Mozilla, and Safari.
`target`	String	Read/Write	The value assigned to the `target` attribute for the form or page; typically the URL of the target page for the output of the form or the response from the server. Supported by Netscape Navigator 2 and later, Internet Explorer 3 and later, Mozilla, and Safari.

you click a form's Reset button. Similarly, submitting a form triggers the `onsubmit` event handler regardless of whether the `submit()` method is called or you click a form's Reset button.

The `onsubmit` event is generally used to start the processing of a form's contents. Form submission can be handled completely in a script, by submitting the form's contents directly to a server for processing, or by using a script to preprocess the form's contents before submitting it to a server.

If you want to preprocess a form before submitting it to a server for final processing, you would need to:

■ Set the submission method using either `method="GET"` to set the HTTP GET method or `method="POST"` to set the HTTP POST method.

■ Set the submission action as a URL of a server page that will process the form's contents or use the `mailto:` action to e-mail the form's contents to a specific e-mail address.

■ Set the form to allow validation of individual form fields or the form as a whole. To validate individual form fields, you can use the `onchange` event handler of the form field itself. To validate the entire form, you can use the `onsubmit` event handler of the form. With the `onsubmit` event handler, be sure to return a Boolean value set to `true` to submit the form for processing or `false` to cancel the form submission.

To see how preprocessing could be handled, consider the example shown in Exhibit 17.1.

EXHIBIT 17.1

```
<form name="myform" method="POST"
action="http://www.pearson.edu/reg.pl"
onsubmit="return validateform()">
...
<p><input type="submit" value="Submit" /></p>
</form>
```

In this example, when the form is submitted, the `onsubmit` event handler is triggered and the `validateform()` function is called. If the function returns `true` after preprocessing the form's contents, the form is submitted to http://www.pearson.edu/reg.pl (a nonexistent URL for the purposes of demonstration). Otherwise, if the function returns `false`, the form submission is cancelled. Hopefully, you have alerted the user as to what must be corrected to submit the form. If you do not, the user will not know that the form was not submitted or that what was entered incorrectly needs to be fixed.

In this exercise, you are going to script the form reset and submit processes. By following this exercise, you will learn techniques for invoking the `reset()` and `submit()` methods. The image files for this exercise can be found on the Companion Web site for this book (www.prenhall.com/webguru). Before you begin, you should copy these images to your current working folder (the one in which you will save the document for this exercise).

STEP 1 – CREATING A PAGE

In your text editor, create a new Web page using the markup shown in Exhibit 17.2 and then save it as C17exercise1.htm. As you enter the source for the page, note that the form uses the POST method to submit the form according to the value of the action attribute. Note also that the form has standard Submit and Reset buttons.

EXHIBIT 17.2

```
<html>
<head>
<title>Registration: Page 2</title>
</head>
<body>
<h1>Registration: Almost Done!</h1>
<form name="entries" method="POST" action="http://www.
  pearson.edu/wgj/cgi-bin/register-user.pl">
<p>To finish your registration, please complete and
  submit the following form. All fields must be filled
  in.</p>
<table border="0" width="75%" id="table1">
<tr><td><b>Full Name</b></td>
<td> </td></tr>
<tr><td>First name:</td>
<td> <input type="text" name="firstName" size="25"
  /></td></tr>
<tr><td>Middle Initial:</td>
<td> <input type="text" name="middleName" size="25"
  /></td></tr>
<tr><td>Last name:</td>
<td> <input type="text" name="lastName" size="25"
  /></td></tr>
<tr><td><b>Current Address</b></td>
<td> </td></tr>
<tr><td>Street address:</td>
<td><input type="text" name="streetaddress" size="40"
  />
</td></tr>
<tr><td>City:</td>
<td> <input type="text" name="city" size="25" /></td>
  </tr>
<tr><td>State:</td>
<td> <input type="text" name="state" size="25"
  /></td></tr>
<tr><td>Zip code:</td>
<td> <input type="text" name="zipcode" size="9"
  /></td></tr>
```

```
</table>
<p><input type="submit" value="Submit" name="Submit"
  /><input type="reset" value="Reset" name="Reset"
  /></p>
</form>
</body>
</html>
```

STEP 2 – LOADING AND TESTING THE PAGE

Open the C17exercise1.htm page in Internet Explorer and then complete the form. Clicking the Reset button should clear the form; clicking the Submit button should submit the form for processing. Note that the form's action in this example is a non-existent URL, so you will receive an error from the browser when you click the Submit button.

STEP 3 – EDITING THE PAGE

In your text editor, edit the page for this exercise. Remove the paragraph in the page that defines the Submit and Reset buttons. It looks like this:

```
<p><input type="submit" value="Submit" name="Submit"
  /><input type="reset" value="Reset" name="Reset" /></p>
```

Insert the markup shown in Exhibit 17.3.

EXHIBIT 17.3

```
<p><a href="javascript:document.forms[0].submit()"><img
  alt="image" src="submit.gif" height="60" width="120"
  border="0" /></a> <a href="javascript:document.
  forms[0].reset()"><img alt="image" src="reset.gif"
  height="60" width="120" border="0" /></a></p>
```

STEP 4 – LOADING AND TESTING THE REVISED PAGE

Open the revised C17exercise1.htm page in Internet Explorer. If you have edited the page correctly, the Submit and Reset buttons should be replaced with images, as shown in Figure 17.1. Clicking the Submit image directly invokes the submit() method of the form. Clicking the Reset image directly invokes the reset() method of the form. You could have also used a function call. However, in this example there is no additional processing of the form, so you do not really need to use a function call.

FIGURE 17.1 Working with forms.

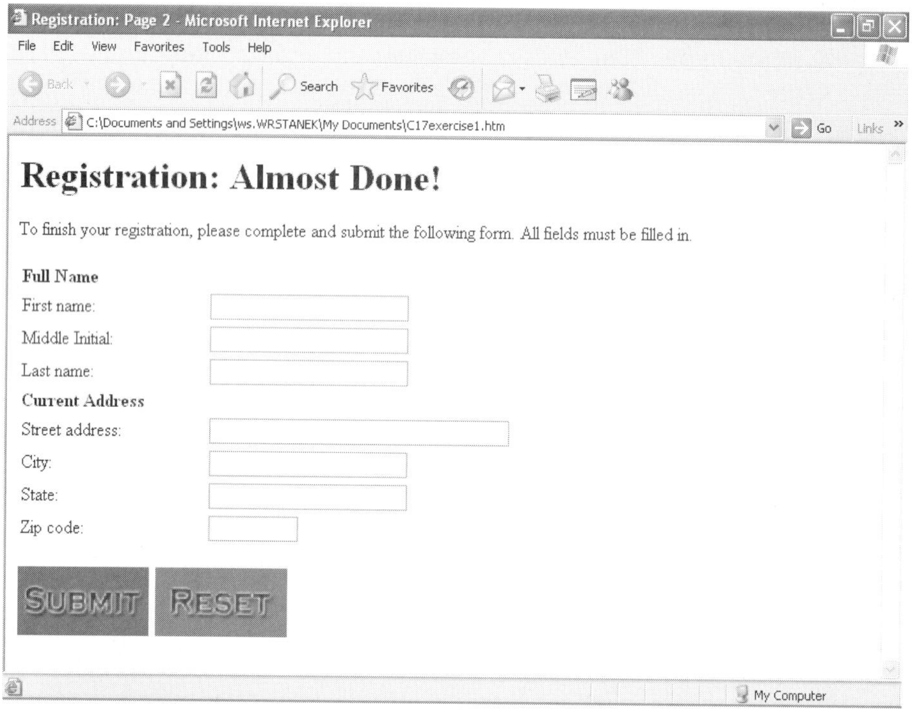

Exercise 17.2 – Working with `button`, `reset`, and `submit` Objects

When you add a form to a page containing an input field with a `type="button"` attribute, you create a ***push button***, and a related `button` object is created by the browser. If you add a form to a page containing an input field of `type="reset"` or `type="submit"`, you create a special type of push button used to reset or submit a form's contents, and a related `reset` or `submit` object is created by the browser.

Table 17.3 provides an overview of the properties, methods, and event handlers for the `button`, `reset`, and `submit` objects. Push buttons—regardless of type—can

TABLE 17.3 Properties, methods, and events of the `button`, `reset`, and `submit` objects.

Properties	Methods	Events
	click()	onclick
form		
name		onmousedown
type		onmouseup
value		

only have a single associated action. They can call a function, detect an event, or sub-mit/clear the contents of a form when pushed.

As Table 17.4 shows, properties of the `button`, `reset`, and `submit` objects let you access the name, type, and value associated with the button definition. You can work with the properties or methods of push buttons in many different ways. The general syntax is:

```
[window.]document.forms[index].elements[buttonindex].
  property
[window.]document.formname.buttonname.property
[window.]document.all.buttonID.property
[window.]document.getElementByID("buttonID").property
[window.]document.getElementsByName("buttonName").property
```

TABLE 17.4 The `button`, `submit`, and `reset` properties summary.

Property	Value	Type	Description
form	form object	Read-only reference	Holds a reference to the `form` object that contains the push button and can be used to access other elements in the form. Supported by Netscape Navigator 6 and later, Internet Explorer 4 and later, Mozilla, and Safari.
name	String	Read-only	The value assigned to the `name` attribute of the push button. Supported by Netscape Navigator 3 and later, Internet Explorer 4 and later, Mozilla, and Safari.
type	String	Read-only	The value assigned to the `type` attribute of the push button. If you do not know what type of form element you are working with, you can use this attribute to determine the type. Supported by Netscape Navigator 3 and later, Internet Explorer 4 and later, Mozilla, and Safari.
value	String	Read/Write	The setting of the push button's `value` attribute. Supported by Netscape Navigator 2 and later, Internet Explorer 3 and later, Mozilla, and Safari.

You can use the onclick event of the button object to create and respond to buttons on your forms. Using the click() method, you can simulate the clicking of a button in your code. The click() method causes the onclick event to occur.

To see how these techniques can be used, consider Exhibit 17.4.

EXHIBIT 17.4

```
<html>
<head>
<title>The button page!</title>
</head>
<body>
<form name="myform">
<input type="button" value="Click Me" name="mybutton"
  id="id1" />
</form>
</body>
</html>
```

The click() method of the push button in Exhibit 17.4 could be accessed using any of the following references:

```
document.forms[0].elements[0].click()
document.myform.mybutton.click()
document.all.id1.click()
document.getElementByID("id1").click()
document.getElementsByName("mybutton").click()
```

In this exercise, you are going to work with push buttons. By following this exercise, you will learn new techniques for managing button clicks and examining forms in general.

STEP 1 – CREATING A PAGE

In your text editor, create a new Web page using the markup shown in Exhibit 17.5 and then save it as C17exercise2.htm. The form on this page defines four push buttons. When one of these buttons is clicked, it calls the booktype() function and uses the this reference to pass the function a reference to the current button object.

EXHIBIT 17.5

```
<html>
<head>
<title>Push buttons</title>
</head>
<body>
<h1>Working with Push Buttons</h1>
```

17

```
<form>
<p><b>Click on your favorite book genres!</b></p>
<input type="button" value="Mystery" onclick=
  "booktype(this)" />
<input type="button" value="Fantasy" onclick=
  "booktype(this)" />
<input type="button" value="Science Fiction" onclick=
  "booktype(this)" />
<input type="button" value="Romance" onclick=
  "booktype(this)" />
</form>
</body>
</html>
```

STEP 2 – ADDING THE FUNCTION

In your text editor, edit the page you created in the previous step. Add a header-defined
script that defines the `booktype()` function using the source provided in Exhibit 17.6.
Not only does this function show how you can handle the `onclick` event, it also shows
you how a single function can be used to handle events for multiple buttons. Here, each
button passes in its own object as a parameter to the `booktype()` function.

EXHIBIT 17.6

```
<script type="text/javascript">
function booktype(btn) {
if (btn.value == "Mystery") {
alert("You selected mystery!");
}
if (btn.value == "Fantasy") {
alert("You selected fantasy!");
}
if (btn.value == "Science Fiction") {
alert("You selected science fiction!");
}
if (btn.value == "Romance") {
alert("You selected romance!");
}
}
</script>
```

STEP 3 – LOADING AND TESTING THE PAGE

Open the C17exercise2.htm page in Internet Explorer and then click one of the buttons.
If you have edited the page correctly, you should see an alert dialog box that specifies
the selection you have made.

STEP 4 – EDITING THE PAGE

In your text editor, edit the page for this exercise. Remove the end-of-function bracket and the end-of-script designator, which look like this:

```
}
</script>
```

Insert the script source and markup shown in Exhibit 17.7.

EXHIBIT 17.7

```
var theOthers = "";
for (var i = 0; i < btn.form.elements.length; i++) {
if (btn.form.elements[i] != btn) {
theOthers += btn.form.elements[i].value + " ";
}
}
alert("You didn't select " + theOthers);
}
</script>
```

STEP 5 – LOADING AND TESTING THE REVISED PAGE

Open the revised C17exercise2.htm page in Internet Explorer. Click one of the buttons to display an alert dialog box that specifies the selection you made and then click OK. If you have edited the page correctly, you should see a second alert dialog box detailing the genres you did not select, as shown in Figure 17.2. Examine the source in Step 4 again. This example is useful because it shows you how to access the related `form` object when you were originally passed a reference to an object within the form. Once you have a reference to the `form` object itself, you can access another object within the form or invoke a method of the form. In this way, you can work with the form without having to reference the form by its index position or name. This technique also makes it possible to create general-purpose functions that service multiple forms.

Exercise 17.3 – Using `checkbox` Objects

Checkboxes are used widely in forms. You will use *checkboxes* when you want the user to make one or more selections from a group of selections. Adding a checkbox to page creates a related checkbox object that can be scripted.

Table 17.5 summarizes the components of the `checkbox` object. Use this object to examine properties of checkboxes and to determine which checkboxes are selected. The `onclick` event occurs when a checkbox is selected. Use the `click()` method to simulate the `onclick` event.

Most of the properties summarized in Table 17.6 have been described earlier in the chapter. Still, there are two new properties: `checked` and `defaultChecked`. You can use the `checked` property to see if a checkbox is currently selected. You can use the `defaultChecked` property to see if a checkbox was selected by default. If the checkbox was selected by default, you may not want to process the results.

FIGURE 17.2 Forms can be manipulated in many ways.

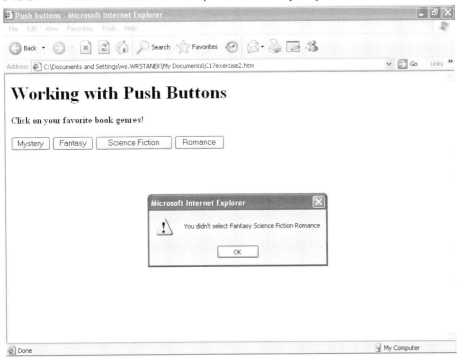

TABLE 17.5 The checkbox object.

Properties	Methods	Events
checked	click()	onclick
form		
defaultChecked		
name		
type		
value		

As with push buttons, you can work with the properties or methods of checkboxes in many different ways. The general syntax follows:

```
[window.]document.forms[index].elements[checkboxindex].
  property
[window.]document.formname.checkboxname.property
[window.]document.all.checkboxID.property
[window.]document.getElementByID("checkboxID").property
[window.]document.getElementsByName("checkboxName")
  .property
```

TABLE 17.6 The checkbox properties summary.

Property	Value	Type	Description
checked	Boolean	Read/Write	Returns true if the object is currently checked (selected). Supported by Netscape Navigator 2 and later, Internet Explorer 3 and later, Mozilla, and Safari.
defaultChecked	Boolean	Read-only	Returns true if the object was checked by default. You can use this property to see if checkboxes were adjusted before the form was submitted. Supported by Netscape Navigator 2 and later, Internet Explorer 3 and later, Mozilla, and Safari.
form	Form object reference	Read-only	Holds a reference to the form object that contains the push button and can be used to access other elements in the form. Supported by Netscape Navigator 6 and later, Internet Explorer 4 and later, Mozilla, and Safari.
name	String	Read-only	The value assigned to the name attribute of the push button. Supported by Netscape Navigator 3 and later, Internet Explorer 4 and later, Mozilla, and Safari.
type	String	Read-only	The value assigned to the type attribute of the push button. If you do not know what type of form element you are working with, you can use this attribute to determine the type. Supported by Netscape Navigator 3 and later,

TABLE 17.6 (*Continued*)

Property	Value	Type	Description
			Internet Explorer 4 and later, Mozilla, and Safari.
value	String	Read/Write	The setting of the checkbox's value attribute. Supported by Netscape Navigator 2 and later, Internet Explorer 3 and later, Mozilla, and Safari.

To see how these techniques can be used, consider the following example shown in Exhibit 17.8.

EXHIBIT 17.8

```
<html>
<head>
<title>Checkboxes</title>
</head>
<body>
<h1>Working with Checkboxes</h1>
<form name="myform">
<p><b>Select your favorite book genres!</b></p>
<p><input type="checkbox" name="C1" value="ON"
  checked />Mystery</p>
<p><input type="checkbox" name="C2" value="ON"
  />Fantasy</p>
<p><input type="checkbox" name="C3" value="ON"
  />Science Fiction</p>
<p><input type="checkbox" name="C4" value="ON"
  />Romance</p>
<p> </p>
</form>
</body>
</html>
```

As you study the example, note that checkboxes are not grouped together with the same name. Each checkbox has its own distinct name. Following this example, you could access the checked attribute of checkbox "C1" using any of the following techniques:

```
document.forms[0].elements[0].checked
document.myform.C1.checked
document.getElementsByName("C1").checked
```

In a script, one way to examine each of these checkboxes would be to use an `if` statement, such as shown in Exhibit 17.9.

EXHIBIT 17.9

```
if (document.myform.C1.checked) {
    //do this
}
if (document.myform.C2.checked) {
    //do this
}
if (document.myform.C3.checked) {
    //do this
}
if (document.myform.C4.checked) {
    //do this
}
```

However, when you have multiple checkboxes, it is usually better to use a general-purpose function. You will use fewer lines of code, and your code will execute more efficiently.

In this exercise, you will develop a general-purpose function for examining checkboxes. It allows you to use the function in any form when you want to examine a series of checkboxes—all you need to do is pass the beginning and ending form index position of the checkboxes you want to examine to the function.

STEP 1 – CREATING A PAGE

In your text editor, create a new Web page using the markup shown in Exhibit 17.10 and then save it as C17exercise3.htm. The form on this page defines a series of checkboxes. When you click the form's Submit button, the `onsubmit` event calls the `validcheck()` function. The `forms[]` array index position of the first checkbox is passed as the first parameter in the function call. The `forms[]` array index position of the last checkbox is passed as the second parameter in the function call.

EXHIBIT 17.10

```
<html>
<head>
<title>Checkboxes</title>
</head>
<body>
<h1>Scripting and Validating Checkboxes</h1>
<form name=myform method=post onsubmit=
  "validcheck(0,4)">
```

```
<p>Select the topics you are interested in:
<p>
<input type=checkbox name="biology" />Biology<br />
<input type=checkbox name="calculus" />Calculus<br />
<input type=checkbox name="organic-chemistry" />Organic
  Chemistry<br />
<input type=checkbox name="physics" />Physics<br />
<input type=checkbox name="world-literature" />World
  Literature</p>
<input type=submit value="Submit" />
</form>
</body>
</html>
```

STEP 2 – ADDING THE FUNCTION

In your text editor, edit the page you created in the previous step. Add a header-defined script that defines the validcheck() function using the source provided in Exhibit 17.11. The function uses a for loop to examine the checked attribute of each check-box. As long as one of them is checked, the value of ischecked will be set to "ok." Otherwise, ischecked will not be set, and an alert is displayed telling you to select at least one of the checkboxes and resubmit the form.

EXHIBIT 17.11

```
<script type="text/javascript">
function validcheck(x,y){
  var ischecked = null;
  for (var i = x; i < y; i++) {
   if (document.forms[0].elements[i].checked) {
     ischecked = "ok";
   }
  }
  if (ischecked == null) {
    alert ("\nPlease select at least one of the
      checkboxes!\n\n Then resubmit the form.");
  }
  return;
}
</script>
```

STEP 3 – LOADING AND TESTING THE PAGE

Open the C17exercise3.htm page in Internet Explorer. Try clicking Submit without making a selection. If you have edited the page correctly, you should see an alert dialog telling you to make a selection and resubmit the form, as shown in Figure 17.3. When you make a selection and then press Submit, no alert should be displayed. In a real-world script, you would then need to process the form's contents or submit the form for processing.

FIGURE 17.3 Checkboxes can be validated easily.

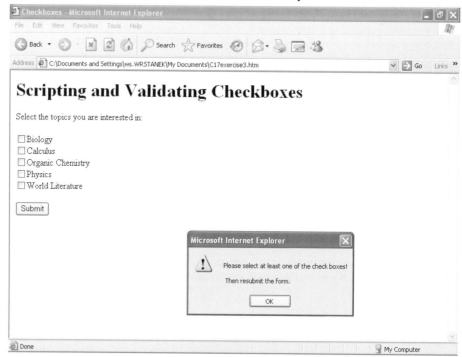

Exercise 17.4 – Using `radio` Objects

Although checkboxes and radio buttons are similar, they serve different purposes. ***Radio buttons*** are used when you want the user to make a single selection from a group of selections.

You use the `radio` object to examine properties of radio buttons and to determine which radio buttons are selected. The `radio` object has the same properties, methods, and event handlers as the `checkbox` object and is referenced in the same way as discussed previously for checkboxes. The key difference is that radio buttons are grouped together with the same name.

You define a group of radio buttons in HTML as shown in Exhibit 17.12.

EXHIBIT 17.12

```
<form>
Select your favorite dessert:
```

```
<input type=radio name=group1 value="none" checked />
  None
<input type=radio name=group1 value="icecream" />Ice
  cream
<input type=radio name=group1 value="pie" />Fruit or
  cream pie
<input type=radio name=group1 value="pudding" />Pudding
  or jello
<input type=radio name=group1 value="candybar" />Candy
  bar
</form>
```

In this example, the first radio button in the group is checked by default. This means that it is selected when the form displays in the user's browser and its `checked` property is set to `true`. The `checked` property of all other radio buttons in the group is set to `false`. If you were to select another radio button in the group, that radio button would be selected and its `checked` property would be set to `true`.

Because radio buttons are grouped with the same name, arrays can be used to track specific instances of a `radio` object within a radio button group. This simplifies the scripting of radio buttons. For example, if the radio button group was named `group1`, you could work with properties of the first radio button defined in the form, as shown in the following example:

```
document.forms[0].group1[0].name;
```

In this exercise, you will use JavaScript to determine which radio button in a group of radio buttons is selected. By following this exercise, you will learn techniques for working with radio buttons and examining their related values.

STEP 1 – CREATING A PAGE

In your text editor, create a new Web page using the markup shown in Exhibit 17.13 and then save it as C17exercise4.htm. The form on this page defines a radio button group called "group1." When you click the Determine Selection button, the `checkselection()` function is called and the current `form` object is passed as the first parameter.

EXHIBIT 17.13

```
<html>
<head>
<title>Radio buttons</title>
</head>
<body>
<form>
<p>Select your favorite dessert:</p>
```

```
<p><input type=radio name=group1 value="none" checked
  />None
<input type="radio" name="group1" value="ice cream"
  />Ice cream
<input type="radio" name="group1" value="pie" />Fruit
  or cream pie
<input type="radio" name="group1" value="pudding"
  />Pudding or jello
<input type="radio" name="group1" value="candy bar"
  />Candy bar</p>
<p><input type=button value="Determine selection"
  onclick="checkselection(this.form)" />
</form>
</body>
</html>
```

STEP 2 – ADDING THE FUNCTION

In your text editor, edit the page you created in the previous step. Add a header-defined script that defines the functions needed to check the radio button group using the source provided in Exhibit 17.14. The `checkselection()` function calls the `checkbutton()` function and passes the `radio` object as its first parameter. In turn, the `checkbutton()` function uses a `for` loop to examine all buttons in `group1` and determine which button is selected. When the radio button with its `checked` property set to `true` is found, the function returns the value of this button's index in the related array. The index into the array is then used to display the value of the radio button in an alert dialog box.

EXHIBIT 17.14

```
<script type="text/javascript">
function checkbutton(radiogroup){
  for (var i = 0; i < radiogroup.length; i++) {
   if (radiogroup[i].checked) {
     return i;
   }
  }
  return 0;
}
function checkselection(form) {
  var i = checkbutton(form.group1);
  alert("You selected " + form.group1[i].value);
}
</script>
```

STEP 3 – LOADING AND TESTING THE PAGE

Open the C17exercise4.htm page in Internet Explorer. If you make a selection and then click the Determine Selection button, you should see an alert dialog telling you which radio button you selected, as shown in Figure 17.4.

FIGURE 17.4 Scripting radio buttons.

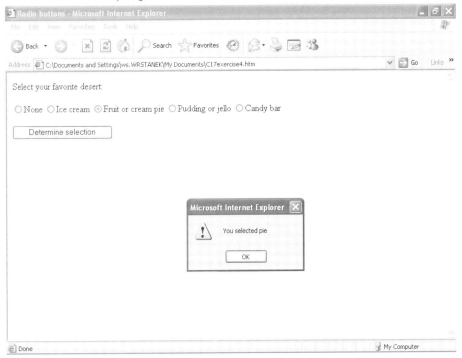

Exercise 17.5 – Working with the `select` and `option` Objects

Selection menus are used widely in forms. You can use *selection menus* to create pop-up lists or scrolling list boxes. Pop-up lists are useful because they provide a very efficient way to present a user with a list of choices; they are especially useful when you want to reduce the screen space used by a form. Scrolling list boxes are useful because they provide an easy way for users to quickly navigate a list and make a selection. Remember, a selection menu or list is created by specifying a `select` element and defining options within this element, as shown in the following example:

```
<select>
<option> </option>
<option> </option>
<option> </option>
```

```
<option> </option>
</select>
```

When you add a selection menu to a page, you create a `select` object that can be scripted. Each option within the selection menu can be scripted as well using the `options[]` array of the `select` object to access its related `option` object.

The `select` object is the most challenging form-related object to work with. As with `radio` objects, you access individual elements of the `select` object using an array. Unlike `radio` objects, you use a named array with many unique properties, as shown in Table 17.7.

TABLE 17.7 The `select` object.

Properties	Methods	Events
form	add()	*onchange*
length	item()	
multiple	namedItem()	
name	options[i].add()	
options[i]	options[i].remove()	
options[i]. defaultSelected	remove()	
options[i].form		
options[i].index		
options[i].selected		
options[i].text		
options[i].value		
selectedindex		
size		
type		
value		

Because JavaScript allows you to modify the options in a selection menu dynamically, you can set many of the `select` object's properties, as shown in Table 17.8. Keep in mind that if you change a selection menu dynamically, you must reset the `length` property for the entire menu and set the `options[i].text` and `options[i].value` properties for each item in the new menu.

TABLE 17.8 The `select` object's properties summary.

Property	Value	Type	Description
`form/options[i].` `form`	form object reference	Read-only	Holds a reference to the `form` object that contains the selection menu and can be used to access other elements in the form. Supported by Netscape Navigator 6 and later, Internet Explorer 4 and later, Mozilla, and Safari.
`length`	Integer	Read/Write	Returns the number of options in the `selection` element. Supported by Netscape Navigator 2 and later, Internet Explorer 3 and later, Mozilla, and Safari.
`multiple`	Boolean	Read/Write	Represents the `multiple` attribute of the `selection` element. If this attribute is set as `multiple=` `"multiple"`, you can make multiple selections. Supported by Netscape Navigator 6 and later, Internet Explorer 4 and later, Mozilla, and Safari. In a script, you can set the multiple property to `true` to allow multiple selections.
`name`	String	Read-only	The value assigned to the `name` attribute of the push button. Supported by Netscape Navigator 3 and later, Internet Explorer 4 and later, Mozilla, and Safari.
`options[i]`	Array	Read-only	Used to reference specific properties of the selection menu. Supported by Netscape

TABLE 17.8 (*Continued*)

Property	Value	Type	Description
			Navigator 2 and later, Internet Explorer 3 and later, Mozilla, and Safari.
options[i].defaultSelected	Boolean	Read-only	Returns `true` if the current option in the `options[]` array was selected by default. Supported by Netscape Navigator 2 and later, Internet Explorer 3 and later, Mozilla, and Safari.
options[i].index	Integer	Read-only	Returns the index value of an option. This is a redundant feature because you must already have the index in the `options[]` array to work with the option. Supported by Netscape Navigator 2 and later, Internet Explorer 3 and later, Mozilla, and Safari.
options[i].selected	Boolean	Read/Write	Returns `true` if the option is currently selected. Supported by Netscape Navigator 2 and later, Internet Explorer 3 and later, Mozilla, and Safari.
options[i].text	String	Read/Write	The text associated with an option as it appears in the selection list. Supported by Netscape Navigator 2 and later, Internet Explorer 3 and later, Mozilla, and Safari.
options[i].value	String	Read/Write	The setting of the `value` attribute for the option, which can be different from the text shown to users. Supported by Netscape Navigator 2 and later, Internet

TABLE 17.8 (*Continued*)

Property	Value	Type	Description
			Explorer 3 and later, Mozilla, and Safari. This is what is sent to the server when a form is submitted.
selectedindex	Integer	Read/Write	Returns the index position of the currently selected item. For lists that allow multiple selections, returns the topmost selected item. Supported by Netscape Navigator 2 and later, Internet Explorer 3 and later, Mozilla, and Safari.
size	Integer	Read/Write	Represents the `size` attribute for the selection list. If you modify the value of this property, you change the number of options that are visible without having to scroll. Supported by Netscape Navigator 6 and later, Internet Explorer 4 and later, Mozilla, and Safari.
type	String	Read-only	Returns the type of the selection list, which is either `select-one` for a list that accepts a single selection or `select-multiple` for a list that accepts multiple selections. Supported by Netscape Navigator 3 and later, Internet Explorer 4 and later, Mozilla, and Safari.
value	String	Read/Write	Returns the string value assigned to the `value` property of the currently selected `option` object. In newer browsers, you

TABLE 17.8 (*Continued*)

Property	Value	Type	Description
			can use this property as a shortcut to obtain the value of the selected option. Supported by Netscape Navigator 6 and later, Internet Explorer 4 and later, Mozilla, and Safari.

In a Web page, you define a selection menu as shown in Exhibit 17.15.

EXHIBIT 17.15

```
<form>
<select name="userPref1">
<option selected="selected">English</option>
<option>French</option>
<option>German</option>
<option>Spanish</option>
</select>
</form>
```

In this example, the first option is selected by default. This means that it is selected when the form displays in the user's browser, and the value of the `selectedIndex` property will point to this option. The `defaultSelected` property for the related `option` is set to `true` as well; the `defaultSelected` property for all other options is `false`.

In this exercise, you will use JavaScript to work with selection menus. By following this exercise, you will learn techniques for working with selection menus and examining their related values.

STEP 1 – CREATING A PAGE

In your text editor, create a new Web page using the markup shown in Exhibit 17.16 and then save it as C17exercise5.htm. Note that the page defines three separate forms, each containing a selection menu. Separate forms are used for convenience and are not required when you want to use multiple selection menus.

EXHIBIT 17.16

```
<html>
<head>
<title>Using selection menus</title>
```

17

```
</head>
<body>
<form name="form1">
<p>Choose the language you plan on studying:</p>
<p><select name="userPref1">
<option selected="selected">English</option>
<option>French</option>
<option>German</option>
<option>Spanish</option>
</select></p>
<p><input type="button" value="Show Selection 1"
  onclick="indexSelection(this.form)"/></p>
</form>
<form name="form2">
<p>Choose one of the following:</p>
<p><select name="userPref2">
<option value="Biology">Biology</option>
<option value="Chemistry">Chemistry</option>
<option value="Physics">Physics</option>
<option value="EarthScience">Earth Science</option>
</select></p>
<p><input type="button" value="Show Selection 2"
  onclick="directSelection(this.form)"/></p>
</form>
<form name="form3">
<p>Choose the areas of math you plan on studying:</p>
<p><select name="userPref3" multiple="multiple">
<option value="Algebra">Algebra</option>
<option value="Trigonometry">Trigonometry</option>
<option value="Calculus">Calculus</option>
<option value="DiscreteMath">Discrete Mathematics
  </option>
</select></p>
<p><input type="button" value="Show Selection 3"
  onclick="multipleSelection(this.form)"/></p>
</form>
</body>
</html>
```

STEP 2 – ADDING THE FIRST FUNCTION

In your text editor, edit the page you created in the previous step. Add Exhibit 17.17 as a header-defined script. This script defines the function needed to check the selection made on the first selection menu. As this example shows, one way to determine the value of the currently selected item is to use the `selectedIndex` property to return the index of the currently selected item and then extract the value or text of this item.

EXHIBIT 17.17

```
<script type="text/javascript">
function indexSelection(form) {
alert(form.userPref1.options[form.userPref1.
  selectedIndex].text);
}
</script>
```

STEP 3 – ADDING THE SECOND FUNCTION

In your text editor, edit the page created for this exercise and add a second function to the header-defined script. This function is used to check the selection made on the second selection menu. As this example shows, you can also determine the value associated with the currently selected option using the `value` attribute of the `select` object. For this technique to work, however, the `option` elements in the form must have `value` attributes, and you must use Internet Explorer 4.0 or later, Netscape Navigator 6.0 or later, Mozilla, or Opera.

```
function directSelection(form) {
 alert(form.userPref2.options.value);
}
```

STEP 4 – ADDING THE THIRD FUNCTION

In your text editor, edit the page you created for this exercise and add a third function to the header-defined script as shown in Exhibit 17.18. This function is used check the selection made on the third selection menu. For a list with multiple selected items, `selectedIndex` and `value` return the value of the last selected item only, and you would not know about other selections. Therefore, if you allow multiple selections or want to use a general-purpose function for checking selected items, you would need to use a function that searches the `options[]` array as shown in this example.

EXHIBIT 17.18

```
function multipleSelection(form) {
var theString = "";
for (var i = 0; i < form.userPref3.length; i++) {
if (form.userPref3.options[i].selected) {
theString += form.userPref3.options[i].text + " \n";
}
}
alert("You have selected: \n\n" + theString);
}
```

STEP 5 – LOADING AND TESTING THE PAGE

In Internet Explorer, open the page you created in Steps 1 through 4. Figure 17.5 shows the page. Work with the page and test out the functions by making a selection on each of the menus in turn and clicking the appropriate buttons. With the third form, you should be able to select multiple options and see all of your selections.

FIGURE 17.5 Scripting selection menus.

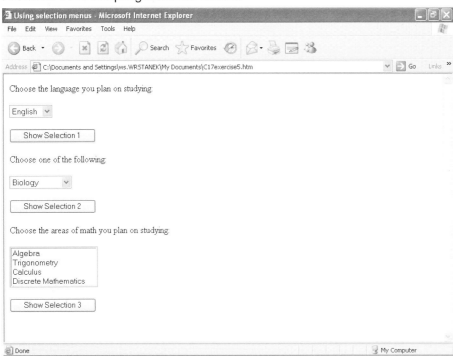

Exercise 17.6 – Working with the `password`, `hidden`, `text`, and `textarea` Objects

The password, hidden, text, and text area fields in a form are all used to obtain input from users or temporarily store information. **Text input fields** are used to enter a single line of data. Password and hidden fields are specialized types of text fields. With a **password field**, any text that is entered is masked with asterisks. With a **hidden field**, you can store information that you want to pass along to the server or use in another page. **Text area fields** are multiple-line input fields into which users can type multiple lines of text.

The related objects for scripting password, hidden, text, and text area fields in forms are `password`, `hidden`, `text`, and `textarea`, respectively. Table 17.9 summarizes the properties, methods, and events of the `text`, `password`, and `hidden` objects.

TABLE 17.9 The `password`, `hidden`, and `text` objects.

Properties	Methods	Events
defaultValue	blur()	onafterupdate
form	focus()	onbeforeupdate
maxLength	select()	onblur
name		onchange
readOnly		onerrorupdate
size		onfocus
type		onselect
value		

Table 17.10 shows the properties, methods, and event handlers supported by the `textarea` object. As you can see, the supported features are similar to those of password, hidden, and text fields.

TABLE 17.10 The `textarea` object.

Properties	Methods	Events
cols	createTextRange()	onafterupdate
defaultValue	blur()	onbeforeupdate
form	focus()	onblur
maxLength	select()	onchange
name		onerrorupdate
readOnly		onfocus
rows		onselect
type		
value		

Most properties of these objects are used to represent attributes of the related form elements. Because many of these properties are the same as those of other objects discussed in this chapter, we will not detail each property. Of the many properties, methods, and events associated with these objects, the `value` property is the one you will use the most. You will use this property to read the text input by users or otherwise stored in a field. You can set values associated with these objects as well, which means you can also use the `value` property to set the values of related form fields at any time.

The methods of the `password`, `hidden`, `text`, and `textarea` objects are used to select or deselect the related objects in the code rather than through a user action:

- `blur()` causes the object to lose focus (and deselects the object).

- `focus()` causes the object to gain focus.

- `select()` selects the object, making it active; an object gains focus before it is selected and active.

Events related to the `password`, `hidden`, `text`, and `textarea` objects are driven by users. If a user selects a text-related element, an `onfocus` event occurs and then an `onselect` event for the related object also occurs. If a user selects a different object, an `onblur` event occurs in the previously selected object.

You can define the password, hidden, text, and text area fields in a form as shown in Exhibit 17.19.

EXHIBIT 17.19

```
<form>
<p>Text field:
<input type="text" name="username" size="16"
  maxlength="16" />
<p>Password field:
<input type="password" name="userpassword" size="16"
  maxlength="16" />
<p>Hidden field:
<input type="hidden" name="memberflag" value=
  "current-member" />
<p>Text area field:
<textarea name="userdata" rows="5" cols=
  "50"></textarea>
</form>
```

In this example, you set various attributes of each field, including `size` and `maxlength` for the text and password fields and `rows` and `cols` for the text area field. Additionally, the `value` attribute is used to set a stored value for the hidden field.

When working with text, password, and text area fields, you often will want to validate the fields before submitting them to a server for processing. Without validation, there is no way to restrict what the user enters. For example, instead of a phone number, a user may enter a bunch of gibberish or you may get a phone number without the area code. With validation, you can determine the acceptable range of values, set the specific type of data you want to obtain, and more.

Using JavaScript, the types of entries can be restricted based on character type. Some of the restrictions you might want to work with include the following:

- **Letters**—Allow or disallow the use of alphabetic characters.

- **Numbers**—Allow or disallow the use of numeric characters.

- **Spaces**—Allow or disallow the use of spaces.

■ **Punctuation**—Allow or disallow specific additional characters, such as commas, periods, or hyphens.

In this exercise, you are going to use JavaScript to validate the entries in a customer registration form. By completing this exercise, you will learn more about working with the text-related fields and validating data entries.

STEP 1 – CREATING A PAGE

In your text editor, create a new Web page using the markup shown in Exhibit 17.20 and then save it as C17exercise6.htm. Note that the page includes the `begin` and `end` form elements but does not include the markup for the form.

EXHIBIT 17.20

```
<html>
<head>
<title>Registration</title>
</head>
<body>
<h2>Customer Registration Form</h2>
<p>Please enter your name and address:</p>
<form>
</form>
</body>
</html>
```

STEP 2 – ADDING THE FORM

In your text editor, edit the page you created in the previous step. Add the form elements shown in Exhibit 17.21 to the form in the body of the page. As you enter the fields, note that each field has a defined `onchange` event handler that calls a function and passes two parameters: the current object for the form field and a special designator that sets the type of characters valid for this field. Usually when you register a user at a site, you will need the user's name and address.

Typically, the user's name is entered with separate fields for first name, middle initial, and last name, and the address is entered with separate fields for street address, city, state/country, and zip code. Each of these entries can be validated by looking for a specific type of value. With name fields, you typically might allow the user to enter only letters and possibly the period or dash characters. With a street address field, you might allow letters, digits, and spaces as well as periods, commas, and hyphens. With city and country fields, you might allow letters, spaces, and dashes. With a zip code field, you might allow only digits and dashes.

EXHIBIT 17.21

```
<p>First <input type="text" size="20" name="firstname"
  onchange="validateinput(this,'letters')" />
 MI <input type="text" size="1" name="middleinitial"
   onchange="validateinput(this,'letters')" />
 Last <input type="text" size="20" name="lastname"
   onchange="validateinput(this,'letters')" /></p>
<p>Street address: <input type="text" size="30"
  name="streetaddress"
onchange="validateinput(this,'special')" /></p>
<p>City: <input type="text" size="30" name=
  "cityaddress" onchange="validateinput(this,'letters')
  " /></p>
<p>State/country: <input type="text" size="30"
  name="countryaddress"
onchange="validateinput(this,'letters')" /></p>
<p>Zipcode: <input type="text" size="20" name="zipcode"
  onchange="validateinput(this,'numbers')" /></p>
<p><input type="submit" value="submit" /></p>
```

STEP 3 – ADDING THE VALIDATION FUNCTION

In your text editor, edit the page you created in the previous step. Add the header-defined script shown as Exhibit 17.22. The function is called with an object reference to the current form field and a character-type parameter. The object reference sets the field you are working with. The character-type parameter is used to set a string containing the acceptable characters for the current form field. Two `for` loops are then used to examine each character entered into the form field in turn and compare it with the list of acceptable characters. If an entered character matches an acceptable character, the inner `for` loop is exited and the next character in the form field is checked. If there is no match between an entered character and the acceptable character list, an error is detected and the `validok` variable is set to `false`, causing an alert to be displayed that tells you to correct the field entry.

EXHIBIT 17.22

```
<script type="text/javascript">
function validateinput(field,type) {
 if (type == "letters") {
  var checkok = "abcdefghijklmnopqrstuvwxyzabcdefghijkl
    mnopqrstuvwxyzABCDEFGHIJKLMNOPQRSTUVWXYZ";
 }
```

```
if (type == "numbers") {
 var checkok = "0123456789";
}
if (type == "lettersnumbers") {
 var checkok = "abcdefghijklmnopqrstuvwxyzabcde
   fghijklmnopqrstuvwxyzABCDEFGHIJK
   LMNOPQRSTUVWXYZ0123456789";
}

if (type == "special") {
 var checkok = "abcdefghijklmnopqrstuvwxyzabcdefghi
   jklmnopqrstuvwxyzABCDEFGHIJKLMNOPQRSTUVWXYZ
   0123456789 .,-";
}
var checkstr = field.value;
var validok = true;
for (i = 0;  i < checkstr.length;  i++) {
 ch = checkstr.charAt(i);
  for (j = 0;  j < checkok.length;  j++) {
   if (ch == checkok.charAt(j)) {
    break;
   }
   if (j == checkok.length - 1) {
    validok = false;
    break;
   }
  }
 }
if (validok == false) {
  alert("The only valid characters for this field are:
    \n \n " + checkok + "\n \n Please go back and
    change this field. Press Shift+Tab");
  return false;
 }
 return true;
}
</script>
```

STEP 4 – LOADING AND TESTING THE PAGE

In Internet Explorer, open the page you created for this exercise. Work with the page and test out the validation function by filling out the form. If you make a mistake, you should see an alert similar to the one shown in Figure 17.6. As you work with the page, consider ways you could improve the validation function for a real Web site. You would probably want to allow spaces, dashes, and periods for a user's last name, for example. If you wanted to validate a phone number, you might want to allow dashes, parentheses, and spaces. For text areas, you would want to make sure that special characters, such as carriage return, form feed, and new line, are considered to be valid characters. The codes for these characters are \r, \f, and \n, respectively.

FIGURE 17.6 Validating text-related fields.

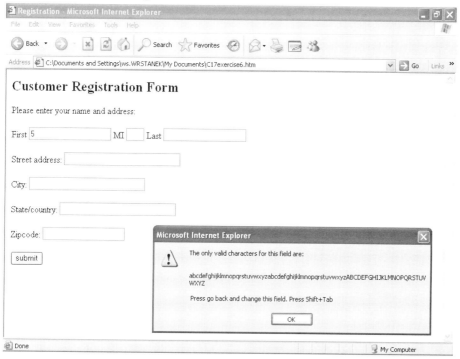

Summary

Forms are widely used on the Web. Anytime you add a form to a Web page, you have access to a related `form` object. Each field in a form also has a related form field object. The `form` object and the form fields objects can be scripted in a variety of ways to examine and validate their contents. In some cases, the only processing the forms will need can be handled by your scripts. In other cases, you will use scripts to preprocess forms before sending the form data to a server for final processing. Either way, processing forms first on the client can save time and reduce the possibility for error.

Test Your Skills

Practice Drill 17.1: Validating Checkboxes

Checkboxes, like any other form field, can be validated. However, checkboxes present a special problem for your validation routines because they are not grouped together; each checkbox has a separate name.

In cases where you want to ensure that the user selects at least one checkbox, you could use a script to examine each individual checkbox in a form. If none of the checkboxes are selected when the form is submitted, a prompt could be displayed telling the user to make a selection.

The following example shows how you can examine the checkboxes in a form and ensure that at least one is selected.

1. In your text editor, create a HTML page with the appropriate HEAD and BODY elements. Use a TITLE element with the text "Validating Checkboxes."

```
<html>
<head>
<title>Validating Checkboxes</title>
</head>
<body>
<h1>Scripting and Validating Checkboxes</h1>
</body>
</html>
```

2. Within the body of the page, add a form that contains a series of checkboxes. Because you want to simulate preprocessing of a form, you set a submission method and action and call a function that returns a Boolean value that can be used to determine if the form should actually be submitted or if the submission should be cancelled.

```
<form name=myform method=post action=
  "http://www.pearson.edu/reg.pl" onsubmit=
  "return validcheck(0,4)">
```

```
<p>Select the topics you are interested in:</p>
<p><input type=checkbox name="biology" />Biology
  <br />
<input type=checkbox name="calculus" />Calculus
  <br />
<input type=checkbox name="organic-chemistry"
  />Organic Chemistry<br />
<input type=checkbox name="physics" />Physics<br />
<input type=checkbox name="world-literature" />World
  Literature</p>
<p><input type=submit value="Submit" /></p>
</form>
```

3. Add a header-defined script containing the `validcheck()` function. Note that the function accepts two parameters. The first parameter is the form index position of the first checkbox. The second parameter is the form index position of the last checkbox. In this example, the first checkbox has an index position of 0 and the last checkbox has an index of 4. Note that a `form` object was not passed to the function, so the form elements are referred to via the `document` object.

```
<script type="text/javascript">
function validcheck(x,y){
  var ischecked = null;
  for (var i = x; i < y; i++) {
    if (document.forms[0].elements[i].checked) {
      ischecked = "ok";
    }
  }
  if (ischecked == null) {
      alert ("\nPlease select at least one of the
        checkboxes!\n\n Then resubmit the form.");
      return false;
  }

  return true;
}
</script>
```

4. Load the page into a Web browser. If you try to submit the form without selecting a checkbox, you should see an alert telling you to make a selection. If you select a checkbox and then submit the form, the browser should attempt to submit the form to the www.pearson.edu server. Note that this is a nonexistent URL, so you will eventually get an error.

Practice Drill 17.2: Using Browser-Specific Code

The problem with radio buttons is that in a standard form, you usually select a default state. The default state ensures that a choice is selected when the form is submitted for processing.

In cases where you want to ensure that the user makes a selection, you may not want to rely on a default state. To work around this, you could use a script to examine the radio buttons in the group. If none of the radio buttons are selected when the form is submitted, a prompt could be displayed that tells the user to make a selection.

When you use scripts to examine radio buttons, you have to examine each radio button according to its index in the radio group. You report an error only when none of the radio buttons are checked.

To see how this could be handled using the techniques you have learned in this chapter, complete the following exercise.

1. In your text editor, create a HTML page with the elements as shown here. Use appropriate HEAD and BODY elements. Use a TITLE element with the text "Checking radio buttons."

```
<html>
<head>
<title>Checking radio buttons</title>
</head>
<body>
<h1>Scripting and Validating Radio Buttons</h1>
</body>
</html>
```

2. Within the body of the page, add a form that contains a radio button group. Because you want to simulate preprocessing of a form, you set a submission method and action and call a function that returns a Boolean value that can be used to determine if the form should actually be submitted or if the submission should be cancelled. Note also that none of the radio buttons are selected by default in this example.

```
<form name="myform" method="POST" action=
  "http://www.pearson.edu/reg.pl" onsubmit=
  "return validradio(this)">
<p>Select your favorite main course:</p>
<p><input type="radio" name="group1" value="pizza"
  />pizza
<input type="radio" name="group1" value="prime rib"
  />prime rib
<input type="radio" name="group1" value="hamburger"
  />hamburger
<input type="radio" name="group1" value="chicken"
  />chicken</p>
<p><input type="submit" value="Submit" /></p>
</form>
```

3. Add a header-defined script that contains the validcheck() function. This function expects to be passed a radio object, and it uses this object to determine if one of the radio buttons in the radio button group is checked (selected).

```
<script type="text/javascript">
function checkradio(radiogroup) {
  for (var i = 0; i < radiogroup.length; i++) {
    if (radiogroup[i].checked) {
        return i;
    }
  }
  return -1;
}
function validradio(rgroup) {
  var isValid = checkradio(rgroup);
  if (isValid == -1) {
      alert ("\n Please select a radio button! \n\n
        Then resubmit the form.");
      return false;
  } else {
  return true;
  }
}
</script>
```

4. Load the page into a Web browser. If you try to submit the form without select-ing a radio button, you should see an alert telling you to make a selection. If you select a radio button and then submit the form, the browser should attempt to submit the form to the www.pearson.edu server. Because this URL does not exist, you will eventually get an error.

MULTIPLE-CHOICE QUESTIONS

1. Submitting a form triggers which method of the `form` object?

    A. `selection()`

    B. `focus()`

    C. `reset()`

    D. `submit()`

2. What event handler is called when a user clicks a form's Submit button?

    A. `onsubmit`

    B. `onfocus`

    C. `onreset`

    D. `onselect`

3. What are the types of push buttons available in forms?

    A. Button

    B. Submit

  C. Reset

  D. All of the above

4. What property of the `checkbox` object do you use to determine if a checkbox has been selected by a user?

  A. `selected`

  B. `checked`

  C. `defaultChecked`

  D. `value`

5. What property of the `select` object can you use to determine the value of the selected option?

  A. Only `selectedIndex`

  B. Only `options.value`

  C. Use `options[i].selected` to determine the selected option and then check its value using `options[i].value`

  D. All of the above

FILL-IN-THE-BLANK QUESTIONS

1. To submit a form to a server for processing, you must set the _____ and _____ attributes.

2. If the `onsubmit` event handler returns _____, the form submission is cancelled.

3. If a checkbox or radio button was selected by default, the value of its _____ property is `true`.

4. Unlike radio buttons, which all have the same name attribute value, each checkbox in a series has a(n) _____.

5. In HTML, you can use the _____ assignment to specify that multiple options can be chosen on a selection menu.

6. In a script, you can set _____ to specify that multiple options can be chosen on a selection menu.

7. The _____, _____, _____, and _____ fields are all used to obtain textual input from users or to temporarily store information.

8. You can use the _____ event handler to determine if the value of an input field has changed.

9. Text areas are very similar to text input fields except that they have _____ and _____ attributes rather than a `size` attribute.

10. To set a default value for a text-related input field, you can use the _____ property of the related object.

DEFINITIONS QUESTIONS

1. What technique would you use to ensure that a form is preprocessed in a user's browser before submitting it to a server for processing?

2. What methods can you call instead of submitting or resetting a form using push buttons?

3. What are two techniques you can use to reference a named form on a page?

4. What are two techniques you can use to reference a named button in a form?

5. What property of the `checkbox` object would you use to determine the value of the selected checkbox?

INTERMEDIATE PROJECTS

The following short projects provide you with additional opportunities to work with forms and form-related objects.

Project 17.1 – Updating Input Fields On-the-Fly

By adding event handlers to an element's markup, you can handle related events in your scripts. Sometimes you will want to dynamically update a form field after an event is triggered. Although JavaScript allows you to dynamically update input fields, these fields must exist on the page before you can update them.

In this project, you will create a page that contains a form with three fields:

- A single text field for entering a full name
- A text area for entering an address
- A text area for displaying a message when either field is updated

Once you have created the HTML page, load it into Internet Explorer to see if it displays correctly. The page should look similar to Figure 17.7. Hint: Use JavaScript to update the `value` attribute of the second text area field to display a confirmation message such as "Thank you for entering your name!"

Project 17.2 – Validating Selection Menus

In forms, selection lists typically allow users to make one or more selections. To give users a pointer that they should make a selection, the first menu item is often a dummy item that reads something like "Make a Selection." This means that sometimes you do not want the first menu item to be selected when a form is submitted.

This project will require you to create a script that validates a selection menu. The script should test for all the appropriate conditions, including the case where no selection

FIGURE 17.7 Updating input fields.

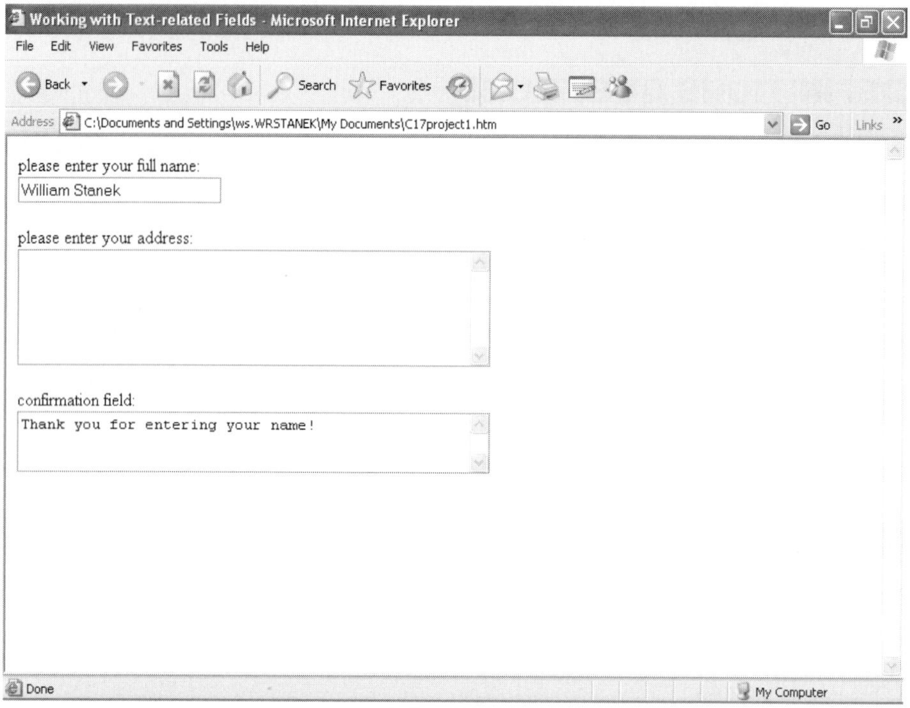

is made (in which case the option text is `null`) and the case where the default option is selected (in which case the option text is equal to the default text you have used, such as "Make a Selection").

Create a selection menu that allows the user to choose a preferred language and has the following options:

- <Choose>
- English
- French
- German
- Spanish
- Italian
- Russian
- Turkish

When you are finished, load the page into Internet Explorer and test the script you have defined. The page should look similar to Figure 17.8. Hint: <> are special characters that must be entered in a special way to get the correct value to display in the selection menu.

FIGURE 17.8 Validating selection menus.

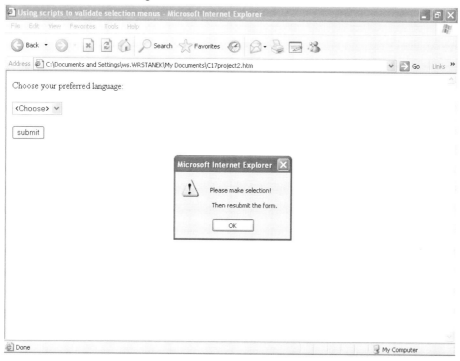

Career Builder

In this Career Builder exercise, you are going to develop a text field validation utility library that you can add to your pages any time you want to validate text fields in forms. If you have followed the chapter exercises, you already have a general-purpose function for checking the characters in a form field. Now you just need to add functions for checking for valid data lengths and valid data ranges.

- Get started by using comments to create a header section that specifies what the library is used for and what functions it contains. This library will contain `checkInput()`, `checkLength()`, and `checkRange()` functions.

```
/*
    The Field Validation Utility
    By William R. Stanek (williamstanek
    Web Guru's Guide to JavaScript

Notes: Utility functions to check for valid
    characters
```

(continued)

```
    data lengths and data ranges
            checkInput() - Checks for valid characters
            checkLength() - Checks for valid data
              lengths
            checkRange() - Checks for valid data ranges
*/
```

- Add the *checkInput()* function along with documentation on how to use the function.

```
/*
Call checkInput() with two parameters
 1. An object reference to the current field
 2. A string designating the type of characters that
    are acceptable. You can optimize the acceptable
    character types based on your local usage.
*/
function checkInput(field,type) {
 if (type == "letters") {
  var checkok = "abcdefghijklmnopqrstuvwxyzabcdefg
    hijklmnopqrstuvwxyzABCDEFGHIJKLMNOPQRSTUVWXYZ";
 }
 if (type == "numbers") {
  var checkok = "0123456789";
 }
 if (type == "lettersnumbers") {
  var checkok = "abcdefghijklmnopqrstuvwxyzabcdefg
    hijklmnopqrstuvwxyzABCDEFGHIJKLMNOPQRS
    TUVWXYZ0123456789";
 }
 if (type == "lspecial") {
  var checkok = "abcdefghijklmnopqrstuvwxyzabcdefgh
    ijklmnopqrstuvwxyzABCDEFGHIJKLMNOPQRSTUV
    WXYZ .,-";
 }
 if (type == "nspecial") {
  var checkok = "0123456789 .,-";
 }
 if (type == "lnspecial") {
  var checkok = "abcdefghijklmnopqrstuvwxyzabcdefg
    hijklmnopqrstuvwxyzABCDEFGHIJKLMNOPQRSTUVWXYZ
    0123456789 .,-";
 }
 var checkstr = field.value;
 var validok = true;
```

(continued)

```
   for (i = 0;  i < checkstr.length;  i++) {
    ch = checkstr.charAt(i);
     for (j = 0;  j < checkok.length;  j++) {
      if (ch == checkok.charAt(j)) {
       break;
       }
       if (j == checkok.length - 1) {
        validok = false;
        break;
       }
     }
    }
  if (validok == false) {
    alert("The only valid characters for this field
       are: \n \n " + checkok + "\n \n Please go back
       and change this field. Press Shift+Tab");
    return false;
   }
  return true;
 }
```

17

- Often you will want to set restrictions on the minimum and maximum length of the text entry. A minimum length of data ensures that users enter correct information. The maximum length restricts the user from entering too much information. By setting the minimum and maximum lengths to the same value, you ensure the user enters the exact number of characters you expect. Add the `checkLength()` function along with documentation on how to use the function.

```
/*
Call checkLength() with three parameters
   1. An object reference to the current field
   2. The minimum number of characters acceptable
   3. The maximum number of characters acceptable
*/
function checkLength(field,theMin,theMax) {
 if (field.value == "") {
   alert("Please enter a value for the " + field.
     name + " field.");
   return false;
 }
 if (field.value.length < theMin || field.value.
   length > theMax)    {
  alert("You must enter between " + theMin + " and "
    + theMax + " characters in the " + field.name + "
    field. \n \n Please go back and change this
    field. Press
```
(continued)

```
                Shift+Tab");
                  return false;
                }
              }
```

- You can also use validation when you need to ensure that entries are within specific value ranges. If you are looking for an answer between 1 and 10, you do not want values less than 1 or more than 10. If you want the user to choose answer A, B, C, or D, you do not want the user to enter E. Add the `checkRange()` function along with documentation on how to use the function.

```
/*
Call checkRange() with up to four parameters
  1. An object reference to the current field
  2. The start character or digit of the range
  3. The end character or digit of the range
  4. An optional Boolean value of true or false to
     indicate whether you are checking input from an
     answer set. With an answer set you give a
     different error message. The value true must be
     entered in lowercase without quotes.
*/
function checkRange(field,startRange,endRange,
  answerSet) {
  if (field.value == "") {
    alert("Please enter a value or make a selection
      for the " + field.name + " field.");
    return false;
  }
  if (field.value < startRange || field.value >
    endRange)    {
      if (!answerSet) {
      alert("You must enter a value between " +
        startRange + " and " + endRange + " in the " +
        field.name + " field. \n \n Please go back and
        change this field. Press
Shift+Tab");
    return false;
    } else {
    alert("You have not made a valid choice. Please
      look at the answer set and choose a valid
        answer. Press Shift+Tab to go back to this
        question.");
    return false;
    }
  }
}
```

(continued)

- Save the library file as C17careerbuilder.js. Note that it does not contain a begin or end script block statement (`<script></script>`). The reason for this is that you will use this file as a utility library and will not be inserting the contents of the file into your pages. Instead, in pages that need to use the utility functions, you will insert the following markup into the page header:

```
<script type="text/javascript" src=
  "C17careerbuilder.js">
</script>
```

- Once you reference the library file, you can call its functions in any of the scripts on the page in the same way you would if the functions were inserted directly into the page. The key thing to keep in mind is that the SRC attribute as shown assumes that the library file is in the current working directory. If the library file is not in the current working directory, you will need to include the appropriate path when you reference the file, such as SRC="/utils/C17careerbuilder.js".

Appendix

Core JavaScript Quick Reference

This appendix provides an at-a-glance guide to the core elements of the JavaScript language. Compatibility notations are provided for all elements referenced.

You can find details on each version of JavaScript supported by Netscape Navigator at www.mozilla.org/js/language/index.html. For Internet Explorer, you will find documentation on JScript (Microsoft's version of JavaScript) at the Windows Scripting Center (msdn.microsoft.com/scripting/default.asp). The official ECMAScript language specification can be found online at www.ecma-international.org/publications/standards/Ecma-262.htm.

Global Elements

Global elements are supported by all JavaScript-compatible browsers except as noted. Most global elements are discussed in Chapters 3 and 4.

Control Statements

```
if (condition) {
  //statementsIfTrue
}

if (condition) {
  //statementsIfTrue
} else {
  //statementsIfFalse
}
```

```
do {
   //statements
} while (condition) [Supported by NN4+, IE4+]

for ([init expr]; [condition]; [update expr]) {
   //statements
}

for (var in object) {
    //statements
}

label : [Supported by NN4+, IE4+]
continue [label] [Supported by NN4+, IE4+]
break [label] [Supported by NN4+, IE4+]

result = condition ? expr1 : expr2

switch (expression) {
 case labelN :
 //statements
 [break]
 ... [default :
 //statements]
} [Supported by NN4+, IE4+]

try {
   //statements to test
}

[catch (errorInfo) {
   //statements if exception
}]
[finally {
   //final statements to run
}] [Supported by NN6+, IE5 for Windows]

while (condition) {
   //statements
}

throw value [Supported by NN6+, IE5 for Windows]

with (object) {
statements
}
```

Functions

`decodeURI("encodedURI")`	Netscape Navigator 6 and later, Internet Explorer 5.5 and later for Windows.
`decodeURIComponent ("encodedComponent")`	Netscape Navigator 6 and later, Internet Explorer 5.5 and later for Windows.
`encodeURI("URIString")`	Netscape Navigator 6 and later, Internet Explorer 5.5 and later for Windows.
`encodeURIComponent ("componentString")`	Netscape Navigator 6 and later, Internet Explorer 5.5 and later for Windows
`escape("string" [,1])`	Deprecated in ECMAScript Version 3. Netscape Navigator 6 and later; Internet Explorer 5.5 and later for Windows should use `encodeURI` but still support `escape()`.
`eval("string")`	
`isFinite(number)`	Netscape Navigator 4 and later, Internet Explorer 4 and later.
`isNaN(expression)`	
`Number(string)`	Netscape Navigator 4 and later, Internet Explorer 4 and later. See also "Number Object."
`parseFloat("string")`	
`parseInt ("string" [,numberBase])`	
`toString([numberBase])`	
`unescape("string")`	Deprecated in ECMAScript Version 3. Netscape Navigator 6 and later; Internet Explorer 5.5 and later for Windows should use `encodeURI` but still support `unescape()`.

Statements

`//`	One-line comment.
`/*...*/`	Block comments.
`const`	Constant. Netscape Navigator 6 and later.
`delete`	Destroy property. Netscape Navigator 4 and later, Internet Explorer 4 and later.

`in item` `in object`	Netscape Navigator 6 and later, Internet Explorer 5.5 and later for Windows.
`instanceof`	Instance of. Netscape Navigator 6 and later, Internet Explorer 5 for Windows.
`new`	Instantiate object.
`this`	Object self-reference.
`typeof`	Value type. Netscape Navigator 3 and later, Internet Explorer 3 and later.
`var`	Declare variable reference.
`void`	Return no value. Netscape Navigator 3 and later, Internet Explorer 3 and later.

Operators

Operators are supported by all JavaScript-compatible browsers except as noted. See Chapter 8 for more information.

Arithmetic

`+`	Add (and string concatenation)
`–`	Subtract
`*`	Multiply
`/`	Divide
`%`	Modulus
`++`	Increment
`--`	Decrement
`-val`	Negation

Assignment

`=`	Equals
`+=`	Add by value
`-=`	Subtract by value
`*=`	Multiply by value
`/=`	Divide by value

%=	Modulus by value
<<=	Left shift by value
>>=	Right shift by value
>>>=	Zero fill right shift by value
&=	Bitwise AND by value
|=	Bitwise OR by value
^=	Bitwise XOR by value

Bitwise

&	Bitwise AND
|	Bitwise OR
^	Bitwise XOR
~	Bitwise NOT
<<	Left shift
>>	Right shift
>>>	Zero fill right shift

Boolean

&&	Logical AND
||	Logical OR
!	Logical NOT

Comparison

==	Equals
===	Strictly equals. Netscape Navigator 4 and later, Internet Explorer 4 and later.
!=	Does not equal
!==	Strictly does not equal. Netscape Navigator 4 and later, Internet Explorer 4 and later.
>	Is greater than
>=	Is greater than or equal to
<	Is less than
<=	Is less than or equal to

Array **Object**

The Array object is supported by all Netscape Navigator 3, Internet Explorer 3, and later versions of these browsers except as noted. See Chapter 6 for more information.

Properties

constructor	Netscape Navigator 4 and later, Internet Explorer 4 and later.
length	
prototype	

Methods

concat(array2)	Netscape Navigator 4 and later, Internet Explorer 4 and later.
join("char")	Netscape Navigator 4 and later, Internet Explorer 4 and later.
pop()	Netscape Navigator 4 and later, Internet Explorer 5.5 and later for Windows.
push()	Netscape Navigator 4 and later, Internet Explorer 5.5 and later for Windows.
reverse()	Netscape Navigator 4 and later, Internet Explorer 4 and later.
shift()	Netscape Navigator 4 and later, Internet Explorer 5.5 and later for Windows.
slice(i,[j])	Netscape Navigator 4 and later, Internet Explorer 4 and later.
sort(compareFunc)	Netscape Navigator 4 and later, Internet Explorer 4 and later.
splice(startIndex, numItemsToDel[, itemsToInsert])	Netscape Navigator 4 and later, Internet Explorer 5.5 and later for Windows.
toLocaleString()	Netscape Navigator 6 and later, Internet Explorer 5.5 and later for Windows.
toString()	Netscape Navigator 4 and later, Internet Explorer 4 and later.
unshift()	Netscape Navigator 4 and later, Internet Explorer 5.5 and later for Windows.

`Boolean` **Object**

The `Boolean` object is supported by Netscape Navigator 3, Internet Explorer 3, and later versions of these browsers. See Chapter 8 for more information.

Properties

`constructor`	Netscape Navigator 4 and later, Internet Explorer 4 and later.
`prototype`	

Methods

`toString()`	Netscape Navigator 4 and later, Internet Explorer 4 and later.
`valueOf()`	Netscape Navigator 4 and later, Internet Explorer 4 and later.

`Date` **Object**

The `Date` object is supported by all JavaScript-compatible browsers except as noted. See Chapter 8 for more information.

Properties

`constructor`	Netscape Navigator 4 and later, Internet Explorer 4 and later.
`prototype`	Netscape Navigator 3 and later, Internet Explorer 4 and later.

Methods

`getDate()`	
`getDay()`	
`getFullYear()`	Netscape Navigator 4 and later, Internet Explorer 3 and later.
`getHours()`	
`getMilliseconds()`	Netscape Navigator 4 and later, Internet Explorer 3 and later.
`getMinutes()`	

A

`getMonth()`	
`getSeconds()`	
`getTime()`	
`getTimezoneOffset()`	
`getUTCDate()`	Netscape Navigator 4 and later, Internet Explorer 3 and later.
`getUTCDay()`	Netscape Navigator 4 and later, Internet Explorer 3 and later.
`getUTCFullYear()`	Netscape Navigator 4 and later, Internet Explorer 3 and later.
`getUTCHours()`	Netscape Navigator 4 and later, Internet Explorer 3 and later.
`getUTCMilliseconds()`	Netscape Navigator 4 and later, Internet Explorer 3 and later.
`getUTCMinutes()`	Netscape Navigator 4 and later, Internet Explorer 3 and later.
`getUTCMonth()`	Netscape Navigator 4 and later, Internet Explorer 3 and later.
`getUTCSeconds()`	Netscape Navigator 4 and later, Internet Explorer 3 and later.
`getYear()`	
`parse("dateString")`	
`setDate(val)`	
`setDay(val)`	
`setFullYear(val)`	Netscape Navigator 4 and later, Internet Explorer 3 and later.
`setHours(val)`	
`setMilliseconds(val)`	Netscape Navigator 4 and later, Internet Explorer 3 and later.
`setMinutes(val)`	
`setMonth(val)`	
`setSeconds(val)`	
`setTime(val)`	
`setUTCDate(val)`	Netscape Navigator 4 and later, Internet Explorer 3 and later.
`setUTCDay(val)`	Netscape Navigator 4 and later, Internet Explorer 3 and later.
`setUTCFullYear(val)`	Netscape Navigator 4 and later, Internet Explorer 3 and later.

setUTCHours(val)	Netscape Navigator 4 and later, Internet Explorer 3 and later.
setUTCMilliseconds(val)	Netscape Navigator 4 and later, Internet Explorer 3 and later.
setUTCMinutes(val)	Netscape Navigator 4 and later, Internet Explorer 3 and later.
setUTCMonth(val)	Netscape Navigator 4 and later, Internet Explorer 3 and later.
setUTCSeconds(val)	Netscape Navigator 4 and later, Internet Explorer 3 and later.
setYear(val)	
toDateString()	Internet Explorer 5.5 and later for Windows.
toGMTString()	
toLocaleDateString()	Internet Explorer 5.5 and later for Windows, Netscape Navigator 6 and later.
toLocaleString()	
toLocaleTimeString()	Internet Explorer 5.5 and later for Windows, Netscape Navigator 6 and later.
toString()toTimeString()	Internet Explorer 5.5 and later.
toUTCString()	Netscape Navigator 4 and later, Internet Explorer 3 and later.
UTC(date values)	

Error **Object**

The Error object is supported by Netscape Navigator 6, Internet Explorer 5 for Windows, and later versions of these browsers except as noted. See Chapter 8 for more information.

Properties

constructor	
description	Internet Explorer 5 and later for Windows.
fileName	Netscape Navigator 6 and later.
lineNumber	Netscape Navigator 6 and later.
message	Netscape Navigator 6 and later, Internet Explorer 5.5 and later.

name	Netscape Navigator 6 and later, Internet Explorer 5.5 and later.
number	Internet Explorer 5 and later for Windows.
prototype	

Method
toString()

Function **Object**

The Function object is supported by Netscape Navigator 3, Internet Explorer 3, and later versions of these browsers except as noted. See Chapter 5 for more information.

Properties

arguments	
arity	Netscape Navigator 4 and later.
caller	
constructor	Netscape Navigator 4 and later, Internet Explorer 4 and later.
length	
prototype	

Methods

apply(this, argsArray)	Netscape Navigator 6 and later, Internet Explorer 5.5 and later for Windows.
call(this[, arg1[,...argN]])	Netscape Navigator 6 and later, Internet Explorer 5.5 and later for Windows.
toString()	
valueOf()	

Math **Object**

The Math object is supported by all JavaScript-compatible browsers except as noted. All properties and methods are of the static Math object. See Chapter 8 for more information.

Properties
E
LN2
LN10

```
LOG2E
LOG10E
PI
SQRT1_2
SQRT2
```

Methods

```
abs(val)
acos(val)
asin(val)
atan(val)
atan2(val1, val2)
ceil(val)
cos(val)
exp(val)
floor(val)
log(val)
max(val1, val2)
min(val1, val2)
pow(val1, power)
random()
round(val)
sin(val)
sqrt(val)
tan(val)
```

Number **Object**

The Number object is supported by Netscape Navigator 3, Internet Explorer 3, and later versions of these browsers except as noted. See Chapter 8 for more information.

Properties

`constructor`	Netscape Navigator 4 and later, Internet Explorer 4 and later.
`MAX_VALUE`	Netscape Navigator 4 and later, Internet Explorer 4 and later.
`MIN_VALUE`	Netscape Navigator 4 and later, Internet Explorer 4 and later.
`NaN`	Netscape Navigator 4 and later, Internet Explorer 4 and later.
`NEGATIVE_INFINITY`	Netscape Navigator 4 and later, Internet Explorer 4 and later.
`POSITIVE_INFINITY`	Netscape Navigator 4 and later, Internet Explorer 4 and later.
`prototype`	

Methods

`toExponential(n)`	Netscape Navigator 6 and later, Internet Explorer 5.5 and later for Windows.
`toFixed(n)`	Netscape Navigator 6 and later, Internet Explorer 5.5 and later for Windows.
`toLocaleString()`	Netscape Navigator 6 and later, Internet Explorer 5.5 and later for Windows, Internet Explorer 5 for Macintosh.
`toString([numBase])`	Netscape Navigator 4 and later, Internet Explorer 4 and later.
`toPrecision(n)`	Netscape Navigator 6 and later, Internet Explorer 5.5 and later for Windows.
`valueOf()`	Netscape Navigator 4 and later, Internet Explorer 4 and later.

RegExp **Object**

The `RegExp` object is supported by Netscape Navigator 4, Internet Explorer 4, and later versions of these browsers. See Chapter 8 for more information.

Properties

`global`	
`ignoreCase`	Internet Explorer 5 for Macintosh, Internet Explorer 5.5 and later for Windows.
`input`	Internet Explorer 5.5 and later. Property of the static `RegExp` object.
`lastIndex`	
`multiline`	Internet Explorer 5.5 and later for Windows. Property of the static `RegExp` object.
`lastMatch`	Internet Explorer 5.5 and later for Windows. Property of the static `RegExp` object.
`lastParen`	Internet Explorer 5.5 and later for Windows. Property of the static `RegExp` object.
`leftContext`	Internet Explorer 5.5 and later for Windows. Property of the static `RegExp` object.
`prototype`	
`rightContext`	Property of the static `RegExp` object.
`source`	
`$1...$9`	

Methods

`compile(regexp)`	
`exec("string")`	Returns an array.
`test("string")`	

See also RegExp functions of the `String` object: `str.match()`, `str.replace()`, `str.search()`, and `str.split()`.

`String` Object

The `String` object is supported by all JavaScript-compatible browsers except as noted. See Chapter 7 for more information.

Properties

`constructor`	Netscape Navigator 4 and later, Internet Explorer 4 and later.
`length`	
`prototype`	

Methods

`anchor("anchorName")`	
`big()`	
`blink()`	
`bold()`	
`charAt(index)`	
`charCodeAt([i])`	Netscape Navigator 4 and later, Internet Explorer 4 and later.
`concat(string)`	Netscape Navigator 4 and later, Internet Explorer 4 and later.
`fixed()`	
`fontcolor(#rrggbb)`	
`fontsize(1to7)`	
`fromCharCode(n1...)`	Netscape Navigator 4 and later, Internet Explorer 4 and later. Property of the static `String` object.
`indexOf ("string" [,i])`	

`italics()`	
`lastIndexOf ("string" [,i])`	
`link(URL)`	
`localeCompare()`	Netscape Navigator 6 and later, Internet Explorer 5.5 and later for Windows.
`match(regexp)`	Netscape Navigator 4 and later, Internet Explorer 4 and later.
`replace(regexp, string)`	Netscape Navigator 4 and later, Internet Explorer 4 and later.
`search(regexp)`	Netscape Navigator 4 and later, Internet Explorer 4 and later.
`slice(i, j)`	
`small()`	
`split(char)`	Netscape Navigator 3 and later, Internet Explorer 4 and later.
`strike()`	
`sub()`	
`substr(start, length)`	
`substring(intA, intB)`	
`sup()`	
`toLocaleLowerCase()`	Netscape Navigator 6 and later, Internet Explorer 5.5 and later for Windows.
`toLocaleUpperCase()`	Netscape Navigator 6 and later, Internet Explorer 5.5 and later for Windows.
`toLowerCase()`	
`toString()`	Netscape Navigator 4 and later, Internet Explorer 4 and later.
`toUpperCase()`	
`valueOf()`	Netscape Navigator 4 and later, Internet Explorer 4 and later.

A

Appendix **B**

Browser Document Object Model Quick Reference

Modern browsers support multiple object models, including:

- The browser document object model (DOM), first implemented in Netscape Navigator 2 and Internet Explorer 3 and supported by all modern browsers.
- The DHTML object model, first implemented in Internet Explorer 4 and supported by Internet Explorer 4 and later.
- The W3C object model, first implemented in Netscape Navigator 6 and Internet Explorer 5 and supported by Netscape Navigator 6, Internet Explorer 5, and later versions of these browsers.

The current HTML/XHTML and DOM specifications are available at www.w3c.org/DOM/ and www.w3c.org/MarkUp/, respectively.

For maximum compatibility and to keep this reference from running a hundred pages, we focus on the original browser document object model and the most commonly used properties. Because it is most important to know that browser X supports features X, Y, and Z, this reference focuses on which browsers support which object model features rather than differentiating between the object models themselves.

anchor **Object**

The anchor object is supported by Netscape Navigator 2, Internet Explorer 3, and later versions of these browsers except as noted. See Chapter 13 for more information.

Properties

charset	Internet Explorer 6 and later, Netscape Navigator 6 and later.
cords	Internet Explorer 4 and later, Netscape Navigator 6 and later.
hash	
host	
hostname	
href	
hreflang	Internet Explorer 6 and later, Netscape Navigator 6 and later.
name	Netscape Navigator 4 and later, Internet Explorer 4 and later.
nameProp	Internet Explorer 4 and later, Netscape Navigator 4 and later.
pathname	
port	
protocol	
protocolLong	Windows Internet Explorer 4 and later only.
rel	Internet Explorer 4 and later, Netscape Navigator 4 and later.
rev	Internet Explorer 4 and later, Netscape Navigator 4 and later.
search	Internet Explorer 3 and later, Netscape Navigator 2 and later.
shape	Internet Explorer 4 and later, Netscape Navigator 6 and later.
target	
text	Netscape Navigator 4 only.
type	Internet Explorer 6 and later, Netscape Navigator 6 and later.
urn	Internet Explorer 4 and later, Netscape Navigator 4 and later.
x	Netscape Navigator 4 only.
y	Netscape Navigator 4 only.

Methods

(None)

Event Handlers

(None)

area **Object**

The area object is supported by Netscape Navigator 2, Internet Explorer 3, and later versions of these browsers except as noted.

Properties

alt	Internet Explorer 4 and later, Netscape Navigator 6 and later.
coords	Internet Explorer 4 and later, Netscape Navigator 6 and later.
hash	
host	
hostname	
href	
pathname	
port	
protocol	
search	
shape	Internet Explorer 4 and later, Netscape Navigator 6 and later.
target	

Methods

(None)

Event Handlers

onclick	Netscape Navigator 4 and later.
onmouseout	
onmouseover	Netscape Navigator 3 and later, Internet Explorer 4 and later.

button, reset, **and** submit **Objects**

The button, reset, and submit objects are supported by Netscape Navigator 2, Internet Explorer 3, and later versions of these browsers except as noted. See Chapter 17 for more information.

Properties

form	
name	
type	Netscape Navigator 3 and later, Internet Explorer 4 and later.
value	

Methods

click()	
handleEvent(evt)	Netscape Navigator 3 and later.

Event Handlers

onclick	
onmousedown	Netscape button Navigator 4 and later, Internet Explorer 4 and later.
onmouseup	Netscape Navigator 4 and later, Internet Explorer 4 and later.

checkbox **Object**

The checkbox object is supported by Netscape Navigator 2, Internet Explorer 3, and later versions of these browsers except as noted. See Chapter 17 for more information.

Properties

checked	
defaultChecked	
form	
name	
type	Netscape Navigator 3 and later, Internet Explorer 4 and later.
value	

Methods

`click()`	
`handleEvent(evt)`	Netscape Navigator 3 and later.

Event Handlers

`onclick`	
`onmousedown`	Netscape Navigator 4 and later, Internet Explorer 4 and later.
`onmouseup`	Netscape Navigator 4 and later, Internet Explorer 4 and later.

`document` Object

The `document` object is supported by Netscape Navigator 2, Internet Explorer 3, and later versions of these browsers except as noted. See Chapter 12 for more information.

Properties

`alinkColor`	
`anchors[]`	
`applets[]`	Netscape Navigator 3 and later, Internet Explorer 4 and later.
`bgColor`	
`cookie`	
`domain`	Netscape Navigator 3 and later, Internet Explorer 4 and later.
`embeds[]`	Netscape Navigator 3 and later, Internet Explorer 4 and later.
`fgColor`	
`forms[]`	
`height`	Netscape Navigator 4 and later.
`images[]`	Netscape Navigator 3 and later, Internet Explorer 4 and later.
`lastModified`	
`layers[]`	Netscape Navigator 4 only.
`linkColor`	
`links[]`	
`location`	

referrer	
selection	Internet Explorer 4 and later for Macintosh only.
title	
URL	Netscape Navigator 3 and later, Internet Explorer 4 and later.
vlinkColor	
width	Netscape Navigator 4 and later.

Methods

captureEvents(type)	Netscape Navigator 4 only.
clear()	
close()	
getSelection()	Netscape Navigator 4 and later.
handleEvent(event)	Netscape Navigator 4 only.
open("mimetype" [,replace])	
releaseEvents(type)	Netscape Navigator 4 only.
routeEvent(event)	Netscape Navigator 4 only.
write("string")	
writeln("string")	

Event Handlers

(None)

fileUpdate Object

The fileUpdate object is supported by Netscape Navigator 3, Internet Explorer 4, and later versions of these browsers except as noted.

Properties

form
name
type
value

Methods

`blur()`	
`focus()`	
`handleEvent(evt)`	Netscape Navigator 4 and later.
`select()`	

Event Handlers

`onblur`
`onfocus`
`onselect`

`form` **Object**

The `form` object is supported by Netscape Navigator 2, Internet Explorer 3, and later versions of these browsers except as noted. See Chapter 17 for more information.

Properties

`action`
`elements[]`
`encoding`
`length`
`method`
`name`
`target`

Methods

`handleEvent(evt)`	Netscape Navigator 4 and later.
`reset()`	Netscape Navigator 3 and later, Internet Explorer 4 and later.
`submit()`	

Event Handlers

`onreset`	Netscape Navigator 3 and later, Internet Explorer 4 and later.
`onsubmit`	

`history` **Object**

The `history` object is supported by Netscape Navigator 2, Internet Explorer 3, and later versions of these browsers except as noted. See Chapter 14 for more information.

Properties

`current`	Netscape Navigator 4 and later with signed scripts.
`length`	
`next`	Netscape Navigator 4 and later with signed scripts.
`previous`	Netscape Navigator 4 and later with signed scripts.

Methods

`back()`
`forward()`
`go(int | "URL")`

Event Handlers

(None)

`image` **Object**

The `image` object is supported by Netscape Navigator 3, Internet Explorer 3 for Macintosh, Internet Explorer 4 for Windows, and later versions of these browsers except as noted. See Chapter 12 for more information.

Properties

`border`	
`complete`	
`height`	
`hspace`	
`lowsrc`	
`name`	
`src`	
`vspace`	
`width`	
`x`	Netscape Navigator 4 only.
`y`	Netscape Navigator 4 only.

Methods

(None)

Event Handlers

```
onabort
onerror
onload
```

`link` Object

The `link` object is supported by Netscape Navigator 2, Internet Explorer 3, and later versions of these browsers except as noted. See Chapter 13 for more information.

Properties

`charset`	Internet Explorer 6 and later, Netscape Navigator 6 and later.
`cords`	Internet Explorer 4 and later, Netscape Navigator 6 and later.
`hash`	
`host`	
`hostname`	
`href`	
`hreflang`	Internet Explorer 6 and later, Netscape Navigator 6 and later.
`name`	Netscape Navigator 4 and later, Internet Explorer 4 and later.
`nameProp`	Netscape Navigator 4 and later, Internet Explorer 4 and later.
`pathname`	
`port`	
`protocol`	
`protocolLong`	Windows Internet Explorer 4 and later only.
`rel`	Netscape Navigator 4 and later, Internet Explorer 4 and later.
`rev`	Netscape Navigator 4 and later, Internet Explorer 4 and later.
`search`	Internet Explorer 3 and later, Netscape Navigator 2 and later.
`shape`	Internet Explorer 4 and later, Netscape Navigator 6 and later.

target	
text	Netscape Navigator 4 only.
type	Internet Explorer 6 and later, Netscape Navigator 6 and later.
urn	Internet Explorer 4 and later, Netscape Navigator 4 and later.
x	Netscape Navigator 4 only.
y	Netscape Navigator 4 only.

B

Methods

(None)

Event Handlers

onclick	
ondblclick	Netscape Navigator 4 and later, Internet Explorer 4 and later.
onmousedown	Netscape Navigator 4 and later, Internet Explorer 4 and later.
onmouseout	Netscape Navigator 4 and later, Internet Explorer 4 and later.
onmouseover	
onmouseup	Netscape Navigator 4 and later, Internet Explorer 4 and later.

location **Object**

The location object is supported by Netscape Navigator 2, Internet Explorer 3, and later versions of these browsers except as noted. See Chapter 14 for more information.

Properties

hash
host
hostname
href
pathname
port
protocol
search

Methods

`assign("URL")`	
`reload([Boolean])`	Netscape Navigator 3 and later, Internet Explorer 4 and later.
`replace("URL")`	Netscape Navigator 3 and later, Internet Explorer 4 and later.

Event Handlers

(None)

`mimeType` **Object**

The `mimeType` object is supported by Netscape Navigator 3, Internet Explorer 4 for Macintosh, and later versions of these browsers except as noted.

Properties

```
description
enabledPlugin
type
suffixes
```

Methods

(None)

Event Handlers

(None)

`navigator` **Object**

The `navigator` object is supported by Netscape Navigator 2, Internet Explorer 3, and later versions of these browsers except as noted. See Chapter 15 for more information.

Properties

`appCodeName`	
`appMinorVersion`	Internet Explorer 4 and later.
`appName`	
`appVersion`	
`browserLanguage`	Internet Explorer 4 and later.
`cookieEnabled`	Netscape Navigator 6 and later, Internet Explorer 4 and later.
`cpuClass`	Internet Explorer 4 and later.

language	Netscape Navigator 4 and later.
mimeTypes[]	Netscape Navigator 3 and later, Internet Explorer 4 and later for Macintosh.
online	Internet Explorer 4 and later.
oscpu	Netscape Navigator 6 and later.
platform	Netscape Navigator 4 and later, Internet Explorer 4 and later.
plugins[]	Netscape Navigator 3 and later, Internet Explore 4 and later for Macintosh.
product	Netscape Navigator 6 and later.
productSub	Netscape Navigator 6 and later.
securityPolicy	Netscape Navigator 4 and later.
systemLanguage	Internet Explorer 4 and later.
userAgent	
userLanguage	Internet Explorer 4 and later.
userProfile	Internet Explorer 4 and later.
vendor	Netscape Navigator 6 and later.
vendorSub	Netscape Navigator 6 and later.

Methods

javaEnabled()	Netscape Navigator 3 and later, Internet Explore 4 and later for Macintosh.
preference(name[, val])	Netscape Navigator 4 and later in signed scripts only.
taintEnabled()	Netscape Navigator 3 and later, Internet Explorer 4 and later.

Event Handlers

(None)

plugin **Object**

The plugin object is supported by Netscape Navigator 3, Internet Explorer 4 for Macintosh, and later versions of these browsers except as noted.

Properties

```
name
filename
description
length
```

Method

```
refresh()
```

Event Handlers

(None)

`radio` **Object**

The `radio` object is supported by Netscape Navigator 2, Internet Explorer 3, and later versions of these browsers except as noted. See Chapter 17 for more information.

Properties

`checked`	
`defaultChecked`	
`form`	
`length`	
`name`	
`type`	Netscape Navigator 3 and later, Internet Explorer 4 and later.
`value`	

Methods

`click()`	
`handleEvent(evt)`	Netscape Navigator 3 and later.

Event Handlers

`onclick`	
`onmousedown`	Netscape Navigator 4 and later, Internet Explorer 4 and later.
`onmouseup`	Netscape Navigator 4 and later, Internet Explorer 4 and later.

screen **Object**

The screen object is supported by Netscape Navigator 4, Internet Explorer 4, and later versions of these browsers except as noted.

Properties

availHeight	
availLeft	Netscape Navigator 4 and later only.
availTop	Netscape Navigator 4 and later only.
availWidth	
bufferDepth	Internet Explorer 4 and later for Windows only.
colorDepth	
fontSmoothingEnabled	Internet Explorer 4 and later for Windows only.
height	
pixelDepth	
updateInterval	Internet Explorer 4 and later for Windows only.
width	

Methods

(None)

Event Handlers

(None)

select **Object**

The select object is supported by Netscape Navigator 2, Internet Explorer 3, and later versions of these browsers except as noted. See Chapter 17 for more information.

Properties

length	
name	
options[i]	
options[i].defaultSelected	
options[i].index	
options[i].selected	
options[i].text	

`options[i].value`	
`selectedIndex`	
`type`	Netscape Navigator 3 and later, Internet Explorer 4 and later.

Methods

`blur()`	Netscape Navigator 3 and later, Internet Explorer 4 and later.
`focus()`	Netscape Navigator 3 and later, Internet Explorer 4 and later.
`handleEvent(evt)`	Netscape Navigator 4 and later.

Event Handlers

`onblur`
`onchange`
`onfocus`

text, textarea, password, and hidden Objects

The text, textarea, password, and hidden objects are supported by Netscape Navigator 2, Internet Explorer 3, and later versions of these browsers except as noted. See Chapter 17 for more information.

Properties

`defaultValue`	Not available for textarea object.
`form`	
`name`	
`type`	Netscape Navigator 3 and later, Internet Explorer 4 and later.
`value`	

Methods

`blur()`	
`focus()`	
`handleEvent(evt)`	Netscape Navigator 4 and later.
`select()`	

Event Handlers

`onblur`	
`onchange`	
`onfocus`	
`onkeydown`	Netscape Navigator 4 and later, Internet Explorer 4 and later.
`onkeypress`	Netscape Navigator 4 and later, Internet Explorer 4 and later.
`onkeyup`	Netscape Navigator 4 and later, Internet Explorer 4 and later.
`onselect`	

window **Object**

The window object is supported by Netscape Navigator 2, Internet Explorer 3, and later versions of these browsers except as noted. See Chapter 11 for more information.

Properties

`appCore`	Netscape Navigator 6 and later.
`clientInformation`	Internet Explorer 4 and later.
`clipboardData`	Internet Explorer 5 and later for Windows.
`closed`	Netscape Navigator 3 and later, Internet Explorer 4 and later.
`components[]`	Netscape Navigator 6 and later.
`controllers[]`	Netscape Navigator 6 and later.
`crypto`	Netscape Navigator 6 and later.
`defaultStatus`	
`dialogArguments`	Internet Explorer 4 and later.
`dialogHeight`	Internet Explorer 4 and later for Windows.
`dialogLeft`	Internet Explorer 4 and later.
`dialogTop`	Internet Explorer 4 and later.

`dialogWidth`	Internet Explorer 4 and later for Windows.
`directories`	Netscape Navigator 4 and later.
`document`	
`event`	Internet Explorer 4 and later.
`external`	Internet Explorer 4 and later for Windows.
`frameElement`	Internet Explorer 5 and later for Windows.
`frames[]`	
`history`	
`innerHeight`	Netscape Navigator 4 and later.
`innerWidth`	Netscape Navigator 4 and later.
`length`	Netscape Navigator 6 and later, Internet Explorer 4 and later.
`loading`	Netscape Navigator 4 only.
`location`	
`locationbar`	Netscape Navigator 4 and later.
`menubar`	Netscape Navigator 4 and later.
`name`	
`navigator`	Netscape Navigator 6 and later, Internet Explorer 4 and later.
`offscreenBuffering`	Internet Explorer 4 and later.
`opener`	Internet Explorer 3 and later, Netscape Navigator 3 and later.
`outerHeight`	Netscape Navigator 4 and later.
`outerWidth`	Netscape Navigator 4 and later.
`pageXOffset`	Netscape Navigator 4 and later.
`pageYOffset`	Netscape Navigator 4 and later.
`parent`	
`personalbar`	Netscape Navigator 4 and later.
`pkcs11`	Netscape Navigator 6 and later.
`prompter`	Netscape Navigator 6 and later.
`returnValue`	Internet Explorer 4 and later for Windows, Internet Explorer 5 and later for Macintosh.
`screen`	Netscape Navigator 6 and later, Internet Explorer 4 and later.
`screenLeft`	Internet Explorer 5 and later for Windows.
`screenTop`	Internet Explorer 5 and later for Windows.
`screenX`	Netscape Navigator 6 and later.

screenY	Netscape Navigator 6 and later.
scrollbars	Netscape Navigator 4 and later.
scrollX	Netscape Navigator 6 and later.
scrollY	Netscape Navigator 6 and later.
self	
sidebar NN4+	
status	
statusbar	Netscape Navigator 4 and later.
toolbar	Netscape Navigator 4 and later.
top	
window	

Methods

alert("msg")	
attachEvent("evt", func)	Internet Explorer 5 and later.
back()	Netscape Navigator 4 and later.
blur()	Netscape Navigator 3 and later, Internet Explorer 4 and later.
captureEvents(type)	Netscape Navigator 4 only.
clearInterval(ID)	Netscape Navigator 4 and later, Internet Explorer 4 and later.
clearTimeout(ID)	
close()	
confirm("msg")	
createPopup()	Internet Explorer 5 and later and 5.5 for Windows.
detachEvent("evt",func)	Internet Explorer 5 and later.
disableExternalCapture()	Netscape Navigator 4 only.
enableExternalCapture()	Netscape Navigator 4 only.
execScript("exprs"[, lang])	Internet Explorer 4 and later.
find(["str"][,case, bkwd])	Netscape Navigator 4 and later.
fireEvent("evt"[, evtObj])	Internet Explorer 5 and later and 5.5 for Windows.

`focus()`	Netscape Navigator 3 and later, Internet Explorer 4 and later.
`forward()`	Netscape Navigator 4 and later.
`handleEvent(event)`	Netscape Navigator 4 only.
`home()`	Netscape Navigator 4 and later.
`moveBy(x,y)`	Netscape Navigator 4 and later, Internet Explorer 4 and later.
`moveTo(x, y)`	Netscape Navigator 4 and later, Internet Explorer 4 and later.
`navigate()`	Internet Explorer 3 and later.
`open(URL,"name","specs")`	
`print()`	Netscape Navigator 4 and later, Internet Explorer 5 and later.
`prompt("msg","reply")`	
`releaseEvents(type)`	Netscape Navigator 4 only.
`resizeBy(x,y)`	Netscape Navigator 4 only, Internet Explorer 4 and later.
`resizeTo(width, height)`	Netscape Navigator 4 only, Internet Explorer 4 and later.
`routeEvent(event)`	Netscape Navigator 4 only.
`scroll(x, y)`	Netscape Navigator 3 and later, Internet Explorer 4 and later.
`scrollBy(x, y)`	Netscape Navigator 4 and later, Internet Explorer 4 and later.
`scrollTo(x, y)`	Netscape Navigator 4 and later, Internet Explorer 4 and later.
`setActive()`	Internet Explorer 5 and later for Windows.
`setInterval(func, msec [, args])`	Netscape Navigator 4 and later, Internet Explorer 4 and later.
`setTimeout(func, msec [, args])`	
`showHelp()`	Internet Explorer 4 and later for Windows.
`showModalDialog()`	Internet Explorer 4 and later.
`showModelessDialog()`	Internet Explorer 5 and later for Windows.
`sizeToContent()`	Netscape Navigator 6 and later.
`stop()`	Netscape Navigator 4 and later.

Event Handlers

onabort	Netscape Navigator 6 and later.
onafterprint	Internet Explorer 5 and later for Windows.
onbeforeprint	Internet Explorer 5 and later for Windows.
onbeforeunload	Internet Explorer 4 and later.
onblur	Netscape Navigator 3 and later, Internet Explorer 4 and later.
onchange	Netscape Navigator 6 and later.
onclick	Netscape Navigator 6 and later.
onclose	Netscape Navigator 6 and later.
ondragdrop	Netscape Navigator 4 only.
onerror	Netscape Navigator 3 only, Internet Explorer 4 and later.
onfocus	Netscape Navigator 3 only, Internet Explorer 4 and later.
onhelp	Internet Explorer 4 and later.
onkeydown	Netscape Navigator 6 and later.
onkeypress	Netscape Navigator 6 and later.
onkeyup	Netscape Navigator 6 and later.
onload	
onmousedown	Netscape Navigator 6 and later.
onmousemove	Netscape Navigator 6 and later.
onmouseout	Netscape Navigator 6 and later.
onmouseover	Netscape Navigator 6 and later.
onmouseup	Netscape Navigator 6 and later.
onmove	Netscape Navigator 4 only.
onreset	Netscape Navigator 6 and later.
onresize	Netscape Navigator 4 and later, Internet Explorer 4 and later.
onscroll	Internet Explorer 4 and later.
onselect	Netscape Navigator 6 and later.
onsubmit	Netscape Navigator 6 and later.
onunload	

Glossary

A

alert—A dialog box used to present a message to users; includes an OK button users can click to close the dialog box.

assignment operator—Assigns a value to a variable.

B

Boolean operator—An operator that computes basic Boolean logic functions such as AND, OR, and NOT.

borderless frames—A frame of a specific size in which all content is showing and the frame border attribute is set to zero. Borderless frames give your page a more cohesive appearance because they do not display scrollbars.

browser cookie—See *cookie*.

browser location—The URL of the current page as referred to by a browser and stored in the `location` object.

C

character escaping—A technique that allows special characters to be quoted within string text.

checkbox—A form-related HTML element that can be toggled between checked and unchecked; used when you want a user to make one or more selections from a group of selections.

child document—A frame created by a parent document. If a script in a child frame needs to access the functions, methods, or properties of the parent document, the script must follow the hierarchy from the parent document.

children—See *child document*.

Common Gateway Interface (CGI)—A technology that allows remote users to execute applications on a Web server and to see the results returned in the form of a Web page. It is a way for the Web server to pass the browser's request to an application and then pass data from the application back to the browser.

confirm—A dialog box with OK and Cancel buttons that is used to display a message to users.

constant—A named value that does not change.

constructor function or method—Displays public code involved in the instantiation of an object.

constructor method—A method that is called when a new object is instantiated.

cookie—Used to store information on the client computer so that it can be retrieved in other pages or in other browser sessions. Many Web sites store user information in cookies to customize their pages for individual users.

D

data dictionary—A document that describes the variables used in a script.

data structure—A structure that holds private data fields of different types, but that lacks methods.

document object—A JavaScript object that represents a Web browser and its windows.

Document Object Model (DOM)—A generic model for working with documents, allowing an application to interface with the document.

Dynamic HTML (DHTML)—A combination of JavaScript and Cascading Style Sheets (CSS) to produce dynamic browser behavior.

E

encapsulated—An object that is self-contained or inaccessible to other sections of code.

event—A procedure that is executed automatically when a certain condition exists. In browsers, there are events for mouse clicks, mouse movements, button clicks, and so on.

event handler—An object property or method that specifies how an object reacts to an event. Events can be triggered by a user action, such as a button click, or a browser action, such as the completion of a document load.

expression—A statement made up of function calls, constants, or operators that evaluates to a value and can be assigned to a variable.

F

form control—A form-related HTML element such as a text input field, push button, or text area field.

function—An encapsulated code block that can take arguments and that returns a single value that can be assigned to a variable.

H

hidden field—A field included in an HTML form that is not displayed on the page; a special HTML form field that is hidden from and cannot be modified by the user (unless a user were to view the HTML source).

history list—A browser-maintained list of places a user has visited.

HTML control—An HTML form element that can be manipulated by scripts. HTML controls include checkboxes, radio buttons, push buttons, text windows, text areas, and selection menus.

Hypertext Markup Language (HTML)—A simple language for marking up Web pages for display, including document structure and hypertext links.

Hypertext Transfer Protocol (HTTP)—The standard protocol for transmitting hypertext documents, written in HTML, on the World Wide Web.

I

identifier—An arbitrary element assigned to variables during interpretation.

initial value—The value to which a variable is set during initialization.

in-line comment—Statements within a script that are ignored by the interpreter and are present for explanatory value only.

interpreter—A program that reads JavaScript statements and executes them.

J

Java Server Pages (JSP)—JSP technology allows Java code to be included in HTML Web pages and compiled at run time to produce dynamic behavior.

JavaScript—An interpreted, object-based programming language primarily used to script dynamic Web pages.

L

looping statement—A statement that ensures that a code block is executed multiple times.

M

method—A function that belongs to an object and can be called by a script to perform an action.

O

object—An abstract entity, modeled from a "real-world" entity, that has both methods and data associated with it.

object initializer—A compact version of the constructor function that initializes private members to specific values during instantiation.

ordered set—A group of related elements that has an ordinal relationship.

P

parameter—An argument to a method or function call.

parent document—Any document that contains a frameset definition.

password field—A text input field in an HTML form in which the characters entered are masked with asterisks so they are hidden from view.

persistent cookie—See *stored cookie*.

prompt—A dialog browser location box that presents a message and allows users to enter information in response to the message. Prompt dialog boxes also have OK and Cancel buttons.

property—Defines a setting of an object.

prototype property—Allows new members to be added to existing JavaScript objects.

push button—A button element in an HTML form that can be clicked.

R

radio button— A form-related HTML element that is a small circular button that is drawn and filled when the user selects it; used when you want a user to make a single selection from a group of selections.

reserved word—A set of names used by JavaScript constructs that cannot be used as variable names; avoids ambiguity during interpretation.

S

scripts—Blocks of JavaScript code that are generally embedded inside a HTML document.

selection menu—A form-related HTML element that creates a menu of choices from which a user can choose.

statement—A syntactically valid code element that is encapsulated.

stored cookie—A cookie with an expiration date. Such a cookie will be persistent and stored on the user's computer and available until its expiration date as long as it is not deleted or the expiration date isn't reset.

string—An object that consists of a set of alphanumeric characters and associated members.

string literal—The character values stored as private data of a string object.

T

temporary cookie—A cookie without an expiration date. A cookie that is only valid for the current session. If the user exits the browser window, the temporary cookie is deleted.

text area field—A HTML form element that provides a large text entry field in which users can type information. A text area field is different from a standard text input field because it can have multiple lines.

text input field—A HTML form element that provides a single-line text entry field in which users can type information.

type declaration—A statement that describes the type of a variable when it is defined.

U

Uniform Resource Locator (URL)—Represents the physical location of a HTML document on the World Wide Web.

V

variable—A script construct that can take on any value that is consistent with the variable's type. JavaScript variables are not strongly typed.

W

Web page—A HTML document designed to be viewed in a Web browser.

window object—The top of the browser object model for all scriptable browsers. As such, `window` is the top-level container for all content you view in a Web browser. Whenever you start a Web browser, the `window` object is defined in memory—even if no document is loaded.

`window.alert()`—See *alert*.

`window.confirm()`—See *confirm*.

`window.prompt()`—See *prompt*.

X

XHTML—The most current form of XML-compatible HTML.

Index